Max Ellery's - EP.Tl
Transmission Re...
Ford 1960 - 2001

Automatic and Manual

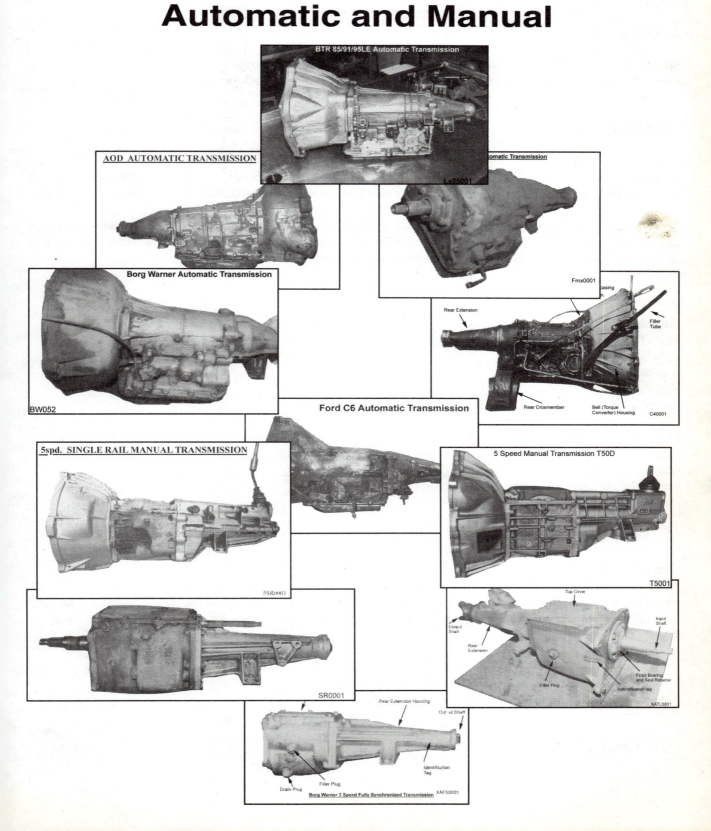

INDEX - GENERAL INFORMATION

This transmission repair and maintenance manual has been published to help provide Ford owners and enthusiasts with an invaluable, comprehensive and thorough guide in all aspects of transmission, maintenance and mechanical repair work.

The manual is published from the latest information obtained by the publishers. Where extensive research is undertaken to obtain the information for the benefit of people who purchase this manual.

Acknowledgements

Special Thanks To Dave Allen from Transmission Services, Bendigo, Victoria.
For his assistance and expertise in helping to produce this specialist publication.

DISCLAIMER

Every endeavour has been made to ensure all information in this manual is accurate. Mistakes and omissions can always occur, and the publisher does not assume any duty or care, or legal responsibility in relation to the contents of this book.

Maintenance, repair and tune-up are essential for safe and reliable use of all motor vehicles. These operations should be undertaken in such a manner as to eliminate the possibility of personal injury or in such a way that could damage the vehicle or compromise the safety of the vehicle, driver, passenger or a third party.

Published By:
Ellery Publications
1974 Eppalock Road,
Axedale
Victoria, 3551
Australia.

Phone: (03) 5439 5000
Fax: (03) 5439 3573
Email   information@ellery.com.au
www.ellery.com.au

© Copyright 2001

Copyright
This publication is copyright. Other than for the purposes of and subject to the conditions prescribed under the Copyright Act, no part of it may in any form or by any means (electronic, mechanical, microcopying, photocopying, recording or otherwise) be reproduced, stored in a retrieval system or transmitted without prior written permission. Enquiries should be addressed to the Publisher.

National Library of Australia Card number and ISBN

ISBN 1-876720-24-7

INDEX

Max Ellery's - EP.TRANF - Transmission Repair Manual - Ford's 1960 - 2001

CONTENTS	Page
GENERAL INFORMATION	4
Transmission Specifications	4
Automatic Transmission Identification by Sumps	10
TOOLS, EQUIPMENT & SAFETY PRECAUTIONS	11
Transmission Overhaul Tool Listing and Description	12
Special Tool Identification	17
Safety Precautions	19
GENERAL TRANSMISSION REPAIR PROCEDURES	20
Maintenance Notes	20
Manual Transmission Removal / Installation	20
Automatic Transmission Removal / Installation	22
Oil Cooler & Pipes	24
Transmission Filters	25
AUTOMATIC TRANSMISSION - BORG WARNER 35/40	26
Maintenance	27
Major Repairs and Rebuild	32
Problem Solving & Diagnosis	43
Specifications	44
FORD C - TYPE Automatic Transmission Identification	46
AUTOMATIC TRANSMISSION - C4, C5, C9 and C10	48
Maintenance	49
Major Repairs and Rebuild	54
Problem Solving & Diagnosis	64
Specifications	65
AUTOMATIC TRANSMISSION - C6	66
Maintenance	67
Major Repairs and Rebuild	71
Problem Solving & Diagnosis	93
Specifications	95
AUTOMATIC TRANSMISSION - FMX	96
Maintenance	97
Major Repairs and Rebuild	104
Problem Solving & Diagnosis	117
Specifications	118
AUTOMATIC TRANSMISSION - AOD	119
Maintenance	120
Major Repairs and Rebuild	122
Problem Solving & Diagnosis	142
Specifications	145
AUTOMATIC TRANSMISSION - M51	146
Maintenance	147
Major Repairs and Rebuild	153
Problem Solving & Diagnosis	164
Specifications	165

INDEX - GENERAL INFORMATION

CONTENTS	Page
AUTOMATIC TRANSMISSION - LE 85/91/93/95/97	166
Maintenance	167
Major Repairs and Rebuild	172
Problem Solving & Diagnosis	186
Specifications	189
MANUAL TRANSMISSION - 3 SPEED PARTIAL SYNCHRONIZED	193
Maintenance	194
Major Repairs and Rebuild	194
Problem Solving & Diagnosis	200
Specifications	200
MANUAL TRANSMISSION - 3 SPEED FULLY SYNCHRONIZED	201
Maintenance	202
Major Repairs and Rebuild	203
Problem Solving & Diagnosis	211
Specifications	211
MANUAL TRANSMISSION - 4 SPEED TOP LOADER	212
Maintenance	214
Major Repairs and Rebuild	214
Problem Solving & Diagnosis	220
Specifications	220
MANUAL TRANSMISSION - 4 SPEED SINGLE RAIL	221
Maintenance	222
Major Repairs and Rebuild	223
Problem Solving & Diagnosis	232
Specifications	232
MANUAL TRANSMISSION - 4 SPEED (0506 series) and 5 SPEED (0507 series) SINGLE RAIL	233
Maintenance	234
Major Repairs and Rebuild	235
Problem Solving & Diagnosis	247
Specifications	247
MANUAL TRANSMISSION - 5 SPEED T5 & 5 SPEED M57	248
Maintenance	249
Major Repairs and Rebuild	250
Problem Solving & Diagnosis	261
Specifications	261

Borg Warner 35/40 AUTOMATIC TRANSMISSION

Model	Years	Engine	Ford Pt No	BW Pt No
XK-XP Falcon	1965-66	177 & 200 cu. in.	--DP7000-	
XR-Falcon	1966-67	170 & 200 cu. in.	ARC6DA-7000A	AS5-35AE (Single)
	1966-67	200 cu. in.	ARC6DA-7000B	AS7-35AE (Dual)
	1966-67	289 cu. in.	ARC6DA-7000C	AS1-35CE
ZA-Fairlane	1966-67	289 cu. in.	ARC6DA-7000C	AS1-35CE
XT-Falcon	1968-69	188 cu. in.	XT-7000A (Ford O Matic)	
				AS1-35BE (Single)
	1968-69	221 cu. in.	XT-7000B (Ford O Matic)	
				AS3-35BE (Single)
	1968-69	221 cu. in.	XT-7000C (Cruise O Matic)	
				AS5-35BE (G.T.A.)
ZB-Fairlane	1968-69	221 cu. in.	ZB-7000A (Cruise O Matic)	
				AS7-35BE (Single)
	1968-69	221 cu. in.	ZB-7000B (Cruise O Matic)	
				AS9-35BE (G.T.A.)
XW-Falcon	1969-70	188 cu. in.	XW-7000B	AS25-35BE (Single)
	1969-70	221 cu. in.	XW-7000C	AS21-35BE (Single)
	1969-70	221 cu. in.	XW-7000D	AS27-35BE (G.T.A.)
ZC-Fairlane	1969-70	221 cu. in.	ZC-7000B	AS23-35BE (G.T.A.)
XY-Falcon	1970-72	200 cu. in.	XYDA-7000-D	AS37-35BE
	1970-72	250 cu. in.	XYDA-7000-C	AS23-35BE
	1970-72	250 cu. in.	XYDA-7000-A	AS25-BE
ZD-Fairlane	1970-72	250 cu. in.	ZDDA-7000-A	AS25-BE
XA-Falcon	1972-73	200 cu. in.	xxDA-7000-xx	0546-002
	1972-73	250 cu. in.	xxDA-7000-xx	0546-001
XB-Falcon	1974-76	200 cu. in.	72DA-7000-CA	0546-011
	1977-76	250 cu. in.	72DA-7000-DA	0546-009
XC-Falcon	1976-79	200 cu. in.	76DA-7000-AA	0546-000071
	1976-79	250 cu. in.	76DA-7000-BA	0546-000070
XD-Falcon	1979-82	200 cu. in.	xxDA-7000-xx	0546-000060
	1979-82	250 cu. in.	xxDA-7000-xx	0546-000070
XE-Falcon	1982-82	200 & 250 cu. in.	82DA-7000EA	0546-0000XX
	1982-83	200 & 250 cu. in.	82DA-7000FA	0546-0000XX

GENERAL INFORMATION

Model	Years	Engine	Ford Pt No	BW Pt No
	1982-83	250cu.in.	82DA-7000HA	0546-0000XX
	1983-84	200cu.in.	82DA-7000FC	0546-0000XX
	1983-84	250 & 250EFI	82DA-7000HC	0546-0000XX
XF - Falcon	1984-88	200cu.in.	84DA-7000-BA	0546-0000XX
	1984-88	250cu.in.	84DA-7000-CA	0546-0000XX
	1984-88	250cu.in. EFI	84DA-7000-AA	0546-0000XX
TC - Cortina	1972-74	200cu.in.	xxDA-7000-xx	0546-000018
		250cu.in.	xxDA-7000-xx	0546-000017
TD - Cortina	1974-77	200cu.in.	xxDA-7000-xx	0546-000066
		250cu.in.	xxDA-7000-xx	0546-000065
TE - Cortina	1977-80	200cu.in.	76DA-7000-AA	0546-000071
		250cu.in.	76DA-7000-BA	0546-000070
TF - Cortina	1980-82	200 & 250cu.in.	xxDA-7000-xx	0546-0000xx

C4, C5, C9 & C10 AUTOMATIC TRANSMISSION

Model	Years	Engine	Part No.
XR - XT Falcon/ZA - ZB Fairlane	1966-69	289cu.in.	PEE-H1
XR - XT Falcon/ZA - ZB Fairlane	1966-69	302cu.in.	PEE-V(column)S(floor)
XW - Falcon/ZC Fairlane	1969-70	302 & 351 cu.in.	PEE-V
XY - Falcon/ZD Fairlane	1970-72	302cu.in.	PEE-AC
	1970-72	351 cu.in.	PEF-C
XA - Falcon/ZF Fairlane	1972-73	250cu.in.	PEE-AC
	1972-73	302cu.in.	PEF-AC
	1972-73	351 cu.in.	PEF-C
XB - Falcon/ZG Fairlane	1974-76	200 & 250cu.in.	PEE-AW
	1974-76	302 & 351 cu.in.	PEF-J
XC - Falcon/ZH Fairlane	1976-79	200 & 250cu.in.	PEE-AW
	1976-79	302cu.in.	PEF-J
	1976-79	351 cu.in.	PEF-J
XD - Falcon/ZJ Fairlane	1979-82	200 & 250cu.in.	PEE-AW
	1979-82	302cu.in.	PEF-J
	1979-82	351 cu.in.	PEF-J
XE - Falcon/ZK Fairlane	1982-84	302cu.in.	PEF-J12
Fairlane & Torino	1962-64	289cu.in.	PCW-W, W1, AB
Mustang	1964-65	170cu.in.	PCS-C, C1
		200cu.in.	PCS-F
		260cu.in.	PCW-G
		289cu.in.	PCW-AS, BA, H, H1, J
Fairlane & Torino	1965	289cu.in.	PCW-AD, AC, AF, M
Cyclone, Fairlane & Torino	1966	289cu.in.	PCW-A2, AN, AY
Mustang	1966	200cu.in.	PCS-Y
		289cu.in.	PCW-AS, BA, H
Cougar	1967	289cu.in.	PEE-C, C1, K
Cyclone Fairlane & Torino	1967	289cu.in.	PEE-J, J1, M, PEF-D, D1, D2
Mustang	1967	200cu.in.	PEB-B
		289cu.in.	PEE-C, C1, K
Mustang	1968	200cu.in.	PEB-B, B1
Mustang & Cougar	1968	289cu.in.	PEE-C, C1
		302cu.in.	PEE-S
Cyclone, Fairlane & Torino	1968-69	302cu.in.	PEE-B, M, V
Cougar	1969	302cu.in.	PEE-AC
Mustang	1969	200cu.in.	PEE-B1; PEB-B, B2
		250cu.in.	PEE-AD, AD6; PED-AA
		302cu.in.	PEE-A, AC
Fairlane & Torino	1970	302cu.in.	PEE-V1, V2, V3, M1, M2, M3
Cougar	1970	302cu.in.	PEE-AC1
Cyclone, Fairlane & Torino	1970	351 cu.in.	PEF-D, D1, D2, E, E1, E2
Mustang	1970	200cu.in.	PEB-B3
		250cu.in.	PEE-AD, AD1, AD6
		302cu.in.	PEE-A, AC, AC1
		351 cu.in.	PEF-C
Mustang	1971	250cu.in.	PEE-AD, AD2, AD3, AD4, AD6
		302cu.in.	PEE-A, AC, AC2, AC3, AC4
Mustang	1972	250cu.in.	PEE-AD, AD3, AD4, AD6
		302cu.in.	PEE-A, AC, AC3, AC4
Mustang	1973	250cu.in.	PEE-AD, AD6
		302cu.in.	PEE-A, AC, AC6
Mustang II	1974	140cu.in.	PEJ-H
		171 cu.in.	PEJ-E, E1, J
Mustang II	1975	171 cu.in.	PEJ-E, E1, J1
		302cu.in.	PEE-BY PEE-CC, CC1, CC3, CC4, CC5
Mustang II	1976	171 cu.in.	PEJ-M1, M2, M3, M4, M5, M6, N
		302cu.in.	PEEBY, CC, CC1, CC2, CC3, CC4, C5
Mustang II	1977	140cu.in.	77DT-BA, 77DT-BC, PEJ-H
		171 cu.in.	PEJ-M1, M2, M3, M4, M5, M6
		302cu.in.	PEE-BY, CC1, CC3, CC4, CC5
Mustang II	1978	140cu.in.	PEJ-P2, P3
		170cu.in.	PEJ-M1, M2, M3, M4, M5, M6
		302cu.in.	PEE-BY2, BY3, BY4
			PEE-CC1, CC3, CC4, CC5
Mustang	1979	170cu.in.	PEJ-M1, M2, M3, M4, M5, M6
			PEJ-S, S1, W, W1
		200cu.in.	PEB-P
		302cu.in.	PEE-BY2, BY3, BY4, FM, FS
Bobcat & Pinto	1980	140cu.in.	PEJ-Z, Z1, Z2, Z3, Z4
Capri, Fairmont, Mustang & Zephyr	1980	140cu.in.	PEJ-AC1, AC2, AC3
Fairmont & Zephyr	1980	140cu.in.	PEJ-AD, AD1, AD2, AD3
Mustang	1980	140cu.in.	PEJ-AC, AC4
Capri, Fairmont, Mustang & Zephyr	1980	200cu.in.	PEB-P4, P5, P6, P7
Cougar & Thunderbird	1980	200cu.in.	PEB-T3, T4
Fairmont & Zephyr	1980	200cu.in.	PEB-N6, N7, N8, N9, S3, S4
			PEB-T1, T2, T3, T4
			PEB-U, U1, U2, U3
Granada & Monarch	1980	250cu.in.	PEL-A, A1, A2, A3
			PEL-B, B1, B2, B3
			PEL-C, C1, D, D1
Cougar, Fairmont, Thunderbird & Zephyr	1980	255cu.in.	PEM-D, D1, D2, D3, D4
			PEM-L, L1, L2, L3, L4
Capri & Mustang	1980	255cu.in.	PEM-B, B1, B2, B3, B4
Capri, Fairmont, Mustang & Zephyr	1980	255cu.in.	PEM-E, E1, E2, E3, E4
			PEM-N, N1, N2, N3, N4
Fairmont & Zephyr	1980	255cu.in.	PEM-C, C1, C2, C3, C4
Fairmont	1980	255cu.in.	PEM-G, G1
Fairmont & Zephyr	1980	255cu.in.	PEM-H, H1, H2, H3, H4
			PEM-M, M1, M2, M3, M4
Granada & Monarch	1980	255cu.in.	PEM-J, J1, J2, J3, J4
			PEM-K, K1, K2, K3, K4
			PEM-P, P1, R, R1
Zephyr	1980	255cu.in.	PEM-G, G1, G2, G3, G4
Pick-up	1980	300 & 302cu.in.	PEA-CE6, CE7, CE8
Cougar & Thunderbird	1980	302cu.in.	PEE-FL, FL1, FL2, FL3, FL4
			PEE-FN, FN1, FN2, FN3, FN4
Ford & Mercury	1980	302cu.in.	PEE-DZ3, DZ4, DZ5, DZ6, DZ7
			PEE-EA3, EA4, EA5, EA6, EA7
			PEE-EM3, EM4, FC1, FC2
			PEE-FE1, FE2, FE3, FE4, FE5
Granada & Monarch	1980	302cu.in.	PEE-CW5, CW6, CW7, CW8, CW9
			PEE-FP, FP1, FP2, FP3, FP4
			PEE-FR, FR1, FR2, FR3, FR4
Versailles	1980	302cu.in.	PEE-EY2, EY3, EY4, EY5, EY6
			PEE-FV, FV1, FV2, FV3, FV4
Capri, Cougar, Fairmont, Granada, Mustang & Zephyr	1981	140cu.in.	PEJ-AC3, AC4
Cougar, Fairmont, Granada & Zephyr	1981	140cu.in.	PEJ-AD3, AD4
Mustang	1981	140cu.in.	PEJ-AC, AC1, AC2
Capri, Cougar, Fairmont, Granada, Mustang & Zephyr	1981	200cu.in.	PEB-P8, P9 PEN-A, A1, B, B1
Cougar, Fairmont, Thunderbird & Zephyr	1981	200cu.in.	PEB-Z, Z1
Cougar, Fairmont, Granada & Zephyr	1981	200cu.in.	PEB-N10, N11
Fairmont & Zephyr	1981	200cu.in.	PEB-U4, U5, PEN-M, N
Mustang	1981	200cu.in.	PEB-P3
Cougar, Fairmont, Granada, Thunderbird & Zephyr	1981	255cu.in.	PEM-D5, D6, AC, AC1
Cougar, Fairmont, Granada & Zephyr	1981	255cu.in.	PEM-C5, C6
Capri, Cougar, Fairmont, Granada, Mustang & Zephyr	1981	255cu.in.	PEM-E5, E6, AD, AD1
Cougar & Mustang	1981	255cu.in.	PEM-AE, AE1
Cougar, Fairmont, Granada & Zephyr	1981	255cu.in.	PEM-AL, AL1, AM, AM1
			PEM-AN, AN1, AN2
Capri & Mustang	1981	255cu.in.	PEM-W, W1, AK, AK1

GENERAL INFORMATION

Model	Years	Engine	Part No.
Pick-up	1981	255 cu.in.	PEA-CP,CP1
Pick-up	1981	300 cu.in.	PEA-CE9,CE10
Thunderbird	1981	255 cu.in.	PEM-AN2
Mustang	1982	200 cu.in.	PEN-W
		255 cu.in.	PEM-AP

C6 AUTOMATIC TRANSMISSION

Model	Years	Engine	Part No
Cyclone, Fairlane & Torino	1966	390 cu.in.	PDD-J,P,E,R,V
Mustang	1966	390 cu.in.	PGA-P,P1,P2
Cougar & Mustang	1967	390 cu.in.	PGA-P,P1,P2
		428 cu.in.	PGA-AF
Cougar & Mustang	1968	390 cu.in.	PGA-P,P1,P2,S
		427 & 428 cu.in.	PGB-AF,W
Cyclone, Fairlane & Torino	1968-69	390 cu.in.	PGA-AC,AD,B,B1,B2,C,C1,C2,M2,R2,V,W
		427 & 428 cu.in.	PGB-AG,AH,Y,Z
Cougar & Mustang	1969	390 cu.in.	PGA-AE,Y
		427 & 428 cu.in.	PGA-AF1
Cyclone, Fairlane & Torino	1970	390 cu.in.	PGA-AC,AD,V,W
		429 cu.in.	PGB-A,B,J; PJC-A,E,F
Cougar & Mustang	1970	390 cu.in.	PGA-AE,Y
		428 cu.in.	PGA-AF1
		429 cu.in.	PGB-AF2
Mustang	1971	351 cu.in.	PGA-AH,AU,AV,AV2
		429 cu.in.	PJC-G
Mustang	1972	351 cu.in.	PGA-AU,AU1,AU3,AV,AV1,AV2,BA,BA1,PJC-G1
Mustang	1973	351 cu.in.	PGA-AV,AV2,AU3
Econoline 150	1980	300 cu.in.	PGD-Z13,Z14
Econoline 100/150	1980	300 cu.in.	PGD-AL9,AL10
Econoline 250/350	1980	300 cu.in.	PJD-A15,A16 PGD-DB,DB1
Pickup 250	1980	300 cu.in.	PGD-AW9,AW10
Pickup 100/150	1980	300 cu.in.	PGD-BC9,BC10
Pickup 100/350	1980	300 cu.in.	PGD-BD9,BD10
Econoline 250	1980	302 cu.in.	PGD-AD8,AD9,DC,DC1
Econoline 100/150	1980	302 cu.in.	PGD-BN4,BN5,BS4,BS5
Ford & Mercury	1980	302 cu.in.	PGD-BH5,CU5
Pickup 100/150	1980	302 cu.in.	PGD-BE8,BE9
Pickup 100/250	1980	302 cu.in.	PGD-BF8,BF9
Pickup 150/250, U150	1980	302 cu.in.	PGD-CZ,CZ1
Econoline 150	1980	351 cu.in.	PGD-Y15,Y16,CM4,CM5 PJA-DR,DR1,DT,DT1
Econoline 100/150	1980	351 cu.in.	PGD-AC12,AC13,CL4,CL5
Econoline 250/350	1980	351 cu.in.	PGD-DR,DS PGA-DL,DL1,DU,DU1
Ford & Mercury	1980	351 cu.in.	PGD-DD,DE,DG
Pickup 150/350	1980	351 cu.in.	PJA-Z10,Z11
Pickup 350	1980	351 cu.in.	PJA-AE10,AE11
Pickup 150/350, U150	1980	351 cu.in.	PJA-AJ10,AJ11
Pickup 150	1980	351 cu.in.	PJA-CJ7,CJ8
Pickup 150/250, U150	1980	351 cu.in.	PJA-DP1,DP11
Pickup 150/250	1980	351 cu.in.	PJA-DS,DS1
Econoline 250/350	1980	400 cu.in.	PJA-DM,DM1,DN,DN1
Pickup 350	1980	400 cu.in.	PJA-AG11,AG12
Pickup 250/350	1980	400 cu.in.	PJA-AH10,AH11
Pickup 250/350, U150	1980	400 cu.in.	PJA-AL11,AL12
Econoline 250/350	1980	460 cu.in.	PJD-W15,W16,Z15,Z16
Econoline 350	1981	300 cu.in.	PGD-A19,A20
Econoline 100/150	1981	300 cu.in.	PGD-AL14,AL15
Econoline 250/350	1981	300 cu.in.	PGD-DB4,DB5
Pickup 250/350	1981	300 cu.in.	PGD-AW9,AW10,AW13,AW14
Pickup 100/150	1981	300 cu.in.	PGD-BC14,BC15
Pickup 150/350	1981	300 cu.in.	PGD-BD14,BD15
Econoline 100/150	1981	302 cu.in.	PGD-BN9,BN10
Econoline 250	1981	302 cu.in.	PGD-DC4,DC5
Pickup 100/150	1981	302 cu.in.	PGD-BE13,BE14
Pickup 150/250	1981	302 cu.in.	PGD-BF13,BF14
Pickup 150/250, U150	1981	302 cu.in.	PGD-CZ4,CZ5
Econoline 100/150	1981	351 cu.in.	PGD-AC17,AC18,CL9,CL10
Econoline 150/250	1981	351 cu.in.	PGD-CM9,CM10
Econoline 150/350	1981	351 cu.in.	PGD-DN,DN1 PGA-DU4
Econoline 250/350	1981	351 cu.in.	PGD-DP,DP1
Pickup 150	1981	351 cu.in.	PGD-DJ,DJ1,DJ2
Pickup 250	1981	351 cu.in.	PGD-DK,DK1
Pickup 150/250, U150	1981	351 cu.in.	PGD-DL,DL1 PJA-DP4
Pickup 100/350	1981	351 cu.in.	PJA-Z15
Pickup 250/350	1981	351 cu.in.	PJA-AE14
Pickup 150/350, U150	1981	351 cu.in.	PJA-AJ14
Pickup 100/150	1981	351 cu.in.	PJA-CJ12
Pickup 250	1981	351 cu.in.	PJA-DS5
Econoline 250/350	1981	400 cu.in.	PJA-DM4,DN4
Pickup 350	1981	400 cu.in.	PJA-AG15
Pickup 250/350	1981	400 cu.in.	PJA-AH15
Pickup 150/350, U150	1981	400 cu.in.	PJA-AL15
Econoline 250/350	1981	460 cu.in.	PJD-W16,Z16
Econoline 350	1982	300 cu.in.	PGD-A21
Econoline 100/150	1982	300 cu.in.	PGD-AL16
Econoline 100/350	1982	300 cu.in.	PGD-DB6
Econoline 100/250	1982	300 cu.in.	PGD-DY
Pickup 250/350	1982	300 cu.in.	PGD-AW15
Pickup 100/150	1982	300 cu.in.	PGD-BC16
Pickup 100/350	1982	300 cu.in.	PGD-BD16
Econoline 100/150	1982	302 cu.in.	PGD-BN11
Econoline 100/250	1982	302 cu.in.	PGD-DC6
Pickup 100/150	1982	302 cu.in.	PGD-BE15
Pickup 150/250	1982	302 cu.in.	PGD-BF15
Pickup 150/250, U150	1982	302 cu.in.	PGD-CZ5,DV
Pickup 100/250	1982	302 cu.in.	PGD-DU
Pickup 150, U150	1982	302 cu.in.	PGD-DW
Econoline 100/150	1982	351 cu.in.	PGD-AC19
Econoline 100/150	1982	351 cu.in.	PGD-CM11
Econoline 150/350	1982	351 cu.in.	PGD-DN2,EC
Econoline 250/350	1982	351 cu.in.	PGD-DP3
Pickup 150	1982	351 cu.in.	PGD-DJ3
Pickup 150/350	1982	351 cu.in.	PGD-DK2
Pickup 150/350, U150	1982	351 cu.in.	PGD-DL1
Pickup 250/350	1982	351 cu.in.	PGD-DW
Econoline 250/350	1982	400 cu.in.	PJA-DM5,DN5
Pickup 250/350	1982	400 cu.in.	PJA-AG16,AH16
Pickup 250/350, U150	1982	400 cu.in.	PJA-AL15
Econoline 250/350	1982	460 cu.in.	PJD-W17,Z17
Econoline 250/350	1983	300 cu.in.	PGD-A32
Econoline 150/350	1983	300 cu.in.	PGD-DB17
Econoline 100/150	1983	300 cu.in.	PGD-DY
F100/350	1983	300 cu.in.	PGD-AW26
F250	1983	300 cu.in.	PGD-EE
F150/250, U150	1983	300 cu.in.	PGD-EF,EG
F150/250	1983	300 cu.in.	PGD-EK10
F100/150	1983	300 cu.in.	PGD-EN
Econoline 150/250	1983	302 cu.in.	PGD-DC17
F150	1983	302 cu.in.	PGD-BE26,EP
F100/250	1983	302 cu.in.	PGD-BF26
F250	1983	302 cu.in.	PGD-DU10
F150/250, U150	1983	302 cu.in.	PGD-DV10,EA10
Econoline 100/250	1983	351 cu.in.	PGD-CM21,DM12
Econoline 250/350	1983	351 cu.in.	PGD-DP13
Econoline 150/250	1983	351 cu.in.	PGD-EC10
Econoline 100	1983	351 cu.in.	PGD-ES
F150/350	1983	351 cu.in.	PGD-DK12
F150/250, U150	1983	351 cu.in.	PGD-DL11
F250/350	1983	351 cu.in.	PGD-DW10
Econoline 250/350	1983	420 cu.in.	DIEPJE-E,D
Econoline 250/350	1983	460 cu.in.	PJD-W27,Z27
Econoline 350	1983	460 cu.in.	PJD-AZ
Econoline 250/350	1984	300 cu.in.	PGD-A32,AW26
Econoline 250	1984	300 cu.in.	PGD-DB17,EK10
Econoline 150	1984	300 cu.in.	PGD-FB,FC
F150/250/350	1984	300 cu.in.	PGD-AW26
F150/250, U150 & Bronco	1984	300 cu.in.	PGD-EG2,EG3
F150/350	1984	300 cu.in.	PGD-EL10,EK10

GENERAL INFORMATION

Model	Years	Engine	Part No.
Econoline 150/250	1984	302 cu.in.	PGD-BE27,DC18
Econoline 150	1984	302 cu.in.	PGD-EP1,EU
F150/250, U150 & Bronco	1984	302 cu.in.	PGD-EA12,EA13,EA14
F150	1984	302 cu.in.	PGD-EP1,BF27
Bronco	1984	351 cu.in.	PGD-EY1,EY2
Econoline 150/350	1984	351 cu.in.	PGD-DK13,DP14,EC11
Econoline 250/350 & F150/350	1984	351 cu.in.	PGD-DW11
Econoline 150/250	1984	351 cu.in.	PGD-EV,EZ
Econoline 150	1984	351 cu.in.	PGD-EW,FA
F150/250	1984	351 cu.in.	PGD-DK13,EV,EW
F150/250, U150	1984	351 cu.in.	PGD-DL13,DL14,DL15, EY1,EY2
Econoline 250/350	1984	420 cu.in. DIE	PJE-A,B,D,E
F250/350	1984	420 cu.in. DIE	PJE-A,B,C,C1
Econoline 250/350	1984	460 cu.in.	PJD-W28,Z28,BB1,B4
F250/350	1984	460 cu.in.	PJD-BB1,BC1
F250/350 4WD	1984	460 cu.in.	PJD-BA3
Econoline 250/350 & F150/250	1985	300 cu.in.	PGD-AW27
Econoline 150	1985	300 cu.in.	PGD-FB
Econoline 150/350	1985	300 cu.in.	PGD-FC1
Econoline 100/350	1985	300 cu.in.	PGD-FC10,F12
F150/250, U150 & Bronco	1985	300 cu.in.	PGD-EG4
F150	1985	300 cu.in.	PGD-EK10,FE,FF
Econoline 150/350	1985	351 cu.in.	PGD-EV1
Econoline 150/250	1985	351 cu.in.	PGD-DW12
Econoline 150	1985	351 cu.in.	PGD-FD
F150/250, U150 & Bronco	1985	351 cu.in.	PGD-DL15
F150/250	1985	351 cu.in.	DW12,EV1
F150/350, U150	1985	351 cu.in.	PGD-EY2
F150	1985	351 cu.in.	PGD-FD
Econoline 250/350	1985	420 cu.in. DIE	PJE-B1
F250/350	1985	420 cu.in. DIE	PJE-A,B1,C1
Econoline 250/350	1985	460 cu.in.	PJD-BB1,BC2
F250/350	1985	460 cu.in.	PJD-BA3,BA4,BB1, BB2,BC2,BC3
Econoline 150/350	1986	300 cu.in.	PDG-AW27
Econoline 150	1986	300 cu.in.	PDG-EK10,EK11,FB,FB1
Econoline 150/250	1986	300 cu.in.	PGD-FC1,FC2
Econoline 150/350	1986	300 cu.in.	PGD-FF,FF1
F150/250	1986	300 cu.in.	PDG-AW27,AW28
F150	1986	300 cu.in.	PGD-EK9,EK10PDG-FE,FE1
F150/350	1986	300 cu.in.	PGD-FF,FF1
F150, U150 & Bronco	1986	300 cu.in.	PGD-EG4,EG5
Econoline 150/250	1986	302 cu.in.	PKB-J5,J6,J7
Econoline 150	1986	302 cu.in.	PKB-N1,N2,N3
F150	1986	302 cu.in.	PGD-FG,FG1
Econoline 150/350	1986	351 cu.in.	PDG-EV1,EV2
Econoline 150	1986	351 cu.in.	PDG-FD,FD1
F150/350	1986	351 cu.in.	PGD-EV1,EV2
F150	1986	351 cu.in.	PGD-FD,FD1
F150/350, U150 & Bronco	1986	351 cu.in.	PGD-EY2,EY3
Econoline 250/350	1986	420 cu.in. DIE	PJE-B2,B3,B4
F250/350	1986	420 cu.in. DIE	PJE-A,A1,A2,B2,B3,B4, C2,C3,C4
Econoline 250/350	1986	460 cu.in.	PJD-BB2,BB3,BC3,BC4
F250/350	1986	460 cu.in.	PJD-BA4,BA5,BB2,BB3, BC3,BC4
Econoline 150	1987	300 cu.in.	PGN-FN,FW
Econoline 150/350	1987	300 cu.in.	PGD-FP
Econoline 250/350	1987	300 cu.in.	PGD-FZ
F150	1987	300 cu.in.	PGD-FN,FR,GD1,GD2
F150/350	1987	300 cu.in.	PGD-FP,FZ,GD
U150 & Bronco	1987	300 cu.in.	PGD-FR,FU
F150	1987	302 cu.in.	PGD-FM,GA
F150/250	1987	302 cu.in.	PGD-GA1
Econoline 150/350	1987	351 cu.in.	PGD-FV
Econoline 150	1987	351 cu.in.	PGD-FY,FY1
F150/350	1987	351 cu.in.	PGD-FK
F150/250	1987	351 cu.in.	PGD-FV
F150	1987	351 cu.in.	PGD-FY,FY1
U150	1987	351 cu.in.	PGD-FK,FT
F250/350	1987	420 cu.in. DIE	PJE-F,G
Econoline 250/350	1987	420 cu.in. DIE	PJE-G
Econoline 250/350 & F250/350	1987	420 cu.in. DIE	PJE-G1
Econoline 250	1987	460 cu.in.	PJD-BF
Econoline 250/350	1987	460 cu.in.	PJD-BG,BH
F250/350	1987	460 cu.in.	PJD-BE,BF,BF1,BH
F250	1987	460 cu.in.	PJD-BG
Bronco	1988	300 cu.in.	PGD-GN1
Econoline 150/350 & F150/250	1988	300 cu.in.	PGD-FN2,FP2
F150	1988	300 cu.in.	PGD-GM1
F150/350	1988	300 cu.in.	PGD-GD2,GW
Bronco	1988	302 cu.in.	PGD-GU
F150	1988	302 cu.in.	PGD-GT
F150/250	1988	302 cu.in.	PGD-FM1,GA1
Bronco	1988	351 cu.in.	PGD-GH,GJ
Econoline 150/350 & F150/350	1988	351 cu.in.	PGD-GE,GF
F150/350	1988	351 cu.in.	PGD-GY,GG,GR
Econoline 250/350 & F250/350	1988	420 cu.in. DIE	PJE-G1
F250/350	1988	420 cu.in. DIE	PJE-H,J
Econoline 250/350 & F250/350	1988	460 cu.in.	PJD-BF1
F250/350	1988	460 cu.in.	PJD-BR,BT
Bronco	1989	300 cu.in.	PGD-JD,HP
Econoline 150/350	1989	300 cu.in.	PGD-HA,HB,HZ
F150	1989	300 cu.in.	PGD-HN,JC
F150/350	1989	300 cu.in.	PGD-HA,HD,HF,HZ
Bronco	1989	302 cu.in.	PGD-HV
F150	1989	302 cu.in.	PGD-GZ,HD,HU
Bronco & F250/350	1989	351 cu.in.	PGD-HL,HM
Econoline 150/350 & F250/350	1989	351 cu.in.	PGD-HG,HH,JA,JE
F250/350	1989	351 cu.in.	PGD-HS,HJ
Econoline 250/350 & F250/350	1989	420 cu.in. DIE	PJE-K,L
F250/350	1989	420 cu.in. DIE	PJE-M
Econoline 250/350 & F250/350	1989	460 cu.in.	PJD-BV,CB
F250/350	1989	460 cu.in.	PJD-BZ

FMX AUTOMATIC TRANSMISSION

Model	Years	Engine	Part No.
Cyclone, Fairlane & Torino	1968-69	351 cu.in.	PHB-C,D,F,G
Cougar	1969	351 cu.in.	PHB-E,H
Mustang	1969	351 cu.in.	PHB-E,E7,E8,H
Cougar	1970	351 cu.in.	PHB-E1,P
Cyclone, Fairlane & Torino	1970	351 cu.in.	PHB-R,S
Mustang	1970	351 cu.in.	PHB-E,E1,E7,E8,P
Mustang	1971	351 cu.in.	PHB-E,E2,E3,E7,E8
Mustang	1972	302 cu.in.	PHA-H,H1,H3
		351 cu.in.	PHB-E,E4,E5,E7,E8
Mustang	1973	302 cu.in.	PHA-H,H3
		351 cu.in.	PHB-E,E7,E8
Ford & Mercury	1980	302 cu.in.	PHB-BH2,H3
Ford & Mercury	1980	351 cu.in.	PHB-BK,K1,BP,P1,BT,T1
Mercury	1980	351 cu.in.	PHB-BU,U1
XW - Falcon	1969-70	351 cu.in.	PHB-F,G
XY - Falcon	1970-72	351 cu.in.	PHB-S
XA - Falcon	1972-73	351 cu.in.	PHB-S
XB - Falcon	1974-76	351 cu.in.	PHB-S
XC - Falcon	1976-79	351 cu.in.	PHB-S
XD - Falcon	1979-82	351 cu.in.	PHB-S
XE - Falcon	1982-84	351 cu.in.	PHB-S

AOD AUTOMATIC TRANSMISSION

Model	Years	Engine	Part No
Cougar	1980	255 cu.in.	PKA-AH
Cougar	1980	302 cu.in.	PKA-Y8
Cougar & Thunderbird	1980	302 cu.in.	PKA-Y1,Y2,Y3,Y4,Y5,Y6
Ford	1980	302 cu.in.	PKA-E1,E2,E3,E4,E5,E6
Lincoln & Mark VI	1980	302 cu.in.	PKA-M1,M2,M3, M4,M5,M6
Mercury	1980	302 cu.in.	PKA-E4,E5,E6
Mercury	1980	302 cu.in.	PKA-W1,W2,W3
Ford & Mercury	1980	351 cu.in.	PKA-C1,C2,C3,C4,C5,C6
Ford & Mercury	1980	351 cu.in.	PKA-R1,R2,R3,R4,R5,R6

GENERAL INFORMATION

Model	Years	Engine	Part No.
Ford	1980	351 cu.in.	PKA-T1, T2, T3
Ford & Mercury	1980	351 cu.in.	PKA-Z1, Z2, Z3, Z4, Z5, Z6
Lincoln & Mark VI	1980	351 cu.in.	PKA-D1, D2, D3, D4, D5, D6
Lincoln & Mark VI	1980	351 cu.in.	PKA-U1, U2, U3, U4, U5, U6
Mercury	1980	351 cu.in.	PKA-T1, T2, T3, T4, T5, T6
Ford & Mercury	1981	255 cu.in.	PKA-AF, T
Thunderbird	1981	255 cu.in.	PKA-AH
F-100/250	1981	302 cu.in.	PKB-A, A1, A6, D, D1
Ford & Mercury	1981	302 cu.in.	PKA-E6
Ford & Mercury	1981	302 cu.in.	PKA-AG, G50, L, U
Lincoln & Mark VI	1981	302 cu.in.	PKA-M8
Thunderbird	1981	302 cu.in.	PKA-Y8
Ford & Mercury	1981	351 cu.in.	PKA-C6, C8
Ford & Mercury	1981	351 cu.in.	PKA-R8
Ford & Mercury	1981	351 cu.in.	PKA-T8
Ford & Mercury	1981	351 cu.in.	PKA-Z8
Ford & Mercury	1981	351 cu.in.	PKA-AR, S, V
Continental	1982	232 cu.in.	PKA-BF
Cougar & Thunderbird	1982	232 cu.in.	PKA-BH
Cougar & Thunderbird	1982	255 cu.in.	PKA-AH5
Continental, Mark VI & Mercury	1982	255 cu.in.	PKA-AF5, T5
Mercury	1982	255 cu.in.	PKA-AG5, U5
F-100/250	1982	302 cu.in.	PKB-A6, A7
Ford	1982	302 cu.in.	PKA-AG5
Ford & Mercury	1982	302 cu.in.	PKA-AY
Ford & Mercury	1982	302 cu.in.	PKA-BB
Mark VI & Town Car	1982	302 cu.in.	PKA-M13
Town Car	1982	302 cu.in.	PKA-BC
Ford & Mercury	1982	351 cu.in.	PKA-CB
Ford & Mercury	1982	351 cu.in.	PKA-AS5
Cougar, Marquis & Thunderbird	1983	232 cu.in.	PKA-BR, BR1, BR2
Cougar, Marquis, Ford & Thunderbird	1983	232 cu.in.	PKA-BT, BT1, BT2, BT3
Ford	1983	232 cu.in.	LTDPKA-BR1, BR2
Ford, Marquis & Thunderbird	1983	232 cu.in.	PKA-CB, CB1, CB2, CB3
Econoline 100/250	1983	300 cu.in.	PKB-F, F1
F-100/250	1983	300 cu.in.	PKB-E, E1, E2, E3, F, F1, F2
Econoline 100/250	1983	302 cu.in.	PKB-A20, A21, A22, A23
Econoline 250	1983	302 cu.in.	PKB-G, G1, G2
F-100/250	1983	302 cu.in.	PKB-A20, A21
Cougar	1983	302 cu.in.	PKA-K, K1, K2, K3
Ford & Mercury	1983	302 cu.in.	PKA-AG17, AG18, AG19, AG20
Ford	1983	302 cu.in.	PKA-AU17, AU18, AU19, AU20
Ford	1983	302 cu.in.	PKA-AY12, AY13, AY14, AY15
Ford	1983	302 cu.in.	PKA-BB12, BB13, BB14, BB15
Ford	1983	351 cu.in.	PKA-C25, C26, C27, C28
Ford	1983	351 cu.in.	PKA-AS17, AS18, AS19, AS20
Capri & Mustang	1984	232 cu.in.	PKA-CD, CD1, CD2, CD3, CD4
Capri & Mustang	1984	232 cu.in.	PKA-BZ, BZ1, BZ2, BZ3, BZ4
& Thunderbird	1984	232 cu.in.	PKA-BT6, BT7, BT8, BT9, BT10
Cougar, Marquis, LTD, Thunderbird & Ford	1984	232 cu.in.	PKA-CB6, CB7, CB8, CB9, CB10
Ford	1984	232 cu.in.	LTDPKA-BT6, BT7, BT8, BT9, BT10
Econoline 150/250	1984	300 cu.in.	PKB-H1, H2
F-150	1984	300 cu.in.	PKB-E6, E7, E8, E9, E10, PKB-F4, F5, F6, F7
F-100/250	1984	300 cu.in.	PKB-E6, E7, E8, E9, E10
F-100/250 & Econoline 150/250	1984	300 cu.in.	PKB-F4, F5, F6, F7, F8, F9
Cougar & Thunderbird	1984	302 cu.in.	PKA-K6, K7, K8, K9, K10
Capri & Mustang	1984	302 cu.in.	PKA-BW, BW1, BW2, BW3, BW4
Capri	1984	302 cu.in.	PKA-BZ1, BZ2, BZ3, BZ4
Cougar, Marquis, LTD, Continental	1984	02 cu.in.	PKA-BD18, BD19, BD20, BD21, BD22
Econoline 250	1984	302 cu.in.	PKB-G5, G6, G7, G8, G9, G10
F-100/150	1984	302 cu.in.	PKB-F8, F9
Ford, LTD & Marquis	1984	302 cu.in.	PKA-CE1, CE2, CE3
Ford, LTD & Marquis	1984	302 cu.in.	PKA-CF1, CF2, CF3
F-150/250 & Econoline 150/250/350	1984	302 cu.in.	PKB-A26, A27, A28, A29, A30, A31
Ford, Mercury, Crown Victoria & Gran Marquis	1984	302 cu.in.	PKA-AG23, AG24, AG25, AG26, AG27
Ford, Mercury, Crown Victoria & Gran Marquis	1984	302 cu.in.	PKA-AU23, AU24, AU25, AU26, AU27
Ford, Mercury, Crown Victoria & Gran Marquis	1984	302 cu.in.	PKA-AY18, AY19, AY20, AY21, AY22
Ford, Mercury, Crown Victoria & Gran Marquis	1984	302 cu.in.	PKA-BB18, BB19, BB20, BB21, BB22
Mark VII	1984	302 cu.in.	PKA-BV1, BV2, BV3, BV4
Town Car	1984	302 cu.in.	PKA-M31, M32, M33, M34, M35
	1984	302 cu.in.	PKA-BC12, BC13, BC14, BC15, BC16
Ford, Mercury, Crown Victoria & Gran Marquis	1984	351 cu.in.	PKA-C31, C32, C33, C34, C35
Ford, Mercury, Crown Victoria & Gran Marquis	1984	351 cu.in.	PKA-AS23, AS24, AS25, AS26, AS27
Cougar, Marquis, LTD & Thunderbird	1985	232 cu.in.	PKA-CB13
Ford	1985	232 cu.in.	LTDPKA-CB13
Mustang	1985	232 cu.in.	PKA-CD7
F-150	1985	300 cu.in.	PKB-E12
Econoline 150/250 & F-150	1985	300 cu.in.	PKB-F12
Bronco	1985	302 cu.in.	PKB-K, M
Capri & LTD	1985	302 cu.in.	PKA-BW17
Continental & Mark VII	1985	302 cu.in.	PKA-BD25
Cougar & Thunderbird	1985	302 cu.in.	PKA-K13
Cougar & Thunderbird	1985	302 cu.in.	PKA-CJ
Econoline 150/250 & F-150/250	1985	302 cu.in.	PKB-A33
Econoline 150/250	1985	302 cu.in.	PKB-G
F-150/250	1985	302 cu.in.	PKB-J, K, L
F-150/250 4WD & U150	1985	302 cu.in.	PKB-M
Ford, Mercury, Crown Victoria & Gran Marquis	1985	302 cu.in.	PKA-AG30
Ford & Mercury	1985	302 cu.in.	PKA-AU30
Ford, Mercury, Crown Victoria & Gran Marquis	1985	302 cu.in.	PKA-AY25
Ford & Mercury	1985	302 cu.in.	PKA-BB25
Ford, Marquis, Mustang & Capri	1985	302 cu.in.	PKA-BW7
Ford, Marquis & LTD	1985	302 cu.in.	PKA-CE6
Ford, Marquis & LTD	1985	302 cu.in.	PKA-CF6
Town Car	1985	302 cu.in.	PKA-M38
	1985	302 cu.in.	PKA-BC19
Ford, Mercury, Crown Victoria & Gran Marquis	1985	351 cu.in.	PKA-C38
Ford & Mercury	1985	351 cu.in.	PKA-AS30
Cougar, LTD, Marquis & Mustang	1986	232 cu.in.	PKA-CD9, CB15
E-150/250 Van & F-150	1986	300 cu.in.	PKB-F17
F-150	1986	300 cu.in.	PKB-E17, E18, F18
Bronco & F-150/250 4WD	1986	302 cu.in.	PKB-K5, K6, K7, M5, M6, M7
Capri & Mustang	1986	302 cu.in.	PKA-CY4
Continental	1986	302 cu.in.	PKA-CS4, CT4
Cougar & Thunderbird	1986	302 cu.in.	PKA-CZ4
Crown Victoria & Gran Marquis	1986	302 cu.in.	PKA-CL4, CM4, DB
Crown Victoria	1986	302 cu.in.	PKA-CN4
E-150/250 & F150/250	1986	302 cu.in.	PKB-J5, J6, J7
E-150/250	1986	302 cu.in.	PKB-N1, N2, N3
F-150/250	1986	302 cu.in.	PKB-J8, L5, L6, L7, L
Mark VII	1986	302 cu.in.	PKA-CU4, CV4, CW4
Town Car	1986	302 cu.in.	PKA-CP5, DC2
Crown Victoria & Gran Marquis	1986	351 cu.in.	PKA-C38
Crown Victoria	1986	351 cu.in.	PKA-AS30
Cougar & Thunderbird	1987	232 cu.in.	PKA-CB15, DK
E-150 Van	1987	300 cu.in.	PKB-T2, T3, U2, U3
Bronco	1987	302 cu.in.	PKB-P2, R2
Continental	1987	302 cu.in.	PKA-CS5, CT5

GENERAL INFORMATION

Model	Years	Engine	Part No.
Cougar & Thunderbird	1987	302 cu.in.	PKA-CZ5,DE1
Crown Victoria & Gran Marquis	1987	302 cu.in.	PKA-CL4,CL5, CM4,CM5,DB,DB1
Crown Victoria	1987	302 cu.in.	PKA-CN4,CN5
E-150/250 Van	1987	302 cu.in.	PKB-J10,N5
F-150/250	1987	302 cu.in.	PKB-J10,L9,P2,R2,T2,T3
Mark VII	1987	302 cu.in.	PKA-CU5,CV4,CW5,DG,DJ
Mustang	1987	302 cu.in.	PKA-DL,DL1,DD3
Town Car	1987	302 cu.in.	PKA-CP5,DC2
Crown Victoria & Gran Marquis	1987	351 cu.in.	PKA-C40
Crown Victoria	1987	351 cu.in.	PKA-AS32
Cougar & Thunderbird	1988	232 cu.in.	PKA-DK1,DK2
E-150 Van & F-150	1988	300 cu.in.	PKB-AA
E-150 Van	1988	300 cu.in.	PKB-AB
Bronco & F-150/250 4WD	1988	302 cu.in.	PKB-Y,Z
Cougar & Thunderbird	1988	302 cu.in.	PKA-DR2,DS2
Crown Victoria	1988	302 cu.in.	PKA-CM8,CN7,CN8,CN9, DB3,DB4,DU,DU1,EM
E-150 Van	1988	302 cu.in.	PKB-N
F-150/250	1988	302 cu.in.	PKB-J12,L11
Gran Marquis	1988	302 cu.in.	PKA-CM8,DB3,DB4
Mark VII	1988	302 cu.in.	PKA-DG4,DG5,DG7,DJ4,DJ6
Mustang	1988	302 cu.in.	PKA-DD4,DD5,DL2,DL3
Thunderbird	1988	302 cu.in.	PKA-DK1,DK2
Town Car	1988	302 cu.in.	PKA-CP7,CP8,CP9, DC4,DC5
Gran Marquis	1988	302 cu.in.	PKA-C42,C43
Thunderbird	1989	232 cu.in.	PKA-DK1,2
E-150 Van	1989	300 cu.in.	PKB-AC,AD
Bronco & F-150/250 4WD	1989	302 cu.in.	PKB-AG,AJ
Cougar & Thunderbird	1989	302 cu.in.	PKA-DR2,DS2
Crown Victoria & Gran Marquis	1989	302 cu.in.	PKA-CM8,DB3,DB4
Crown Victoria	1989	302 cu.in.	PKA-CN7,CN8,CN9,DU,DU1,EM1
E-150 Van	1989	302 cu.in.	PKB-AF
F-150/250	1989	302 cu.in.	PKB-AC,AE,AH
Mark VII	1989	302 cu.in.	PKA-DG4,DG5, DG7,DJ4,DJ6
Mustang	1989	302 cu.in.	PKA-DZ,DZ1,EK,EK1, DD4,DD5,DL2,DL3
Thunderbird	1989	302 cu.in.	PKA-DK1,DK2
Town Car	1989	302 cu.in.	PKA-CP7,CP8,CP9,DC4,DC5
Gran Marquis	1989	351 cu.in.	PKA-C42,C43
Mustang	1990-		PKA-XXX

85/91/85 LE AUTOMATIC Transmission

Model	Years	Engine	Trans. Model	BTR Part No
EA-ED-Falcon	1988-94	6 Cyl	85LE	90 DA 7000 AA
(XG-Utility,	1988-94	6 Cyl	91LE	91 DA 7000 AA/BA
NJ-Fairlane)	1988-94	6 Cyl	95LE	91 DA 7000 CA

93/97 LE AUTOMATIC TRANSMISSION

Model	Years	Engine	Trans. Model
EF-EL-Falcon	1994-98	6 Cylinder	93LE
(XG-XH Utility,	1994-98	8 Cylinder	97LE
NF-NL-Fairlane)			
AU-Falcon	1998-2001	6 Cylinder	93LE
(Utility and Fairlane)	1998-2001	8 Cylinder	97LE

3spd. P.S. MANUAL TRANSMISSION

Model	Years	Engine	Part No
XK to XY - Falcon	1960-72	144,170,200,221 250 cu.in.	130032
XA - Falcon	1972-73	200 & 250 cu.in.	199333

3spd. F.S. MANUAL TRANSMISSION

Model	Years	Engine	Part No
XR-XY Falcon	1966-67	170, 188, 200, 221, 302, 351 cu.in.	130033
XA - Falcon	1972-73	200 & 250 cu.in.	199332
	1972-73	302 cu.in.	199331
XB - Falcon	1974-76	200 & 250 cu.in.	199332
	1974-76	302 cu.in.	199331
XC - Falcon	1976-79	200 & 250 cu.in.	199332
XD - Falcon	1979-82	200 & 250 cu.in.	0501-001
XE - Falcon	1982-84	200 & 250 cu.in.	0501-001
XF - Falcon	1984-88	200 & 250 cu.in.	0501-001
TC,TD,TE,TF-Cortina	1972-82	200 & 250 cu.in.	199332

4spd. TOP LOADER Manual Trans

Model	Years	Engine	Part No.	Ford Pt No
XR Falcon	1966-67	289 cu.in. code L	RUG-xx	C60Z-7003-D
XT Falcon	1968-69	302 cu.in.	RUG-xx	C60Z-7003-G
XW Falcon/ZC Fairlane	1969-70.	221/302/351	RUG-AR	XW-7003-D
XW Falcon GT-HO	1969-70	351 Cleveland	RUG-AS	XW-7003-E
XY Falcon	1970-72	250/302/351.	RUG-AR	XW-7003-D
XY Falcon GT-HO	1970-72	Handling Option	RUG-BA	DOOZ-7003-J
XA - Falcon	1972-73		RUG-xx	
XB - Falcon	1974-76		RUG-BF	

4spd. SINGLE RAIL MANUAL

Model	Years	Engine	Part No
XB - Falcon	1974-76	250 cu.in.	0503-003
	1974-76	302 cu.in.	0503-00x
	1974-76	351 cu.in.	0503-00x
XC - Falcon	1976-79	250 cu.in.	0503-009
	1976-79	302 cu.in.	0503-009
	1976-79	351 cu.in.	0503-008
XD - Falcon	1979-82	250 cu.in.	0503-009
	1979-82	302 cu.in.	0503-009
	1979-82	351 cu.in.	0503-008
XE - Falcon	1982-84	200 cu.in.	0503-00x
	1982-84	250 cu.in.	0503-00x
	1982-84	302 cu.in.	0503-00x
	1982-84	351 cu.in.	0503-00x
XF - Falcon	1984-88	200 cu.in.	0506-00x
	1984-88	250 cu.in.	0503-00x
TC - Cortina	1972-74	200 & 250 cu.in.	0503-00x
TD - Cortina	1974-77	200 & 250 cu.in.	0503-004
TE - Cortina	1977-80	200 & 250 cu.in.	0503-009/010
TF - Cortina	1980-82	200 & 250 cu.in.	0503-00x

5spd. SINGLE RAIL MANUAL TRANS

Model	Years	Engine	Part No
XE - Falcon	1982-84	200 cu.in.	0507-xxx
	1982-84	200 cu.in.	0506-xxx (no 5th)
XF - Falcon	1984-88	200 cu.in.	0507-xxx

5spd. T5 MANUAL TRANS

Model	Years	Part No
EA,EB,ED,EF,EL-Falcon	1988-98	T50D

5spd. M57 MANUAL TRANS

Model	Years	Part No.
AU and AU11	1998-2001	M57

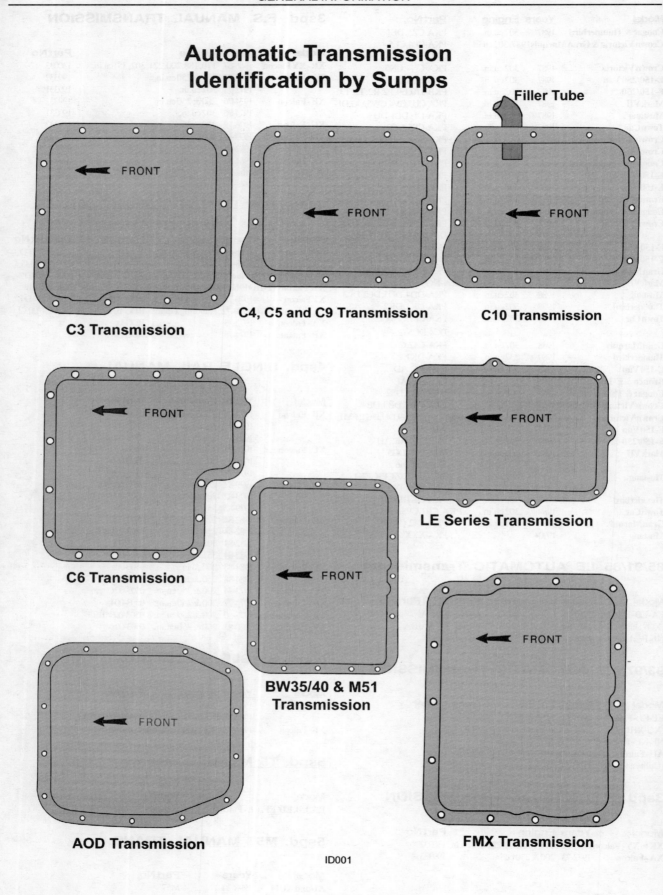

TOOLS, EQUIPMENT & SAFETY PRECAUTIONS

Subject	Page
Transmission Overhaul Tool Listing & Description	12
Torque Wrench	12
Cir-clip/Snap-ring Pliers	12
Hammer/Mallet	12
Cold Chisels	12
Centre/Pin Punches	12
Files	12
Taps & Dies	13
Pullers	13
Bench Vice	13
Slide Hammer	13
Micrometer	13
Dial Indicator	13
Vernier Calipers	14
E-Z-Out Extractors	14
Stethoscope	14
Vacuum Gauge	14
Hydraulic Pressure Gauge	14
Drill/Drill Bits	15

Subject	Page
Die Grinder	15
Work Gloves	15
Face Mask/Safety Glasses	15
Fire Extinguishers	15
Bench Grinder	15
Sockets/Ratchet	16
Screw Drivers	16
Spanners	16
Pliers	16
Magnetic Rod or Magnetic Finger	16
Wash-up Bay	17
Sturdy Work Bench	17
Special Tool Identification	17
Safety Precautions	19
Fire	19
Electrical Equip./Tools	19
Fuels	19
General Practice	19

TOOLS, EQUIPMENT & SAFETY PRECAUTIONS

Transmission Overhaul Tool Listing & Description

Torque Wrench:
Torque wrenches are an important necessity for the work shop to allow bolts and screws to be tightened to the correct torque specifications. Torque wrenches are available in either lb. ft. or Nm, they are also available with both.

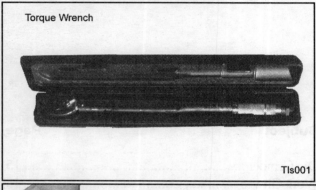

Torque Wrench

Tls001

Torque wrench being used to tighten bolt to specified torque.

Tls018

Cir-clip/Snap-ring Pliers:
Cir-clip and Snap-ring pliers are essential for rebuilding transmissions. These are available as either individual pliers designed purely for certain types of clips or is available as a single set with interchangeable heads.

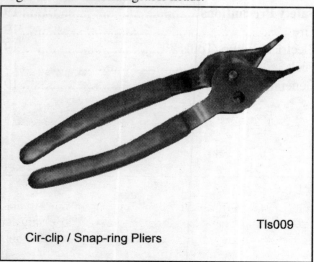

Cir-clip / Snap-ring Pliers

Tls009

Hammer/Mallet:
A good steel hammer preferably a ball-peen hammer and a rubber mallet are vital tools for all workshops. If possible it's best not to use a hammer, although at times they are required for removing or installing parts.

Steel hammers are also essential for when using punches and chisels.

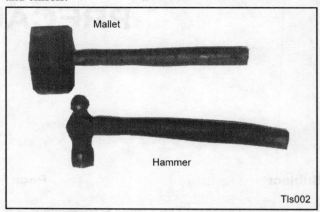

Mallet

Hammer

Tls002

Cold Chisels:
Cold chisels are generally used for removing seized or rusted bolt heads, or removing bolts which have had the heads rounded.

Centre/Pin Punches:
Punches are used for removing and installing roll pins and also for placing a small indent in a location to be drilled and is used to help centre and align the drill piece while starting.

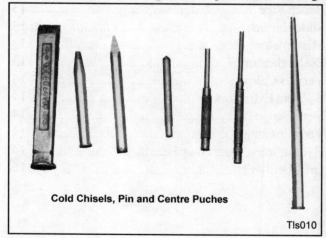

Cold Chisels, Pin and Centre Puches

Tls010

Files:
Files are used for removing burrs and rough edges from parts of the transmission to assist in removal or before installation of parts. They are also used for marking parts, removing rust and filing of rivet and bolt heads where needed. Files are available in a number of shapes and sizes and are usually single-cut or double-cut files.

TOOLS, EQUIPMENT & SAFETY PRECAUTIONS

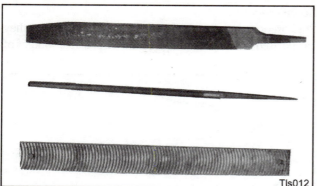

Taps & Dies:
Taps are used for restoring and cutting internal threads to bolt holes, while dies are used for restoring and cutting external threads such as bolts.

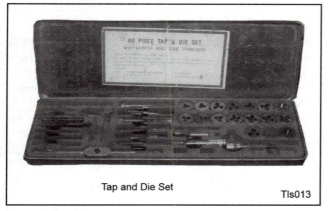

Tap and Die Set

Pullers:
Pullers are used to remove bearings, bad bushings and seized or corroded parts. Pullers are available in different sizes and are available as multipurpose or designed for a specific purpose.

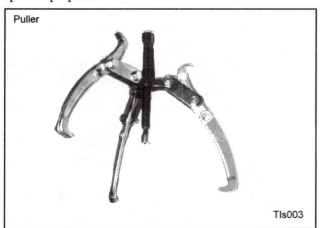

Puller

Bench Vice:
Bench vices are a vital accessory for any workshop, vices are used for holding parts secure while working, soft jaws are also a necessity for the holding of parts which are soft and may be damaged by the hard jaws.

Bench Vice

Slide Hammer:
Slide hammers are used to remove components such as the pump body on the Hydra-matic Turbo 400. The slide hammers are also used for bushing removal and other components as required.

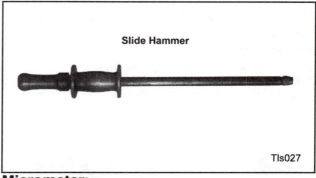

Slide Hammer

Micrometer:
Micrometers are used for measuring the thickness of washers, snap rings and shims. Micrometers are available as conventional read-out or they are available with a digital read-out.

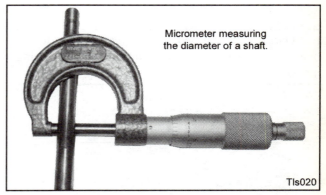

Micrometer measuring the diameter of a shaft.

Dial Indicator:
Dial indicators are used to measure endplay of transmissions and other movement clearances. Ensure a good quality dial indicator is used with at least a one inch travel on the pin.

TOOLS, EQUIPMENT & SAFETY PRECAUTIONS

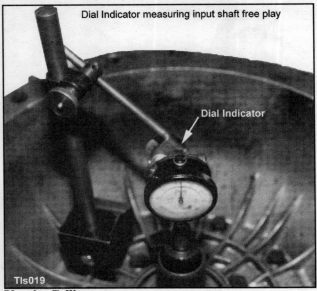
Dial Indicator measuring input shaft free play
Tls019

Vernier Callipers:
Vernier callipers are used for measuring the diameter of parts or the inner diameter of holes. Vernier callipers are less accurate than micrometers but are also available in conventional and digital read-outs. The callipers can also be used to measure the depth of various parts/holes.

E-Z-Out Extractors:

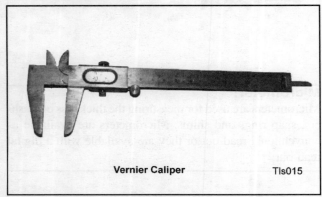
Vernier Caliper — Tls015

E-Z-Out extractors are used for removing broken of studs and bolts, they are sold in sets and can be used for removing a number of different sized studs and bolts.

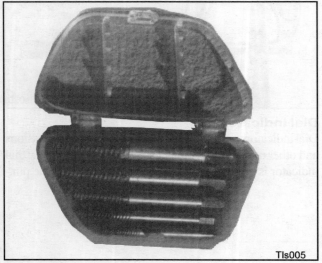
Tls005

Stethoscope:
Stethoscopes are very good in diagnosis of problems as they can be used to amplify noise to diagnose possible sources of trouble.

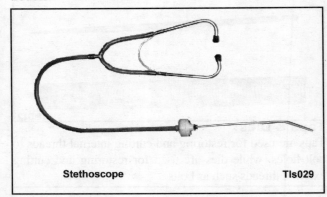
Stethoscope — Tls029

Vacuum Gauge:
Vacuum gauges are used to check the amount of vacuum at the intake manifold, and is required to check in certain transmissions the vacuum modulator system.

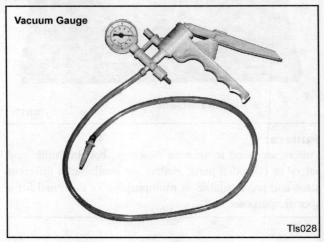
Vacuum Gauge
Tls028

Hydraulic Pressure Gauge:
The hydraulic pressure gauge is used to measure the oil pressure being generated by the oil pump. The gauge must read a minimum of 300 psi.

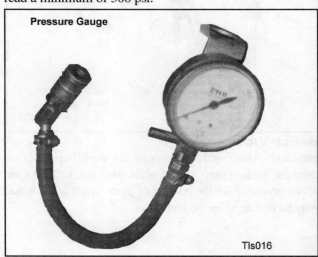
Pressure Gauge
Tls016

TOOLS, EQUIPMENT & SAFETY PRECAUTIONS

Drill/Drill Bits:
A good quality drill and drill bits are a essential part of any workshop, a variety of different sized drill pieces in both metric and imperial are handy for drill holes, drilling out rivets and pins.

Drill Bits — Tls011

Die Grinder:
Die grinders are useful to chamfer oil holes, debar parts, cut and grind. They allow a job to be finished much quicker than doing it by hand although extreme care must be taken as they remove a large amount of material very quickly.

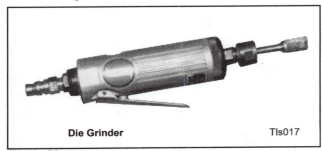
Die Grinder — Tls017

Work Gloves:
A good quality pair of heavy gloves are good for handling and components which are hot or have been heated for any reason. Also good for holding components with sharp edges to prevent cut hands.

Work Gloves — Tls023

Face Mask / Safety Glasses:
Face masks and especially safety glasses are very important protective wear which should be used whenever grinding, cutting or doing anything which could cause shrapnel or fluids to fly or splash into your face.

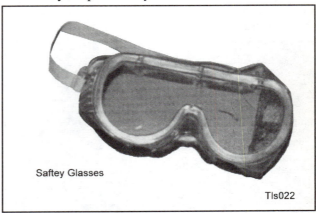
Saftey Glasses — Tls022

Fire Extinguisher:
A chemical fire extinguisher should be kept in close proximity incase of fire. As in workshop environments fire is a very dangerous hazard.

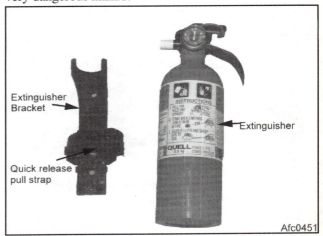
Afc0451

Bench Grinder:
Bench grinders are a useful tool for removing rust and cleaning components, sharpening tools and grinding parts if required. Care must be taken to ensure the grinder is secured to a bench or stand and that it will not vibrate around.

Bench Grinder — Tls006

TOOLS, EQUIPMENT & SAFETY PRECAUTIONS

Sockets/Ratchet:
A good quality ratchet and socket set is the best way of removing bolts and nuts, as it is easier, quicker and most the time more secure on the bolt heads than conventional spanners.

Ratchet and socket sets are available in a number of drive sizes as well as being available in both metric and imperial.

Socket and Ratchet Set — Tls007

Screw Drivers:
A large number of different sized screw drivers of both phillip head and flat blade screw drivers will be used frequently in disassembly of transmissions.

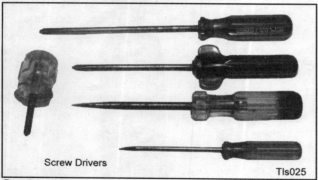
Screw Drivers — Tls025

Spanners:
A full set of metric and imperial spanners of both ring and open end are a essential set of tools to have in a work shop. Spanners are used allot in areas where access is not accessible with a ratchet and socket.

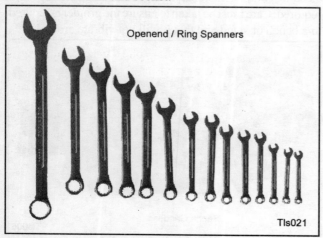
Openend / Ring Spanners — Tls021

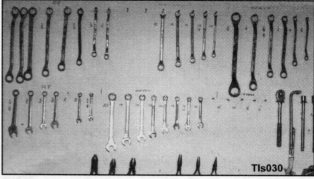
Tls030

Pliers:
Both small and large conventional and pointed nose pliers are used frequently in rebuilding transmissions to disconnect springs remove clips and other small jobs.

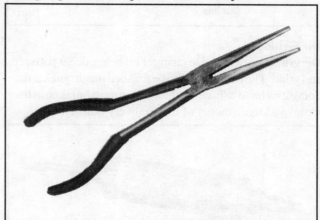

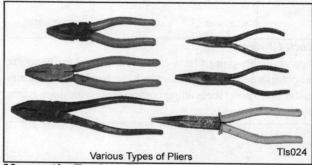
Various Types of Pliers — Tls024

Magnetic Rod or Finger:
A magnetic rod or finger and preferably an extendable unit is a necessity to remove small locking pins or balls, which are located in hard to access bores or cavities. A magnetic rod or finger is also particularly handy retrieve a small steel

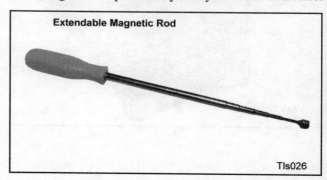
Extendable Magnetic Rod — Tls026

TOOLS, EQUIPMENT & SAFETY PRECAUTIONS

component or small steel tool falls into a partly assembled engine or transmission.

Wash-up Bay:
A good wash-up bay is essential for cleaning components before inspecting for damage and before reassembly. A professional wash bay with flowing fluid can be purchased from a accessories/tools supplier or a bay can be made from using an old sink or similar.

Washup Bay — Tls008

Sturdy Work Bench:
A good sturdy clean work bench is essential when working on transmissions, ensure the bench has a large work area to enable the components to be laid out in order to assist in repairs and assembly of the transmission.

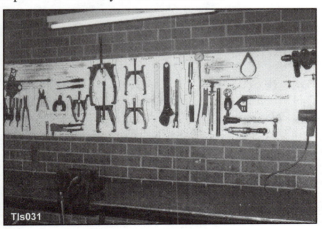
Tls031

SPECIAL TOOL IDENTIFICATION

Manual 3 spd. Partial & Full Synchronized

Tool (Litchfield)	Description
E9273	Input Shaft Housing Seal Installer
E1524	Extension Housing Seal Remover
E1506	Extension Housing Seal Installer
E9261	Extension Housing Bush Remover/Installer
E6673	Bearing Remover Separator 100 mm
E3C10AE	Input Shaft Bearing Installer
Cluster Gear Dummy Shaft	202.0 mm (long)
	19.0 mm (diam)

Manual 4 spd. Top Loader

Tool (Litchfield)	Description
E9217	Shift Rail Pin Remover/Installer
E9273	Input Shaft Housing Seal Installer
E1524	Extension Housing Seal Remover
E1506	Extension Housing Seal Installer
E9261	Extension Housing Bush Remover/Installer
E6673	Bearing Remover Seperator 100 mm
E3C10AE	Input Shaft Bearing Installer
Cluster Gear Dummy Shaft	202.0 mm (long)
	19.0 mm (diam)

Manual 4 spd. (0503) Single Rail

Tool (Litchfield)	Description
E9217	Shift Rail Pin Remover/Installer
E9274	Input Shaft Housing Seal Installer
E1524	Extension Housing Seal Remover
E1506	Extension Housing Seal Installer
E9261	Extension Housing Bush Remover/Installer
E6673	Bearing Remover Seperator 100 mm
E21M21	Gear Lever Retaining Nut Spanner
E3C10AE	Input Shaft Bearing Installer
Cluster Gear Dummy Shaft	228.6 mm (long)
	24.0 mm (diam)

TOOLS, EQUIPMENT & SAFETY PRECAUTIONS

Manual 4 spd. (0506) & 5 spd. (0507) Single Rail

Tool (Litchfield)	Description
E9217	Shift Rail Pin Remover/Installer
E21M10	Adaptor Shift Rail Pin
E9275	Input Shaft Housing Seal Installer
E6606	Extension Housing Seal Remover
E21M12	Extension Housing Seal Installer
E9285	Extension Housing Bush Remover/Installer
E6673	Bearing Remover Seperator 100 mm
E21M21	Gear Lever Retaining Nut Spanner

Manual T5 & M57

Tool (Litchfield)	Description
T40	Torx Bit
T50	Torx Bit
E9320	Input Shaft Seal Installer Kit
E7518B	Bearing Installation Tool (Countershaft) Attachment for E7511-A Handle
E1673P or E1673MT	Puller (use with E1673U15A)
E9321	Extension Housing Seal Installer Kit
E1673U15A	Puller Adaptor (Use with E1673P or E1673MT)
E9319	Snap Ring Expander/Installer
E9318	Countershaft Bearing Cup Remover/Installer
E9322	Dial Indicator Mounting Rod
E7511A	Countershaft Bearing Installer (handle)
E9261	Extension Housing Bush Remover/Installer

Automatic BW35/40 & M51

Tool (Litchfield)	Description
E1384	Transmission Cradle
E9264	Clutch Spring Compressor
E1387A	Rear Clutch Piston Installer
E1388	Front Clutch Piston Installer
E1282	Front Servo Adjustment Gauge
E1284	Front Band Adjust Adaptor
E1294-1	Rear Band Adjustment Spanner
E9261	Extension Housing Bush Remover/Installer
E1506	Extension Housing Seal Installer
E1524	Extension Housing Seal Remover
E9055	Front Pump Oil Seal Installer
E1375	Hydraulic Pressure Test Set
E9046	Banjo Adaptor

Automatic C4, C5, C9 & C10

Tool (Ford)	Description
T66L-7003-B	Bushing Adaptor Remover/Replacer
T63L-77837-A	Front Pump Oil Seal Replacer
T61L-7675-A	Extension Housing Oil Seal Replacer
T65L-77515-A	Clutch Spring Compressor
AT-7697-B	Extension Housing Bush Replacer
AF2-4405-TV	Crowfoot Wrench Vacuum Control Unit

Automatic C6

Tool (Ford)	Description
T66L-7003-B	Bushing Adaptor Remover/Replacer
T63L-77837-A	Front Pump Oil Seal Replacer
T61L-7675-A	Extension Housing Oil Seal Replacer
T65L-77515-A	Clutch Spring Compressor
AT-7697-B	Extension Housing Bush Replacer
AF2-4405-TV	Crowfoot Wrench Vacuum Control Unit

Automatic FMX

Tool (Ford)	Description
T66L-7003-B	Bushing Adaptor Remover/Replacer
T63L-77837-A	Front Pump Oil Seal Replacer
T61L-7675-A	Extension Housing Oil Seal Replacer
T65L-77515-A	Clutch Spring Compressor
AT-7697-B	Extension Housing Bush Replacer
AF2-4405-TV	Crowfoot Wrench Vacuum Control Unit

Automatic AOD

Tool (Ford)	Description
T66L-7003-B	Bushing Adaptor Remover/Replacer
T63L-77837-A	Front Pump Oil Seal Replacer
T61L-7675-A	Extension Housing Oil Seal Replacer
T65L-77515-A	Clutch Spring Compressor
AT-7697-B	Extension Housing Bush Replacer
AF2-4405-TV	Crowfoot Wrench Vacuum Control Unit

Automatic LE Series

Tool (Litchfield)	Description
E1531	Transmission Bench Cradle
E1542	Pump Puller
E1539	Cross Shaft Pin Remover/Installer
E1543	Clutch Spring Compressor Bridge
E1546	Clutch Spring Compressor Shaft
E1545	Clutch Pack Clearance Kit
E9322	End Float Measuring Shaft & Adaptor
E1540	Cross Shaft seal remover
E1541	Cross Shaft Seal Installer
E90261	Extension Housing Bush Remover/Installer
J21426	Extension Housing Seal Installer
E1536	Pump Aligner
17-010A	Pump Seal Installer
E1544	Band Adjusting Spanner
E1544-1	Band Adjusting Adaptor

SAFETY PRECAUTIONS

Fire:
Remember that in a work shop you are working with and around flammable liquids. When working ensure nothing that can ignite is in the vicinity if possible especially when sparks are being created by the job. Ensure the chemical fire-extinguisher is available.

Note: Never use water on a fire in a work shop which is caused by electrical fault or a flammable liquid as water will only spread the flammable liquid enlarging the fire.

Electrical Equipment/Tools:
Be extremely careful when using electrical equipment not to use in damp areas or have cords laying in water, also be careful not to damage the power leads by cutting or having near heat as the result may be electrocution.

Fuels:
Do not store or use petrol or other fuels in plastic containers unless they are approved for transporting or storing fuels as many plastics will be eaten through (melted) by fuel. Metal or glass containers are best for storing and using fuels in.

General Practice:
* When siphoning toxic chemicals never use your mouth to start the liquid drawing, always use a suction pump, or proper siphon hose.
* Do not remove radiator cap before firstly allowing coolant to cool down.
* Do not drain transmission fluid until it has cooled sufficiently to prevent burning.
* Do not inhale brake or clutch dust as it is hazardous to health.
* Always ensure correct sized spanners are use to prevent slipping as it may cause injury.
* Wear protective clothing where necessary.

GENERAL TRANSMISSION REPAIR PROCEDURES

Subject	Page
GENERAL INFORMATION	20
Maintenance Notes	20
TRANSMISSIONS	20
Manual Transmission	20
Removal	20
Installation	21
Automatic Transmission	22
Fluid Level	22
Removal	22
Installation	23

Subject	Page
FLUID COOLER & COOLER PIPES	24
Transmission Cooler	24
External Transmission Cooler	25
Transmission Cooler Pipes	25
TRANSMISSION FLUID COOLER & PIPES	25

MAINTENANCE NOTES

While maintaining the transmission, all parts should be cleaned and inspected. Individual units should be reassembled before disassembly of other units to avoid confusion and interchanging of parts.

1. Thoroughly clean the exterior before disassembly of the unit.
2. Disassembly and assembly must be made on a clean work bench. Cleanliness is of the utmost importance. The bench tools, and parts must be kept clean at all times.
3. Before installing screws into aluminium parts, dip screws into transmission fluid prevent galling aluminium threads and to prevent screws from seizing.
4. To prevent thread stripping, always use a torque wrench when installing screws.
5. If threads in aluminium parts are stripped or damaged the part can be made serviceable by the use of suitable thread inserts.
6. Protective tools must be used when assembling seals to prevent damage. The slightest flaw in the sealing surface of the seal can cause an oil leak.
7. Aluminium castings and valve are very susceptible to nicks, burns, burrs, etc., and should be handled with care.
8. Internal snap rings should be expanded and external snap rings compressed if they are to be reused. This will ensure proper seating when reinstalled.
9. "O" rings, gaskets and oil seals that are removed should not be reused.
10. Teflon oil seal rings should not be removed unless damaged.
11. During assembly of each unit, all internal moving parts must be lubricated with transmission fluid.

SPECIAL NOTE: *Photographs included throughout this chapter are of Ford transmissions, but are not of any specific transmission and are included only as a reference.*

MANUAL TRANSMISSION

REMOVAL
1. Disconnect battery earth lead and raise vehicle (front and rear) and support on safety stands.
(a) Remove propeller shaft.

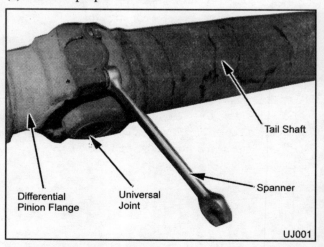

(b) Insert a suitable plug in the end of transmission extension.
3. Disconnect the hand brake cable from the equalizer
4. Disconnect wiring harness connector from back-up lamp switch.

GENERAL TRANSMISSION REPAIR PROCEDURES

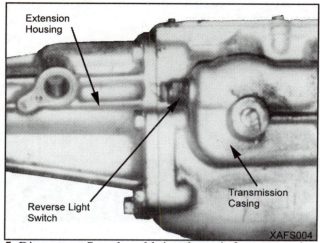

5. Disconnect Speedo cable/sender unit from extension housing.

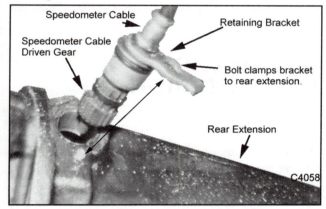

6. (a) Disconnect engine front exhaust pipe from engine.
(b) Place a lifting jack beneath transmission and support weight of transmission.
7. (a) Remove rear cross-member of engine to frame bolts and washers.
(b) Remove cross-member to rear attaching bolts mounting and remove cross-member.
(c) Lower jack and remove from under vehicle.
9. Remove transmission case attaching bolts to clutch housing and withdraw transmission.
* Keep the transmission assembly supported so that it will not tilt in relation to the engine, until the maindrive gear splines are clear of the clutch plate.
* If the transmission is allowed to hang on the splines, the clutch plate will be damaged.

INSTALLATION

1. Make sure that the clutch housing and engine block mating surfaces are clean and free of burrs.
2. Lubricate clutch throw-out bearing surface of the maindrive gear bearing retainer and spigot bearing.

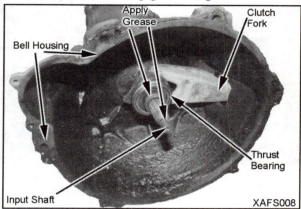

3. Lift transmission into position and support on transmission stand.
4. Fully lift transmission into position and carefully manoeuvre forward until the transmission is fully installed and clutch housing is seated against the engine block.
5. Install the transmission clutch housing to engine block retaining bolts and finger tighten.
6. Install cross-member to transmission then install rear cross-member to mount retaining bolts and tighten to specification for that particular model.
7. Install the rear cross-member to body retaining bolts and tighten cross-member and clutch housing bolts to specification bolts for that particular model.
8. Lower jack and remove from under vehicle.
9. (a) Make sure that the front exhaust pipe to the engine manifold is clean and free of any gasket material.
(b) Install new gasket and tighten front exhaust pipe to manifold bolts to specification.
10. Reconnect Speedo cable/sender unit to transmission extension housing.

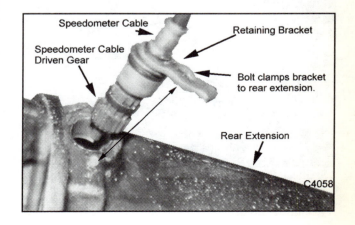

GENERAL TRANSMISSION REPAIR PROCEDURES

11. Reconnect wiring harness connector to back-up lamp switch.

12. Reconnect the hand brake cable to the equalizer

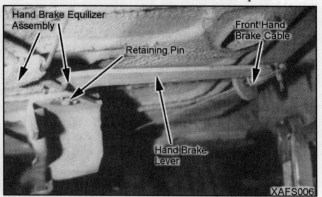

13. Remove plug (dummy yoke) from the end of transmission extension then install propeller shaft and tighten bolts to specification for that particular model.

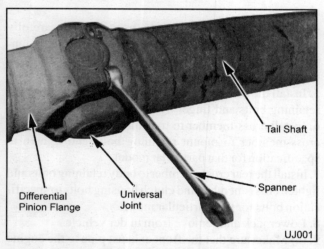

14. Install the starter motor and tighten retaining bolts to specification for that particular model.

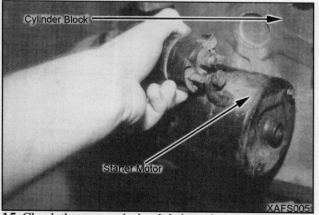

15. Check that transmission lubricant is at correct level.

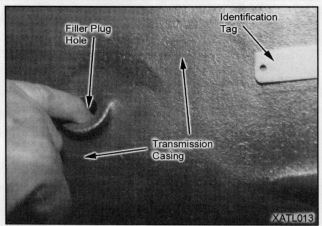

16. Adjust clutch and shift linkage (where required) to specifications and reinstall the centre console into vehicle, if removed.

17. Reconnect battery earth lead, remove safety stands and lower vehicle.

AUTOMATIC TRANSMISSION

FLUID LEVEL
Some automatic transmissions need oil levels to be checked with engine running, while others with engine off. At all times engine must have been running before checking level.

REMOVAL
1. Disconnect the earth cable from the battery, disconnect

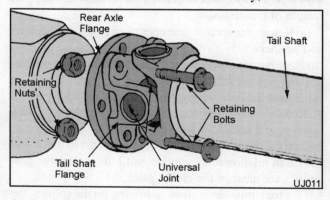

the downshift cable.

2. Place vehicle on safety stands.

3. Place drip tray beneath transmission.

4. Remove the tail shaft and install a plug or seal into the extension housing to stop oil from leaking out.

5. Remove the converter cover attaching bolts at the lower side of converter housing, remove the cover. Where fitted remove drain plug from converter, drain converter and replace drain plug.

6. Disconnect the speedometer cable/sender unit from extension housing.

GENERAL TRANSMISSION REPAIR PROCEDURES

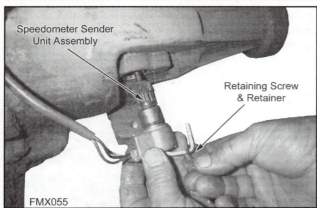

7. Remove the extension housing to cross-member bolts.
8. Remove the sump to drain the fluid from transmission, re-tighten the sump.
9. Remove the filler tube and oil cooler tubes.

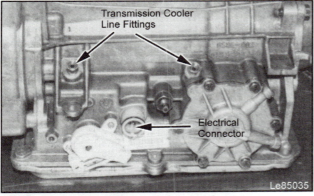

10. Disconnect the selector linkage rod.
11. Remove the neutral start switch wiring connector and any other electrical connections.

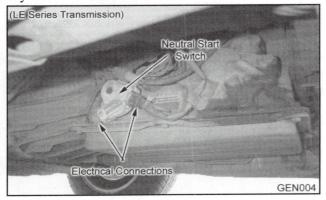

12. Remove the starter motor.
13. Remove the 4 bolts attaching the converter to the flywheel.
14. Place a jack underneath the transmission and secure the transmission to the jack if possible.
15. Remove the cross-member to body retaining bolts and then lower and remove the cross-member.
16. Remove the bolts attaching the converter housing to the engine.

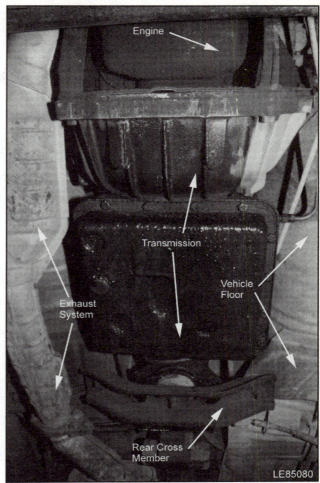

17. Lower and move back the transmission and converter assembly to free from engine.

Note: *Ensure converter moves back with transmission on removal.*

18. Once transmission assembly is free from the engine carefully lower and remove assembly from vehicle.

INSTALLATION

1. Install the converter to the transmission.

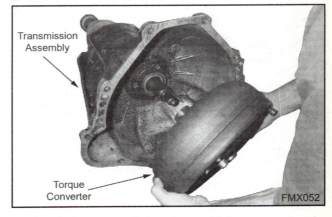

When fitting transmissions into vehicles ensure that the converter is fully installed into transmission before installing transmission. Under no circumstances fit con-

23

GENERAL TRANSMISSION REPAIR PROCEDURES

verter to engine ansd then try to install transmission, as this will lead to damage of the fluid pump and converter.
2. Place the transmission on a mobile jack and secure the transmission.
3. Move the transmission under the car, lift and slide forward the transmission up to the rear of the engine. Install the bolts attaching the converter housing to the engine, torque to specification for that particular model.
4. Install the cross-member to rear mount, then raise transmission and torque cross-member bolts to specification for that particular model.
5. Fit the 4 flywheel to converter bolts and tighten to specification for that particular model.
6. Remove the mobile jack.
7. Connect the fluid cooler tubes to transmission ensuring that they are installed in the correct order.
(return pipe to return fitting)

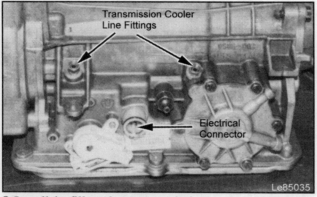

8. Install the filler tube to transmission and install dip stick.
9. Reconnect the neutral start wiring connector then reconnect the selector linkage rod to the transmission.
10. Install the speedometer cable/sender unit to extension housing.

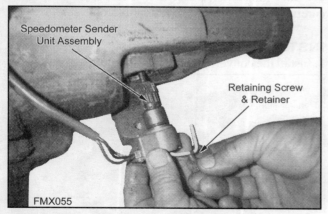

11. Install the park brake cable and adjust.
12. Fit the converter housing cover and tighten to specification for that particular model.
13. Install the starter motor and tighten bolts to specification for that particular model.

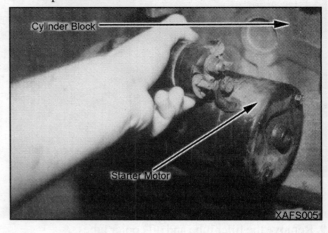

14. Remove plug (dummy yoke) from extension housing then install the tail shaft tightening bolts to specification for that particular model.

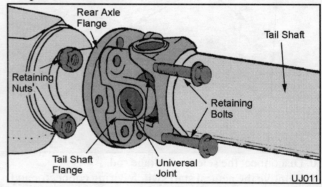

15. Remove vehicle from safety stands.
16. Fill transmission with correct amount of specified automatic transmission fluid for that particular model.
17. Install and adjust kickdown cable.
 # Kickdown adjustments are importent for Borg Warner automatic transmissions as this also controls the transmission pressure. Kickdown slipping will occur if the kickdown cable is not hooked up at all.
18. Adjust gear selector linkages.
19. Reconnect the earth cable to the battery and road test vehicle.

TRANSMISSION FLUID COOLER & PIPES

Transmission Cooler
As the transmission cooler is incorporated into the radiator, the radiator needs to be replaced if the cooler needs replacement.
Unless the vehicle is fitted with an external transmission cooler which is usually mounted in front of the radiator.

GENERAL TRANSMISSION REPAIR PROCEDURES

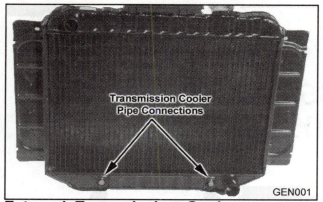

External Transmission Coolers

External transmission coolers are mandatory for vehicles towing, working under heavy loads or street performance use.

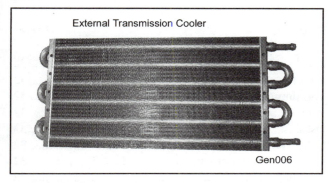

Also if the vehicle has a tendency to overheat it is advisable to install an external cooler to relieve the strain on the cooling system and to assist in keeping the transmission cool.
When choosing an external transmission cooler the size of the cooler is very important as it has to be adequate to keep the transmission fluid cool.
External coolers can be used in-line with the original in radiator cooler or can be used independently, disconnecting the in radiator cooler. If the vehicle is used in cold climates it is advised to install the external cooler in-line with the original as it will assist in initial warm-up in cold weather.

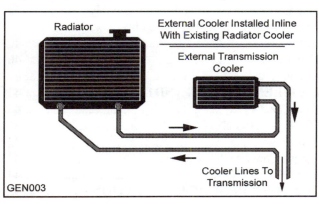

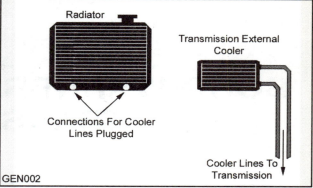

When selecting a transmission cooler choose a cooler which is rated in excess of your vehicle. Coolers are rated on gross vehicle weight (GVW) therefore choose a cooler rated well above your vehicle's GVW.

Transmission Cooler Pipes

If replacement of transmission steel tubing cooler pipes is required, only use double wrapped and brazed steel tubing meeting transmission manufactures specifications or equivalent. Under no condition use copper or aluminium tubing to replace steel tubing. These materials do not have satisfactory fatigue durability to withstand normal car vibrations.
Steel tubing should be flared using the double flare method.

Transmission In-line Filters

One of the main cause of transmission failure is due to metallic particles and the installation of an In-line transmission filter will add extra filtration to the transmission fluid in addition to the internal filter.
In-line transmission filters are extremely easy to install into

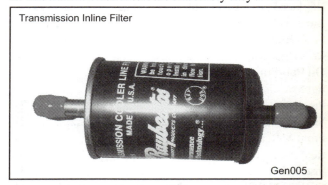

the transmission cooler lines. Take extra care when installing an In-line filter to ensure it is installed with the flow in the correct direction, as a filter installed in the wrong direction will prevent flow and may result in server transmission damage. The direction of flow is clearly marker on the filter.

BORG-WARNER 35/40 AUTOMATIC TRANSMISSION

Subject	Page
MAINTENANCE AND ADJUSTMENT	**27**
Transmission Identification	27
Lubrication	27
Fluid Level	27
Changing Fluid	27
Lubricant	27
Maintain Strainer	28
Maintenance Notes	28
Oil Cooler Pipes	28
Clean and Inspect	28
Console Shift Lever Assembly	**29**
Removal	29
Installation	29
Accelerator Linkage & Down Shift Cable	**29**
Check and Adjust	29
Down Shift Cable Adjustment	29
Replace Kickdown Cable	**29**
Band Adjustment	**29**
Front Brake Band	29
Rear Brake Band	30
Oil Pan/Sump & Valve Body Assembly	**30**
Remove	30
Installation	31
SERVO VALVES	**31**
Front & Rear Servos	31
Remove	31
Installation	31
COOLER REPLACEMENT	**31**
SELECTOR LINKAGE	**31**
Remove	31
Inspect	32
Install	32
Adjust	32
Speedometer Cable & Gear Assembly	**32**
Remove	32
Install	32
MAJOR REPAIR	**32**
Dismantle Transmission	**32**
Housing	32
Valve Bodies	36
Pump	36
Front Clutch & Input Shaft Assembly	36
Rear Clutch & Forward Sun Gear Assembly	37
Front Servo	38
Rear Servo	38
Governor	38
Assemble Transmission	**39**
Governor	39
Rear Servo	39
Front Servo	39
Rear Clutch & Forward Sun Gear Assembly	39
Front Clutch & Input Shaft Assembly	39
Pump	40
Valve Bodies	40
Housing	41
PROBLEM SOLVING AND DIAGNOSIS	**43**
Fluid Checks	43
Oil Pressure Check	43
Road Test	43
Torque Converter Evaluation	44
SPECIFICATIONS	**44**
TORQUE WRENCH SPECIFICATIONS	**45**

MAINTENANCE AND ADJUSTMENT

Transmission Identification
Transmissions are fitted with and identification plate for easy identification when servicing and repairing.

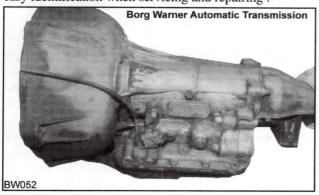

The model code for vehicles equipped with different transmissions are listed in General Information Chapter at the front of this manual.

LUBRICATION
If adding or changing the transmission fluid, use only specified Automatic Transmission fluid M2C33F (Dextron II).

FLUID LEVEL
The dipstick is located at the right rear of the engine near the fire wall. Check fluid level is done in the following procedure:
Parking brake engaged and engine idling with transmission at normal operating temperature, select each gear briefly, and selector the "P" park position.
* The transmission must be at normal operating temperature to obtain an accurate dipstick reading.
* Do not overfill the transmission. Overfilling will cause foaming of the fluid, loss of fluid, shift complaints and possible damage to the transmission.
Remove dipstick and wipe with clean lint free cloth. Turn the engine off, then within 10 sec of turning off replace dipstick into transmission, then remove and check the level.

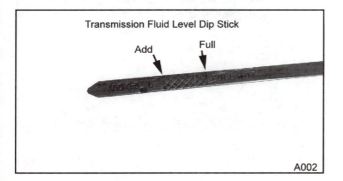

The level must be indicated within the low and full marks on the "hot" range on dipstick, refer below.
NOTE: Ensuring dipstick is properly seated in dipstick tube to prevent fluid contamination. Maintaining transmission fluid at correct level, use recommended fluid in the transmission.

CHANGING FLUID
Overfill the transmission will cause fluid to foaming, loss of fluid, shift complaints and possible damage to the transmission.
1. Raise vehicle and place a large drain tray under transmission oil pan. Clean all dirt from around oil pan and transmission case.
2. Remove all but 2 oil pan retaining bolts, loosen one of the two bolts and tap pan at one corner to break seal loose, allow fluid to drain from the pan.
3. Carefully remove oil pan from the transmission, as pan will still have fluid within it.

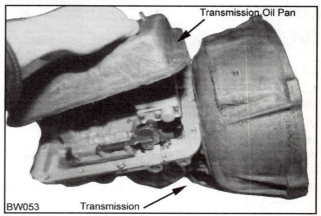

4. Clean oil pan and remove gasket, also clean the transmissions pan mounting surface.
5. Install oil pan with a new gasket, tighten bolts to specified torque.
**Oil pan bolt torque specification: (BW35) 11-14 Nm
                                        (BW40) 14-17 Nm**
6. Pour 3.5L of automatic transmission fluid M2C33F (Dextron II) into the transmission through the dipstick tube.
7. Start engine and allow to idle for at least two minutes. With park brake on, move selector lever momentarily to each position ending in "P" park position.
8. Remove dipstick and wipe with clean lint free cloth. Turn the engine off, then within 10 sec of turning off replace dipstick into transmission, then remove and check the level. The level must be indicated within the low and full marks on the "hot" range on dipstick, refer below.
9. Add more fluid if necessary, until correct level is obtained.

LUBRICANT
BW35 - 8.1 litres including converter M2C33F (Dextron II)
BW40 - 8.5 litres including converter M2C33F (Dextron II)

MAINTAIN STRAINER

Take care when removing sump from transmission as hot oil can cause serious burns. Avoid this by allowing transmission to cool down.

1. Remove the oil pan as described above in the Changing Fluid section, from step 1 to 3.
2. Remove the four screws and washers securing the oil filter to the valve body, then remove filter from valve body and gasket.

3. Fit the new strainer and gasket into position, and refit the retaining screws.
4. Replace the oil pan as described above in the Changing Fluid section, from step 4 to 9.

MAINTENANCE NOTES

While maintaining the transmission, all parts should be cleaned and inspected. Individual units should be reassembled before disassembly of other units to avoid confusion and interchanging of parts.

1. Thoroughly clean the exterior before disassembly of the unit.
2. Disassembly and assembly must be made on a clean work bench. Cleanliness is of the utmost importance. The bench tools, and parts must be kept clean at all times.
3. Before installing screws into aluminium parts, dip screws into transmission fluid prevent galling aluminium threads and to prevent screws from seizing.
4. To prevent thread stripping, always use a torque wrench when installing screws.
5. If threads in aluminium parts are stripped or damaged the part can be made serviceable by the use of suitable thread inserts.
6. Protective tools must be used when assembling seals to prevent damage. The slightest flaw in the sealing surface of the seal can cause an oil leak.
7. Aluminium castings and valve are very susceptible to nicks, burns, burrs, etc., and should be handled with care.
8. Internal snap rings should be expanded and external snap rings compressed if they are to be reused. This will ensure proper seating when reinstalled.
9. "O" rings, gaskets and oil seals that are removed should not be reused.
10. Teflon oil seal rings should not be removed unless damaged.
11. During assembly of each unit, all internal moving parts must be lubricated with transmission fluid.

OIL COOLER PIPES

If replacement of transmission steel tubing cooler pipes is required, only use double wrapped and brazed steel tubing meeting transmission manufactures specifications or equivalent. Under no condition use copper or aluminium tubing to replace steel tubing. These materials do not have satisfactory fatigue durability to withstand normal car vibrations. Steel tubing should be flared using the double flare method.

Clean and Inspect

After complete disassembly of a unit, wash all metal parts in a clean solvent and dry with compressed air. Blow oil passages out and check to make sure they are not obstructed. Small passages should be checked with tag wire. All parts should be inspected to determine which parts are to be replaced.

Pay particular attention to the following:

1. Inspect the magnet in the sump pan for metal filings, to help determine problems with transmission.

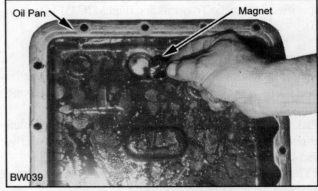

2. Inspect the transmission case for cracking a major problem is cracking in the section shown in below diagram.

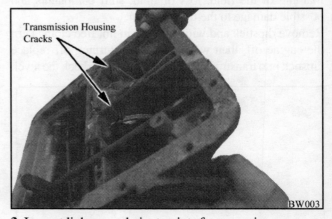

3. Inspect linkage and pivot points for excessive wear.
4. Bearing and thrust surfaces of all parts should be checked

for excessive wear and scoring.
5. Check for broken score seal rings, damaged ring lands and damaged threads.
6. Inspect seal and 'O' rings.
7. Mating surfaces of castings should be checked for burrs. Irregularities may be removed by lapping the surface with emery paper. The emery paper is laid on a flat surface, such as a piece of plate glass.
8. Castings should be checked for cracks and sand holes. Do not use solvents on neoprene seals, composition faced clutch plates or thrust washers as damage to parts may occur.

CONSOLE SHIFT LEVER ASSEMBLY
* Column shift autos refer to the Steering Section under Steering Column Removal (Column Shift).

Removal
1. Raise vehicle to enable the shift rod to be disconnected from the shift lever under the vehicle.
2. Loosen the selector lever handle lock nut, then remove the handle, lock control rod, bush and locknut.
3. Centre Console is to be removed.
4. Disconnect the shift indicator light, then unscrew the shift assembly retaining screws and lift the assembly from the floor pan.

Installation
1. Clean mating surfaces of floor pan and shift lever assembly.
2. Apply a bead of sealer around opening in floor pan between the screw holes.
3. Place the shift lever assemble into the floor pan, then screw the shift assembly retaining screws into position and connect the shift indicator light.
4. Centre Console is to be replaced.
5. Replace the locknut, bush, lock control rod and the handle onto the shift assembly, then tighten the selector lever handle lock nut.
6. Raise vehicle to enable the shift rod to be connected to the shift lever under the vehicle.
7. Adjust linkage as described in this chapter.

ACCELERATOR LINKAGE & DOWN SHIFT CABLE

CHECK & ADJUST
* *Ensure accelerator linkage/cable is correctly adjusted before resetting down shift cable (i.e. Check that wide open throttle can be achieved).*

1. Transmission and engine to be at normal operating temperature before any adjustments are carried out. Engage the hand brake to ensure the vehicle will not move.
2. Connect a tachometer to the engine, with selector in "D" position adjust the idle speed to specification.
Note: For correct procedure refer to appropriate fuel chapter.

Downshift Cable Adjust
1. With engine off press accelerator cable to floor and check that throttle is fully open.
2. Disconnect the downshift inner cable from the bell crank assembly.
3. Adjust trunnion into hole so the stop on the kickdown inner cable just touches to specification off the outer cable (no slack) then replace clip.

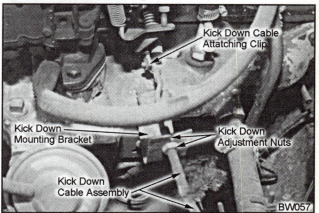

Cable specification: 1.6 mm
4. At full throttle check that the cable pull is at minimum specification.
Cable pull specification: 44.45 mm

REPLACE KICKDOWN CABLE:
1. Remove the oil pan as previously described in this chapter.
2. Remove the inner cable from kick down cam located in the transmissions left hand front corner.
3. Unclip the inner cable from throttle lever, then loosen the adjuster screws and disconnect it from its bracket.
4. To remove the assembly from the transmission casing, press the outer cable retaining lugs together from the inside of the transmission and push the assembly out.
5. With new seal fitted to the retainer, push it into the transmission case until the lugs lock into position.
6. Fit the inner cable to the downshift valve cam, then refit the oil pan with a new gasket as described previously in the chapter.
7. Fit the kickdown cable to the adjuster bracket and then to the throttle lever.
8. Ensure cable is placed correctly, then adjust cable as described above.

BAND ADJUSTMENT
Front Brake Band
1. Place vehicle on safety stands.
2. Place an oil collect tray under transmission.

3. Remove oil pan as described above.
4. Loosen adjusting screw locknut, to allow the servo lever to move outwards, then place a 6.35 mm spacer into the gap between the servo piston pin and adjusting screw.

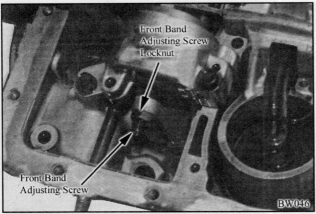

5. The adjusting screw can then be tensioned.
Torque Adjusting screw: 1.130 Nm
6. Once screw is tensioned the locknut can then be tightened, then remove the spacer.
7. Refit oil pan as described above.
8. The vehicle can then be taken for a test drive.

Rear Brake Band
1. Place vehicle on safety stands.
2. With adjusting screw locknut loosened, located on the right hand side of the transmission case.

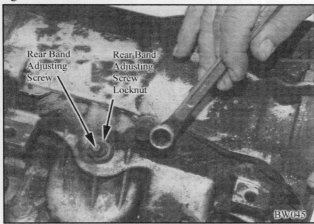

3. Tighten the adjusting screw to a torque of 14 Nm, then slacken adjusting screw 3/4 of a turn.
4. Tighten the adjusting screw locknut.
5. Remove vehicle from safety stands and test run.

OIL PAN / SUMP & VALVE BODY ASSEMBLY
Remove
1. Place vehicle on safety stands.
2. Place an oil collection tray underneath the transmission, then lower the oil pan as described above.
3. Disconnect the transfer pipes, pipes are pushed into the valve body and servo's and many need to be levered from the valve body.

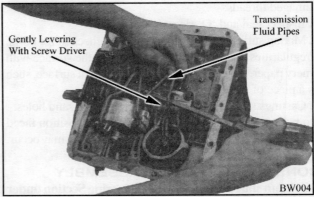

* Do not damage the pipes when levering from the body.
4. Remove the oil strainer as described previously.
5. Unclip the kick down cable from the downshift cam, then the retaining bolts can be removed.

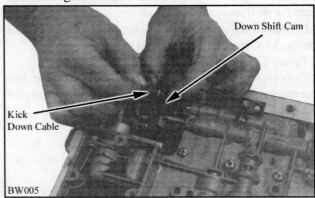

6. There are 3 retaining bolts, they must be withdrawn to allow the valve body to be removed.

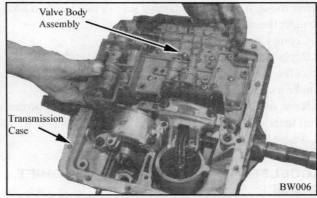

7. The valve body assembly has to be removed evenly to protect the valve body to main casing and pump pipes.

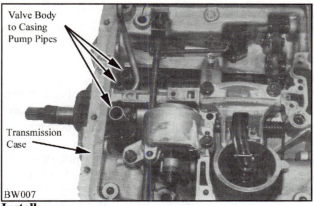

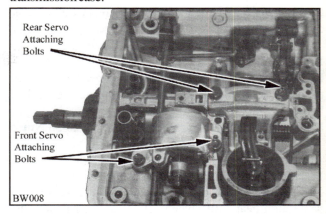

transmission case.

Install

1. Oil pick-up tubes will need to be refitted to the pump if they have been removed, ensure "O" ring is fitted to large pipe into pump.
2. The valve body can be lifted into position ensuring that the oil tubes are fitted into the oil tube collector correctly. Ensure the manual control valve has engaged the peg of the operating lever.
3. The valve body retaining bolts can be fitted, the 2 long bolts go to the rear of the valve body and 1 short in the centre of the valve body near the filter, securing the valve body assembly.

4. The kickdown cable is able to be fitted and adjustment checked.
5. Install the fluid pipes to the valve body assembly.
6. Adjust the front band as previously described.
7. Refit oil pan as previously described.
8. Remove from safety stands and road test vehicle.

SERVO VALVES
Front and Rear Servo
Remove

1. Place vehicle on safety stands.
2. Place an oil collection tray underneath the transmission.
3. Detach the oil pan and valve body from the housing.
4. Remove two bolts which attach the particular servo to the

5. Remove servo take care the operating strut, that transfers the movement from the servos to bands does not fall out and get bent or distorted..

Install

1. Fit operating strut to the servo with petroleum jelly, then manoeuvre into place until strut engages the band.
2. The servo retaining bolts can now be fitted and tensioned. (The front servo bolts are the same) (The rear servo, rear bolt is longer and has a reduced diameter at one end to locate the centre support). Torque bolts to specification.

BW-35
Front Servo Bolts: 11-14 Nm **Rear Servo Bolts:** 14-18 Nm
BW-40
Front Servo Bolts: 14-20 Nm
Rear Servo Bolts: (2 x 3/8 bolt) 21-33 Nm
EFI (1 x 5/16 bolt) 14-20 Nm

3. Proceed with band adjustments as previously described.
4. Fit the oil pan as previously described in this chapter.
5. Remove from safety stands and road test vehicle.

COOLER REPLACEMENT

The cooler is located inside the radiator, if the cooler is to be replaced the radiator must also be replaced. See cooling system for radiator replacement.

There is an optional transmission cooler that is mounted in front of the radiator for models that do not have an air-conditioner fitted.

SELECTOR LINKAGE
Remove

Set transmission selector lever to 'PARK' position. Raise front of vehicle. Remove locking bolt, dished washer, flat washer, insulator and sleeve from lower end of selector lever. Slide trunnion from selector rod. Remove retaining nut, rod and lever assembly from the transmission manual shaft.

BORG-WARNER 35/40 AUTOMATIC TRANSMISSION

Inspect
Check all items for wear and/or damage, replace all worn or damaged items.

Install
Installation is the reverse of the removal procedure. Tighten the nut to the specified torque. Adjust linkage as described below.
Manual shaft nut torque specification: 26-30 Nm

Adjust
1. Loosen locking bolt at selector lever.
2. Position transmission selector lever in "PARK".
3. Position gear shift lever in 'PARK', then tighten the locking bolt at the selector lever, to the specified torque.
Selector lever locking bolt: 18-24 Nm
4. Lower vehicle and test.
5. Ensure that engine can be started only in 'PARK' and 'Neutral'. The Park /Neutral/Backup switch is automatically adjusted when linkage is correctly adjusted.

SPEEDOMETER CABLE & DRIVEN GEAR ASSEMBLY
Remove
1. Raise rear of vehicle and place on safety stands. Place drip tray beneath speedometer driven gear.
2. Remove screw and bracket retaining speedometer cable and driven gear.
3. Withdraw cable and gear assembly from case extension.

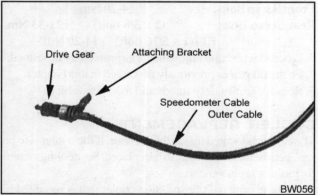

Install
1. Inspect 'O' ring seal and replace it if unsatisfactory.
2. Installation is the reverse of the removal procedure.
3. Tighten retainer bolt to specified torque.
Retainer bolt torque specification: 8-14 Nm

MAJOR REPAIR

Dismantle Transmission
Housing
1. Carefully slide the torque converter from the bell housing, placing it on a clean work area, cover pump drive lugs and sleeve to protect from contamination. Ensure both lugs are intact and undamaged.
2. Loosen the bell housing retaining bolts, place the auto upside down in a transmission cradle with the bell housing over the end of the bench.
3. Remove the screw and plate securing the speedo cable and slide the cable and driven gear assembly from the extension housing, then withdraw the bell housing bolts and the bell housing can be levered from the housing if needed.
4. Extension housing bolts can be undone, then slide the extension housing from transmission case and place to one side.

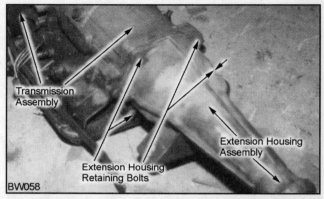

5. Press the speedo clip down and withdraw the gear from the output shaft, place gear and clip together on the bench.

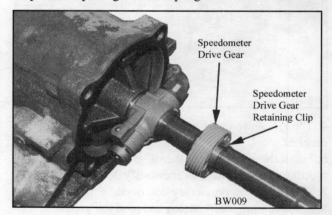

6. The centre support screws can now be removed, which are located 120° from the rear servo on both sides.

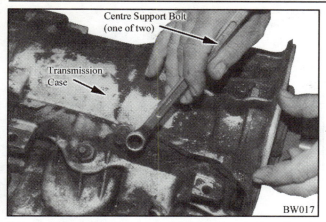

7. Remove oil pan and valve body as previously described in this chapter, also remove the safety 'P'/'N' switch.

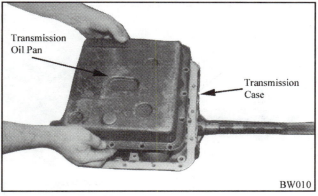

8. Remove the front and rear servo piston assemblies as described previously.

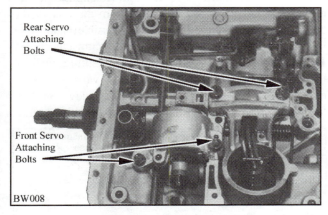

9. Loosen the governor retaining bolt 2.5 turns, then the governor should be able to be slid off the output shaft. Also remove the servos as previously described in this chapter.
10. The end float of the gear train will need to be checked, this is done by levering the front clutch backwards until there is no movement, then place a dial indicator on the input shaft and release the lever and then levering the assemble towards the dial indicator.

End Float Specifications: 0.25-0.76 mm
if not within specification replace shim pack.

11. The transmission fluid pump is retained by 6 bolt, once the bolts have been withdrawn the pump assembly, gasket and thrust washer can be removed from the housing.

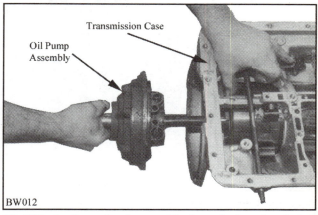

12. Slide the front clutch assembly from the housing, being careful to keep the thrust washers and needle roller bearing in order of where they come from.

13. Rear clutch and sun gears can now be slid from the casing as an assembly, located behind the assembly is a washer and needle roller thrust bearing which can also be removed and placed in order.

14. Before the centre support can be released the front band will need to be removed by squeezing the top together and sliding out.

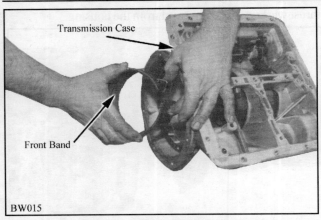

15. Using a rubber mallet lightly hit the output shaft to release the centre support and allow it to be slid from the case.

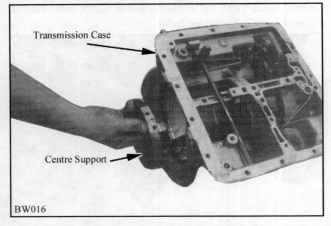

16. Remove the planet gear assembly, needle thrust bearing and steel washer, then the rear band can be removed in a similar way to the front band.

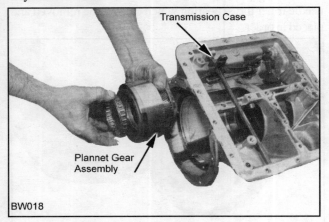

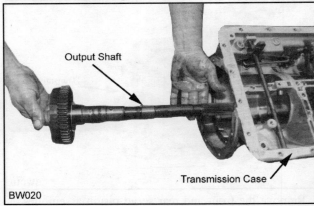

17. Remove the output shaft from the casing, ensuring that the thrust washer is still in place.

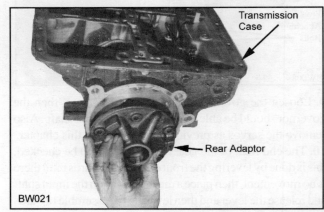

18. Loosen and withdraw the rear adaptor retaining bolts and remove the adaptor body and plate from the rear of the transmission case, there will be three rings visible made of cast iron that can not be damaged under any circumstances.

19. To remove the cross shaft, withdraw the spring clip from the end furthest from the shaft to the manual valve lever, then compress the cross shaft spring with the valve lever until the drive pin is released and withdraw the pin from the shaft.

20. Slide the cross shaft from the casing, the manual valve lever spring and detent ball are spring loaded, so do not loose. Withdraw the manual valve lever and parking pawl link after detaching it from the parking pawl operating mechanism.

21. Release the spring clip from the parking pawl operating

BORG-WARNER 35/40 AUTOMATIC TRANSMISSION

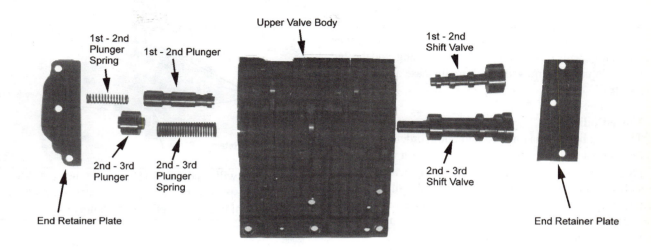

Lower Valve Body Assembly

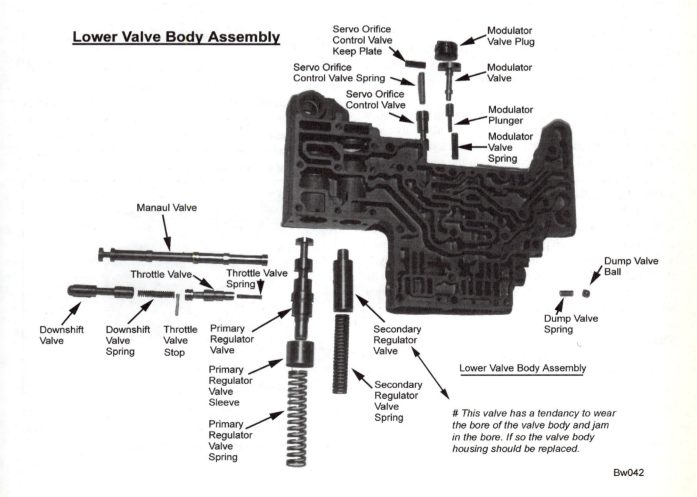

This valve has a tendency to wear the bore of the valve body and jam in the bore. If so the valve body housing should be replaced.

mechanism, take note of the fitment of the spring before it is released, then withdraw the assembly from the casing.

22. The band adjusters can be removed from the casing, if necessary the parking pawl pivot pin can be removed by pushing the tension pin from the parking pawl pivot pin, then push the parking pawl pivot pin from the casing, and the 2nd pivot pin can be removed by tilting the case and taping in lightly.

Valve Bodies

The valve body parts must be laid out in order when being dismantled to ensure the correct installation on reassembling. The best place to lay them out is on clean paper.

1. If not previously removed withdraw the filter element retaining screws, then detach the filter element from the valve body and place to one side. Slide the reverse pressure boost cam and manual control valve (if fitted).

2. Release down shift cam assembly and bracket from the valve body, placing to one side, then slide the throttle and down shift valves with springs from the valve body.

3. Withdraw the 6 lower valve body screws and 2 upper valve body screws to divide that valve body into two pieces.

4. With the valve body split unscrew the 6 screws from the retaining plates on the upper body, then withdraw the 1-2 shift valve, 2-3 shift valve, 2-3 plunger & spring from one side and the 1-2 plunger & spring from the other side.

5. With the lower valve body facing up on a bench, withdraw the retaining screws for the oil tube collector and the retaining screws for the governor line plate, then lift them away including the separator plate.

6. With the separator plate lifted the 2-3 dump valve (spring & ball), throttle valve keep plate and throttle valve stop rollercam be withdrawn and placed to one side.

7. From the lower valve body detach the regulator valve retainer plate, then withdraw the primary regulator valve spring, sleeve and valve, then the secondary regulator spring and valve.

8. Withdraw the orifice control valve keep plate from the lower body, with keep plate withdrawn the orifice control valve and spring can be slid from the lower valve body.

9. Modulator valve dowel pin is to be withdrawn from the valve body to allow the modulator valve plug, plunger, spring and valve to be slid from the lower valve body.

Pump

To divide the pump assembly there is 1 screw and 5 bolts that need to be unscrewed, this will allow the body to be removed from the adaptor.

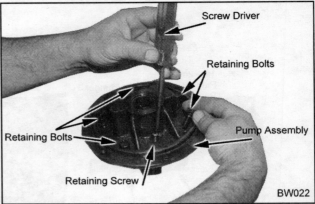

Pump gears will need marking to ensure they are installed correctly, inspect all components and seals for damage, if any need replacing do so prior to assembly.

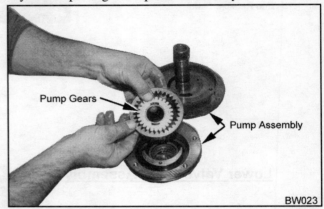

Front Clutch & Input Shaft Assembly

When dismantling this assembly ensure that all components are laid out in order as they are removed from the assembly, this will help with correct installation when assembling.

1. Pry input shaft retaining cir-clip from the clutch cylinder and remove the input shaft assembly.

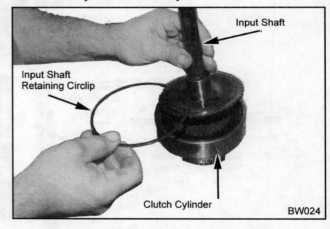

2. Withdraw the front clutch hub to allow the clutch pack to be withdrawn easier, taking note of the order that the steel and composition plates are being removed.

BORG-WARNER 35/40 AUTOMATIC TRANSMISSION

3. The last plate that is removed is a pressure plate which has a wave through it, this can be determined by placing it on a flat surface. Then the lower cir-clip will need prying from the clutch cylinder to enable the diaphragm spring and piston to be removed.

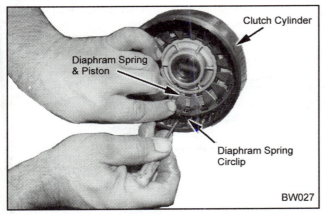

4. The piston is released from the clutch cylinder by applying compressed air to the clutch cylinder piston guide, this will push the piston off its seat and enable it to be removed.

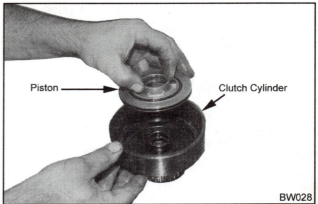

5. All components will need inspection and be replaced if necessary.

Rear Clutch & Forward Sun Gear assembly

When dismantling this assembly ensure that all components are laid out in order as they are removed from the assembly, this will help with correct installation when assembling.

2. Pull the forward sun gear shaft from the rear clutch cylinder, then pry the sealing rings from the shaft with out damaging the shaft.

3. Pry the clutch plate retaining cir-clip from the clutch cylinder, then withdraw the pressure plate. The clutch pack have three different plate designs and must be replaced in the same order as they are removed, they use a fibre plate, flat steel plate and a dished steel plate.

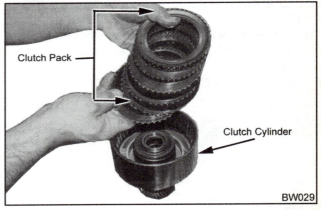

4. Apply the clutch spring compressor to the clutch spring, compressing the spring to enable the cir-clip to be release. Then

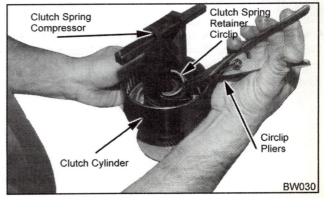

37

remove the cir-clip, compressor, retainer, and spring.

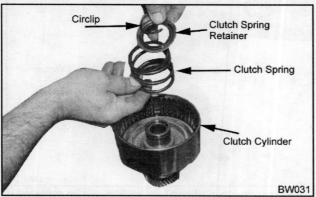

5. The piston is released from its seat by applying compressed air to the port located beside the sealing ring near the front drum.

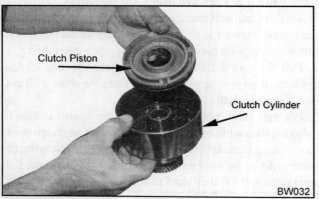

Front Servo
Press the piston guide down the servo housing bore until the cir-clip is clear of the guide and is able to be released from the housing.

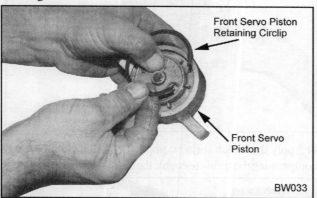

Once the cir-clip has been removed from the housing release the piston guide and allow the spring to push the piston and guide from the housing, then withdraw the piston from the guide.

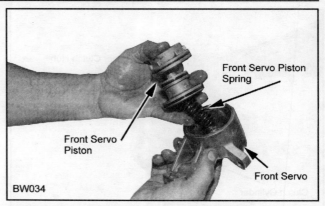

All seals are to be replaced with new seals before assembly.

Rear Servo
To withdraw the piston from the assembly depress the straight arm of the spring, then disconnect it from the lug cast in the servo body. Spring can then be withdrawn as well as the piston.

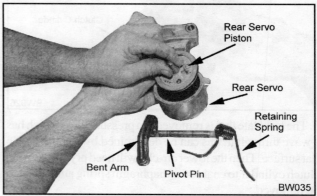

If the lever is to be disconnected, push the retaining pin from the housing using a 3 mm drift.

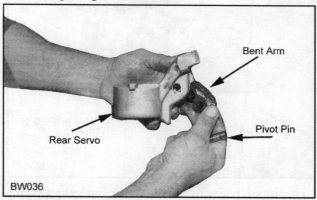

Governor
The governor is dismantled by disconnecting the cir-clip from the weight stem and sliding the weight from the stem, then the stem, valve and spring are all withdrawn through the main shaft bore of the governor.

BORG-WARNER 35/40 AUTOMATIC TRANSMISSION

Assemble Transmission
Governor
Place the weight stem, spring and valve into position through the governor main bore, then slide weight into place and fit the cir-clip.

Rear Servo
Replace the seals, install the piston spigot to the seat of the operating lever, then move the piston into the bore, then apply spring to pivot pin and engage the bent arm to the servo lever, press the straight spring arm to connect the servo body lug.

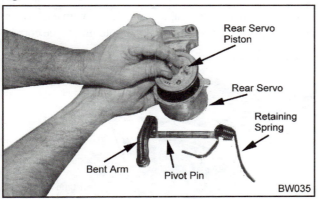

Front Servo
All seals are to be replaced with new seals before assembly, if lever has be disconnected, fit into place and push the retaining pin into the housing using a 3 mm drift.
Install the piston into the guide, then place the spring, piston and guide into the housing, then press the piston guide down the servo housing bore compressing the spring until the cir-clip grove is clear of the guide and the cir-clip is able to be installed into the housing.

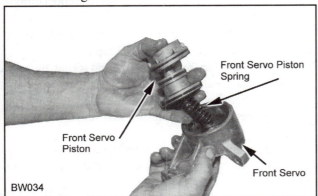

Rear Clutch & Forward Sun Gear Assembly
All seals are to be replaced with new seals before assembly, also inspect the needle roller bearings that support the forward sun gear shaft.
1. Place the piston into position in the rear clutch cylinder, pressing it into place by hand, then fit the spring, retainer and compressor into place and compress the spring until cir-clip groove is visible, then install cir-clip and remove the compressor.

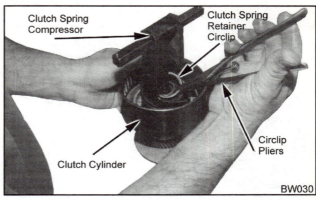

2. Install the clutch plates into the rear clutch cylinder in the reverse order as they were removed, starting with a outer spline, then inner spline, as follows below:
* dished - fibre - flat - fibre - dished - fibre - flat - fibre - dished - fibre *

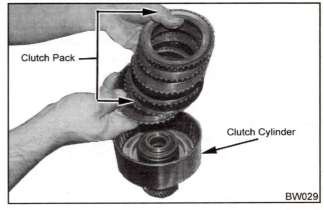

The dish drops in towards the piston when assembling the plates.
3. Once the clutch plates are fitted into place the pressure plate and cir-clip are able to be fitted into position and secure the clutch pack into the housing.
4. Replace the seal on the forward sun gear shaft, then fit the forward needle thrust race, placing the forward sun gear shaft into the rear clutch assembly.
5. Install the seals to the forward sun gear shaft and then fit the needle thrust race and steel washer onto the rear of the forward sun gear shaft.

Front Clutch & Input Shaft Assembly
All seals are to be replaced with new seals before assembly.
1. (a) Place the piston into position and push down until it is fully seated, then install the diaphragm spring, retaining it with the cir-clip. Once the cir-clip has been installed the pressure plate and clutch plates can be fitted.

BORG-WARNER 35/40 AUTOMATIC TRANSMISSION

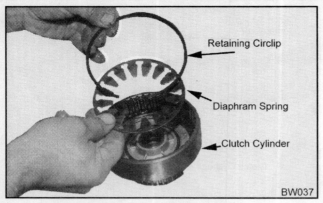

(b) The clutch plates are fitted in the order of:
   * steel - fibre - steel - fibre - steel - fibre - steel - fibre - steel - fibre *

The steel plates have an outer spline and the fibre plates have an inner spline.

2. The clutch clearances need to be checked after installation, this is done by applying a 3.0 kg load to the clutch pack, then measuring the distance from the input shaft seat to the top of the clutch pack, using vernia callipers is the easiest way of measuring this distance.
   * Clearance should be 0.38 mm maximum

If out of specs use external tooth plates to bring within specifications.

3. Install the inner front clutch hub aligning the inner toothed plates, until the hub has bottomed out in the front clutch cylinder, then fit input shaft into position and install the circlip, ensuring that it is locked in its groove properly.

Pump

Replace all seals and components that are damaged in any way before assembling the pump body to the adaptor. Fit the pump gears into the pump body, then aligning up the holes in the pump adaptor with the pump body segment.

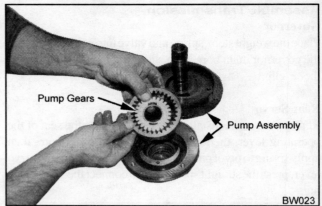

When pump body and adaptor are aligned with each other install the retainer bolts and screw, tightening to the correct tension.

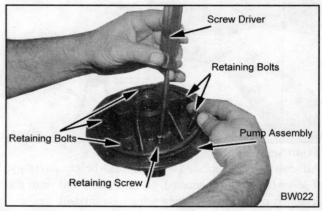

Valve Body

Valve body parts were laid out in order when dismantled to provide easier installation on reassembling.

1. In the lower valve body install the modulator valve spring, plunger, valve, plug and then plug dowel to secure components into place.

2. The servo orifice valve and spring can be fitted into the housing and secured using the valve keep plate

3. Install the secondary regulator valve and spring, then the primary regulator valve, sleeve and spring. Once they are fitted the regulator valve retainer plate can be installed, the springs will need to be compressed to install the retaining screws.

4. The 2-3 dump valve (spring & ball), throttle valve keep plate and throttle valve stop roller will need installing before the separator plate can be fitted.

5. With the lower valve body facing up on a bench place the separator plate, governor line plate and oil tube collector into place, then install the retaining screws for the governor line plate and oil tube collector tensioning them to correct tension.

6. The upper valve body can have the 2-3 plunger, spring, 2-3 shift valve and the 1-2 shift valve fitted into one side, the 1-2 plunger and spring fitted into the other side. The retainer plates can then be installed and screws tensioned.

7. Place the upper valve body onto the lower valve body

BORG-WARNER 35/40 AUTOMATIC TRANSMISSION

securing them together with 6 lower valve body screws and 2 upper valve body screws.

8. Slide the throttle valve spring and valve, then the down shift valve spring and valve , then the manual valve into the valve body before securing the down shift cam assembly and bracket on the valve body.

9. Install the filter element and filter element retaining screws, then the reverse pressure boost cam and manual control valve can be reinstalled (if originally fitted).

Housing

1. Replace the band adjuster into the case and if the parking pawl pivot pin needs to be refitted to the casing repeat the remove process in reverse.

2. Place the park pawl operating mechanism into position in the case, the spring is to be fitted the same way as it was removed, and the spring clip to be installed.

3. Connect the park pawl linkage to the operating mechanism, then lower the manual valve lever into place with detent ball & spring fitted and slide the cross shaft through the lever.

4. Install the spring clip in place, then the cross shaft spring can be compressed with the manual valve lever, until the drive pin is able to be inserted into the shaft. Once the drive pin is in place the manual valve lever can be released into position.

5. Replace the adaptor body and plate into place over the output shaft, once the adaptor body and plate are aligned, insert the retaining bolts tensioning them to the correct torque.

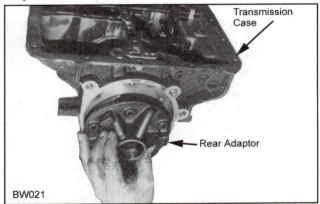

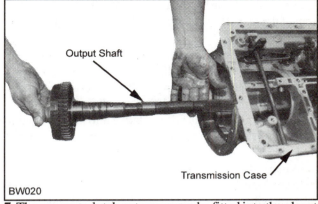

6. The thrust washer is to be installed to the transmission casing, where it aligns with lugs in the casing to stop thrust washer turning. Fit the output shaft assembly in the casing.

7. The one way clutch outer race can be fitted into the planet gear carrier making sure the lugs are engaged. Install the retaining circlip and then the one way clutch.

8. The centre support is to be fitted to the planetary gear assembly with the centre boss inside the one way clutch. On the rear of the planet gear assemble fit the steel washer, lip facing out , and then the needle thrust race.

9. Install the rear band into the casing, placed on the adjuster.

10. Carefully manoeuvre the planet gear assembly and centre support as one into the casing slotting correctly into place with the ring gear and aligning centre support with the pre-dismantle markings. Fit the retaining bolts in through the casing to the centre support.

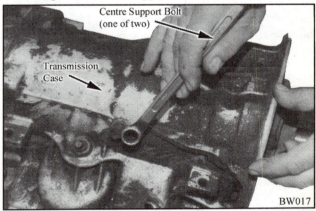

11. Replace the front band into position the casing with the band attached to the casing lug.

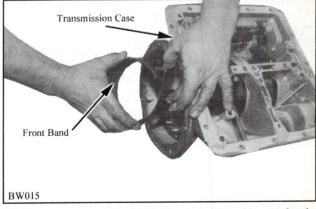

12. The next process is to fit the front clutch to the rear clutch, fit the steel thrust washer then the needle roller bearing to the front of the rear clutch. Carefully slide the two clutch packs together.

13. (a) Before installing the clutch assemblies into the casing, ensure that the needle thrust race and steel thrust washer are positioned at the rear of the front sun gear shaft, then the assembly can be installed into the casing.

(b) Once the assembly is fully installed into the casing turn the assembly to ensure that it all moves freely and does not bind up.

14. When installing the pump the preload will need setting, if the reading obtained on the dismantling procedure is incorrect the shims will need altering to obtain the correct reading before the pump is fitted.

End Float Specifications: 0.25-0.76 mm
, if not within specification replace shim pack.

15. Once the correct shim thickness is obtained, fit the shims to the face of the pump, then install the pump into the casing, then install and tension the retaining bolts to correct torque.

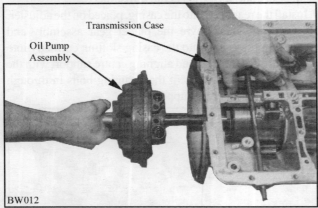

16. Position the governor drive hole up, then install the governor into place over the output shaft, the cast projection towards the rear of the assembly. The locking screw can then be tensioned to the correct torque.

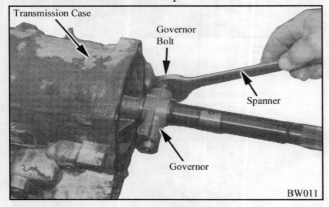

17. Refit the servos and valve body as previously described in this chapter, then adjust the bands as previously described in this chapter.

18. Replace oil pan as previously described in this chapter, also fit the safety 'P'/'N' switch into place.

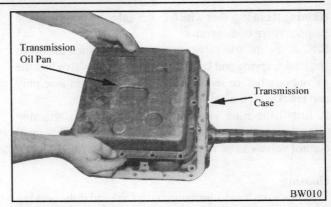

19. With the speedo clip positioned on the output shaft, slide the gear over the output shaft and the clip until gear locks into the clip.

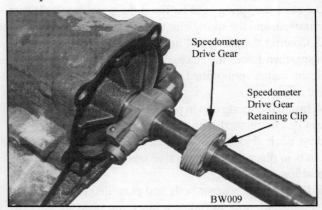

20. Slide the extension housing into place on the transmission case, then the extension housing bolts can be fitted and tensioned.

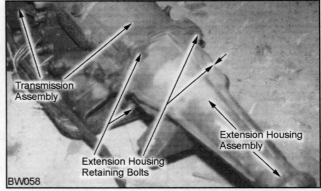

21. Slide the speed sensor unit into the extension housing, then install and tension the speed sensor retaining bolt.

22. Fit the bell housing into place tipping lightly with a soft face hammer if needed, insert and tension the bell housing retaining bolts. Remove the transmission from the cradle and place with the bell housing over the end of the bench.

23. Carefully slide the torque converter over the input shaft, taking care not to damage the front pump seal. Transmission can then be installed into the vehicle.

PROBLEM SOLVING & DIAGNOSIS

FLUID CHECK

Transmission fluid changes colour and smell very early in life, these indicators should not necessarily be relied on to diagnose either transmission internal condition nor fluid deterioration.

The chart on the next page shows that a dark brown fluid colour, coupled with a delayed shift pattern, may only indicate that the fluid requires replacement and alone, is not a definite indication of a potential transmission failure.

Fluid level should only be checked when transmission reaches normal operating temperature (82-93 degrees Celsius).

Transmission fluid colour when new and unused, is red. A red dye is added so that it can be distinguished from other oils and lubricants. The red dye is not an indicator of fluid quality and is not permanent. As the vehicle is driven, the transmission fluid will begin to look darker in colour. The colour will then appear light brown. A DARK brown colour with a distinctively burnt odour MAY indicate fluid deterioration and a need for the fluid to be changed.

Details of transmission oil pressure check procedures refer to 'Oil pressure check information' chart at the start of this chapter.

OIL PRESSURE CHECK

Preliminary Check Procedure
Check transmission oil level and condition
Check and adjust Kickdown Cable
Check outside manual linkage and correct
Check engine tune

Engine Idle Test

With pressure gauge fitted to the transmission, hand brake applied and service brake applied, start the vehicle and check the fluid pressures in all gears.
Pressure should be within the specs indicated on the Pressure Table under the specifications section of this chapter.

Stall Test

With pressure gauge fitted to the transmission, hand brake applied and service brake applied, start the vehicle and check the fluid pressures in all gears at full throttle.
The pressures and speeds should be within the specs indicated on the Pressure Table under the specifications section of this chapter.
Engine not to be held at full throttle for any longer than 5 sec, then select 'N' and run at about 1200 rpm to cool torque converter before continuing.

After Cut Back

With pressure gauge fitted to the transmission, this test is conducted on the road. Accelerating at full throttle and the pressure should drop at modulator operation.
The pressure should be within the specs indicated on the Pressure Table under specifications section of this chapter.

ROAD TEST

Drive and Reverse Engagement Shift Check.

1. Start engine.
2. Depress brake pedal.
3. Move gear selector:
    a) 'P' (Park) to 'R' (Reverse)
    b) 'R' (Reverse) to 'N' (Neutral) to 'D' (Drive).
    c) Gear selections should be immediate and not harsh.

Transmission Upshifts

With gear selector in 'D' :-
1. Accelerate using a steady increasing throttle application.
2. Note the shift speed point gear engagements for:
    a) 2nd gear
    b) 3rd gear

Throttle Downshift

At a speed of 70-90 km/h, quickly depress the accelerator to half open position and observe:
   Transmission downshift to 2nd gear immediately.

Full Throttle (Detent) Downshift

Operate the vehicle at 30 km/h in 'D', then quickly depress to wide open throttle position and observe:
   Transmission downshift to 1st gear immediately.

Manual Downshift

1. Operate the vehicle at 65 km/h in 'D', then release the accelerator pedal (closed throttle position) and simultaneously move the gear selector to 1st gear, and observe:
    a) Transmission downshift 3rd to 2nd gear immediately.
    b) Vehicle should slow under engine braking.
    c) Should downshift 2nd to 1st gear under 30 km/h..
2. Operate the vehicle at 30 km/h in 1st.
   Check the transmission for no up shifts, slippage and squawking.

Manual Gear Range Selection.

Manual Third "D".
1. With vehicle stopped, place gear selector in 'D' (Drive) and accelerate to observe:
    a) The first to second gear shift point.
    b) The second to third gear shift point.

Manual Second (2).
1. With vehicle stopped, place gear selector in '2' (second) and accelerate to observe:
    a) The first to second gear shift point.
2. Accelerate to 60 km/h and observe:
    a) That a second to third gear shift does not occur.

Manual First (1)
1. With vehicle stopped, place gear selector in '1' (first) and accelerate to 40 km/h and observe:

a) That no upshift occurs.

Reverse.

1. With vehicle stopped. Place gear selector in 'R' (Reverse) and slowly accelerate to observe reverse gear operation.

* **This publication does not include all possible throttle positions and the corresponding shift point information. Actual shift points will vary in accordance with transmission build variation.**

Kickdown Cable

Kickdown adjustments are importent for Borg Warner automatic transmissions as this also controls the transmission pressure. Kickdown slipping will occur if the kickdown cable is not hooked up at all.

TORQUE CONVERTER EVALUATION

Torque Converter Stator

The torque converter stator roller clutch can have one of two different type malfunctions:

a) Stator assembly freewheels in both directions.
b) Stator assembly remains locked up at all times.

Condition A:- Poor Acceleration, Low Speed

The vehicle tends to have poor acceleration from a standstill. The engine tune is correct and the transmission is in first (1st) gear when starting out.

Checking for poor performance in 'D' (Drive) and 'R' (Reverse) will help determine if the stator is free wheeling at all times.

Condition B:- Poor Acceleration, High Speed

Engine rpm and car speed limited or restricted at high speeds. Performance when accelerating from a standstill is normal.

Engine may overheat. Visual examination of the converter may reveal a blue colour from over heating.

If converter has been removed, the stator roller clutch can be checked by inserting a finger into the splined inner race of the roller clutch and trying to turn the race in both directions. The inner race should turn freely clockwise, but not turn or be very difficult to turn counter-clockwise.

The Converter Should be Replaced if:-

Leaks externally, such as the hub weld area.

Converter has an imbalance which can not be corrected.

Converter is contaminated with engine coolant containing anti freeze.

The Converter Should Not be Replaced if:-

The oil has an odour, is discoloured, and there is no evidence of metal or clutch facing particles.

The threads in one or more of the converter bolt holes are damaged. Correct with thread insert.

SPECIFICATIONS

Trans. Models

Application	Ford No.	Borg Warner No.
XA: 3.3L		0546-002
4.1L		0546-001
XB: 3.3L	72DA-7000-CA	0546-011
4.1L	72DA-7000-DA	0546-009
XC: 3.3L	76DA-7000-AA	0546-000071
4.1L	76DA-7000-BA	0546-000070

Lubricant

BW35 - 8.1 litres including converter M2C33F (Dextron II)
BW40 - 8.5 litres including converter M2C33F (Dextron II)

Gear Ratios:	BW-35	BW-40
Reverse (R)	4.18 - 2.09:1	2.09:1
Drive (D)	2.00 - 1.00:1	1.00:1
Second (2)	2.90 - 1.45:1	1.45:1
First (1)	4.78 - 2.39:1	2.39:1

Shift Points
Diff Ratio 3.23:1

Manual Shift		Throttle	Km/h
D	1-2	KD	50-63
D	2-3	KD	85-98
D	3-2	KD	71-87
D	3-1	KD	31-47
Manual Shift		Throttle	Km/h
D	1-2	Zero	13-16
D	2-3	Zero	16-21
D	3-1	Zero	6-13
1	2-1	Zero	16-29

Line Pressure (kPa)

	Idle	Stall	K.D. after cutback
D	400-483	1379-1723	620-793
2	400-483	1379-1723	620-793
1	400-483	1379-1723	620-793
R	400-483	1379-1723	
N	400-483		

Torque Converter:

Stall Speed	R.P.M.
3.3 L	1800-1900
4.1 L	1850-1950

Torque Specifications

BW-35	Nm
Transmission Case to Converter Housing	23-30
Extension Housing to Transmission	11-14
Converter to Flywheel/Drive plate	34-41
Pump Adaptor to Pump Body set screw	33-48
5/16 in. bolt	23-30
Pump Adaptor to Transmission Case	11-25
Rear Adaptor to Trans. Case 1/4 in. bolt	5-7
Centre Support to Trans. Case	14-18
Transmission Oil Pan (Sump)	11-14
Front Servo to Transmission Case	11-14
Rear Servo to Transmission Case	14-18
Outer Lever to Manual Valve Shaft	14-20
Lower Body End Plate to Lower Body	2-3
Upper Body End Plate to upper Body	2-3
Upper Valve Body to Lower Valve Body	2-3
Valve Body to Trans. Case	5-7
Downshift Valve Cam Bracket to Valve Body	2-3
Front Servo Lever Adjusting Screw Nut	20-27
Rear Servo Adjusting Screw Locknut	34-41
Governor body to Shaft	20-24

BW-40	Nm
Transmission Case to Converter Housing	16-24
Extension Housing to Transmission	50-60
Converter to Flywheel/Drive plate	34-40
Pump Adaptor to Pump Body set screw	6-11
5/16 in. bolt	24-29
Pump Adaptor to Transmission Case	17-24
Rear Adaptor to Trans. Case 1/4 in. bolt	6-10
Centre Support to Trans. Case	21-33
Transmission Oil Pan (Sump)	14-17
Front Servo to Transmission Case	14-20
Rear Servo to Transmission Case	
(2 x 3/8 bolt)	21-33
EFI (1 x 5/16 bolt)	14-20
Outer Lever to Manual Valve Shaft	14-16
Lower Body End Plate to Lower Body	6-10
Upper Body End Plate to upper Body	6-10
Upper Valve Body to Lower Valve Body	6-10
Valve Body to Trans. Case	6-10
Downshift Valve Cam Bracket to Valve Body	6-11
Front Servo Lever Adjusting Screw Nut	21-27
Rear Servo Adjusting Screw Locknut	34-40
Governor body to Shaft	35-40

Memo

Ford "C" type Automatic Transmissions

C - Type automatic transmissions are code named and identified by a Ford system. "C" is Fords decade identification for the 1960's, starting at year 1 of the decade. The "C" is followed by a number which stands for the year of the decade, Therefore C4 represents the year 1964. Ford have identified their automatic transmissions by the year the transmission was developed.

C4, C9 and C10, represent the years 1964, 1969 and 1970 respectively.

The "C" transmissions can be grouped according to their use. C4, C5, C9 and C10 are all very similar in appearance and maintenance procedures. These transmissions were manufactured to be installed behind six cylinder and V8 engines and used in vehicles designed for general type of passenger transport plus some of the "F" series have C5 transmissions. These transmissions were installed into Falcon and Fairlane vehicles behind larger six cylinder and medium sized V8 engines such as 302 and 351 c.i.d.

C4 and C9 were installed behind six cylinders, 289 and 302 V8 engines. C10 was used for high performance V8 engines such as 2 barrel 302 and 351 cu.in. cleveland block engines. U.S. refer to C4 type transmissions.

C5 is very similar to a C9 except for a slightly deeper oil pan, and is installed in many 6 cylinder "F" series pick-ups that do not have the stronger C6 transmissions installed. Also fitted to small bodied passenger vehicles such as Mustang, Cougar, Capri with larger six cylinder and small V8 engines.

C6 transmissions are a stronger transmission and manufactured for heavier duty and performance type of vehicles. Initially C6 transmissions were installed into passenger vehicles behind powerful performance engines such as 390, 428 and 427 c.i.d. engines, the type of cars were Ford Mustang, Cyclone, Fairlane, Torino and Mercury Cougar. Later the transmissions were installed into many of the "F" series pick-up, light trucks and commercial Econoline vehicles. Ford continued to manufacture C6 transmissions up to and including 1989.

C6 have became a popular performance transmission and will bolt up to Windsor and Cleveland V8 engines.

C3 transmissions were designed for lighter vehicles with four and small six cylinder displacement engines. Fitted to passenger vehicles such as Ford Cortina, Capri, small body Mustangs produced in the mid-1980's.

C4, C5, C9 and C10 transmissions are similar in appearance and also similar too repair and rebuild, we have included these 4 transmissions in the same chapter with any differences noted. The valve bodies are not interchangable, however many components are as an assembly. Gasket kits are provided which are suitable for C4, C5, C9 and C10.

Even though these transmissions are similar in external appearance there are minor differences, we will list these differences because our automatic transmission expert has had many experiences of people purchasing a replacement transmission and not purchasing the transmission they required. C6 and C3 transmissions are different in appearance. The C6

Ford C6 Automatic Transmission

does not have a seperate bell housing for the torque converter. C3 transmissions are different in appearance and have many different internal components. The rear servo is located inside the transmission, under the valve body.

C3 Ford Transmission

C3 Ford Transmission

Transmission Case

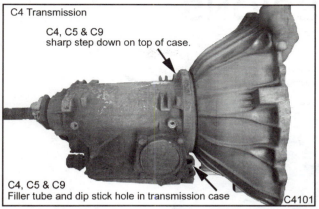

The top of the transmission case for the C4, C5 and C9 has a sharp step down near the bell housing while C10 cases have a curved slope down from the bell housing to the top of the case.

Filler Tube / Dip Stick

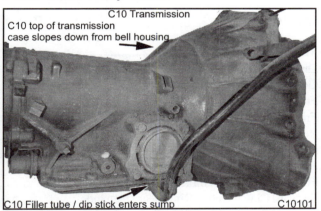

The filler tube / dip stick on C4, C5 and C9 transmissions enters through a hole in the front of the transmission case, while on C10 transmissions the entry is through the transmission sump.

Transmission Oil Pan

C5 and C9 transmissions are almost identical, one way of external identification is the oil pan, C5 have a 20-25mm deeper and 1.5 litre larger capacity oil pan compared to a C9. C5 has a depper oil filter.

Bell Housing Attaching Bolts

C9 has the same bolts attaching the bell housing and oil pump to the front of the transmission case. C10 have a seperate row of bolts as shown by the C10 illustration along side.

Transmission Breather

The transmission breather on C4 transmissions consists of a small breather tube on the side of the case.

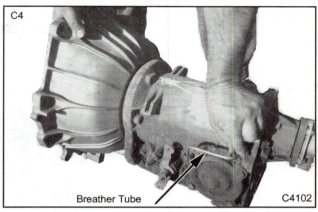

Breather on C5, C9 and C10 consists of a small screw in breather cap in the rear extension housing as shown.

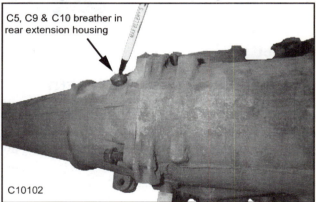

Input Shaft

The input shaft for C4 has a slightly smaller diameter than a C5, C9 and C10. The shaft looks similar but if a C4 input shaft is installed on to a C5, C9 or C10 torque converter, the transmission will not drive, because the torque converter spins on the transmission input shaft.

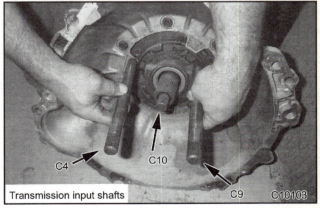

Alternatively you can not install a C4 torque converter onto a C5, C9 or C10 transmission input shaft, because the torque converter inside diameter is too small for the input shaft.

C4, C5, C9 and C10 AUTOMATIC TRANSMISSIONS

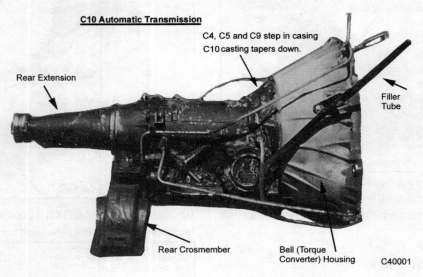

Subject	Page
MAINTENANCE AND ADJUSTMENT	**49**
Lubrication	49
Fluid Level	49
Changing Fluid	49
Lubricant	49
Maintain Strainer	49
Maintenance Notes	50
Oil Cooler Pipes	50
Clean and Inspect	50
Console Shift Lever Assembly	**50**
Removal	50
Installation	50
Column Shift Linkage Assembly	**51**
Removal	51
Installation	51
Accelerator Linkage & Down Shift Cable	**51**
Check and Adjust	51
Down Shift Rod Adjustment	51
Replace Kickdown Cable	51
Band Adjustment	**51**
Intermediate Band	51
Low/Reverse Band	51
Oil Pan/Sump & Valve Body Assembly	**52**
Remove	52
Installation	52
Servo Valves	**53**
Intermediate Servo	53
Low/Reverse Servo	53
Cooler Replacement	**54**
Speedometer Cable & Driven Gear Assembly	**54**
Remove	54
Installation	**54**

Subject	Page
Major Repair	**54**
Dismantle	54
Gear Train Separation	56
Front Pump Dismantle	56
Front Pump Assemble	56
Reverse/High Clutch Dismantle	57
Reverse/High Clutch Assemble	57
Forward Clutch Dismantle	57
Forward Clutch Assemble	57
Forward Clutch Hub & Ring Gear Dismantle	58
Forward Clutch Hub & Ring Gear Assemble	58
Input Shell & Sun Gear Dismantle	58
Input Shell & Sun Gear Assemble	58
Reverse Sun Gear & Hub Dismantle	58
Reverse Sun Gear & Hub Assemble	58
Governor & Oil Distributor Dismantle	58
Governor & Oil Distributor Assemble	58
Valve Body Dismantle	58
Valve Body Assemble	60
Gear Train Assemble	61
Transmission Assemble	62
PROBLEM SOLVING AND DIAGNOSIS	**64**
Oil Pressure Check	64
Hydraulic Diagnosis	64
Road Test	64
Transmission Fluid Checking Procedure	64
Torque Converter Evaluation	64
SPECIFICATIONS	**65**
TORQUE WRENCH SPECIFICATIONS	**65**

C4, C5, C9 and C10 AUTOMATIC TRANSMISSIONS

GENERAL INFORMATION

The illustration on the previous page shows the C4 automatic transmission.

A metal identification plate is attached to the transmission. The model code for vehicles equipped with different transmissions are listed in General Information Chapter at the front of this manual.

MAINTENANCE AND ADJUSTMENT

LUBRICATION
If adding or changing the transmission fluid, use only specified Automatic Transmission fluid M2C-33F.

FLUID LEVEL
The dipstick is located in the right section of engine compartment. To check level, follow this procedure:
Apply parking brake and with engine idling and transmission at normal operating temperature, engage each gear briefly, ending with selector in "N" neutral.
* The transmission must be at normal operating temperature to obtain an accurate dipstick reading.
* Do not overfill the transmission. Overfilling will cause foaming of the fluid, loss of fluid, shift complaints and possible damage to the transmission.
Withdraw dipstick and wipe clean with a lint free cloth. Install dipstick into transmission, withdraw and check level. The level must be within "hot" range on dipstick, refer below.
NOTE: Avoid entry of dirt into transmission by ensuring that

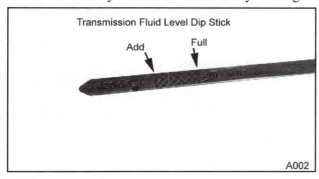

dipstick is properly seated. Maintaining transmission to correct level with recommended fluid is essential for correct operation of unit.

CHANGING FLUID
* Do not overfill the transmission. Overfilling will cause foaming of the fluid, loss of fluid, shift complaints and possible damage to the transmission.
1. Raise vehicle and place a large drain tray under transmission in drain plug and oil pan.
2. Remove transmission drain plug and allow fluid to drain, refer below.
3. Remove oil pan retaining bolts and tap pan at one corner to break it loose, allow remaining fluid to drain and then remove pan.
4. Install transmission in drain plug and tighten to specified torque.
5. Clean transmission case gasket surface and oil pan.
6. Install oil pan with a new gasket, tighten bolts to specified torque.

Oil pan bolt torque specification: 16 - 22 Nm

7. Firstly pour sufficient automatic transmission fluid M2C-

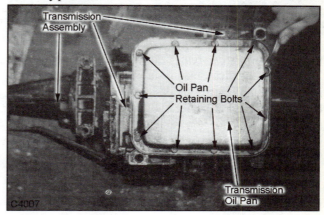

33F to bring fluid level to lower mark on dipstick. Add automatic transmission fluid into transmission through dipstick hole.

8. Start engine and allow to idle for at least two minutes. With park brake on, move selector lever momentarily to each position ending in "N" neutral position.
9. Add sufficient automatic transmission fluid to bring fluid level to lower mark on dipstick. Re-check fluid level after transmission has reached operating temperature. The fluid level should be between upper and lower marks of "HOT" range on dipstick. Insert the dipstick fully to prevent dirt entry into transmission.

LUBRICANT
9.4 litres including converter   M2C-33F

MAINTAIN STRAINER
* Take care when removing sump from transmission as hot oil can cause serious burns. Avoid this by allowing transmission to cool down.
1. Raise vehicle and support on safety stands.
2. Clean all dirt from around oil pan and transmission case, place drain tray under transmission.
3. Hold oil pan in place, leaving one bolt loose at the front of the oil pan, remove the remaining bolts. Allow the rear of the oil pan to drop, emptying oil into drain tray.
4. Remove remaining bolt and oil pan and empty fluid from pan.
5. If necessary, remove strainer and 'O'-ring and discard.

C4, C5, C9 and C10 AUTOMATIC TRANSMISSIONS

6. If necessary install new strainer and 'O' ring.

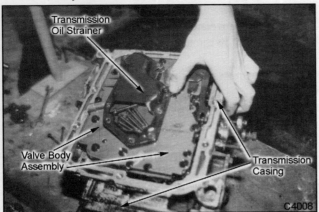

 # C5, C9 & C10 have a spring and valve under the thumb, if this is lost whilst changing filter, trans will not drive at all.

7. Clean oil pan and case mating surfaces. Check that magnet is functional and located in the designated position in the oil pan.
8. Install new gasket and reinstall oil pan. Tighten bolts to specified torque.

Oil pan bolt torque specification: 13 - 17 Nm

9. Lower vehicle and add automatic transmission fluid. Check transmission fluid level.

MAINTENANCE NOTES

While maintaining the transmission, all parts should be cleaned and inspected. Individual units should be reassembled before disassembly of other units to avoid confusion and interchanging of parts.

1. Thoroughly clean the exterior before disassembly of the unit.
2. Disassembly and assembly must be made on a clean work bench. Cleanliness is of the utmost importance. The bench tools, and parts must be kept clean at all times.
3. Before installing screws into aluminium parts, dip screws into transmission fluid prevent galling aluminium threads and to prevent screws from seizing.
4. To prevent thread stripping, always use a torque wrench when installing screws.
5. If threads in aluminium parts are stripped or damaged the part can be made serviceable by the use of suitable thread inserts.
6. Protective tools must be used when assembling seals to prevent damage. The slightest flaw in the sealing surface of the seal can cause an oil leak.
7. Aluminium castings and valve are very susceptible to nicks, burns, burrs, etc., and should be handled with care.
8. Internal snap rings should be expanded and external snap rings compressed if they are to be reused. This will ensure proper seating when reinstalled.
9. "O" rings, gaskets and oil seals that are removed should not be reused.
10. Teflon oil seal rings should not be removed unless damaged.
11. During assembly of each unit, all internal moving parts must be lubricated with transmission fluid.

OIL COOLER PIPES

If replacement of transmission steel tubing cooler pipes is required, only use double wrapped and brazed steel tubing meeting transmission manufactures specifications or equivalent. Under no condition use copper or aluminium tubing to replace steel tubing. These materials do not have satisfactory fatigue durability to withstand normal car vibrations. Steel tubing should be flared using the double flare method.

CLEAN AND INSPECT

After complete disassembly of a unit, wash all metal parts in a clean solvent and dry with compressed air. Blow oil passages out and check to make sure they are not obstructed. Small passages should be checked with tag wire. All parts should be inspected to determine which parts are to be replaced.

* Pay particular attention to the following:

1. Inspect linkage and pivot points for excessive wear.
2. Bearing and thrust surfaces of all parts should be checked for excessive wear and scoring.
3. Check for broken score seal rings, damaged ring lands and damaged threads.
4. Inspect seal and 'O' rings.
5. Mating surfaces of castings should be checked for burrs. Irregularities may be removed by lapping the surface with emery paper. The emery paper is laid on a flat surface, such as a piece of plate glass.
6. Castings should be checked for cracks and sand holes.

* Do not use solvents on neoprene seals, composition faced clutch plates or thrust washers as damage to parts may occur.

CONSOLE SHIFT LEVER ASSEMBLY
Removal

1. Raise vehicle. From beneath vehicle, disconnect rod from shift lever by withdrawing securing pin at transmission end.
2. Withdraw centre console from the vehicle, then disconnect electrical connector for the dial indicator light.
3. Release four retaining screws from the shift assembly to floor pan and lift shift assembly from the vehicle.

Installation

1. Clean mating surfaces of floor pan and shift lever assembly.
2. Apply a bead of sealer around opening in floor pan between the screw holes.
3. Install shift lever assembly using the four screws to retain it in position.
4. The remainder of the installation is the reverse of the removal procedure.
5. Adjust linkage.

COLUMN SHIFT LINKAGE ASSEMBLY
Removal
1. Disconnect shift linkages from the bottom of the steering column, then the linkage onto the transmission selector shaft.
2. Release the bolts holding the linkage assembly to the chassis rail.
3. Release linkage assembly retaining bolts from the transmission casing, then withdraw linkage assembly from the vehicle.

Installation
1. Fit linkage assembly to the vehicle, then fit linkage assembly to the transmission casing using retaining bolts.
2. Fit the bolts holding the linkage assembly to the chassis rail.
3. Connect shift linkages to the bottom of the steering column, then the linkage onto the transmission selector shaft.
4. Adjust linkage

ACCELERATOR LINKAGE & DOWN SHIFT
CHECK & ADJUST
* *Ensure accelerator linkage/cable is correctly adjusted before resetting down shift cable (i.e. Check that wide open throttle can be achieved). Have engine and transmission at operating temperatures.*

Downshift Cable Adjustment
1. Engine must be turned off and the accelerator pressed down to wide open throttle.
2. Disconnect downshift cable.
3. Hold down shift lever against internal stop and refit kickdown cable
4. Adjust kickdown cable so it is taut.

Downshift Rod Adjustment
1. Remove the accelerator and downshift return springs from the carburettor throttle lever.
2. Have the transmission rod installed and hold carburettor throttle lever in wide open position against the stop.
3. Hold the transmission in full kickdown position against the integral stop.
4. Turn the adjusting screw on the carburettor kickdown lever to within 1.0-2.0mm gap of contacting pick-up surface of carburettor throttle lever.
5. Release carburettor and transmission to free positions.
6. Reconnect accelerator cable and springs to accelerator cable and kickdown cables

REPLACE KICKDOWN CABLE:
1. Unclip cable from kickdown level at the transmission.
2. Unclip cable from throttle linkage assembly.
3. Withdraw the cable from the vehicle.
4. Connect cable from kickdown level at the transmission.

6. Connect cable from throttle linkage assembly.
7. Ensure cable is routed correctly, then adjust cable as described above.

BAND ADJUSTMENT
Intermediate Band
1. Place vehicle on safety stands.
2. Loosen the adjusting screw locknut on the left hand side of the transmission case.
3. Tighten the adjusting screw to a torque of 14Nm.
4. Slacken the adjusting screw $1\frac{3}{4}$ turns.

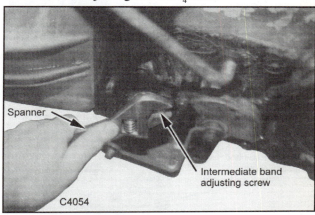

5. Tighten the adjusting screw locknut.
* Never reuse the locknut a second time.

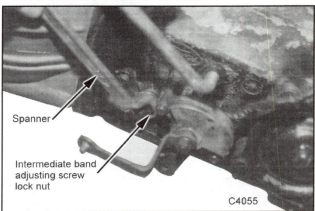

6. Remove vehicle from safety stands and test run.

Low-Reverse Band
1. Place vehicle on safety stands.
2. Loosen the adjusting screw locknut on the right hand side of the transmission case.
3. Tighten the adjusting screw to a torque of 14Nm.

C4, C5, C9 and C10 AUTOMATIC TRANSMISSIONS

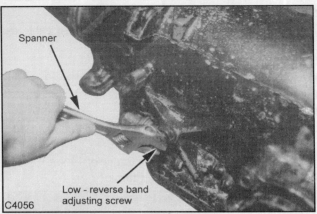

4. Slacken the adjusting screw 3 turns.
5. Tighten the adjusting screw locknut.
* Never reuse the locknut a second time.

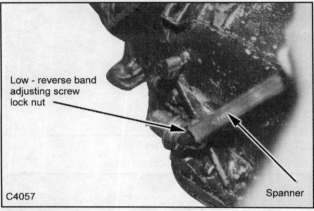

6. Remove vehicle from safety stands and test run.

OIL PAN / SUMP & VALVE BODY ASSEMBLY
Remove
1. Place vehicle on safety stands.
2. Place an oil collection tray underneath the transmission.
3. Remove the oil pan / sump and gasket.

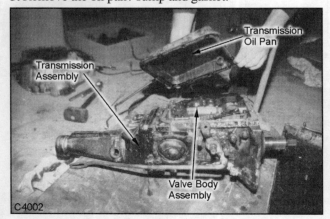

4. Place the transmission selector into "P" position.
5. Remove the 2 bolts holding the detent spring to the valve body and trans case.
6. Remove the remaining valve body to trans case attaching bolts.

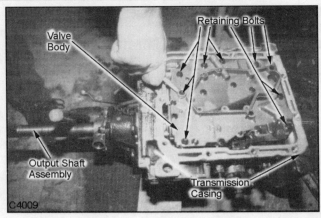

7. Hold the manual valve body (so it is not bent or damaged) and remove the valve body from the trans case.

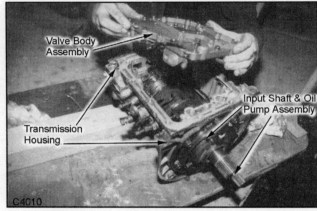

Replace
1. Shift the manual lever at the transmission into the P detent position.
2. Lift the valve body into position. Position the inner downshift lever between the downshift lever stop and the downshift valve. Make sure the 2 lands on the end of the manual valve engage the actuating pin on the manual detent lever. Fit the valve body to trans case attaching bolts, do not tighten.
3. Fit the detent valve spring to the lower valve body and install the spring to trans case bolt, do not tighten.
4. Tighten all the valve body bolts to specification.

Valve body retaining bolts: 4.5 - 6.2 Nm

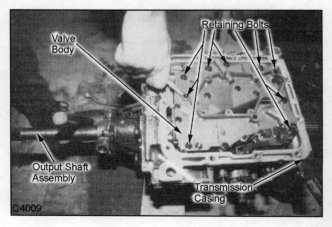

C4, C5, C9 and C10 AUTOMATIC TRANSMISSIONS

5. Refit oil pan / sump with an new gasket.
6. Tighten the sump bolts to specification.

Torque Transmission Oil Sump   16 - 22 Nm

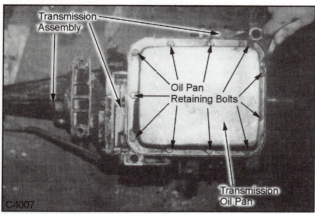

7. Fill transmission with fluid.
8. Remove from safety stands and road test vehicle.

INTERMEDIATE SERVO
Remove
1. Place vehicle on safety stands.
2. Remove the 4 servo cover bolts.

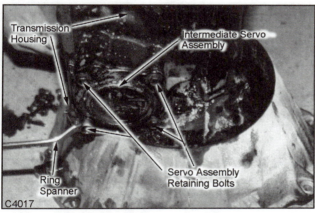

3. Remove the cover, piston and return spring, remove the piston from the cover.

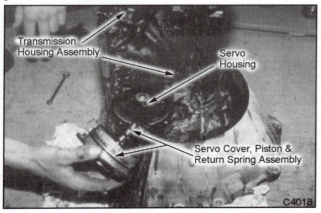

4. Remove the piston seals and cover gasket.

Install
1. Install new seals to piston and new gasket to cover.
2. Install the piston return spring in the case, the new gasket. Install the piston and cover to the transmission, make sure the slot in the end of the piston is horizontal, so that it will engage the strut (it may help to use longer bolts to start with and replace them with the correct bolts when the strut has been engaged). Tighten the cover bolts to specification.

Torque Servo Cover Bolts: 22 - 30 Nm

3. Adjust the intermediate band as previously described.
4. Remove from safety stands and road test vehicle.

LOW REVERSE SERVO
1. Place vehicle on safety stands.
2. Loosen the reverse band adjusting screw, and tighten the adjusting screw to 14Nm (this is to ensure the band strut does not fall down).
3. Remove the 4 servo cover bolts, servo cover and seal.

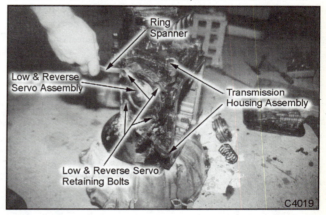

4. Remove the servo piston.
* Note: The seal can not be replaced with out replacing the piston.

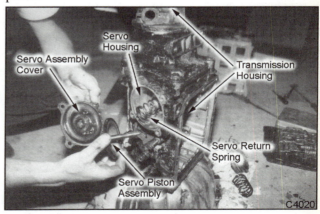

Install
1. Install the piston into the trans case, ensure the return spring is in place.
2. Install the servo cover and a new seal (following the same procedure as for the intermediate servo cover). Tighten the cover bolts to specification.

Torque Servo Cover Bolts: 16 - 27 Nm

3. Adjust the low reverse band as previously described.
4. Remove from safety stands and road test vehicle.

COOLER REPLACEMENT
The cooler is located inside the radiator, if the cooler is to be replaced the radiator must also be replaced. See cooling system for radiator replacement.

There is an optional transmission cooler that is mounted in front of the radiator for models that do not have an air conditioner fitted.

SPEEDOMETER CABLE & DRIVEN GEAR ASSEMBLY
Remove
1. Raise rear of vehicle and place on safety stands. Place drip tray beneath speedometer driven gear.
2. Remove screw and bracket retaining speedometer cable and driven gear.
3. Withdraw cable and gear assembly from case extension.

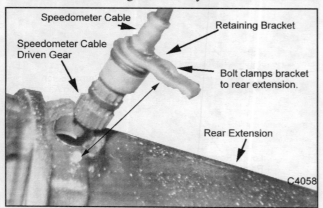

Install
1. Inspect 'O' ring seal and replace it if unsatisfactory.
2. Installation is the reverse of the removal procedure.
3. Tighten retainer bolt.

MAJOR REPAIR

Transmission Dismantle
1. Remove the bolts retaining the converter housing to transmission case and remove converter housing.
2. Remove the vacuum unit, gasket and control rod then from the hole remove the primary throttle valve.

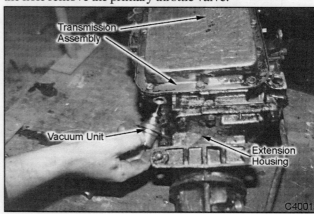

3. Remove the oil pan retaining bolts and lift oil pan from transmission.

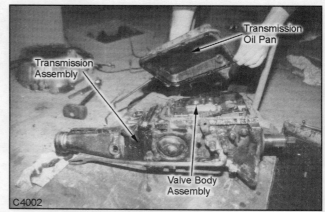

4. Remove the bolts retaining the rear extension housing to the transmission case and remove extension.

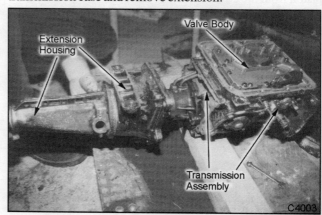

5. Remove the valve body as described previously.
6. Loosen the adjusting screw for the intermediate band then remove the band struts from the case.

7. Loosen the adjusting screw for the low-reverse band then remove the band struts from the case.

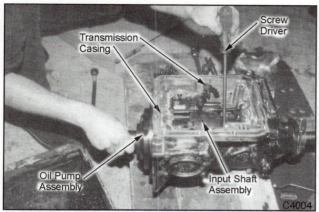

8. Remove the seven bolts retaining the front pump to the transmission casing, then remove pump by levering out with a screwdriver inserted behind the input shell. Remove the No.1 thrust washer if it did not come out with the front pump.

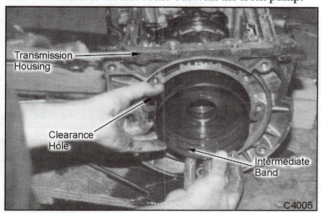

9. Fully remove the intermediate and low-reverse band adjusting screws, then remove the intermediate band from transmission case by aligning with clearance hole in case.

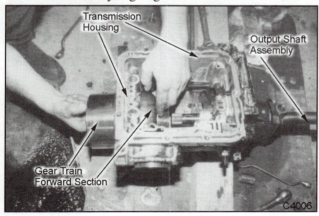

10. Remove the forward section of the gear train as an assembly by firstly lifting the input shell upwards using a screwdriver between the input shell and rear planet carrier.
11. Remove the No.6 thrust washer from the reverse planet carrier, then remove the reverse planet carrier and thrust washer No.7 from the ring gear hub.

12. With the output shaft pushed forward remove the retaining ring for the reverse ring gear hub.

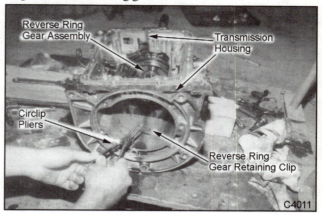

13. From the output shaft remove the reverse ring gear and hub, then remove the No.8 thrust washer from the low and reverse drum.
14. From the transmission case remove the low-reverse band, then from the one-way clutch inner race remove the low-reverse drum.

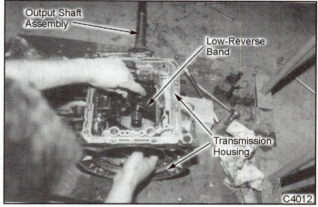

15. Rotate the one-way clutch inner race clockwise while removing from transmission case.

16. From the outer race remove the 12 one-way clutch rollers, springs and spring retainer.
17. Pull upward on the output shaft and remove the output shaft and governor distributor assembly from the governor distributor sleeve.

C4, C5, C9 and C10 AUTOMATIC TRANSMISSIONS

18. Remove the retaining bolts securing the distributor sleeve to the transmission case, and remove the distributor sleeve.
19. From the transmission case remove the park pawl return spring, park pawl and retaining pin, then remove the park gear and No.10 thrust washer.

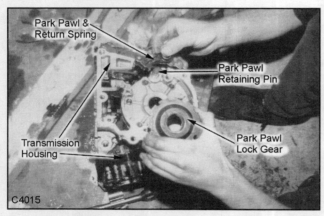

20. Inside the transmission case hold the outer race in position and remove the bolts securing the one-way clutch outer race from the outside of the case.

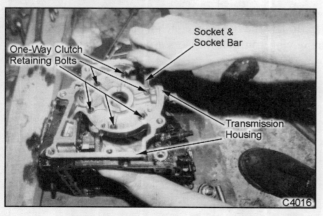

21. Remove the outer race and No.9 thrust washer from the inside of the transmission case.

Gear Train Separation
1. Remove the reverse-high clutch from the forward part of the gear train and also remove drum from the forward clutch.
2. Remove thrust washer No.2 if not already removed, then from the forward clutch hub and ring gear remove the forward clutch.
3. Remove thrust washer No.3 from the forward clutch hub if not already removed, then from the front planet carrier remove the forward clutch hub and ring gear.
4. From the input shell remove the No.4 thrust washer and the front planet carrier.

Front Pump
Dismantle
1. From the stator support remove the four seal rings, then remove the five stator support to pump housing bolts and separate.
2. From the pump housing remove the drive and driven gears.

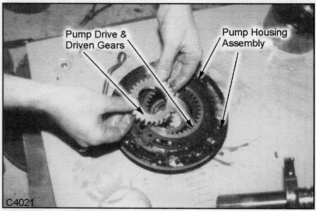

Assemble
1. To the pump housing install the driven and drive gears ensuring the chamfered side is positioned downward against the pump housing.
2. Install the stator support to the pump housing and tighten the five retaining bolts to specification.

Front pump to stator support bolts: 2.8 - 3.9 Nm

3. To the stator support replace the four seal rings, then check that the pump gears have free rotation.

Reverse High Clutch
Dismantle
1. Remove the snap ring for the pressure clutch plate, then remove the pressure plate and the drive and driven clutch plates.

2. Using a piston compressor, compress the piston and remove the snap ring for the piston spring retainer.
3. Release the compressor them remove the spring retainer and piston return spring.
4. Use air pressure in the piston apply hole of the clutch hub to release piston and remove.

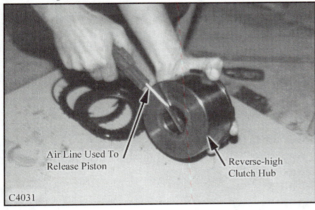

5. From the piston remove the outer seal and also remove the inner seal from the clutch drum.

Assemble
1. To the clutch drum install a new inner seal and a new outer seal to the piston, then coat the new seals with clean transmission fluid.
2. Install the clutch piston spring into place on the piston, then install the spring retainer to the spring.
3. Using the compressor compress the assembly and install the snap ring, then release compressor.
4. Install the clutch plates into assembly starting with a steel plate then friction plate.
Note: If new clutch plates are to be used soak plates in transmission fluid for at least 15 minutes before installing.
5. Lastly install the pressure plate and secure with snap ring retaining.

6. Using a feeler gauge check the clearance between the snap ring and pressure plate ensuring to hold down pressure plate while checking clearance.
Pressure plate to snap ring clearance: 1.27 - 1.80 mm
Note: If note within specification replace snap ring should be replaced.

Forward Clutch
Dismantle
1. Remove the snap ring for the pressure clutch plate, then remove the pressure plate and the drive and driven clutch plates.

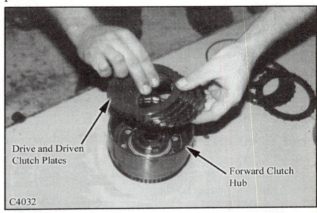

2. Remove the snap ring for the disc spring, then using air pressure in the piston pressure hole of the clutch hub to release piston and remove.

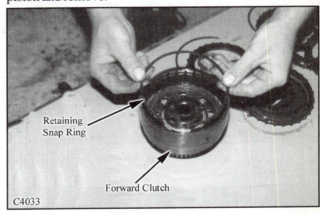

3. From the piston remove the outer seal and also remove the inner seal from the clutch drum.

Assemble
1. To the clutch drum install a new inner seal and a new outer seal to the piston, then coat the new seals with clean transmission fluid.
2. Install the clutch piston into place, then install the steel ring onto piston, install disc spring and secure with retaining snap ring.
3. Install the lower pressure plate into assembly with the flat side facing up, then install the clutch plates starting with a non-metallic plate.

Note: *If new clutch plates are to be used soak plates in transmission fluid for at least 15 minutes before installing.*
4. Lastly install the pressure plate snap ring retaining.
5. Using a feeler gauge check the clearance between the snap ring and pressure plate ensuring to hold down pressure plate while checking clearance.
Pressure plate to snap ring clearance: 0.64 - 1.27 mm
Note: *If not within specification snap ring should be replaced.*

Forward Clutch Hub and Ring Gear
Dismantle
Remove the retaining snap ring for the forward clutch hub, then remove the forward clutch hub from the ring gear.

Assemble
To the ring gear install the forward clutch hub ensuring the hub is bottomed in the ring gear groove, then install the retaining snap ring.

Input Shell and Sun Gear
Dismantle
1. From the sun gear remove the external snap ring, then remove the No. 5 thrust washer.

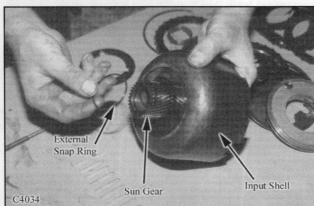

2. From the input shell remove the sun gear, then remove the sun gear internal snap ring.

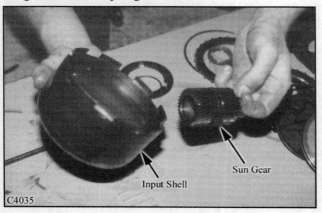

Assemble
1. To the sun gear install the internal snap ring, then install the sun gear to the input shell.
2. Install the No. 5 thrust washer to the sun gear and input shell, then install the external snap ring.

Reverse Ring Gear and Hub
Dismantle
From the reverse ring gear remove the hub retaining snap ring, then remove the hub.

Assemble
To the reverse ring gear install the hub, then install the retaining snap ring ensure it is secured correctly.

Governor and Oil Distributor
Dismantle
1. From the governor oil distributor remove the rings, then the bolts securing the governor housing to the distributor, then remove the distributor and oil screen.
2. Remove the retaining ring for the primary governor valve, then remove the washer, spring and valve from the housing.
3. Remove the retaining ring for the secondary governor valve, then remove the spring and valve from the housing.

Assemble
1. To the housing install the secondary governor valve, spring and retaining snap ring.
2. To the housing install the primary governor valve, spring, washer and retaining snap ring.
3. Install the governor oil screen then install the governor assembly to oil distributor and tighten bolts to specification.
Governor to distributor bolts: 9.0 - 13.5 Nm
4. To the distributor install the rings then check the rings have free rotation.

Valve Body
Dismantle
1. If not already removed remove the filter screen from the valve body by removing the retaining screws, being careful not to lose the throttle pressure limit valve and spring.
 # C5, C9 & C10 have a spring and valve under the thumb,

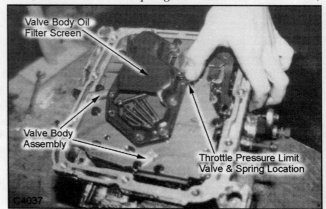

if this is lost whilst changing filter, trans will not drive at all.
2. Remove the screws securing the lower valve body to the upper valve body and separate the valve bodies, separator plate and hold down plate.
Caution: *Be careful not to lose the upper valve body shuttle valve and check valve.*

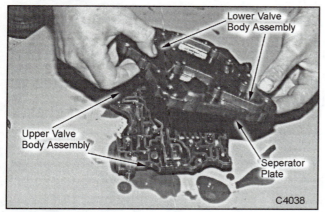

3. From the upper valve body remove the manual valve.
4. From the upper valve body remove the retainer for the low servo modulator valve, then remove the retainer plug, spring and valve.
5. Remove the downshift valve retainer and remove the spring and downshift valve.

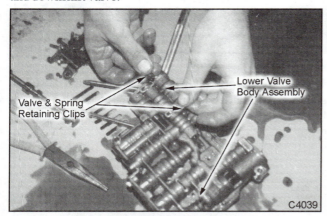

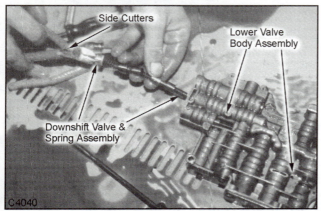

6. Remove the retaining pin for the throttle booster plug then remove plug, valve and spring.
Note: *250 2V and 302 2V remove the ball.*

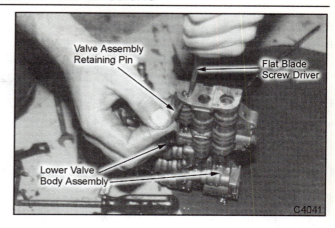

7. From the valve body remove the cover plate for the cut-back valve and transition valve, then remove the cut back valve.

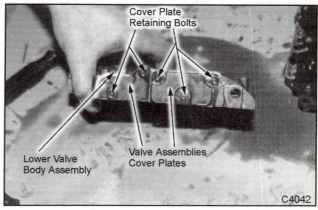

8. Remove the transition valve spring, transition valve, 2-3 back-out valve and the spring.

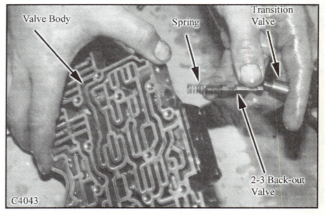

9. From the valve body remove the cover plate for the 1-2 shift valve and 2-3 shift valve, then remove the 2-3 shift valve, spring and throttle modulator valve.

59

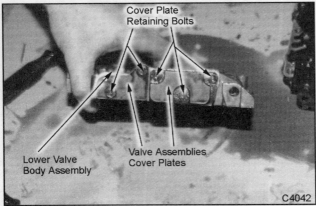

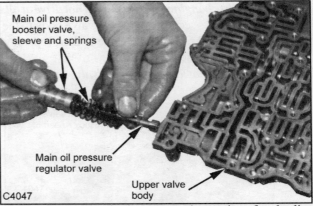

10. From the valve body remove the 1-2 shift valve, D2 valve and spring, then remove the retaining pin for the intermediate servo.

13. From the valve body remove the retainer for the line coasting boost then remove the spring and line coasting boost valve.

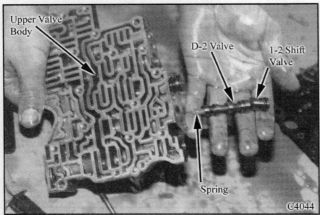

11. Remove the retainer for the intermediate accumulator valve, valve and the spring.

Assemble

1. To the lower valve body install the two shuttle valves as shown, then install the separator plate and hold-down plate to lower valve body retaining with the two retaining screws.

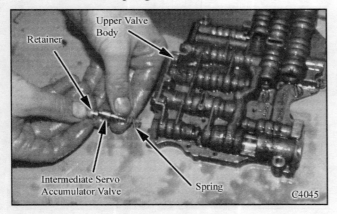

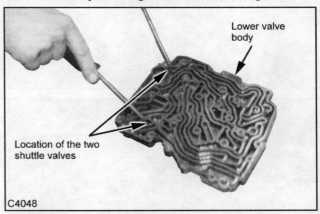

12. Remove the retaining pin for the main oil pressure booster valve, then remove the valve, sleeve, springs, retainer and main oil pressure regulator valve.

2. To the main valve body install the down shift valve, spring and retainer then install the low servo modulator valve, spring, retainer plug and install the retainer.

3. To the valve body install the throttle booster valve spring, valve, plug and retaining.

Note: *Install the ball on 250 2V and 302 2V.*

4. To the valve body install the spring, 2-3 back-out valve, transition valve and spring.

5. Install the cut-back valve, then retain by installing the transition valve cover plate and tighten the retaining screws to specification.

Transition valve cover plate screws: 2.2 - 4.0 Nm

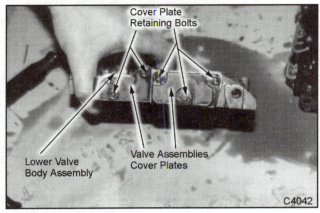

6. To the valve body install the throttle modulator valve, spring and 2-3 shift valve, then install the springs, D2 valve and 1-2 shift valve.

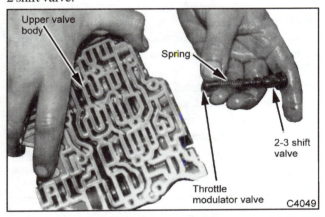

7. Install the cover plate for the 2-3 shift valve and 1-2 shift valve assemblies and tighten retaining screws to specification.

2-3 & 1-2 shift valve cover screws: 2.2 - 4.0 Nm

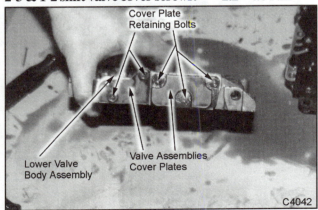

8. To the valve body install the spring, intermediate servo accumulator valve, retainer and retaining pin.
9. To the valve body install the line coating boost valve, spring and secure with retainer.
10. To the valve body install the main oil pressure regulator valve and spring retainer, then install the two springs, sleeve, main oil pressure booster valve and retaining pin.
11. Install the manual valve to the upper valve body, then install the rubber ball shuttle valve and servo check valve in the upper valve body as shown.

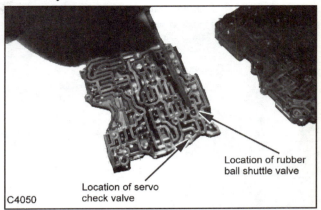

12. Install the lower valve body to the upper valve body, then install and tighten the retaining screws to specification.

Lower to upper valve body screws: 4.5 - 6.2 Nm

13. To the lower valve body install the throttle pressure limit valve and spring, then install the filter screen and gasket to the valve body and tighten retaining screws.

Filter screen to valve body screws: 4.5 - 6.2 Nm

Gear Train Assembly

1. Install the No.2 thrust washer or washer and spacer to the stator support.

Note: Use end play result to select correct thrust washer.

2. To the stator support install the reverse-high clutch and forward clutch.
3. Select a nylon washer No.1 which will still maintain a minimal clearance when inserted between the stator support and intermediate brake drum, then remove the intermediate brake drum and forward clutch unit from stator support.
4. To the front pump stator support install the selected No.1 and 2 thrust washers (hold with small amount of vaseline).
5. To the forward clutch install the No.3 thrust washer, then install the forward clutch hub and ring in the forward clutch ensuring splines and clutch plates mesh properly.

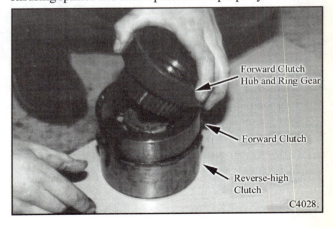

6. To the front planet carrier install the No.4 thrust washer, then install the planetary carrier into the forward clutch hub and ring gear.

7. To the gear train assembly install the input shell and sun gear rotating the input shell to engage reverse-high clutch drive lugs.

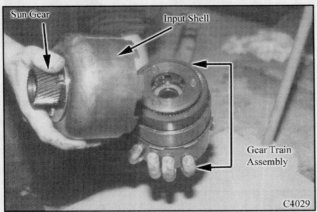

Transmission Assembly

1. To the transmission case install the No. 9 thrust washer, then install the one-way clutch outer race into the transmission case, install and tighten retaining bolts.

2. To the transmission case install the park pawl retaining pin, park pawl and return spring, then install the No. 10 thrust washer to the park pawl gear and install gear to transmission case.

3. To the governor distributor sleeve install the two fluid tubes, then install the distributor sleeve to the case, ensuring the fluid tubes insert into the holes correctly and the retaining pin for the park pawl inserts to the alignment hole.

4. Replace and tighten the retaining bolts securing the distributor sleeve to the transmission case.

Oil distributor sleeve bolts: **16-27 Nm**

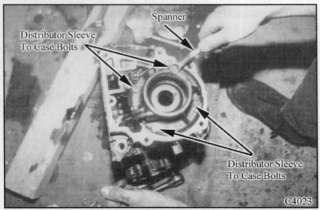

5. To the output shaft install the governor distributor and secure with retaining snap ring, then install the output shaft and governor assembly in the distributor sleeve.

6. To the outer race install the one-way clutch spring retainer, then install inner race inside spring retainer.

7. Between the inner and outer race install the individual springs, then install the one-way clutch rollers between springs and retainer. Rotate inner race clockwise to centre rollers.

8. To the transmission case install the low and reverse drum, then rotate the low and reverse drum to check the one way clutch.

Note: *The drum should only rotate clockwise and not anticlockwise.*

9. To the top of the low and reverse drum install the No. 8 thrust washer, then install the low-reverse band to the transmission case.

10. To the output shaft install the reverse ring gear, then move the output shaft forward and install the reverse ring gear hub to output shaft retaining ring.

11. To the reverse planet carrier insert the No.6 and 7 thrust washers, then install the planet carrier in the reverse ring gear engaging the tabs on the carrier with the slots in the low reverse drum.

12. To the transmission case install the forward part of the gear train ensure all splines and gears mesh together properly.

C4, C5, C9 and C10 AUTOMATIC TRANSMISSIONS

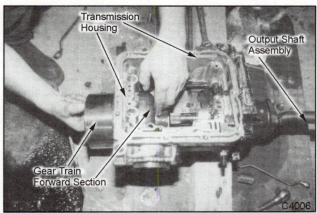

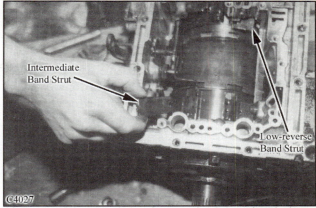

13. Through the front of the case install the intermediate band, ensuring the arrow on the end of the band points towards the front of transmission.

14. Install a new front pump gasket and the front pump assembly to transmission, align bolt holes and tighten bolts to specification.

Front pump to transmission case: **38-54 Nm**

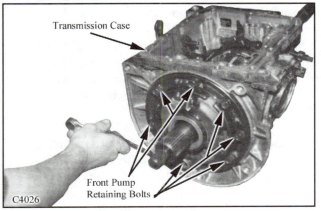

15. Using a new gasket install the extension housing and tighten retaining bolts to specification.

Rear extension housing bolts: **38 - 54 Nm**

16. To the transmission casing install the converter housing and tighten the retaining bolts to specification.

Converter housing to case bolts: **38 - 54 Nm**

17. Install the input shaft to transmission with the short splined end toward the rear of the transmission, then check the end play as described previously.

Note: *If end play is not within specification the wrong selective thrust washers were used or one of the 10 thrust washers is not correctly seated.*

18. To the transmission case install the intermediate and low-reverse band adjusting screws and install the band struts, then adjust bands as described previously.

19. Ensure the gear train has free rotation by turning the input and output shafts in both directions.

20. Install the valve body as described previously, then install the oil pan using a new gasket and tighten bolts to specification.

Oil pan to transmission case bolts: **16 - 22 Nm**

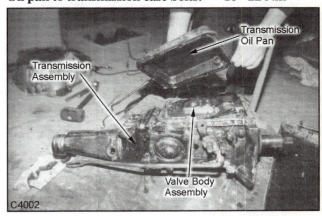

21. To the transmission case install the primary throttle valve, then install the control rod, vacuum unit and new gasket.

PROBLEM DIAGNOSIS

Oil Pressure Check
FLUID CHECK
Transmission fluid changes colour and smell very early in life, these indicators should not necessarily be relied on to diagnose either transmission internal condition nor fluid deterioration. A dark brown fluid colour, coupled with delayed shift pattern, may only indicate that the fluid requires replacement and is not a definite indication of a potential transmission failure.

The fluid level should only be checked when the transmission reaches normal operating temperature.

Transmission fluid colour when new and unused, is red. A red dye is added so that it can be distinguished from other oils and lubricants. The red dye is not an indicator of fluid quality and is not permanent. As the vehicle is driven, the transmission fluid will begin to look darker in colour. The colour will then appear light brown. A DARK brown colour with a distinctively burnt odour MAY indicate fluid deterioration and a need for the fluid to be changed.

Details of transmission oil pressure check procedures refer to 'Oil pressure check information' chart at start of this chapter.

HYDRAULIC DIAGNOSIS
OIL PRESSURE CHECK INFORMATION
Preliminary Check Procedure
* Check transmission oil level and condition
* Check and adjust Kickdown Cable
* Check outside manual linkage and correct
* Check engine tune
* Install oil pressure gauge
* Connect tachometer to engine
* Check oil pressure as follows:

Minimum Kickdown Line Pressure Check
Set the Kickdown cable to specification; and with the brakes applied, take the line pressure readings in the ranges and at the engine r.p.m.'s indicated in the chart below.

Full Kickdown Line Pressure Check
Full Kickdown line pressure readings are obtained by tying or holding the Kickdown cable to the full extent of it's travel; and with the brakes applied, take the line pressure readings in the ranges and at the engine r.p.m.'s indicated in the chart shown later.

NOTICE - Total running time for this combination not to exceed 2 mins.
CAUTION - Brakes must be applied at all times.

Road Test
Drive and Reverse Engagement Shift Check.
1. Start engine.
2. Depress brake pedal.
3. Move gear selector:
   a) 'P' (Park) to 'R' (Reverse)
   b) 'R' (Reverse) to 'N' (Neutral) to 'D' (Drive).
   c) Gear selections should be immediate and not harsh.

Upshifts Application
With gear selector in 'D' :-
1. Accelerate using a steady increasing throttle application.
2. Note the shift speed point gear engagements for:
   a) 1st gear, b) 2nd gear, c) Drive

Part Throttle Downshift
At a speed of 70-90 km/h, quickly depress the accelerator to half open position and observe:
Transmission downshifts to 2nd gear immediately.

Full Throttle (Detent) Downshift
Operate the vehicle at 70-90 km/h in 'D', then quickly depress to wide open throttle position and observe:
Transmission downshifts to 2nd gear immediately.

Manual Downshift
1. Operate the vehicle at 70-80 km/h in 'D' .
Release the accelerator pedal and simultaneously move the gear selector '2' (second) gear position, and observe:
Transmission downshifts to 2nd gear immediately.
Engine should slow vehicle.
2. Move gear selector to 'D' and accelerate to 40 km/h Release the accelerator pedal (closed throttle position) and simultaneously move the gear selector to '1' (first) gear and observe:
   a) Transmission downshifts to 1st gear immediately.
   b) Engine should slow vehicle.

TORQUE CONVERTER EVALUATION
Torque converters can have two different malfunctions:
a) Stator assembly freewheels in both directions.
b) Stator assembly remains locked up at all times.

Condition A:- Poor Acceleration, Low Speed
The vehicle tends to have poor acceleration from a standstill. The engine tune is correct and the transmission is in first (1st) gear when starting out.
Checking for poor performance in 'D' (Drive) and 'R' (Reverse) will help determine if the stator is free wheeling at all times.

Condition B:- Poor Acceleration, High Speed
Engine rpm and car speed limited or restricted at high speeds. Performance when accelerating from a standstill is normal. Engine may overheat. Visual examination of the converter may reveal a blue colour from over heating.

The Converter Should be Replaced if:-
Leaks externally, such as the hub weld area.
Converter has an imbalance which can not be corrected.
Converter is contaminated with engine coolant containing anti freeze.

The Converter Should Not be Replaced if:-
The oil has an odour, is discoloured, and there is no evidence of metal or clutch facing particles.
The threads in one or more of the converter bolt holes are damaged. Correct with thread insert.

Line Pressure at Nil output speed

Gear Lever	Throttle position	Manifold vac	Control Pres
P-N-D	Idle	Approx 18 ins	52-85
1-2	Idle	Approx 18 ins	52-115
R	Idle	Approx 18 ins	52-180
D-2-1	Fast Idle	17 ins	increasing
D-2-1	Partly open	10 ins	96-110
D-2-1	Fully open	3- ins	143-160
R	Fully open	3- ins	230-260

SPECIFICATIONS

Type — Code
- 200 & 250 cu.in. — PEE-AW
- 302 & 351-2V cu.in. — PEF-J
- Lubricant 9.4 litres including converter — M2C-33F

Gear Ratios:
- Reverse (R) 2.09
- Drive (D) 1.00:1
- Second (2) 1.45:1
- First (1) 2.39:1

Shift Speeds 4.1 litre 2.92:1 Diff Ratio

Manual	Shift	Throttle	Km/h
D	1-2	KD	56-72
D	2-3	KD	80-97
D	3-2	KD	80-97
D	3-1	KD	45-55

4.1 litre 3.23:1 Diff Ratio

Manual	Shift	Throttle	Km/h
D	1-2	KD	51-65
D	2-3	KD	72-88
D	3-2	KD	72-88
D	3-1	KD	41-50

4.9 litre 2.92:1 Diff Ratio

Manual	Shift	Throttle	Km/h
D	1-2	KD	58-77
D	2-3	KD	90-116
D	3-2	KD	87-93
D	3-1	KD	45-48

Torque Converter: Stall Speed R.P.M.
- 3.3 litre — 1500-1750
- 4.1 litre — 1600-1800
- 4.9 litre — 1780-2000

Torque Specifications Nm

- Converter Housing to Engine .... 54 - 68
- Transmission Case to Converter Housing .... 54 - 68
- Extension Housing to Transmission .... 40 - 54
- Converter to Flywheel/Drive plate .... 27 - 41
- Converter Housing Lower Cover to Housing .... 16 - 22
- Transmission Oil Pan (Sump) .... 13 - 17
- Control Valve Body to Case .... 11 - 13
- Intermediate Servo to Transmission Case .... 21 - 30
- Front Servo to Transmission Case .... 40 - 47
- Rear Servo to Transmission Case .... 15 - 22
- Downshift Valve Control Cable .... 14 - 16
- Downshift Valve Cam Bracket to Valve Body .... 6 - 11
- Converter Drain Plug .... 20 - 38
- Band Adjusting Screw Locknut to Case .... 47 - 61
- Fluid Cooler Line to Case .... 20 - 27
- Front Pump to Case .... 23 - 30
- Regulator Assembly to Case .... 23 - 30
- Rear Bearing to Extension .... 38 - 42
- Governor body to Shaft .... 35 - 40

C6 AUTOMATIC TRANSMISSIONS

Subject	Page
GENERAL DESCRIPTION	**67**
MAINTENANCE AND ADJUSTMENT	**67**
Lubrication	67
Fluid Level	67
Changing Fluid	67
Lubricant	67
Maintain Strainer	67
Maintenance Notes	68
Oil Cooler Pipes	68
Clean and Inspect	68
Band Adjustment	**69**
Oil Pan/Sump & Valve Body Assembly	**69**
Remove	69
Replace	69
Intermediate Servo	**69**
Remove	69
Install	70
Extension Housing Rear Seal	**70**
Remove	70
Install	70
Speedometer Cable & Driven Gear Assembly	**70**
Remove	70
Install	70
MAJOR REPAIR	**71**
Transmission Dismantle	71
Front Pump	**76**
Dismantle	76
Clean & Inspect	76
Assemble	77
Gear Train	**77**
Dismantle	77
Reverse/High Clutch	**77**
Dismantle	77
Clean & Inspect	78

Subject	Page
Assemble	78
Forward Clutch	**79**
Dismantle	79
Clean & Inspect	79
Assemble	80
Low-Reverse Clutch Hub	**80**
Dismantle	80
Clean & Inspect	80
Assemble	80
Input Shell & Sun Gear	**81**
Dismantle	81
Assemble	81
Governor & Oil Distributor	**81**
Dismantle	81
Clean & Inspect	81
Assemble	81
Valve Body	**82**
Dismantle	82
Clean & Inspect	85
Assemble	85
Transmission Assemble	**86**
PROBLEM SOLVING AND DIAGNOSIS	**93**
TORQUE WRENCH SPECIFICATIONS	**95**

C6 AUTOMATIC TRANSMISSIONS

GENERAL DESCRIPTION

The C6 automatic transmission was a transmission option in many Ford vehicle with V8 engines.

A metal identification plate is attached to the transmission. The model code for vehicles equipped with different transmissions are listed in General Information Chapter at the front of this manual.

MAINTENANCE AND ADJUSTMENT

LUBRICATION
If adding or changing the transmission fluid, use only specified Automatic Transmission fluid DEXRON III

FLUID LEVEL
The dipstick is located in the right section of engine compartment. To check level, follow this procedure:
Apply parking brake and with engine idling and transmission at normal operating temperature, engage each gear briefly, ending with selector in "N" neutral.
* The transmission must be at normal operating temperature to obtain an accurate dipstick reading.
* Do not overfill the transmission. Overfilling will cause foaming of the fluid, loss of fluid, shift complaints and possible damage to the transmission.
Withdraw dipstick and wipe clean with a lint free cloth. Install dipstick into transmission, withdraw and check level. The level must be within "hot" range on dipstick, refer below.
NOTE: Avoid entry of dirt into transmission by ensuring that dipstick is properly seated. Maintaining transmission to correct level with recommended fluid is essential for correct operation of unit.

CHANGING FLUID
* Do not overfill the transmission. Overfilling will cause foaming of the fluid, loss of fluid, shift complaints and possible damage to the transmission.
1. Raise vehicle and place a large drain tray under transmission drain plug and oil pan.
2. Remove transmission drain plug and allow fluid to drain, refer below.
3. Remove oil pan retaining bolts and tap pan at one corner to break it loose, allow remaining fluid to drain and then remove pan.
4. Install transmission drain plug and tighten.
5. Clean transmission case gasket surface and oil pan.
6. Install oil pan with a new gasket, tighten bolts to specification.

Oil Pan to Transmission Case Bolts:
1980-82 .... 12 - 16 lb.ft.
1983-88 .... 8 - 12 lb.ft.

7. Firstly pour sufficient automatic transmission fluid M2C-33F to bring fluid level to lower mark on dipstick. Add automatic transmission fluid into transmission through dipstick hole.
8. Start engine and allow to idle for at least two minutes. With park brake on, move selector lever momentarily to each position ending in "N" neutral position.
9. Add sufficient automatic transmission fluid to bring fluid level to lower mark on dipstick. Re-check fluid level after transmission has reached operating temperature. The fluid level should be between upper and lower marks of "HOT" range on dipstick. Insert the dipstick fully to prevent dirt entry into transmission.

LUBRICANT
11.0 litres including converter   DEXRON II

MAINTAIN STRAINER
* Take care when removing sump from transmission as hot oil can cause serious burns. Avoid this by allowing transmission to cool down.
1. Raise vehicle and support on safety stands.
2. Clean all dirt from around oil pan and transmission case, place drain tray under transmission.
3. Hold oil pan in place, leaving one bolt loose at the front of the oil pan, remove the remaining bolts. Allow the rear of the oil pan to drop, emptying oil into drain tray.
4. Remove remaining bolt and oil pan and empty fluid from pan.

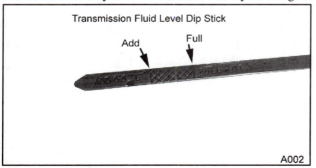

C6 AUTOMATIC TRANSMISSIONS

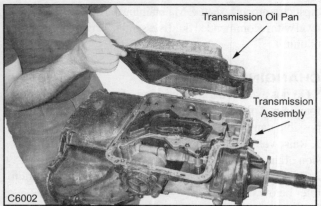

5. Remove the 11 strainer retaining screws and strainer from transmission assembly.
6. Install new strainer using a new gasket/seal and tighten retaining screws to specification.

Strainer Retaining Screws .... 40 - 55 lb.in.

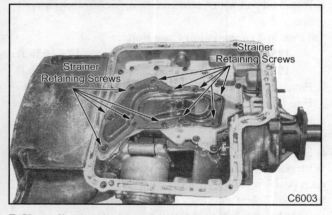

7. Clean oil pan and case mating surfaces. Check that magnet is functional and located in the designated position in the oil pan.
8. Install new gasket and reinstall oil pan. Tighten bolts to specified torque.

Oil Pan to Transmission Case Bolts:
- 1980-82 .... 12 - 16 lb.ft.
- 1983-88 .... 8 - 12 lb.ft.

9. Lower vehicle and add automatic transmission fluid. Check transmission fluid level.

MAINTENANCE NOTES

While maintaining the transmission, all parts should be cleaned and inspected. Individual units should be reassembled before disassembly of other units to avoid confusion and interchanging of parts.

1. Thoroughly clean the exterior before disassembly of the unit.
2. Disassembly and assembly must be made on a clean work bench. Cleanliness is of the utmost importance. The bench tools, and parts must be kept clean at all times.
3. Before installing screws into aluminium parts, dip screws into transmission fluid prevent galling aluminium threads and to prevent screws from seizing.
4. To prevent thread stripping, always use a torque wrench when installing screws.
5. If threads in aluminium parts are stripped or damaged the part can be made serviceable by the use of suitable thread inserts.
6. Protective tools must be used when assembling seals to prevent damage. The slightest flaw in the sealing surface of the seal can cause an oil leak.
7. Aluminium castings and valve are very susceptible to nicks, burns, burrs, etc., and should be handled with care.
8. Internal snap rings should be expanded and external snap rings compressed if they are to be reused. This will ensure proper seating when reinstalled.
9. "O" rings, gaskets and oil seals that are removed should not be reused.
10. Teflon oil seal rings should not be removed unless damaged.
11. During assembly of each unit, all internal moving parts must be lubricated with transmission fluid.

OIL COOLER PIPES

If replacement of transmission steel tubing cooler pipes is required, only use double wrapped and brazed steel tubing meeting transmission manufactures specifications or equivalent. Under no condition use copper or aluminium tubing to replace steel tubing. These materials do not have satisfactory fatigue durability to withstand normal car vibrations. Steel tubing should be flared using the double flare method.

CLEAN AND INSPECT

After complete disassembly of a unit, wash all metal parts in a clean solvent and dry with compressed air. Blow oil passages out and check to make sure they are not obstructed. Small passages should be checked with tag wire. All parts should be inspected to determine which parts are to be replaced.

* Pay particular attention to the following:

1. Inspect linkage and pivot points for excessive wear.
2. Bearing and thrust surfaces of all parts should be checked for excessive wear and scoring.
3. Check for broken score seal rings, damaged ring lands and damaged threads.
4. Inspect seal and 'O' rings.
5. Mating surfaces of castings should be checked for burrs. Irregularities may be removed by lapping the surface with emery paper. The emery paper is laid on a flat surface, such as a piece of plate glass.
6. Castings should be checked for cracks and sand holes.

* Do not use solvents on neoprene seals, composition faced clutch plates or thrust washers as damage to parts may occur.

C6 AUTOMATIC TRANSMISSIONS

BAND ADJUSTMENT
1. Place vehicle on safety stands.
2. Loosen the adjusting screw locknut on the left hand side of the transmission case.
3. Tighten the adjusting screw to a torque of 120 lb.in.
4. Slacken the adjusting screw $1\frac{1}{2}$ turns.

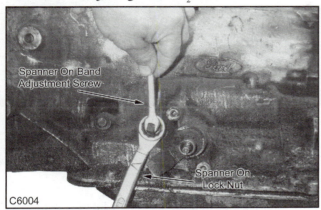

5. Tighten the adjusting screw locknut to 40 lb.ft.
* Never reuse the locknut a second time.
6. Remove vehicle from safety stands and test run.

OIL PAN / SUMP & VALVE BODY ASSEMBLY
Remove
1. Place vehicle on safety stands.
2. Place an oil collection tray underneath the transmission.
3. Remove the oil pan / sump and gasket.
4. Place the transmission selector into "P" position.
5. Remove the 8 bolts retaining the valve body assembly to transmission case, then carefully remove valve body from transmission case.

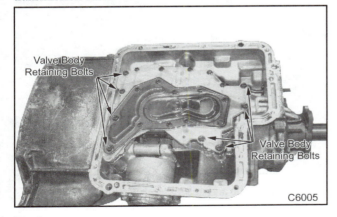

Replace
1. Position the valve body onto transmission assembly, lining up the manual valve with the post on the inner manual valve lever.

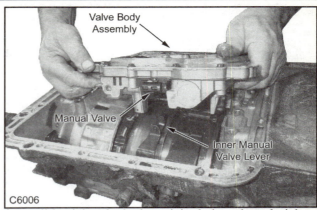

2. Install the eight valve body retaining bolts and evenly tighten bolts to specification.

Valve Body Bolts .... **95 - 125 lb.in.**

3. Ensure the oil pan and transmission case mating surfaces are clean then install a new oil pan gasket.
4. Install oil pan to transmission case aligning bolt holes then install and tighten the 17 oil pan retaining bolts tightening to specification.

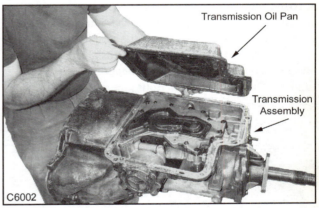

Oil Pan to Transmission Case Bolts:
   1980-82 .... 12 - 16 lb.ft.
   1983-88 .... 8 - 12 lb.ft.

5. Fill transmission with fluid.
6. Remove from safety stands and road test vehicle.

INTERMEDIATE SERVO
Remove
1. Place vehicle on safety stands.
2. Remove the band adjustment locknut and screw then remove the four cover bolts for the intermediate servo cover and remove cover.
3. From the transmission case remove the servo spring then from the servo cover remove the piston, seal and any gasket material.

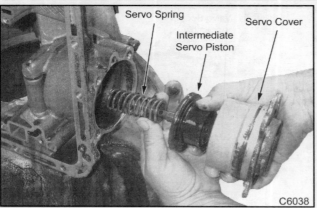

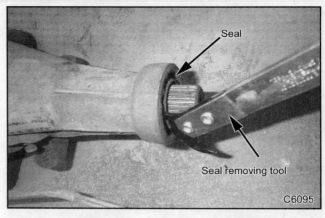

Install

1. To the intermediate servo piston install the outer and inner seals which have been lubricated with clean transmission fluid.

2. To the intermediate servo cover install the cover seal which has been lubricated with clean transmission fluid, then lubricate the inside of the cover with clean transmission fluid and install piston into cover.

3. To the intermediate servo cover install a new gasket then install the piston return spring into the transmission case.

4. To the transmission case install the servo cover assembly pressing down until fully seated, then install and tighten the four cover retaining bolts to specification.

Intermediate Servo Cover Bolts .... 14-20 lb.ft.

5. To the intermediate band adjusting screw install a new lock nut and seal then adjust intermediate band.
a) Tighten the adjusting screw to 10 lb.ft.
b) Back off adjusting screw exactly $1^1/_2$ turns.
c) Hold adjusting screw firmly in position and tighten lock nut to 35-45 lb.ft.
6. Remove from safety stands and road test vehicle.

Extension Housing Rear Seal
Remove

1. Jack vehicle up and safely support vehicle to allow access to the transmission and drive / tail shaft..
2. (a) Place a drain tray beneath transmission extension.
 (b) Remove drive / tail shaft.
3. Remove seal using seal remover and discard seal.

4. (a) Inspect seal lip surface on slip yoke of propeller shaft for damage.
(b) Clean (or replace) as necessary.

Install

1. (a) Apply a little transmission lubricant to seal lip.
(b) Install seal into the extension with a seal insertion tool.
2. Replace tail / drive shaft.
3. Check transmission lubricant level as previously described in this Chapter.

SPEEDOMETER CABLE & DRIVEN GEAR ASSEMBLY
Remove

1. Raise rear of vehicle and place on safety stands. Place drip tray beneath speedometer driven gear.
2. Remove screw and bracket retaining speedometer cable and driven gear.

3. Withdraw cable and gear assembly from rear extension.

Install

1. Inspect 'O' ring seal and replace it if unsatisfactory.
2. Install cable and gear assembly into rear extension.
3. Install retaining bracket and tighten retaining bolt.
4. Lower vehicle and test drive to ensure speedometer is working correctly.

C6 AUTOMATIC TRANSMISSIONS

MAJOR REPAIR

TRANSMISSION

Transmission Dismantle

1. Remove the 6 bolts retaining the rear extension housing to the transmission case and remove rear extension housing.

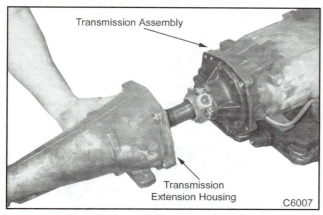

2. Remove the 4 bolts securing the governor to the governor collector and remove governor from shaft.

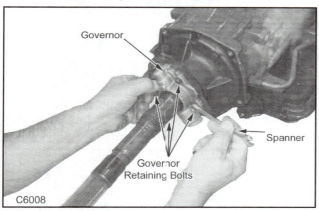

3. Remove the nut from the kickdown lever and remove the 2 neutral/safety switch retaining bolts, then remove the kickdown lever, shift lever and neutral safety switch.

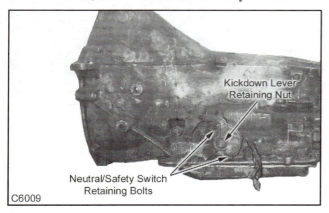

4. Remove the band adjustment locknut and screw.
5. Remove the bolt and hold-down clamp for the vacuum modulator then slowly withdraw the modulator from the transmission case.

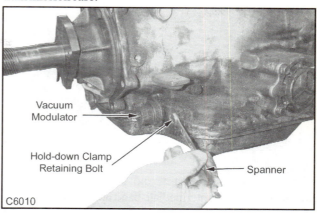

Note: Some models the modulator needs to be unscrewed from the transmission case.

6. From the vacuum modulator remove the modulator rod.
7. Remove the oil pan retaining bolts and remove oil pan from transmission case, then remove the strainer retaining bolts and remove strainer.

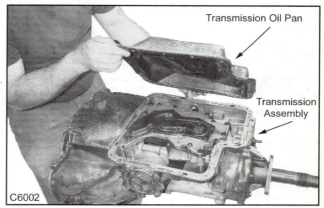

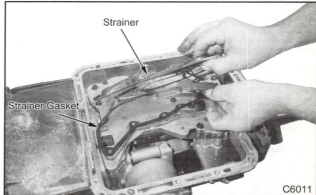

8. Remove the six remaining valve body retaining bolts and lift valve body from transmission assembly.

71

C6 AUTOMATIC TRANSMISSIONS

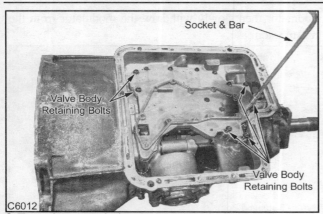

9. From the transmission case remove the intermediate band anchor strut and the intermediate band apply strut.

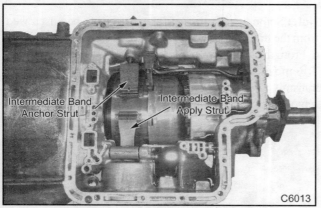

10. Check end play.
a) Install a dial indicator to the front pump assembly and position the indicator needle on the end of the input shaft.
b) Use a screw driver to pry the gear train rearward, then press the input shaft in and zero dial indicator.
c) Using the screw driver pry forward the gear train and record endplay.
11. Remove the seven bolts retaining the front pump to the transmission case, then insert a screw driver between the input shell and case and lever out the front pump assembly, removing pump from case.

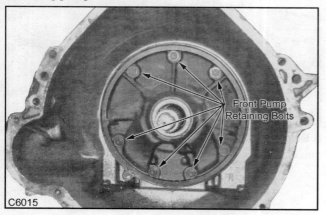

12. From inside transmission case remove the No. 1 selective thrust washer then, remove the intermediate band by squeezing the ends together.

13. From inside transmission case ensure the high reverse clutch assembly and input shell and sungear assembly (gear train) is held together and slid forward as a unit.

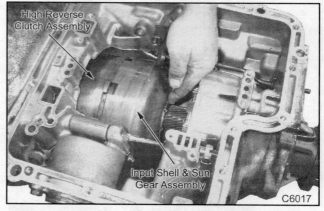

14. Remove the gear train as an assembly from the transmission case.

72

15. From transmission case if not already removed, remove the vacuum modulator valve.

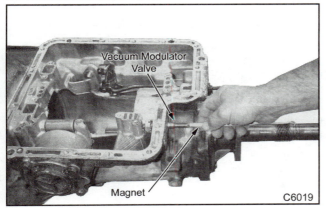

16. Where fitted remove the snap-ring securing the reverse ring gear to the output shaft then remove the output shaft assembly from transmission case.

17. From the transmission case remove the Reverse planetary assembly and low-reverse clutch as an assembly.

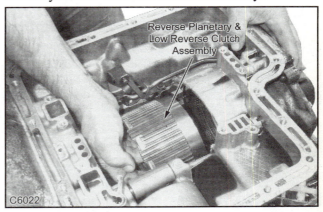

18. From inside the transmission case remove the snap ring retaining the low reverse clutch plates then remove the low reverse clutch pressure plate, friction discs and steel plates.

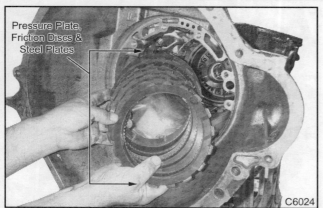

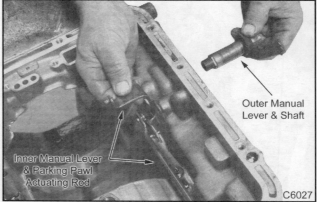

19. From the manual shaft slide out the inner downshift lever, then remove the retaining nut securing the inner manual lever to the manual shaft.

21. Where installed remove the bolt securing the detent spring and roller assembly to transmission case and remove assembly.

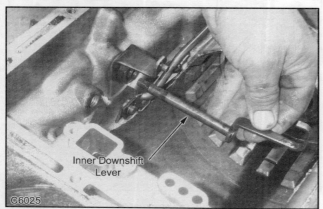

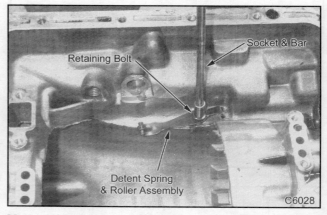

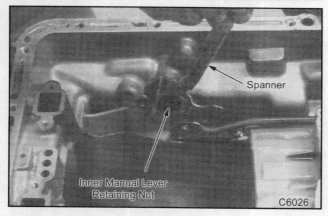

20. From the transmission case remove the parking pawl actuating rod and inner manual lever, then remove the outer manual lever and shaft.

Note: *Some models the detent spring and roller assembly is attached to the valve body and is remove with the valve body assembly.*

22. From transmission pry out the manual shaft seal using a screwdriver.

23. Remove the bolts securing the governor distributor sleeve to the transmission case then remove the distributor sleeve and oil feed tubes from transmission case by gently levering with screw driver.

C6 AUTOMATIC TRANSMISSIONS

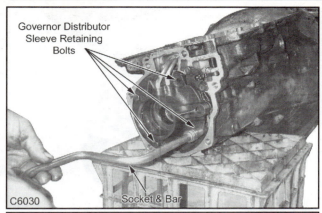

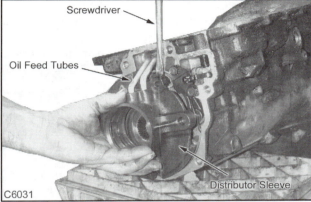

24. Remove the parking gear and the No. 10 thrust washer then from the transmission case.

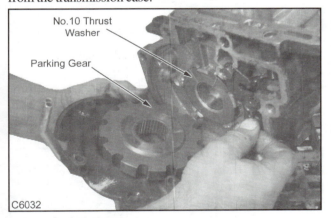

25. From the transmission case remove the parking pawl and spring.

26. Remove the five bolts that retain the one-way clutch inner race to the transmission case, ensuring to loosen bolts evenly.

27. From transmission case remove the one-way clutch inner race.

28. Remove the snap ring and spring retainer then remove the springs from the case.

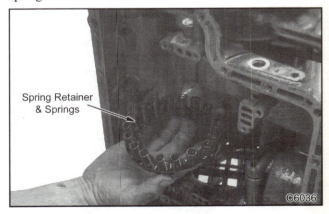

29. Place rags in the bottom of the transmission case to catch the low reverse piston when released.

30. Apply air pressure to the low reverse clutch to release the low-reverse piston then remove the piston from the transmission case.

75

31. Remove the four cover bolts for the intermediate servo cover and remove cover.

32. From the transmission case remove the servo spring then from the servo cover remove the piston, seal and any gasket material.

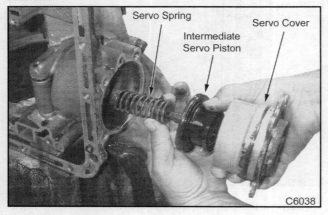

Front Pump
Dismantle

1. From the stator support remove the input shaft, then remove the five stator support to pump housing bolts and separate.

2. From the pump housing remove the drive and driven gears.
3. From the pump remove the front pump seal being careful not to damage pump bushing.

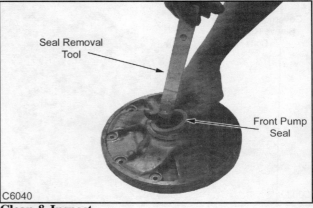

Clean & Inspect

1. Using a solvent cleaner, clean the oil pump components then allow to air dry.
2. Inspect the drive and driven gears for damage or scoring.

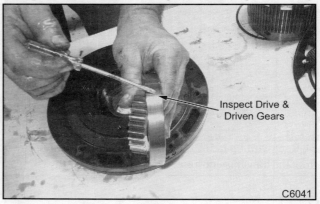

3. Inspect the pump body and cover for damage such as nicks and burrs.
4. Inspect the sealing ring grooves for damage.
5. Inspect stator shaft bushings for wear and damage.
6. Inspect the pump body gear area for wear, nicks, burrs or scoring.

7. Install the pump body to the cover and inspect for warpage.
8. Ensure oil passages and lubrication holes are clean and not restricted.

Assemble

1. To the oil pump housing install a new front pump seal.
2. To the pump housing install the driven and drive gears ensuring the drive gears flat side is to the rear of the pump when installed.
3. Install the stator support to the pump housing and tighten the five retaining bolts to specification.

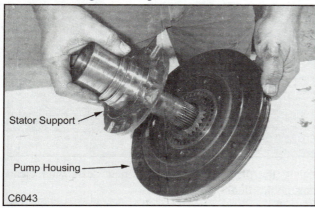

Front pump to stator support bolts .... 12-16 lb.ft.
4. Check that the pump gears have free rotation.

Gear Train
Dismantle

1. Separate the forward and reverse-high clutch assembly from the input shell and sun gear assembly.
2. Separate the forward clutch assembly from the reverse-high clutch.

3. From the input shell and sun gear assembly remove the No.4 thrust washer and the forward planetary ring gear, then remove the No.5 thrust washer and forward planetary assembly.

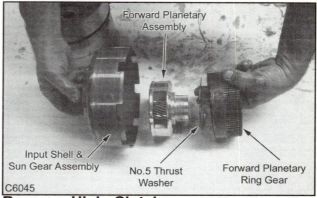

Reverse High Clutch
Dismantle

1. Remove the snap ring for the pressure clutch plate, then remove the pressure plate and the friction discs and steel plates.

2. Using a piston compressor, compress the piston and remove the snap ring for the piston spring retainer.

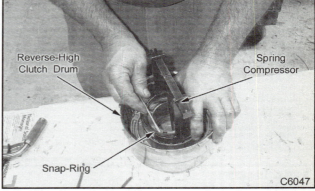

3. Release the compressor them remove the spring retainer and piston return springs.

C6 AUTOMATIC TRANSMISSIONS

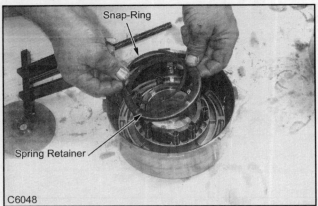

4. Use air pressure in the piston apply hole of the clutch hub to release piston and remove.

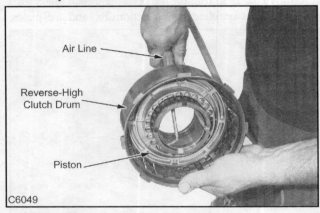

5. From the piston remove the outer seal and also remove the inner seal from the clutch drum.

Clean & Inspect

1. Clean components with a suitable cleaning solvent then allow components to air dry.
2. Inspect the bushings and overdrive band for wear and damage.
3. Inspect piston for damage, also inspect piston check ball is clean and moves freely.
4. Inspect clutch plates for overheating and damage.
5. Inspect the friction plates for flaking, cracking, pitting or wear.
6. Check the return springs for signs of over heating or damage.
7. Inspect the input shaft splines for damage.

8. Replace any components in which are damaged or suspect.

Assemble

1. To the clutch drum install a new inner seal and a new outer

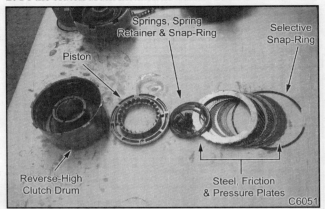

seal to the piston, then coat the new seals with clean transmission fluid.
2. Install piston into reverse drum then install the clutch piston springs into place on the piston as shown in diagram.
3. Install the spring retainer to the springs then using the spring compressor compress the assembly and install the snap ring, then release compressor.

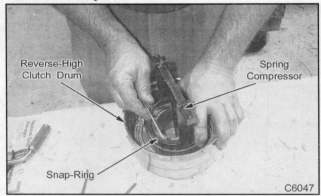

4. To the drum assembly install a steel plate then install a friction plate and continue process until all plates are installed.
Note: If new friction plates are to be used soak plates in transmission fluid for at least 15 minutes before installing.
5. Lastly install the pressure plate and secure with snap ring retaining.
6. Using a feeler gauge check the clearance between the snap ring and pressure plate ensuring to hold down pressure plate while checking clearance.

Pressure plate to snap ring clearance .. 0.022 - 0.036 in.
Note: *If note within specification the snap ring should be replaced.*

Forward Clutch
Dismantle

1. From the forward clutch assembly remove the No.4 thrust washer.

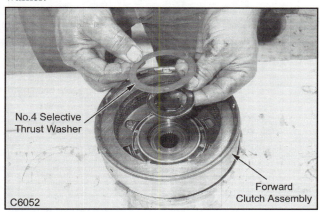

2. Remove the selective snap ring for the pressure clutch plate, then remove the pressure plate, and the friction and steel plates.

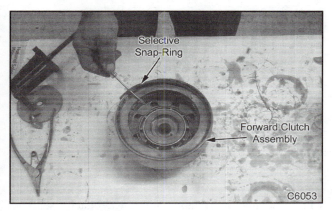

3. Remove the snap ring securing the disc spring, then remove disc spring.

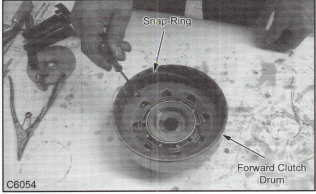

4. Remove the steel pressure ring from the piston.

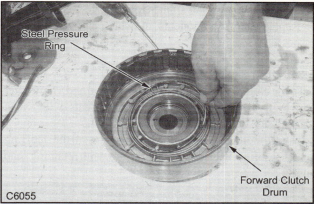

4. Remove the piston from the drum, if piston will not release easily using air pressure in the piston pressure hole of the clutch hub to release piston.

5. From the piston remove the outer seal and also remove the inner seal from the clutch drum.

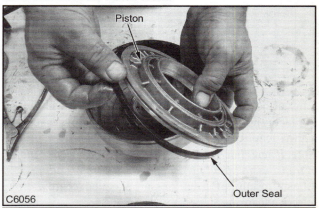

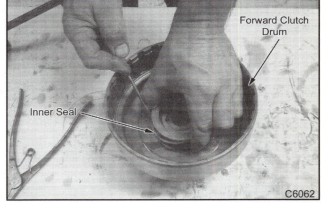

Clean & Inspect

1. Clean components with a suitable cleaning solvent then allow components to air dry.
2. Inspect the bushings and overdrive band for wear and damage.
3. Inspect piston for damage, also inspect piston check ball is clean and moves freely.
4. Inspect clutch plates for overheating and damage.
5. Inspect the friction plates for flaking, cracking, pitting or wear.
6. Check the return springs for signs of over heating or damage.

C6 AUTOMATIC TRANSMISSIONS

7. Inspect the input shaft splines for damage.
8. Replace any components in which are damaged or suspect.

Assemble
1. To the clutch drum install a new inner seal and a new outer seal to the piston, then coat the new seals with clean transmission fluid.
2. Install the clutch piston into place, then install the steel ring onto piston, install disc spring and secure with retaining snap ring.

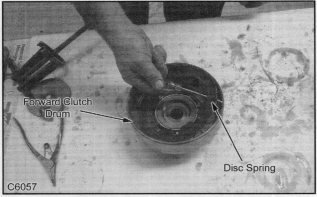

3. Install the forward pressure plate into assembly with the flat side facing up, then install the friction and steel plates starting with a friction plate.
Note: *If new clutch plates are to be used soak friction plates in transmission fluid for 15 minutes before installing.*
4. Lastly install the flat rear pressure plate and secure with the selective snap ring.
5. Using a feeler gauge check the clearance between the snap ring and pressure plate ensuring to hold down pressure plate while checking clearance.
Pressure plate to snap ring clearance ... 0.021 - 0.046 in.
Note: *If not within specification snap ring should be replaced.*

Low-Reverse Clutch Assembly
Dismantle
1. Remove the snap ring securing the reverse planetary gear assembly to the low-reverse clutch hub.

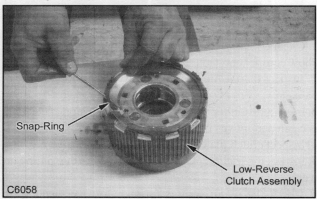

2. From the low reverse clutch hub remove the reverse planetary gear, the No.8 thrust washer and the reverse ring gear.

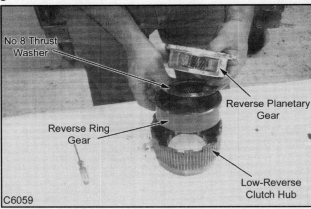

3. From the low-reverse clutch hub remove the inner snap-ring securing the one-way clutch.

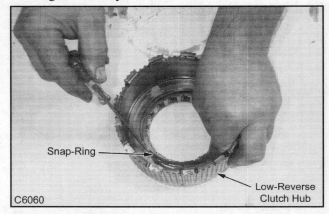

4. From the clutch hub remove the one-way clutch assembly.

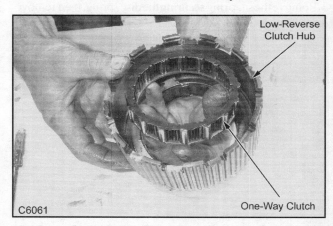

Clean & Inspect
1. Clean components with a suitable cleaning solvent then allow components to air dry.
2. Inspect one-way clutch for worn or damaged rollers and for damaged or broken springs.
3. Check race finish for wear, scoring or damage.
4. Inspect clutch plates for overheating and damage.
5. Inspect the friction plates for flaking, cracking, pitting or

wear.

6. Replace any components in which are damaged or suspect.

Assemble

1. To the low-reverse clutch hub install the one-way clutch assembly.

2. Secure the one-way clutch assembly to the low-reverse clutch hub with the retaining snap-ring.

3. To the low reverse clutch hub install the reverse ring gear, the No.8 thrust washer and the reverse planetary gear.

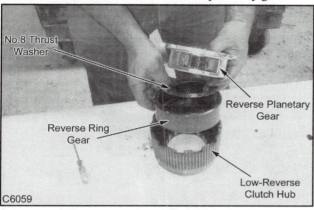

4. Fit the snap ring to securing the reverse planetary gear assembly to the low-reverse clutch hub.

Input Shell and Sun Gear
Dismantle

1. From the sun gear remove the external snap ring, then remove the No. 6 thrust washer wear plate.

2. From the input shell remove the sun gear, then remove the sun gear internal snap ring.

Assemble

1. To the sun gear install the internal snap ring, then install the sun gear to the input shell.

2. Install the No. 6 thrust washer wear plate to the sun gear and input shell, then install the external snap ring.

Governor and Oil Distributor
Dismantle

1. Remove the secondary valve spring retaining plate from the valve body.

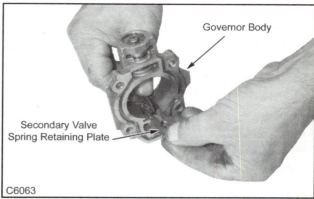

2. Remove the secondary valve spring and secondary valve from governor body.

3. From the governor body remove the primary valve assembly retaining snap-ring and washer.

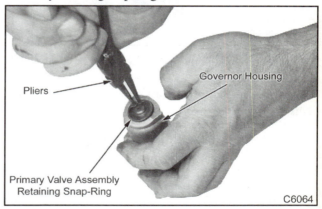

4. Remove the primary valve spring and primary valve from governor body.

Clean and Inspect

1. Ensure all components are carefully laid out in order of removal.

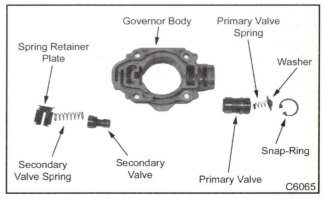

2. Clean valves and springs carefully and allow to air dry.

3. Inspect valves for scoring, cracks or any other form of damage.

C6 AUTOMATIC TRANSMISSIONS

4. Inspect the springs to ensure they are not distorted, broken or have any collapsed coils.
5. Carefully inspect the governor body bores for scoring, cracks or any other form of damage.

Assemble
1. To the governor body install the primary valve and primary valve spring.
2. Secure the primary valve assembly into governor body by installing retaining washer and snap-ring.

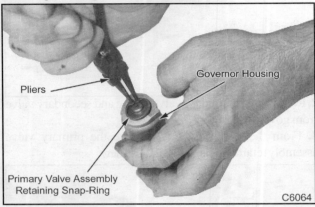

3. To the governor body install the secondary valve and secondary valve spring.
4. Secure the secondary valve assembly into governor body by installing retainer plate.

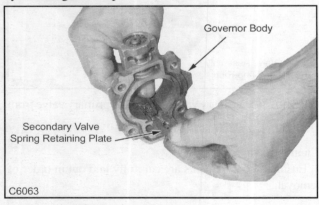

Valve Body
Dismantle
1. If not already removed remove the filter screen from the valve body by removing the retaining screws.
2. Remove the screws securing the lower valve body and separator plate to the upper valve body.

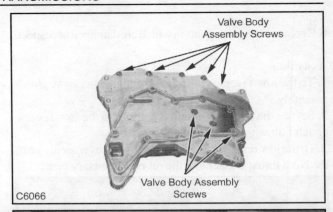

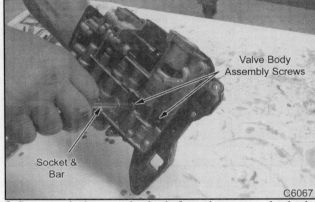

3. Separate the lower valve body from the upper valve body.
Caution: *Be careful not to lose the check balls and relief ball from valve bodies.*

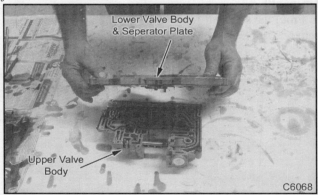

4. From the upper valve body remove the throttle pressure relief ball and spring.

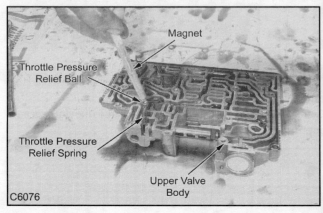

C6 AUTOMATIC TRANSMISSIONS

5. From the upper valve body remove the converter pressure relief valve and spring, then remove the two check balls from the valve body.

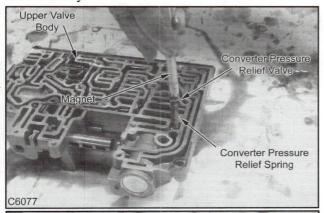

3. Remove the screws retaining the two reinforcement plates to the separator plate then remove reinforcement plates from separator plate and lower valve body assembly.

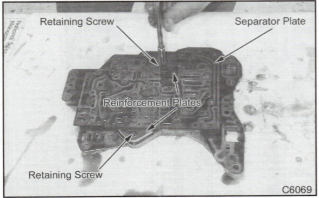

4. Remove the separator plate and gasket from the lower valve body assembly.
5. From the upper valve body remove the manual valve.
6. From the upper valve body remove the retainer for the downshift valve then remove the downshift valve spring and valve.

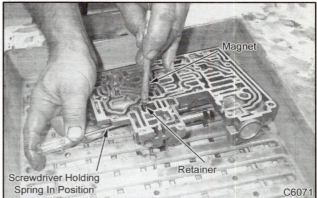

7. Remove the retainer securing the pressure boost valve sleeve then remove the sleeve and the pressure booster valve.

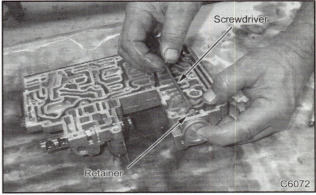

8. From the same bore of the upper valve body remove the two springs and main regulator valve.
9. Remove the two screws securing the throttle booster valve retaining plate then remove retaining plate, throttle boost valve and spring, also remove the manual low 2-1 scheduling valve and spring from the valve body.

10. From the remaining valve retaining plate remove the eight retaining screws while holding plate in position, then slowly remove retaining plate from valve body.

C6 AUTOMATIC TRANSMISSIONS

UPPER VALVE BODY ASSEMBLY

(1) Retainer
(2) Boost Valve Sleeve
(3) Boost Valve
(4) Intermediate Spring
(5) Pressure Regulator Spring
(6) Spring Seat
(7) Main Regulator Valve
(8) Manual Valve
(9) Retainer
(10) Downshift Valve Spring
(11) Throttle Downshift Valve
(12) Throttle Pressure Boost Valve
(13) Throttle Pressure Boost Spring
(14) 2-1 Scheduling Valve Spring
(15) 2-1 Scheduling Valve
(16) Throttle Boost Plate
(17) Internal Servo Modulator Valve
(18) Internal Servo Modulator Valve Spring
(19) Internal Servo Accumulator Valve
(20) Lg. Internal Servo Accumulator Valve Spring

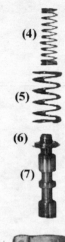
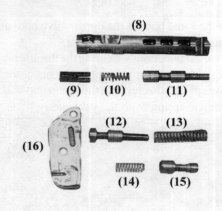

(21) Sm. Internal Servo Accumulator Valve Spring
(22) 2-3 Backout Valve
(23) 2-3 Backout Valve Spring
(24) Throttle Modulator Valve
(25) 2-3 Shift Spring
(26) 2-3 Shift Valve
(27) 1-1 Shift Valve Spring
(28) DR-2 Shift Valve
(29) 1-2 Shift Valve
(30) Line Pressure Control Valve
(31) Cutback Control Valve
(32) Shift Valve Plate
(33) Upper Valve Body

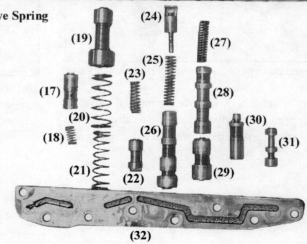

C60100

84

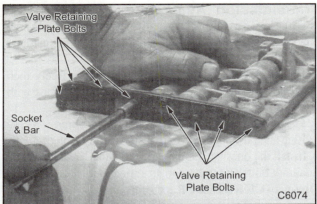

11. From the valve body remove the 1-2 shift capacity scheduling and accumulator valves and springs, then remove the 2-3 back out valve and spring.

NOTE: *Do not remove the 3-2 shift timing valve plug if it is peened, preventing its removal.*

12. Remove the 2-3 shift valve, spring and throttle modulator valve from the valve body.
13. From the upper valve body remove the 1-2 shift valve, D2 shift valve and spring, then remove the coasting boost valve and spring.
14. Remove the cut-back control valve from valve body assembly.

Clean & Inspect

1. Ensure all components are carefully laid out in order of removal.
2. Clean all valves, springs and bushings carefully and air dry.
3. Inspect all valves and bushings for scoring, cracks or any other form of damage.
4. Inspect the springs to ensure they are not distorted, broken or any collapsed coils.
5. Carefully inspect the valve body bores for scoring, cracks or any other form of damage.

Assemble

1. Install the cut-back control valve to the valve body assembly.
2. To the upper valve body install the coasting boost valve and spring then install the D2 shift valve and spring, and the 1-2 shift valve.
3. To the valve body install the throttle modulator valve, spring and the 2-3 shift valve.
4. To the valve body install the 2-3 back out valve and spring then install the 1-2 shift capacity scheduling and accumulator valves and springs.
5. Install the large valve retaining plate into position on the valve body and tighten the eight retaining screws to specification.

Retaining Plate Screws .... **20 - 45 lb.in.**

6. To the upper valve body install the manual low 2-1 scheduling valve spring and valve then install the throttle boost valve spring and valve.
7. Install the throttle booster valve retaining plate and tighten the two retaining screws to specification.

Retaining Plate Screws .... **20 - 45 lb.in.**

8. To the upper valve body install the main regulator valve and the two springs, then install the pressure booster valve, sleeve and secure in valve body with retainer.

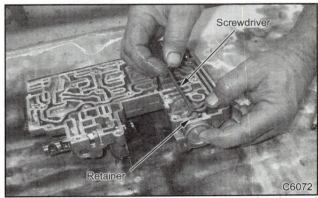

9. To the upper valve body install the downshift valve and spring then secure in valve body with retainer.
10. To the upper valve body install the manual valve.
11. To the upper valve body install the two check balls, the throttle pressure relief ball and spring and also install the converter pressure relief valve.

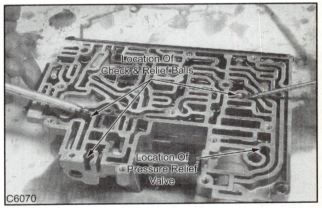

11. To the lower valve body assembly fit the separator plate and gasket.

12. To the separator plate and lower valve body install the two reinforcement plates and secure with retaining screws tighten-

C6 AUTOMATIC TRANSMISSIONS

ing to specification.
Reinforcement Plate Retaining Screws ..... 20 - 45 lb.in.

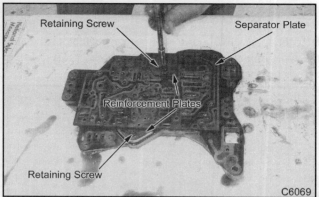

13. To the upper valve body install the lower valve body and separator plate, then install retaining screws and tighten to specification.
Valve Body Assembly Screws .... 40 - 50 lb.in.

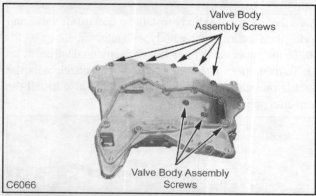

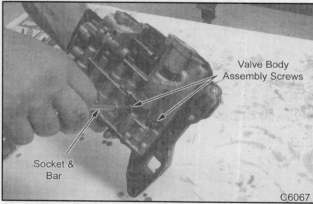

14. Install the filter screen to the valve body tightening the retaining screws to specification.
Filter Retaining Screws .... 40 - 50 lb.in.

Transmission Assembly

1. To the low-reverse piston install a new inner seal and a new outer seal which have both been lubricated with clean transmission fluid.
2. Ensure the check ball in the piston moves freely then lubricate the piston and bottom of the transmission case with clean transmission fluid.
3. Install the low-reverse piston into the transmission case turning and pushing down until piston is fully seated.
4. Install the one-way clutch inner race then install the five retaining bolts and tighten to specification.
One-way Clutch Inner Race Bolts .... 18 - 25 lb.ft.

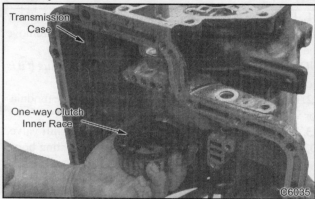

5. Lubricate the No.10 thrust washer with petroleum jelly then install trust washer to rear of case. With thrust washer aligned stake the case tabs to retain washer.

6. Install the parking gear to the transmission case over the No.10 thrust washer.
7. To the transmission case install the parking gear then install the parking pawl shaft and to the shaft slide on the parking pawl.

C6 AUTOMATIC TRANSMISSIONS

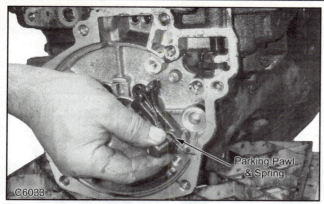

8. Install the parking pawl return spring with the straight end of spring installed into transmission case and the hooked end on the parking pawl.

9. To the governor distributor sleeve install the oil fed tubes then install the governor distributor sleeve to the transmission case over the parking pawl ensuring oil feed tubes are seated into transmission case.

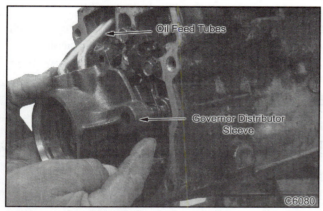

10. Install the four retaining bolts for the governor distributor sleeve and tighten to specification.
Governor Distributor Sleeve Bolts .... 12 - 16 lb.ft.
11. Install the parking pawl actuating rod guide plate and tighten the two retaining bolts to specification.
Guide Plate Bolts .... 12 - 16 lb.ft.

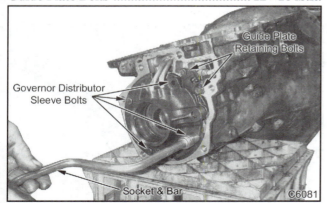

12. To the intermediate servo piston install the outer and inner seals which have been lubricated with clean transmission fluid.
13. To the intermediate servo cover install the cover seal which has been lubricated with clean transmission fluid, then lubricate the inside of the cover with clean transmission fluid and install piston into cover.
14. To the intermediate servo cover install a new gasket then install the piston return spring into the transmission case.
15. To the transmission case install the servo cover assembly pressing down until fully seated, then install and tighten the four cover retaining bolts to specification.
Intermediate Servo Cover Bolts .... 14 - 20 lb.ft.

16. To the transmission case install the vacuum modulator valve which has been lubricated with petroleum jelly.

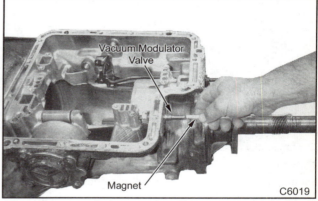

17. To the transmission case install a new manual shaft seal with the aid of a seal installation tool, then install the outer manual which has been lubricated with clean transmission fluid.
18. To the transmission case install the detent spring and roller, tightening retaining bolt to specification.
Detent Spring Retaining Bolt .... 90 - 100 lb.in.

C6 AUTOMATIC TRANSMISSIONS

Note: *Some models have the detent spring and roller attached to valve body assembly.*

19. To the parking pawl actuating rod guide plate install the actuating rod then to the outer manual shaft attach the inner manual lever and parking pawl actuating rod.
20. Install the inner manual lever retaining nut to the outer manual shaft and tighten to specification.

Inner Manual Lever Retaining Nut .... 30 - 40 lb.ft.

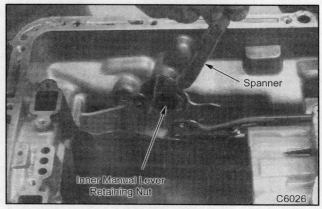

21. Ensure that the detent roller is engaged correctly with the manual lever and it operates smoothly through all notches.
22. To the outer manual shaft install the inner downshift lever and shaft then to the end of the outer manual shaft install the downshift shaft O-ring.
23. To the low reverse piston install the return springs then install the spring retainer and secure to the inner one-way clutch race with the nonselective snap ring.

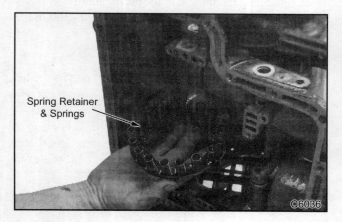

24. To the transmission case onto the low-reverse piston install a steel plate then install a friction plate and continue process until all plates are installed.

Note: *If new friction plates are to be used soak plates in transmission fluid for at least 15 minutes before installing.*

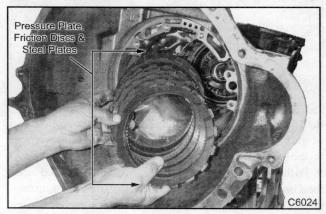

25. Lastly install the pressure plate and secure with nonselective snap ring.
26. Check for proper operation of the low-reverse clutch assembly by applying air pressure to the apply passage.
27. To the governor collector body install the three seal rings which have been lubricated with petroleum jelly.

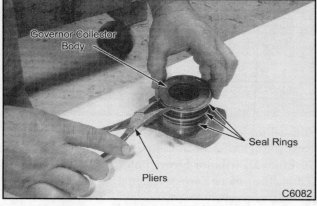

28. To the output shaft fit the governor collector body and secure with retaining snap-ring.

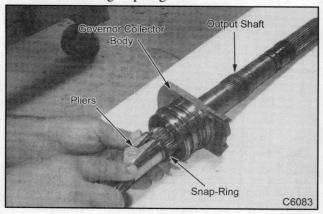

C6 AUTOMATIC TRANSMISSIONS

29. Use petroleum jelly to lubricate the distributor sleeve then to the transmission case install the output shaft and governor collector body.

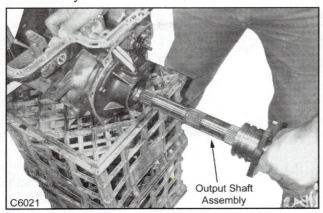

30. To the back of the reverse ring gear install the No.9 thrust washer, retaining in position with petroleum jelly then to the low-reverse clutch hub install the reverse ring gear.

31. To the reverse planetary gear set install the No.8 thrust washer to the backside and the No.7 thrust washer onto the top side holding then in place with petroleum jelly.

32. Install the planetary gear set to reverse ring gear meshing pinion gears with the reverse ring gear, then secure in position with nonselective snap ring.

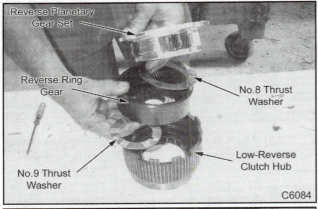

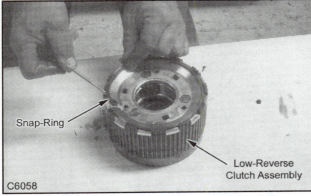

33. To the transmission case install the low-reverse clutch and reverse ring gear assembly over the output shaft engaging splines, then install the ring gear-to-output shaft retaining snap ring.

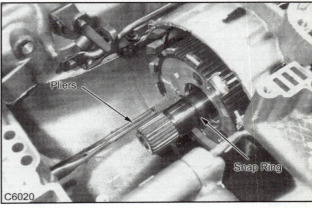

34. Check to ensure one-way clutch rotates on a clockwise direction and locks up in a counter-clockwise direction.

35. To the reverse-high clutch hub install the No.2 thrust washer which has been lubricated with petroleum jelly, then install the forward clutch assembly to the reverse-high clutch engaging splines with friction plates.

36. To the forward clutch drum install the No.3 thrust washer needle bearing race, then install the No.3 thrust washer needle bearing, both of which have been lubricated with petroleum jelly.

37. Install the No.4 thrust washer which has been lubricated with petroleum jelly, then install the forward clutch hub into the forward clutch assembly engaging splines with the friction discs.

C6 AUTOMATIC TRANSMISSIONS

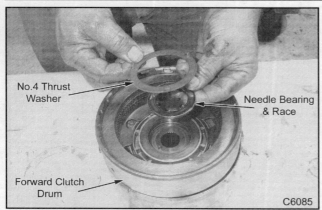

38. To the forward planetary gearset install the No.5 thrust washer and the No.3 needle bearing outer race, both of which have been lubricated with petroleum jelly.

39. To the forward clutch hub and ring gear install the forward planetary gear set engaging the pinion gears with the ring gear.

40. To the forward clutch assembly install the input shell and sun gear assembly engaging the reverse-high clutch tabs into the input shell.

41. To the transmission case install the gear train until the input shell seats against the No.7 thrust washer.

42. To the transmission install the intermediate band around the reverse-high drum, then install the apply strut with the narrow end against the servo and the wide end locked into the band.

43. Fit the anchor strut into transmission case with the narrow end into the band, then install the adjustment screw into transmission case until the end of the adjuster locks into the anchor strut.

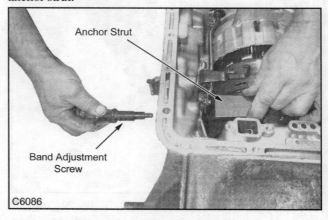

44. If necessary replace the stator support seal ring ends and ensure they are properly locked in the grooves, then lubricate with petroleum jelly.

45. Install a new front pump gasket and the front pump assembly to transmission, align bolt holes and tighten bolts to specification.

Front pump to transmission case .... 16 - 30 lb.ft.
Note: The use of alignment studs or a screw driver will assist in pump installation.

46. To the stator support install the input shaft and ensure it is fully seated, do not force the input shaft into stator support.

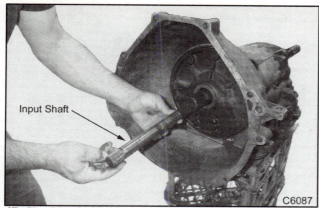

47. Check end play.
a) Install a dial indicator to the front pump assembly and position the indicator needle on the end of the input shaft.
b) Use a screw driver to pry the gear train rearward, then press the input shaft in and zero dial indicator.
c) Using the screw driver pry forward the gear train and record endplay.
End Play Specification .... **0.008 - 0.044 in.**
Note: If not to specification remove front pump and replace No.1 selective thrust washer.
48. To the intermediate band adjusting screw install a new lock nut and seal then adjust intermediate band.
a) Tighten the adjusting screw to 10 lb.ft.
b) Back off adjusting screw exactly $1\frac{1}{2}$ turns.
c) Hold adjusting screw firmly in position and tighten lock nut to 35-45 lb.ft.

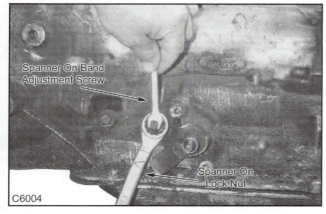

49. Lower the valve body onto transmission assembly, lining up the manual valve with the post on the inner manual valve.

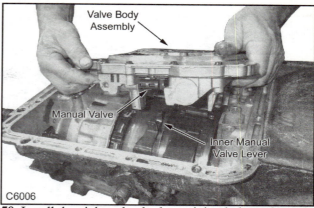

50. Install the eight valve body retaining bolts and evenly tighten bolts to specification.
Valve Body Bolts .... **95-125 lb.in.**

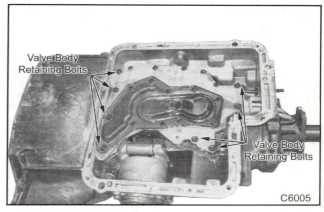

51. Ensure the oil pan and transmission case mating surfaces are clean then install a new oil pan gasket.
52. Install oil pan to transmission case aligning bolt holes then install and tighten the 17 oil pan retaining bolts tightening to specification.
Oil Pan to Transmission Case Bolts:
   1980-82 .... **12 - 16 lb.ft.**
   1983-88 .... **8 - 12 lb.ft.**

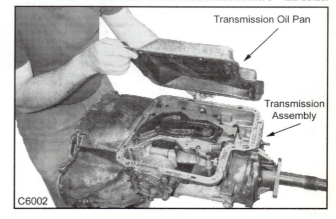

53. To the modulator valve install the vacuum control rod which has also been lubricated with petroleum jelly, then to the vacuum modulator install a new O-ring lubricated with transmission fluid and install vacuum modulator into transmission case.

C6 AUTOMATIC TRANSMISSIONS

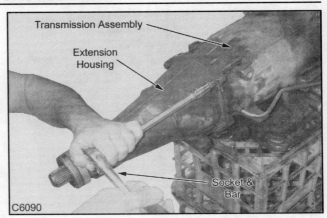

54. To the vacuum modulator install the hold down clamp and tighten retaining bolt to specification.

Hold Down Bolt .... **128 - 16 lb.ft.**

Note: *Some models have a screw in vacuum modulator valve, these type do not have a hold down clamp.*

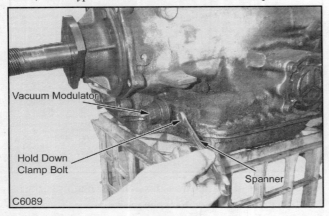

55. To the transmission assembly install the governor tightening the 4 retaining bolts to specification.

Governor Retaining Bolts .... **80 - 120 lb.in.**

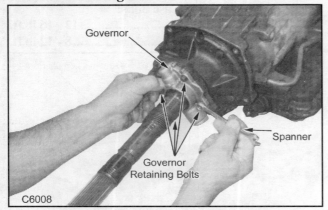

56. To the output shaft install a new O-ring which has been lubricated with petroleum jelly, then install a new extension housing gasket.

57. To transmission assembly install the extension housing tightening retaining bolts to specification.

Extension Housing Retaining Bolts .... **25 - 35 lb.ft.**

PROBLEM SOLVING & DIAGNOSIS

PROBLEM	POSSIBLE CAUSE	CORRECTION
* Slow Initial Engagment	* Improper fluid level * Damaged or improperly adjusted linkage * Contaminated fluid * Faulty clutch and band application, or oil control pressure system.	* Add fluid as required * Repair or adjust linkage * Perform fluid level check * Perform control pressure test
* Rough initial engagment in either forward or reverse	* Improper fluid level * High engine idle * Looseness in driveshaft, U-joints or engine mounts. * Incorrect linkage adjustment * Faulty clutch or band aplication, or oil control pressure system * Sticking or dirty valve body	* Perform fluid level check * Adjust idle to specification * Repair as required * Repair or adjust linkage * Perform control pressure test * Clean, repair or replace valve body
* No drive in any gear	* Improper fluid level * Damaged or improperly adjusted linkage * Faulty clutch or band aplication, or oil control pressure system * Internal linkage * Valve body loose * Faulty clutches * Sticking or dirty valve body	* Perform fluid level check * Repair or adjust linkage * Perform control pressure test * Check and repair as required * Tighten to specification * Perform air pressure test * Clean, repair or replace valve body
* No drive forward - reverse OK	* Improper fluid level * Damaged or improperly adjusted linkage * Faulty clutch or band aplication, or oil control pressure system * Faulty forward clutch or governor * Valve body loose * Sticking or dirty valve body	* Perform fluid level check * Repair or adjust linkage * Perform control pressure test * Perform air pressure test * Tighten to specification * Clean, repair or replace valve body
* No drive, slips or chatters in reverse - forward OK	* Improper fluid level * Damaged or improperly adjusted linkage * Looseness in driveshaft, U-joints or engine mounts. * Bands or clutches out of adjustment * Faulty oil control pressure system * Faulty reverse clutch servo * Valve body loose * Sticking or dirty valve body	* Perform fluid level check * Repair or adjust linkage * Repair as required * Adjust low reverse clutch * Perform control pressure test * Perform air pressure test * Tighten to specification * Clean, repair or replace valve body
* No drive, slips or chatters in first gear in D - all others OK	* Faulty one-way clutch	* Repair or replace one-way clutch
* No drive, slips or chatters in second gear	* Improper fluid level * Damaged or improperly adjusted linkage * Intermediate band out of adjustment * Faulty band or clutch application, or oil pressure control system * Faulty servo and/or internal leaks * Sticking or dirty valve body * Polished, glazed intermediate band or drum	* Perform fluid level check * Repair or adjust linkage * Adjust intermediate band * Perform control pressure test. * Perform air pressure test * Clean, repair or replace valve body * Replace or repair as required
* Starts in high - in D drag or lockup at 1 2 shift pint or in 2 or 1	* Improper fluid level * Damaged or improperly adjusted linkage * Faulty governor * Faulty clutches and/or internal leaks * Valve body loose * Dirty sticking valve body * Poor mating of valve body to case mounting surfaces	* Perform fluid level check * Repair or adjust linkage * Repair or replace governor, clean screen * Perform air pressure test. * Tighten to specification * Clean, repair or replace valve body * Replace valve body or case

C6 AUTOMATIC TRANSMISSIONS

PROBLEM	POSSIBLE CAUSE	CORRECTION
* Starts up in 2nd or 3rd but no lockup at 1-2 shift points	* Improper fluid level * Damaged or improperly adjusted linkage * Improper band and/or clutch application, or oil pressure control system * Faulty governor * Valve body loose * Dirty sticking valve body * Cross leaks between valve body ans case mating surface	* Perform fluid level check * Repair or adjust linkage * Perform control pressure test * Perform governor check. Replace or repair governor, clean screen * Tighten to specification * Clean, repair or replace valve body * Replace valve body and/or case as required
* Shift points incorrect	* Improper fluid level * Improper vacuum hose routing or leaks * Improper operation of EGR system * Linkage out of adjustment * Improper speedometer gear installed * Improper band or clutch application, or oil pressure control system * Faulty governor * Dirty sticking valve body	* Perform fluid level check * Correct hose routing * Repair or replace as required * Repair or adjust linkage * Replace gear * Perform shift test and control pressure test * Repair or replace governor - clean screen * Clean, repair or replace valve body
* No upshift at any speed in D	* Improper fluid level * Vacuum leak to diaphragm unit * Linkage out of adjustment * Improper band or clutch application, or oil pressure control system * Faulty governor * Dirty sticking valve body	* Perform fluid level check * Repair vacuum line or hose * Repair or adjust linkage * Perform control pressure test * Repair or replace governor - clean screen * Clean, repair or replace valve body
* Shifts 1-3 in D	* Improper fluid level * Intermediate band out of adjustment * Faulty front servo and/or internal leaks * Polished, glazed band or drum * Improper band or clutch application, or oil pressure control system * Sticking or dirty valve body	* Perform fluid level check * Adjust band * Perform air pressure test. Repair front servo and/or internal leaks * Repair or replace band or drum * Perform control pressure test * Clean, repair or replace valve body
* Engine over-speeds on 2-3 shift	* Improper fluid level * Linkage out of adjustment * Improper band or clutch application, or oil control system * Faulty high clutch and/or intermediate servo * Sticking or dirty valve body	* Perform fluid level check * Repair or adjust linkage * Perform control pressure test. * Perform air pressure test. Repair as required * Clean, repair or replace valve body
* Mushy 1-2 shift	* Improper fluid level * Incorrect engine idle and/or performance * Improperly adjusted linkage * Intermediate band out of adjustment * Improper band or clutch application, or oil pressure control system * Faulty high clutch and/or intermediate servo release * Polished, glazed band or drum * Dirty sticking valve body	* Perform fluid level check * Tune adjust engine idle as required * Repair or adjust linkage * Adjust intermediate band * Perform control pressure test * Perform air pressure test. Repair as required * Repair or replace as required * Clean, repair or replace valve body
* Rough 1-2 shift	* Improper fluid level * Incorrect engine idle and/or performance * Intermediate band out of adjustment * Improper band or clutch application, or oil pressure control system * Faulty intermediate servo * Dirty sticking valve body	* Perform fluid level check * Tune and adjust engine idle as required * Adjust intermediate band * Perform control pressure test * Air pressure checkintermediate servo * Clean, repair or replace valve body

C6 AUTOMATIC TRANSMISSIONS

PROBLEM	POSSIBLE CAUSE	CORRECTION
* Rouh 2-3 shift	* Improper fluid level * Incorrect engine idle and/or performance * Improper band or clutch application,or oil pressure control system * Faulty intermediate servo apply and release and high clutch piston check ball * Dirty sticking valve body	* Perform fluid level check * Tune and adjust engine idle as required * Perform control pressure test * Air pressure test the intermediate servo apply and release and hogh clutch piston check ball. Repair as required * Clean, repair or replace valve body
* Rough 3-1 shift at closed throttle in D	* Improper fluid level * Incorrect engine idle and/or performance * Improperly adjusted linkage * Improper band or clutch application,or oil pressure control system * Faulty governor operation * Dirty sticking valve body	* Perform fluid level check * Tune and adjust engine idle as require * Repair or adjust linkage * Perform control pressure test * Perform governor test. Repair as required * Clean, repair or replace valve body
* No forced downshifts	* Improper fluid level * Improperly adjusted linkage * Improper band or clutch application,or oil pressure control system * Faulty internal kickdown linkage * Dirty sticking valve body	* Perform fluid level check * Repair or adjust linkage * Perform control pressure test * Repaire internal kickdown linkage * Clean, repair or replace valve body
* No 3-1 shift in D	* Improper fluid level * Incorrect engine idle and/or performance * Faulty governor * Dirty sticking valve body	* Perform fluid level check * Tune and adjust engine idle as required * Perform governor test. Repair as required * Clean, repair or replace valve body
* Runaway engine on 3-2 downshift	* Improper fluid level * Improperly adjusted linkage * Improper band or clutch application,or oil pressure control system * Faulty intermediate servo * Faulty intermediat servo * Polished, glazed band or drum * Dirty sticking valve body	* Perform fluid level check * Repair or adjust linkage * Adjust intermediate band * Perform control pressure test * Perform air pressure testcheckthe intermediate servo and/or seals. * Repair or replace as required * Clean, repair or replace valve body
* No engine braking in manual first gear	* Improper fluid level * Improperly adjusted linkage * Band or clutches out of adjustment * Faulty oil pressure control system * Faulty reverse servo * Polished, glazed band or drum	* Perform fluid level check * Repair or adjust linkage * Adjust low-reverse clutch * Perform control pressure test * Perform air pressure test of reverse servo. Repair reverse clutch or rear servo as required * Repair or replace as required

Torque Specifications

Description	lb.ft.
Intermediate Servo Cover to Case	14-20
Parking Rod Guide Plate to Case	12-16
Downshift Lever to Shaft	12-16
Distributor Sleeve to Case	12-16
Stator Support to Pump	12-16
Oil Pump to Case	16-30
Oil Pan to Case	
1980-82	12-16
1983-88	8-12
Vacuum Diaphragm Unit to Case	12-16
One-way Clutch Inner Race to Case	18-25
Flywheel to Converter	
1980-82	20-30
1983-88	20-34
Extension Housing to Case	25-35
Manual Control Lever Nut	30-40
Transmission to Engine	40-50
Filler Tube to Engine	20-25
Converter Drain Plug	8-28
Band Adjusting Screw Locknut	35-45

Description	lb.in.
Converter Cover to Converter Housing	30-60
Plate to Control Valve	20-45
Lower to Upper Valve Body	40-50
Screen and Lower Valve Body to Upper Body	40-55
Neutral Switch to Case	55-75
Control Valve to Case	95-125
Governor Body to Collector Body	80-120

FMX AUTOMATIC TRANSMISSIONS

Subject	Page
GENERAL INFORMATION	97
MAINTENANCE AND ADJUSTMENT	97
Lubrication	97
Fluid Level	97
Changing Fluid	97
Lubricant	97
Maintain Strainer	98
Console Shift Lever Assembly	98
Removal	98
Installation	98
Column Shift Linkage Assembly	98
Removal	98
Installation	98
Accelerator Linkage & Down Shift Cable	98
Check and Adjust	98
Down Shift Rod Adjustment	98
Replace Kickdown Cable	98
Band Adjustment	99
Front Band	99
Rear Band	99
Oil Pan/Sump & Valve Body Assembly	99
Removal	99
Install	100
Front Servo Assembly	100
Removal	100
Installation	101
Rear Servo Assembly	102
Remove	102
Install	102
Selector Linkage	103
Remove	103
Inspect	103
Install	103
Adjust	103
Speed Sender Unit and Fitting Assembly	103
Remove	103
Install	103

Subject	Page
MAJOR REPAIR	104
TRANSMISSION DISMANTLE	104
SUB ASSEMBLIES	106
Rear Clutch Drum	106
Dismantle	106
Assemble	106
Front Clutch Drum	107
Dismantle	107
Assemble	107
Pump Assembly	108
Dismantle	108
Clean & Inspect	108
Assemble	109
Governor	109
Dismantle	109
Clean & Inspect	109
Assemble	109
Pressure Regulator	109
Dismantle	109
Clean & Inspect	109
Assemble	109
Valve Body	110
Dismantle	110
Clean & Inspect	113
Assemble	113
TRANSMISSION ASSEMBLY	114
PROBLEM SOLVING & DIAGNOSIS	117
Fluid Check	117
Hydraulic Diagnosis	117
Road Test	117
Torque Converter Evaluation	118
SPECIFICATIONS	118
TORQUE WRENCH SPECIFICATIONS	118

FMX AUTOMATIC TRANSMISSIONS

GENERAL INFORMATION

The illustration on this page shows the FMX automatic transmission.

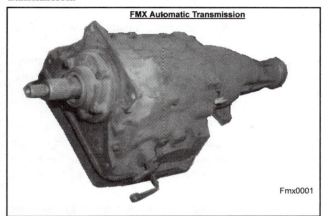

A metal identification plate is attached to the transmission. The model code for vehicles equipped with different transmissions are listed in General Information Chapter at the front of this manual.

MAINTENANCE AND ADJUSTMENT

Lubrication
If adding or changing the transmission fluid, use only specified Automatic Transmission fluid M2C-33F.

Fluid Level
The dipstick is located in the right section of engine compartment. To check level, follow this procedure:
Apply parking brake and with engine idling and transmission at normal operating temperature, engage each gear briefly, ending with selector in "N" neutral.
* The transmission must be at normal operating temperature to obtain an accurate dipstick reading.
* Do not overfill the transmission. Overfilling will cause foaming of the fluid, loss of fluid, shift complaints and possible damage to the transmission.
Withdraw dipstick and wipe clean with a lint free cloth. Install dipstick into transmission, withdraw and check level. The level must be within "hot" range on dipstick, refer below.
NOTE: Avoid entry of dirt into transmission by ensuring that dipstick is properly seated. Maintaining transmission to correct level with recommended fluid is essential for correct operation of unit.

Changing Fluid
* Do not overfill the transmission. Overfilling will cause foaming of the fluid, loss of fluid, shift complaints and possible damage to the transmission.
1. Raise vehicle and place a large drain tray under transmission drain plug/trans fluid pan.
2. Release transmission in drain plug and allow fluid to drain.
3. Release oil pan retaining bolts and tap pan at one corner to break it loose, allow remaining fluid to drain and then withdraw pan.
4. Refit drain plug and tighten to specified torque.
5. Clean transmission case gasket surface and oil pan.
6. Fit oil pan with a new gasket, tighten bolts to specified torque.
Oil pan bolt torque specification: 11-14 Nm

7. Firstly pour sufficient automatic transmission fluid M2C-33F to bring fluid level to lower mark on dipstick. Add automatic transmission fluid into transmission through dipstick hole.
8. Start engine and allow to idle for at least two minutes. With park brake on, move selector lever momentarily to each position ending in "N" neutral position.
9. Add sufficient automatic transmission fluid to bring fluid level to lower mark on dipstick. Re-check fluid level after transmission has reached operating temperature. The fluid level should be between upper and lower marks of "HOT" range on dipstick. Insert the dipstick fully to prevent dirt entry into transmission.

Lubricant
V8   10.5 litres including converter   M2C-33F

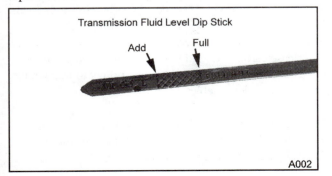

FMX AUTOMATIC TRANSMISSIONS

Maintain Strainer
* Take care when removing sump from transmission as hot oil can cause serious burns. Avoid this by allowing transmission to cool down.
1. Raise vehicle and support on safety stands.
2. Clean all dirt from around oil pan and transmission case, place drain tray under transmission.
3. Hold oil pan in place, leaving one bolt loose at the front of the oil pan, remove the remaining bolts. Allow the rear of the oil pan to drop, emptying oil into drain tray.
4. Remove remaining bolt and oil pan and empty fluid from pan.
5. If necessary, withdraw strainer and 'O'-ring and discard.

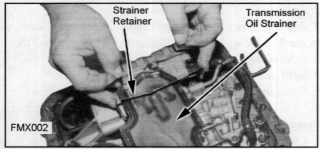

6. If necessary install new strainer and 'O' ring.
7. Withdraw oil pan gasket and discard.
8. Clean oil pan and case mating surfaces. Check that magnet is functional and located in the designated position in the oil pan.
9. Install new gasket and reinstall oil pan. Tighten bolts to specified torque.

Oil pan bolt torque specification: 11-14 Nm

10. Lower vehicle and add automatic transmission fluid. Check transmission fluid level.

CONSOLE SHIFT LEVER ASSEMBLY
Removal
1. Raise vehicle. From beneath vehicle, disconnect rod from shift lever by withdrawing securing pin at transmission end.
2. Withdraw centre console from the vehicle, then disconnect electrical connector for the dial indicator light.
3. Release four retaining screws from the shift assembly to floor pan and lift shift assembly from the vehicle.

Installation
1. Clean mating surfaces of floor pan and shift lever assembly.
2. Apply a bead of sealer around opening in floor pan between the screw holes.
3. Install shift lever assembly using the four screws to retain it in position.
4. The remainder of the installation is the reverse of the removal procedure.
5. Adjust linkage.

COLUMN SHIFT LINKAGE ASSEMBLY
Removal
1. Disconnect shift linkages from the bottom of the steering column, then the linkage onto the transmission selector shaft.
2. Release the bolts holding the linkage assembly to the chassis rail.
3. Release linkage assembly retaining bolts from the transmission casing, then withdraw linkage assembly from the vehicle.

Installation
1. Fit linkage assembly to the vehicle, then fit linkage assembly to the transmission casing using retaining bolts.
2. Fit the bolts holding the linkage assembly to the chassis rail.
3. Connect shift linkages to the bottom of the steering column, then the linkage onto the transmission selector shaft.
4. Adjust linkage

ACCELERATOR LINKAGE & DOWN SHIFT

CHECK & ADJUST
* *Ensure accelerator linkage/cable is correctly adjusted before resetting down shift cable (i.e. Check that wide open throttle can be achieved). Have engine and transmission at operating temperatures.*

Downshift Cable Adjustment
1. Engine must be turned off and the accelerator pressed down to wide open throttle.
2. Disconnect downshift cable.
3. Hold down shift lever against internal stop and refit kickdown cable
4. Adjust kickdown cable so it is taut.

Downshift Rod Adjustment
1. Remove the accelerator and downshift return springs from the carburettor throttle lever.
2. Have the transmission rod installed and hold carburettor throttle lever in wide open position against the stop.
3. Hold the transmission in full kickdown position against the integral stop.
4. Turn the adjusting screw on the carburettor kickdown lever to within 1.0-2.0mm gap of contacting pick-up surface of carburettor throttle lever.
5. Release carburettor and transmission to free positions.
6. Reconnect accelerator cable and springs to accelerator cable and kickdown cables

REPLACE KICKDOWN CABLE:
1. Unclip cable from kickdown lever at the transmission.
2. Unclip cable from throttle linkage assembly.

3. Withdraw the cable from the vehicle.
4. Connect cable from kickdown level at the transmission.
6. Connect cable from throttle linkage assembly.
7. Ensure cable is routed correctly, then adjust cable as described above.

Band Adjustment
Front Band
1. Place vehicle on safety stands.
2. Place an oil collect tray under transmission.
3. Remove oil pan and gasket.
4. Loosen the adjusting screw locknut, pull the actuating rod back and insert a 6.35mm feeler gauge between the servo piston pin and the adjusting screw.

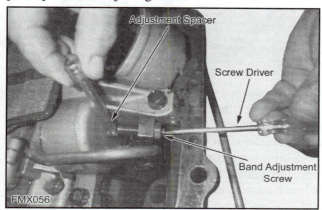

5. Tighten the adjusting screw.
Torque Adjusting screw: **10 in-lb.**

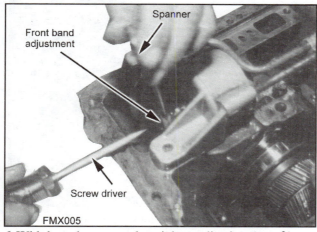

6. Withdraw the spacer, then tighten adjusting screw $^3/_4$ turn and tension the lock nut.
7. Replace the oil pan with a new gasket and tighten the oil pan screws to specification.
Torque Oil Pan Bolts   **11-14 Nm**
8. Refill transmission with fluid.
9. Remove vehicle from safety stands and test run.

Rear Band
1. Place vehicle on safety stands.
2. Release the adjusting screw locknut on the side of the transmission case.
3. Tension the adjusting screw to specified torque of 11.6 Nm.
4. Slacken the adjusting screw 1.5 turns.

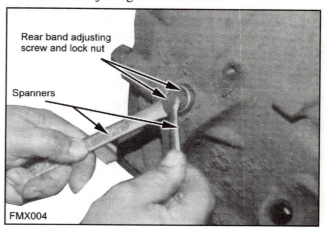

5. Tension the adjusting screw locknut.
6. Remove vehicle from safety stands and test run.

Oil Pan/Sump & Valve Body Assembly
Remove
1. Place vehicle on safety stands.
2. Place an oil collection tray underneath the transmission.
3. Withdraw the oil pan/sump and gasket.
4. Release the vacuum diaphragm unit and hose, take care when removing unit from the transmission, withdraw the push rod, the filter screen clip and screen.

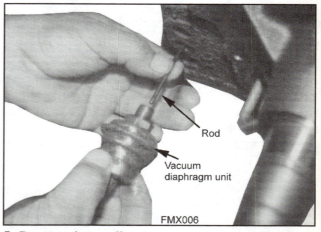

5. Remove the small compensator pressure tube, main pressure oil tube (remove the end that connects to the main control valve assembly first).

FMX AUTOMATIC TRANSMISSIONS

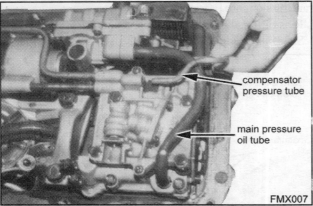

6. Loosen the front servo attaching bolts approximately 3 turns.
7. Remove the 3 control valve body attaching bolts, lower the body gently and pull it off the front servo tubes.
* Take care.

Install
1. Replace the control valve body, align the front servo tubes into position. Move the manual lever to the 1 detent position and place the inner downshift lever between the downshift lever stop and downshift valve, the lever must engage the actuating pin in the manual detent lever.

2. Install the control valve body bolts, move the valve body to the centre of the case until the clearance is less than 1.27mm between the manual valve and actuating pin on the manual detent lever. Fluid screen filter clip under centre back bolt. Tighten bolts to specification.

Control Valve Body bolts: 11-13Nm

3. Install the main pressure oil tube, the end that connects to the pressure regulator first. Tap other end of tube in with rubber hammer.
4. Install the compensator pressure tube to the pressure regulator and valve body.

5. Turn the manual valve one full turn in each manual lever detent position. If the manual valve binds against the actuating pin in any position, loosen the valve body and move it away from the centre of the case to relieve the binding. Torque the valve body bolts to specification and re-check the manual valve for binding.
6. Install the push rod into the threaded opening of the case and install vacuum diaphragm unit and hose.

Torque Vacuum Unit   20-31Nm

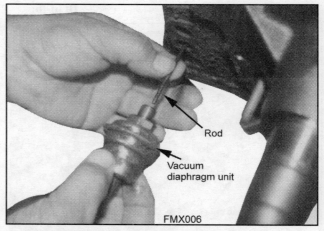

7. Adjust the front band as previously described.
8. Install the fluid screen and oil pan with a new gasket. Torque oil pan bolts to specification.

Oil Pan Attaching Bolts   13-17Nm

9. Adjust the rear band as previously described.
10. Fill transmission with fluid.
11. Remove from safety stands and road test vehicle.

Front Servo Assembly
Remove
1. Place vehicle on safety stands.
2. Place an oil collection tray underneath the transmission.

3. Remove the oil pan / sump and gasket.
4. Remove the vacuum diaphragm unit and hose, take care when removing unit, remove the push rod, the filter screen clip and screen.

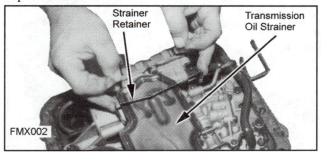

5. Remove the small compensator pressure tube, main pressure oil tube (remove the end that connects to the main control valve assembly first).
6. Loosen the front servo attaching bolts approximately 3 turns.

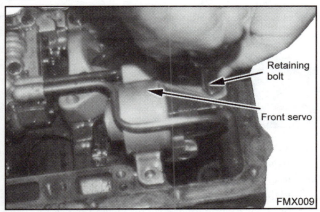

7. Remove the front servo attaching bolts, hold the strut with your fingers, and remove the servo.

Install

1. Push the front band forward in the case, with the end of the band face down. Make sure the front servo anchor pin is in position in the case. Align the large end of the servo strut with servo actuating lever, align the small end with the band end.
2. Rotate the band, strut, and servo to align the anchor end of the band with the anchor in the case. Install the front servo body on to the control valve body tubes.
3. Install the attaching bolts and torque to specification.
Front servo attaching bolts: **40-47Nm**

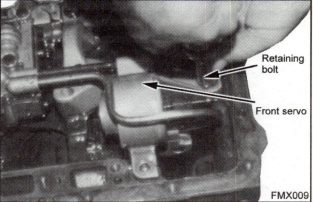

4. Install the control valve body bolts, move the valve body to the centre of the case until the clearance is less than 1.27mm between the manual valve and actuating pin on the manual detent lever. Fluid screen filter clip under centre back bolt. Tighten bolts to specification.
Control Valve Body bolts: **11-13Nm**

5. Install the main pressure oil tube, the end that connects to the pressure regulator first. Tap other end of tube in with rubber hammer.
6. Install the compensator pressure tube to the pressure regulator and valve body.
7. Turn the manual valve one full turn in each manual lever detent position. If the manual valve binds against the actuating pin in any position, loosen the valve body and move it away from the centre of the case to relieve the binding. Torque the valve body bolts to specification and re-check the manual valve for binding.
8. Install the push rod into the threaded opening of the case and install vacuum diaphragm unit and hose.
Torque Vacuum Unit: **20-31Nm**

FMX AUTOMATIC TRANSMISSIONS

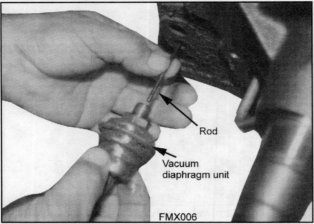

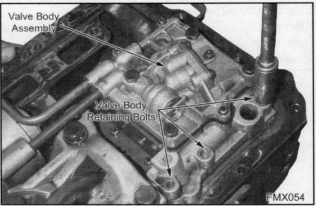

8. Remove the rear servo attaching servo bolts, hold the actuating struts with your fingers and remove the servo.

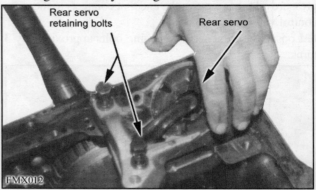

9. Adjust the front band as previously described.
10. Install the fluid screen and oil pan with a new gasket. Torque oil pan bolts to specification.

Oil Pan Attaching Bolts: 13-17Nm

11. Adjust the rear band as previously described.
12. Fill transmission with fluid.
13. Remove from safety stands and road test vehicle.

Rear Servo Assembly
Remove
1. Place vehicle on safety stands.
2. Place an oil collection tray underneath the transmission.
3. Remove the oil pan / sump and gasket.
4. Remove the vacuum diaphragm unit and hose, take care when removing unit, remove the push rod, the filter screen clip and screen.
5. Remove the small compensator pressure tube, main pressure oil tube (remove the end that connects to the main control valve assembly first).
6. Remove the 3 control valve body attaching bolts, lower the body gently and pull it off the front servo tubes.
* Take care.

Install
1. Position the servo anchor strut on the servo band, rotate the band to engage the band to the strut.
2. Hold the servo anchor strut in position with your fingers, position the actuating lever strut and install the servo.
3. Install the servo bolts (longest bolt to inner bolt hole of servo), move the rear servo (might take some force - without servo bolts tightened) toward the centre line of the case against the servo bolts. While in this position torque servo bolts.

Torque servo bolts: 40-47Nm

4. Replace the control valve body, align the front servo tubes

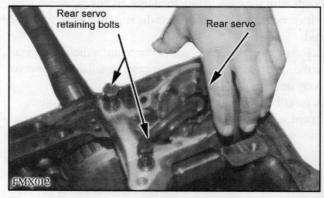

into position. Move the manual lever to the 1 detent position and place the inner downshift lever between the downshift lever stop and downshift valve, the lever must engage the actuating pin in the manual detent lever.
5. Install the control valve body bolts, move the valve body

to the centre of the case until the clearance is less than 1.27mm between the manual valve and actuating pin on the manual detent lever. Fluid screen filter clip under centre back bolt. Tighten bolts to specification.

Control Valve Body bolts: 11-13Nm

6. Install the main pressure oil tube, the end that connects to

the pressure regulator first. Tap other end of tube in with rubber hammer.

7. Install the compensator pressure tube to the pressure regulator and valve body.

8. Turn the manual valve one full turn in each manual lever detent position. If the manual valve binds against the actuating pin in any position, loosen the valve body and move it away from the centre of the case to relieve the binding. Torque the valve body bolts to specification and re-check the manual valve for binding.

9. Install the push rod into the threaded opening of the case and install vacuum diaphragm unit and hose.

Torque Vacuum Unit   20-31Nm

10. Adjust the front band as previously described.
11. Install the fluid screen and oil pan with a new gasket. Torque oil pan bolts to specification.

Oil Pan Attaching Bolts   13-17Nm

12. Adjust the rear band as previously described.

13. Fill transmission with fluid.
14. Remove from safety stands and road test vehicle.

Selector Linkage
Remove
Set transmission selector to lever to 'PARK' position. Raise front of vehicle. Remove locking bolt, dished washer, flat washer, insulator and sleeve from lower end of selector lever. Slide trunnion from selector rod. Remove retaining nut, rod and lever assembly from the transmission manual shaft.

Inspect
Check all items for wear and/or damage, replace all worn or damaged items.

Install
Installation is the reverse of the removal procedure. Tighten the nut to the specified torque. Adjust linkage as described below.

Manual shaft nut torque specification: 26-30 Nm

Adjust
1. Loosen locking bolt at selector lever.
2. Position transmission selector lever in "PARK".
3. Position gear shift lever in 'PARK', then tighten the locking bolt at the selector lever, to the specified torque.

Selector lever locking bolt: 18-24 Nm

4. Lower vehicle and test.
5. Ensure that engine can be started only in 'PARK' and 'Neutral'. The Park/Neutral/Backup switch is automatically adjusted when linkage is correctly adjusted.

Speed Sender Unit & Fitting Assembly
Remove
1. Raise rear of vehicle and place on safety stands. Place drip tray beneath speed sender.
2. Disconnect sender unit electrical connector.
3. Unscrew vehicle speed sender unit and remove.
4. Unscrew bolt securing fitting assembly retainer to extension and remove retainer. Withdraw fitting assembly including driven gear from case extension.

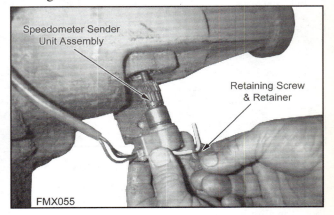

FMX AUTOMATIC TRANSMISSIONS

Install

1. Inspect fitting assembly 'O' ring seal and replace it if unsatisfactory.
2. Installation is the reverse of the removal procedure.
3. Tighten retainer bolt to specified torque.
Retainer bolt torque specification: 8-14 Nm
* The vehicle speed unit is tightened by hand only.

MAJOR REPAIR

DISMANTLE TRANSMISSION
Dismantle
1. (a) Carefully slide the torque converter from the transmission bell housing.
(b) Release and withdraw the bell housing from the transmission assembly.
2. Release the extension housing, using soft face hammer to release then slide from the transmission.

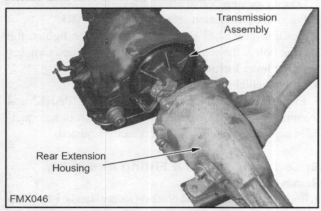

3. Release the centre support retaining bolts, locking tabs will need bending back first.

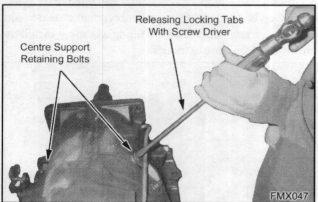

4. (a) Release the governors retaining cir-clip then slowly slide the governor assembly from its position.
(b) When sliding the governor from the output shaft do not loose the aligning ball.

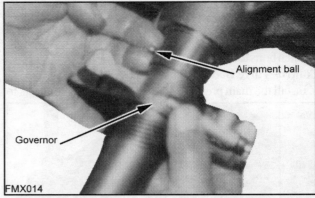

5. (a) Release and withdraw the transmission pump retaining bolts.
(b) Using a soft face hammer tap the pump assembly to release its bond to the housing, then withdraw.

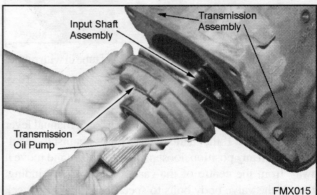

6.(a) Release the oil pan bolts, then lift from the transmission.
(b) Unclip the pressure regulator valve spring retainer, and withdraw the spring.
(c) Remove the compensator and main pressure tubes from the valve body assemblies.

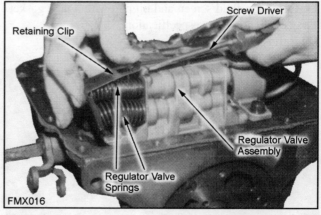

(d) Release the pressure regulator bolts and lift regulator body from the transmission.

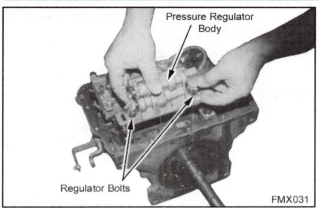

(e) Release the servo and valve body retaining bolts, then lift the two components from the transmission as an assembly.
(f) As the assembly is lifted do not lose the band strut.

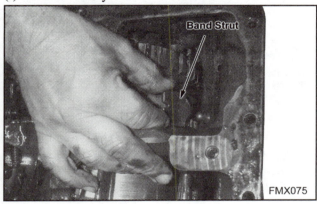

7.(a) Carefully withdraw the rear support from the transmission assembly.
(b) Ensure that the fluid pipes do not get damaged as the support is released.

8. Withdraw the output shaft from the transmission, ensuring that the thrust washer is also withdrawn.

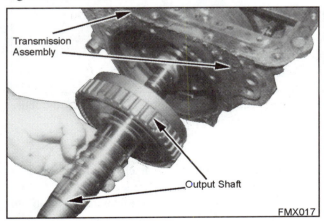

9. Pull the rear drum from the casing, then the roller bearing, ensure that the one-way clutch is still fitted to the rear drum assembly.

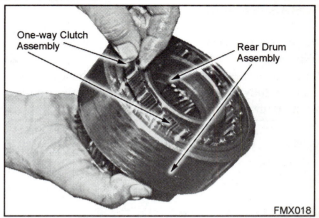

10. Remove the rear band from the casing, then the centre support and rear clutch drum assembly are able to be withdrawn.

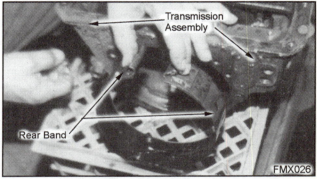

12. Withdraw the front clutch drum from the casing, ensure that the thrust washer are not misplaced or lost.

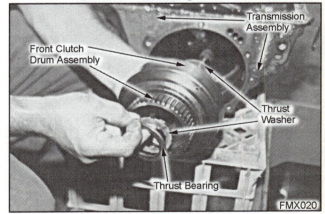

14.(a) Slide the front band from the transmission casing.
(b) If necessary release the linkage and park pawl assembly from the transmission.

SUB ASSEMBLIES

Rear clutch drum
Dismantle
1. Release the metal sealing rings from the primary sun gear shaft, carefully withdraw the shaft and thrust washer from the assembly, then remove remaining metal sealing rings.

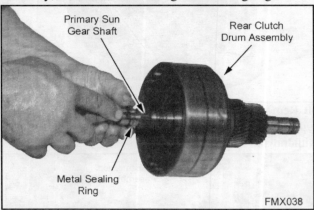

2. Withdraw the primary sun gear shaft needle rollers from the rear clutch drum assembly, then release the clutch pack retaining cir-clip.

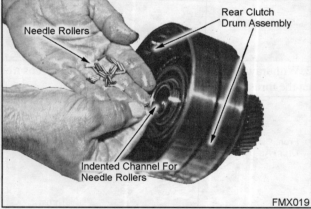

3. Remove clutch pack keeping the plates and clutches in order of removal.

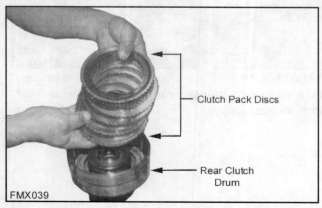

4. Fit a piston spring compressor, compress piston and remove retaining cir-clip then withdraw spring.

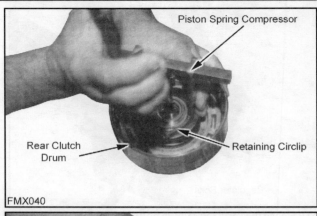

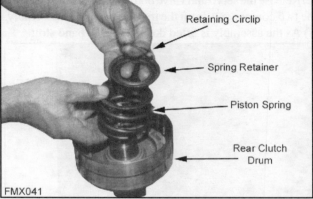

5. Remove the piston by applying compressed air to the inner fluid port to release piston then remove from drum.

Note :- The piston should have a check ball fitted to the under side of it, ensure it is in place.

Assemble
1. Install the piston into the rear clutch drum until it is bottomed out hard, then fit the spring and retainer.
2. Use the spring compressor until the retaining clip is able to be fitted, then release the spring compressor.

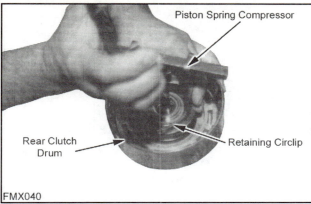

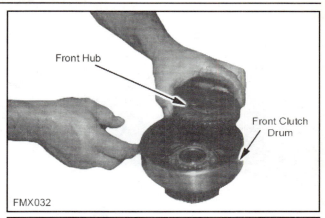

3. Fit the clutch packs in the reverse to what they were removed, then install the cir-clip.

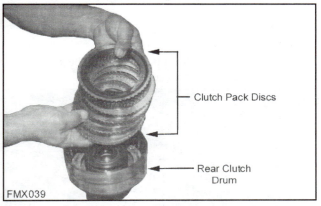

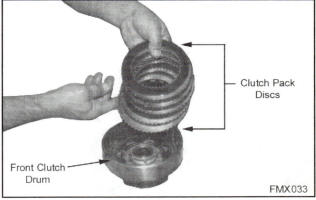

3. Release piston spring cir-clip, then the spring and piston spring runner can be removed from the assembly.

4. Fit the primary sun gear shaft needle rollers into the rear clutch drum.

5. With the thrust washer and inner metal sealing rings fitted to the primary sun gear shaft, slide the shaft through the rear clutch drum assembly, then fit the outer metal sealing rings.

Front clutch drum
Dismantle

1. Release the input shaft retaining cir-clip, then lift the input shaft and thrust bearing from the assembly.

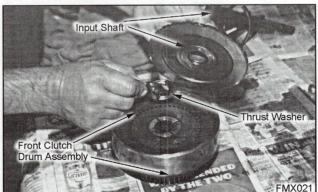

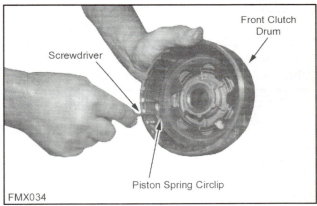

Note : Ensure that the piston spring cir-clip and input shaft cir-clip are not mixed up, the piston spring cir-clip is heavier that the input shaft cir-clip.

4. Apply air to the fluid port and push the piston from its seat, then withdraw the piston.

2. Lift the front hub from the assembly, then the clutch pack keeping plates and clutches in order of removal.

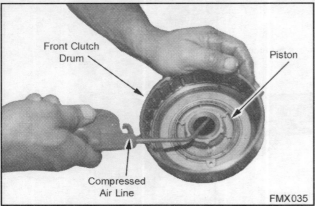

Note :- The piston should have a check ball fitted to the under side of it, ensure it is in place.

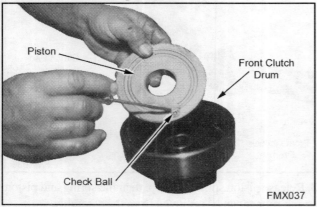

Assemble
1. Fit the piston into the bottom of the clutch drum, ensure that it has seated correctly.
2. Place the piston spring runner in the top of the piston, then fit the spring, securing it with the cir-clip.

3. Place the hub in the front clutch drum, then fit the clutch pack in the reverse order that it was removed.

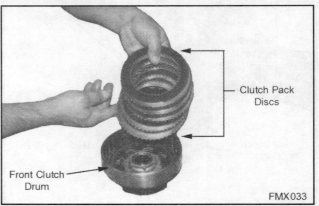

4. With the thrust bearing positioned, lower the input shaft into the assembly and secure with the retaining cir-clip.

Pump Assembly
Dismantle
1. Remove the four stator support to pump housing screws and separate stator support and pump body.

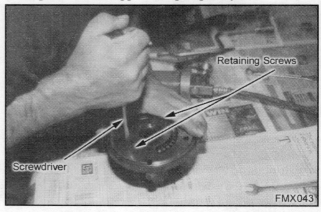

2. Mark the top of the driven gear for assembly (do not scratch) then from the pump housing remove the drive and driven gears.

Inspection
1. Inspect the pump housing, for scores or damage.
2. Inspect drive and driven gears for wear scoring or damage.
3. If required replace pump housing bushing.

Assemble

1. To the pump housing install the driven and drive gears ensuring the chamfered side is positioned downward against the pump housing.
2. Install the stator support to the pump housing and tighten the four retaining bolts to specification.

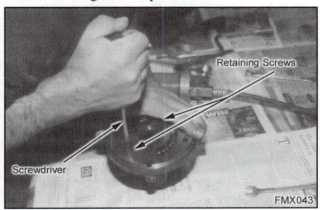

Front pump to stator support: **23-30Nm**

Governor
Dismantle
1. From the governor assembly remove the valve body cover.
2. Remove the governor valve body from the counter weight.
3. From the valve body remove the plug and sleeve.
4. Remove the spring clip from the valve body then remove the spring and valve from the valve body.

Clean and Inspect
1. Clean all components thoroughly and dry with compressed air.
2. Inspect all components for nicks, burrs or damage.

Assemble
1. To the bore of the valve body install the valve and spring then install spring clip.
2. To the valve body install the sleeve and plug then install counter weight to valve body.
3. To the governor body install the valve body cover and tighten retaining screws.

Cover to Governor Body:

Pressure Regulator
Dismantle
1. Remove the valve assembly retainer then remove the pressure valve springs.
2. Remove the valve retainer and valve stop from regulator housing.
3. From the pressure regulator assembly remove the control pressure valve and converter pressure valve.

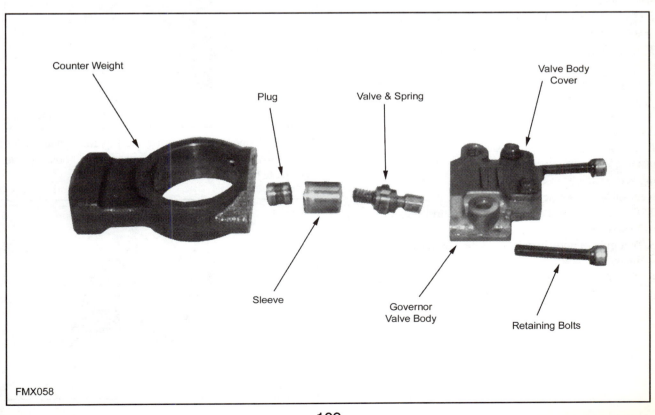

FMX AUTOMATIC TRANSMISSIONS

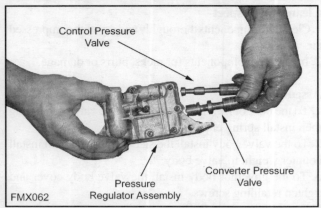
FMX062

Valve Body
When dismantling the valve body it is important to keep all the valves laid out in their correct position as they are removed, this ensures that they will be correct on assembly.

Dismantle
1. From the valve body assembly remove the manual valve.
2. From the valve body assembly remove the throttle valve body and separator plate being careful not to lose the check valve.

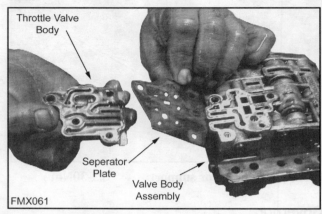
FMX061

4. Remove the regulator body cover retaining screws then remove regulator cover and separator plate.

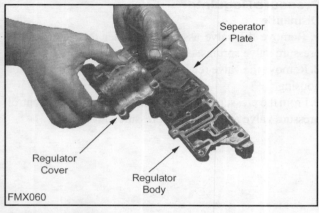
FMX060

Clean and Inspect
1. Clean all components with a suitable cleaning solvent then dry with compressed air.
2. Check to ensure all fluid passages are clean and have no obstructions.
3. Inspect regulator cover and body for burrs, nicks or damage.
4. Inspect valves for nicks, burrs or damage also inspect valve springs for breakage or damage.

Assemble
1. To the regulator cover install the separator plate then install cover assembly to regulator body and tighten retaining screws to specification.
Regulator Cover Screws:
2. To the regulator body install the control pressure valve and valve stop.
3. To regulator body install the converter pressure valve and retainer.
4. To pressure regulator assembly install the converter pressure valve springs and secure with spring retainer.

3. From the throttle valve body remove the plug and throttle valve.

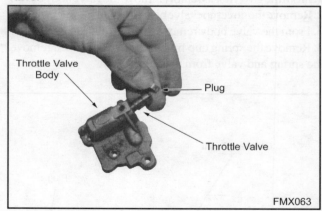
FMX063

4. Remove one screw securing the separator plate to the lower valve body then from the upper valve body remove front plate being careful as it is spring loaded.

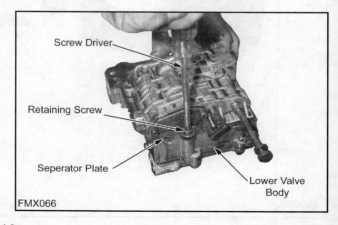
FMX066

FMX AUTOMATIC TRANSMISSIONS

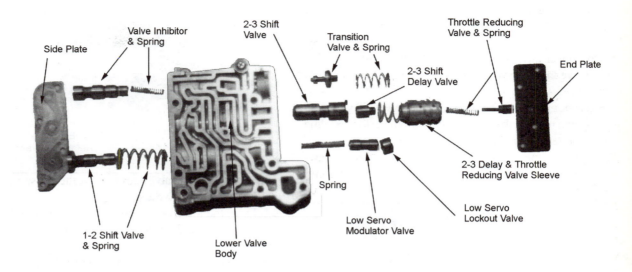
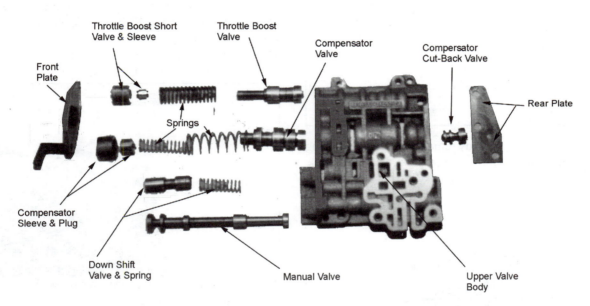
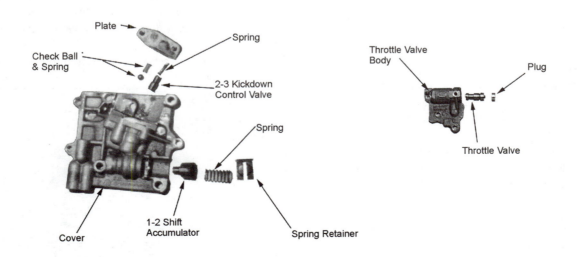

FMX AUTOMATIC TRANSMISSIONS

Note: *Hold front plate firmly while removing retaining screws.*

5. From the upper valve body remove the compensator sleeve and plug, then remove compensator valve springs and valve.

6. From upper valve body remove the throttle boost short valve and sleeve then remove the valve spring and throttle boost valve.

7. From the upper valve body remove the downshift valve and spring then remove the valve retainer for the 2-1 scheduling valve and remove valve from valve body.

8. From the upper valve body remove the three screws securing the rear plate then remove the compensator cutback valve.

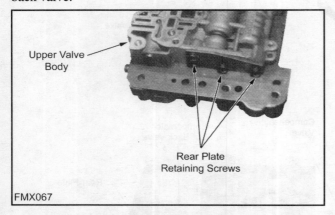

9. From the lower valve body remove the screws securing the side plate while holding plate in position, then remove side plate being careful as it is spring loaded.

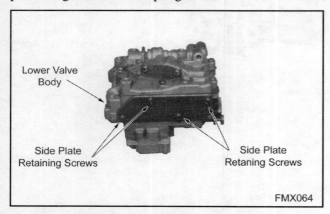

10. From the lower valve body remove the 1-2 shift valve and spring, then remove the inhibitor valve and spring.

11. Remove the two screws securing the separator plate to the valve body cover.

12. From the lower valve body remove the screws securing the end plate while holding plate in position, then remove end plate being careful as it is spring loaded.

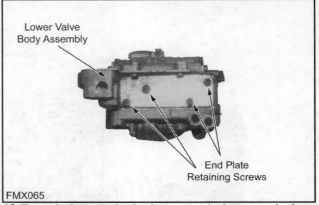

13. From the lower valve body remove the low servo lockout valve, modulator valve and spring.

14. From the lower valve body remove the 2-3 delay and throttle reducing valve sleeve, throttle reducing valve and spring.

15. From the lower valve body remove the 2-3 shift delay valve then remove the 2-3 shift valve spring and valve.

16. From the lower valve body remove the transition valve spring and valve.

17. From the valve body cover remove the plate then remove the check ball spring and check ball.

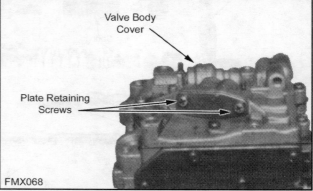

18. From the valve body cover remove the 2-3 kickdown control valve spring and valve.

19. From the valve body cover remove the spring retainer for the 1-2 shift accumulator valve assembly then remove the 1-2 shift accumulator valve spring, valve and the lockout valve.

20. Remove the valve body assembly through bolts and retaining screws.

FMX AUTOMATIC TRANSMISSIONS

21. Separate valve bodies and separator plates being careful not to lose the check valves.

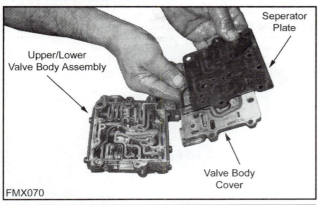

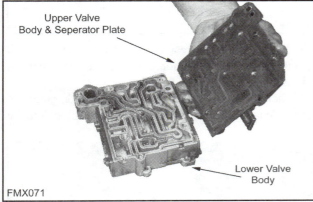

Clean And Inspection

Clean all components in a suitable cleaner, then wash down and dry all components.

Check all components for wear and damage, damaged components will need to be replaced.

Fit new seals and gaskets throughout the transmission, especially to the pistons.

Assembly

When installing valves and plugs rotate as installing to prevent damage to valve, plug or valve body.

1. To the upper valve body install the check valve then to the valve body position the separator plate.

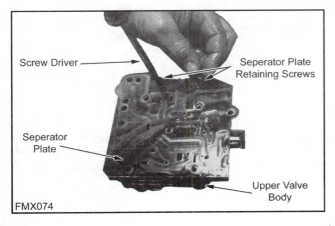

2. To the upper valve body assembly position the lower valve body then install and start the attaching screws (do not tighten).
3. To the valve body cover install the check valve then install the cover and separator plate to the lower valve body and start the four through bolts (do not tighten).

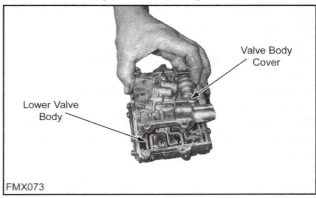

4. Align the separator and valve body bolt holes then tighten valve body bolts to specification.

Valve Body Assembly Bolts:

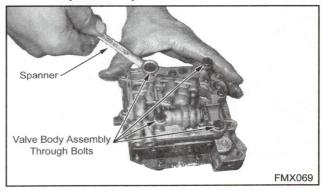

5. To the valve body cover install the 2-3 kickdown control valve and valve spring.
6. To the valve body cover install the check ball and check ball spring then install the plate and tighten retaining screws.
7. To the valve body cover install the 1-2 shift accumulator lockout valve, accumulator valve, valve spring and the spring retainer.
8. To the lower valve body install the transition valve and valve spring.
9. To the lower valve body install the 2-3 shift valve and spring then install the 2-3 shift delay valve and valve spring.
10. To the lower valve body install the 2-3 delay and throttle reducing valve sleeve then install the throttle reducing valve and spring.
11. To the lower valve body install the low servo modulator valve and spring then install the low servo lockout valve.
12. To the lower valve body install the end plate and tighten retaining screws.
13. To the lower valve body install the inhibitor valve spring and valve then install the 1-2 shift valve spring and valve.
14. To the lower valve body install the side plate and tighten retaining screws.

15. To the upper valve body install the compensator cut-back valve then install the rear plate and tighten retaining screws.
16. To the upper valve body install the 2-1 scheduling valve, spring and spring retainer then install the downshift valve spring and valve.
17. To the upper valve body install the throttle boost valve and spring then install the throttle boost short valve and sleeve.
18. To the upper valve body install the compensator valve, inner and outer compensator springs and then install the compensator sleeve and plug.
19. To the upper valve body install the front plate and tighten retaining screws.
20. To the throttle valve body install the throttle valve and plug then install the check valve into the throttle body.
21. To the upper valve body install the separator then install

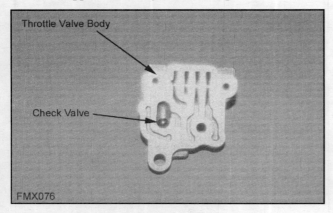

the throttle valve body and the retaining screws.
22. Install the four cover to lower valve body screws, the two

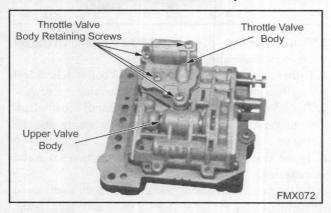

separator plate to upper valve body screws and the one separator plate to lower valve body screw.
23. Tighten all cover and valve body screws to specification.
Cover to Lower Body Screws:
Separator Plate to Upper Body Screws:
Separator Plate to Lower Body Screw:
24. Install the manual valve to the valve body assembly.

ASSEMBLE TRANSMISSION

1.(a) Fit parking pawl and shift assembly if removed during dismantle procedures.
(b) Slide the front band into the transmission casing.

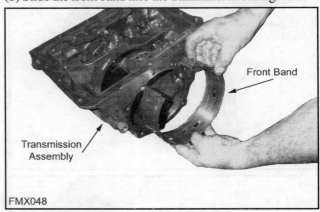

4.(a) Fit the front and rear clutch drums together as an assembly ready for installation, ensure the thrust washer and bearing are fitted between the two.
(b) Fit the thrust washer to the input shaft, then holding the front band slide the front and rear clutch drum assembly into the casing.

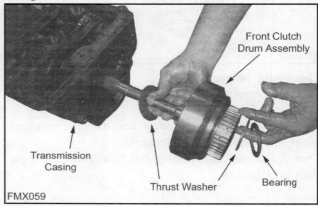

(c) Once in position fit the centre support and install retaining bolts finger tight.

5.(a) Position the rear band in the transmission housing.

FMX AUTOMATIC TRANSMISSIONS

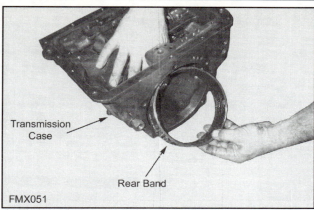
FMX051

(b) Fit the rear drum assembly into the casing, ensure the thrust bearing is fitted between the two.
(c) Ensure that the rear drum engages the front and rear clutch drum assembly correctly.

6. Fit the thrust washer to the output shaft, then install the output shaft in the casing.

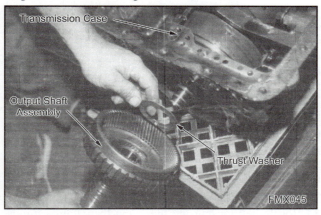

7.(a) Slide the rear support over the output shaft, until it is in position, being careful of the pipes.
(b) Make sure that the fluid pipes are fitted in the correct position.

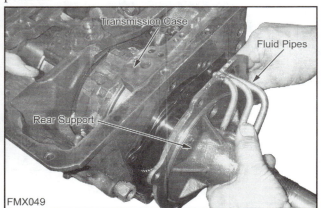
FMX049

8.(a) Position the band struts on the bands, then fit the rear servo aligning the band struts, bolt the servo into place.
Torque Rear Servo Bolts to Trans Case: 20-33Nm

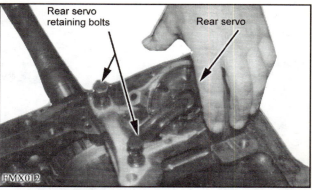

(b) Lower the servo and valve body assembly into position, align the band struts then bolt the assembly to the casing.
Torque Front Servo Bolts to Trans Case: 15-20Nm
Torque Valve Body Bolts   6-10Nm

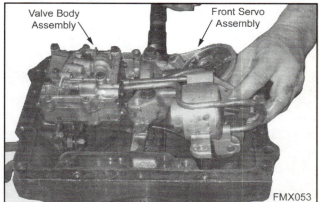
FMX053

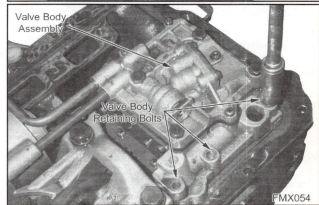
FMX054

(c) Install the pressure regulator, then fit the compensator and main pressure oil pipes.
(d) Position the pressure regulator valve springs, then secure with the retaining clip.

FMX AUTOMATIC TRANSMISSIONS

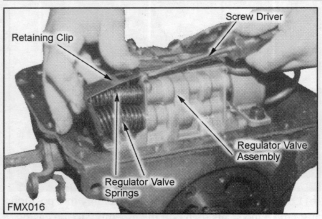

(e) Fit the filter assembly, then the oil pan.
Torque Transmission Oil Sump   11-14Nm

9. With the oil pump assembled, slide it over the input shaft, then fit bolts tensioning to specifications.
Pump Assembly to Trans Case: 17-25Nm

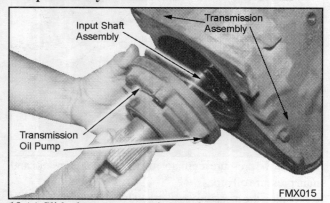

10.(a) Slide the governor unit over the output shaft.
(b) Fit the alignment ball to the output shaft, then slide the governer over the top.
(c) Install the governer retaining circlip.

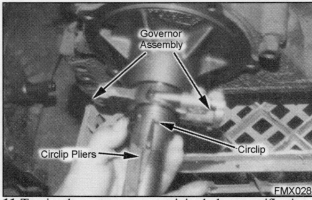

11. Tension the centre support retaining bolts to specifications.
Centre Support to Trans Case: 20-33Nm
12. Slide the extension housing over the output shaft, then fit and tension the retaining bolts.
Rear Extension housing to Trans: 50-60Nm

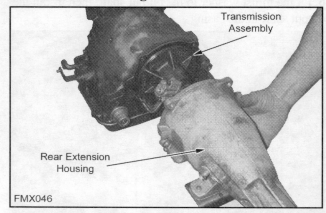

13. With transmission assembled check the end float.
14. Bolt the bell housing onto the casing, then slide the torque convertor into position.

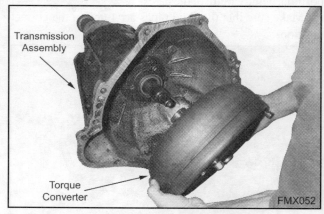

116

PROBLEM SOLVING & DIAGNOSIS

Fluid Check

Transmission fluid changes colour and smell very early in life, these indicators should not necessarily be relied on to diagnose either transmission internal condition nor fluid deterioration.

The chart on the next page shows that a dark brown fluid colour, coupled with a delayed shift pattern, may only indicate that the fluid requires replacement and alone, is not a definite indication of a potential transmission failure.

The fluid level should only be checked when the transmission reaches normal operating temperature (82-93 degrees Celsius).

Transmission fluid colour when new and unused, is red. A red dye is added so that it can be distinguished from other oils and lubricants. The red dye is not an indicator of fluid quality and is not permanent. As the vehicle is driven, the transmission fluid will begin to look darker in colour. The colour will then appear light brown. A DARK brown colour with a distinctively burnt odour MAY indicate fluid deterioration and a need for the fluid to be changed.

Details of transmission oil pressure check procedures refer to 'Oil pressure check information' chart at the start of this chapter.

HYDRAULIC DIAGNOSIS

Oil Pressure Check Information

Preliminary Check Procedure
* Check transmission oil level and condition
* Check and adjust Kickdown Cable
* Check outside manual linkage and correct
* Check engine tune
* Install oil pressure gauge
* Connect tachometer to engine
* Check oil pressure as follows:

Minimum Kickdown Line Pressure Check
Set the Kickdown cable to specification; and with the brakes applied, take the line pressure readings in the ranges and at the engine r.p.m.'s indicated in the chart below.

Full Kickdown Line Pressure Check
Full Kickdown line pressure readings are obtained by tying or holding the Kickdown cable to the full extent of it's travel; and with the brakes applied, take the line pressure readings in the ranges and at the engine r.p.m.'s indicated in the chart shown later.

* **NOTICE** - Total running time for this combination not to exceed 2 mins.
* **CAUTION** - Brakes must be applied at all times.

Road Test

Drive and Reverse Engagement Shift Check.
1. Start engine.
2. Depress brake pedal.
3. Move gear selector:
** 'P' (Park) to 'R' (Reverse)
** 'R' (Reverse) to 'N' (Neutral) to 'D' (Drive).
** Gear selections should be immediate and not harsh.

Upshifts Application
With gear selector in 'D' :-
1. Accelerate using a steady increasing throttle application.
2. Note the shift speed point gear engagements for:
** 2nd gear
** 3rd gear

Part Throttle Downshift
At a speed of 70-90 km/h, quickly depress the accelerator to half open position and observe:
** Transmission downshift to 2nd gear immediately.

Full Throttle (Detent) Downshift
Operate the vehicle at 70-90km/h in 'D', then quickly depress to wide open throttle position and observe:
** Transmission downshifts to 2nd gear immediately.

Manual Downshift
1. Operate the vehicle at 70-90km/h in 'D', then release the accelerator pedal (closed throttle position) and simultaneously move the gear selector to 'D' (Drive), and observe:
** Transmission downshifts to 2nd gear immediately.
** Engine should slow vehicle.
2. Operate the vehicle at 70-80 km/h in 'D'.
Release the accelerator pedal and simultaneously move the gear selector '2' (second) gear position, and observe:
** Transmission downshifts to 2nd gear immediately.
** Engine should slow vehicle.
3. Move gear selector to 'D' and accelerate to 40km/h. Release the accelerator pedal (closed throttle position) and simultaneously move the gear selector to '1' (first) gear and observe:
** Transmission downshifts to 1st gear immediately.
** Engine should slow vehicle.

Coastdown Downshift
1. With the gear selector in 'D', accelerate to engage 3rd (approx 60km/h).
2. Release the accelerator pedal (closed throttle position) and lightly apply the brakes to observe:
** The point at which downshift occurs.

Manual Gear Range Selection.
Manual Third "D".
1. With vehicle stopped, place gear selector in 'D' (Drive) and accelerate to observe:
** The first to second gear shift point.
** The second to third gear shift point.

Manual Second (2).
1. With vehicle stopped, place gear selector in '2' (second) and accelerate to observe:

FMX AUTOMATIC TRANSMISSIONS

** The first to second gear shift point.
2. Accelerate to 60km/h and observe:
** That a second to third gear shift does not occur.

Manual First (1)
1. With vehicle stopped, place gear selector in '1' (first) and accelerate to 40km/h and observe:
** That no upshift occurs.

Reverse.
1. With vehicle stopped. Place gear selector in 'R' (Reverse) and slowly accelerate to observe reverse gear operation.

* This publication does not include all possible throttle positions and the corresponding shift point information. Actual shift points will vary in accordance with transmission build variation.

Torque Converter Evaluation
The Converter Should be Replaced if:-
Leaks externally, such as the hub weld area.
Converter has an imbalance which can not be corrected.
Converter is contaminated with engine coolant containing anti freeze.
The Converter Should Not be Replaced if:-
The oil has an odour, is discoloured, and there is no evidence of metal or clutch facing particles.
The threads in one or more of the converter bolt holes are damaged. Correct with thread insert.

SPECIFICATIONS

TYPE: FMX
CODE: XW: PHB-F
  PHB-G
  XY/XA/XB/XC: PHB-S
  XD/XE: PHB-S

LUBRICANT:
Type: M2C-33F
Capacity: XW-XC: 10.5 litres (inc. converter)
  XD-XE: 7.7 litres (6 Cylinder)
  8.25 litres (V8)

GEAR RATIOS:
  Reverse (R) 2.09
  Drive (D) 1.00:1
  Second (2) 1.45:1
  First (1) 2.39:1

SHIFT SPEEDS:

XW - Models — 3.00:1 & 3.25:1 Diff Ratio

Manual	Shift	Throttle	MPH
D	1-2	KD	41 - 50
D	2-3	KD	65 - 76
D	3-2	KD	59 - 70
D	3-1	KD	28 - 37

XY - Models — 2.75:1 Diff Ratio

Manual	Shift	Throttle	MPH
D	1-2	KD	49 - 58
D	2-3	KD	75 - 89
D	3-2	KD	62 - 79
D	3-1	KD	33 - 44

XA/B - Models — 2.75:1 Diff Ratio

Manual	Shift	Throttle	Km/h
D	1-2	KD	79-93
D	2-3	KD	121-143
D	3-2	KD	100-127
D	3-1	KD	53-71

XC/XD/XE - Models — 2.75:1 Diff Ratio

Manual	Shift	Throttle	Km/h
D	1-2	KD	70-84
D	2-3	KD	104-123
D	3-2	KD	92-108
D	3-1	KD	45-59

TORQUE CONVERTER: 1650-1850

TORQUE SPECIFICATIONS

Description	Nm
Converter Housing to Engine	54-68
Transmission Case to Converter Housing	54-68
Extension Housing to Transmission	40-54
Converter to Flywheel/Drive plate	27-41
Converter Housing Lower Cover to Housing	12-18
Transmission Oil Pan (Sump)	11-14
Front Servo to Transmission Case	11-14
Front Servo to Transmission Case	40-47
Rear Servo to Transmission Case	15-22
Downshift Valve Control Cable	14-16
Downshift Valve Cam Bracket to Valve Body	6-11
Converter Drain Plug	20-38
Band Adjusting Screw Locknut to Case	47-61
Fluid Cooler Line to Case	20-27
Front Pump to Case	23-30
Front Pump to Case	38-52
Regulator Assembly to Case	23-30
Rear Bearing to Extension	38-42
Governor body to Shaft	35-40
Filler Tube to Transmission	43-57

AOD AUTOMATIC TRANSMISSIONS

AOD001

Subject	Page
GENERAL INFORMATION	**120**
MAINTENANCE AND ADJUSTMENT	**120**
Lubrication	120
Fluid Level	120
Changing Fluid	120
Lubricant	120
Maintain Strainer	120
Maintenance Notes	121
Oil Cooler Pipes	121
Clean and Inspect	121
Band Adjustment	**122**
Speed Sender Unit/ Speedo Gear Assembly	**122**
Remove	122
Install	122
Cooler Replacement	**122**
MAJOR REPAIR	**122**
Transmission Dismantle	**122**
Transmission Case Inspection	**125**
Planet Gear Set Inspection	**126**
Output Shaft & Governor Inspection	**126**
Transmission Sub-Assemblies	**126**
Pump Assembly	**126**
Dismantle	126
Clean & Inspect	126
Assemble	127
Reverse Clutch Assembly	**127**
Dismantle	127
Clean & Inspect	128
Assemble	128

Subject	Page
Forward Clutch Assembly	**129**
Dismantle	129
Clean & Inspect	130
Assemble	130
Direct Clutch Assembly	**130**
Dismantle	130
Clean & Inspect	131
Assemble	131
Valve Body Assembly	**132**
Dismantle	132
Clean & Inspect	134
Assemble	134
Governor Valve Assembly	**135**
Dismantle	135
Clean & Inspect	135
Assemble	135
Transmission Assembly	**136**
PROBLEM SOLVING AND DIAGNOSIS	**142**
Fluid Check	142
Road Test	142
Problems and Diagnosis Charts	143
TORQUE WRENCH SPECIFICATIONS	**145**

AOD AUTOMATIC TRANSMISSIONS

GENERAL INFORMATION

The AOD automatic transmission is a 4 speed overdrive transmission used primarily in large cars and trucks. It was introduced in 1980 to replace the C4/C5 and was used until 1994 where it was replaced by a electronic version.
The AOD transmission was not used in Australian built vehicles, it was an import transmission.
A metal identification plate is attached to the transmission. The tag is attached to the lower rear extension housing bolt.

MAINTENANCE AND ADJUSTMENT

LUBRICATION
If adding or changing the transmission fluid, use only specified Automatic Transmission fluid.

Dexron 11, Dexron 111 or Mercon ATF.

FLUID LEVEL
The dipstick is located in the engine compartment. To check level, follow this procedure:
Apply parking brake and with engine idling and transmission at normal operating temperature, engage each gear briefly, ending with selector in "N" neutral.
* The transmission must be at normal operating temperature to obtain an accurate dipstick reading.
* The transmission should not be overfilled, otherwise the transmission fluid will cause undue transmission-fluid high pressure, this could result in fluid leakages, foaming and difficulty in gear changes.
Withdraw dipstick and wipe clean with a lint free cloth. Install dipstick into transmission, withdraw and check level. The level must be within "hot" range on dipstick, refer below.

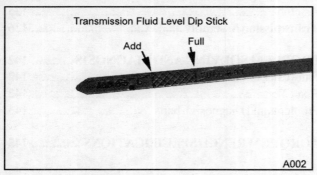

NOTE: Avoid entry of dirt into transmission by ensuring that dipstick is properly seated. Maintaining transmission to correct level with recommended fluid is essential for correct operation of unit.

CHANGING FLUID
* The transmission should not be overfilled, otherwise the transmission fluid will cause undue transmission-fluid high pressure, this could result in fluid leakages, foaming and difficulty in gear changes.
1. Raise vehicle and place a large drain tray under transmission oil pan.
2. Remove oil pan retaining bolts and tap pan at one corner to break it loose, allow fluid to drain and then remove pan.

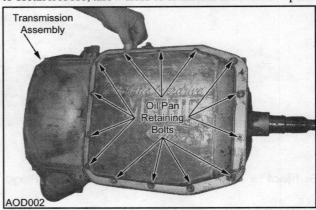

3. Clean transmission case gasket surface and oil pan.
4. Install oil pan with a new gasket, tighten bolts to specification.
Oil Pan to Case:
1980-84 .... 12-16 lb.ft.
1985-88 .... 6-10 lb.ft.
5. Firstly pour sufficient automatic transmission fluid in through the dipstick tube to bring fluid level to lower mark on dipstick.
6. Start engine and allow to idle for at least two minutes. With park brake on, move selector lever momentarily to each position ending in "N" neutral position.
7. Add sufficient automatic transmission fluid to bring fluid level to lower mark on dipstick. Re-check fluid level after transmission has reached operating temperature. The fluid level should be between upper and lower marks of "HOT" range on dipstick. Insert the dipstick fully to prevent dirt entry into transmission.

LUBRICANT
10.0 litres including converter

Dexron 11, Dexron 111 or Mercon ATF.

MAINTAIN STRAINER
* Take care when removing sump from transmission as hot oil can cause serious burns. Avoid this by allowing transmission to cool down.
1. Raise vehicle and support on safety stands.
2. Clean all dirt from around oil pan and transmission case, place drain tray under transmission.
3. Hold oil pan in place, leaving one bolt loose at the front of the oil pan, remove the remaining bolts. Allow the rear of the

oil pan to drop, emptying oil into drain tray.

4. Remove remaining bolt and oil pan and empty fluid from pan.

5. If necessary, remove strainer, by removing the three retaining screws.

6. If necessary install new strainer and gasket tightening screws strainer screws to specification.

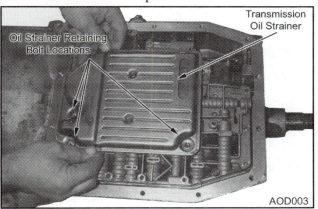

Transmission Strainer Screws:
1980-84 .... 80-100 lb.in.
1985-88 .... 80-120 lb.in.

7. Clean oil pan and case mating surfaces. Check that magnets are functional and located in the designated position in the oil pan.

8. Install new seal and reinstall oil pan. Tighten bolts to specification.

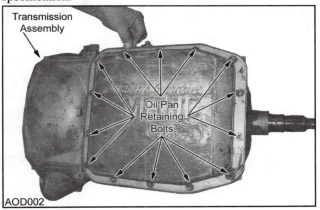

Oil Pan to Case:
1980-84 .... 12-16 lb.ft.
1985-88 .... 6-10 lb.ft.

9. Lower vehicle and add automatic transmission fluid. Check transmission fluid level.

MAINTENANCE NOTES

* While maintaining the transmission, all parts should be cleaned and inspected. Individual units should be reassembled before disassembly of other units to avoid confusion and interchanging of parts.

1. Thoroughly clean the exterior before disassembly of the unit.

2. Disassembly and assembly must be made on a clean work bench. Cleanliness is of the utmost importance. The bench, tools, and parts must be kept clean at all times.

3. Before installing screws into aluminium parts, dip screws into transmission fluid prevent galling aluminium threads and to prevent screws from seizing.

4. To prevent thread stripping, always use a torque wrench when installing screws.

5. If threads in aluminium parts are stripped or damaged the part can be made serviceable by the use of thread inserts.

6. Protective tools must be used when assembling seals to prevent damage. The slightest flaw in the sealing surface of the seal can cause an oil leak.

7. Aluminium castings and valve are very susceptible to nicks, burns, burrs, etc., and should be handled with care.

8. Internal snap rings should be expanded and external snap rings compressed if they are to be reused. This will ensure proper seating when reinstalled.

9. "O" rings, gaskets and oil seals that are removed should not be reused.

10. During assembly of each unit, all internal moving parts must be lubricated with transmission fluid.

OIL COOLER PIPES

If replacement of transmission steel tubing cooler pipes is required, only use double wrapped and brazed steel tubing meeting transmission manufactures specifications or equivalent. Under no condition use copper or aluminium tubing to replace steel tubing. These materials do not have satisfactory fatigue durability to withstand normal car vibrations. Steel tubing should be flared using the double flare method.

CLEAN AND INSPECT

After complete disassembly of a unit, wash all metal parts in a cleaning solvent and dry with compressed air. Blow oil passages out and check to make sure they are not obstructed. Small passages should be checked with tag wire. All parts should be inspected to determine which parts are to be replaced.

Pay particular attention to the following:

1. Inspect linkage and pivot points for excessive wear.

2. Bearing and thrust surfaces of all parts should be checked for excessive wear and scoring.

3. Check for broken score seal rings, damaged ring lands and damaged threads.

4. Inspect seal and 'O' rings.

5. Mating surfaces of castings should be checked for burrs. Irregularities may be removed by lapping the surface with emery paper. The emery paper is laid on a flat surface, such as a piece of plate glass.

6. Castings should be checked for cracks and sand holes.

* Do not use solvents on neoprene seals, composition faced clutch plates or thrust washers as damage to parts may occur.

AOD AUTOMATIC TRANSMISSIONS

BAND ADJUSTMENT
AOD Transmissions do not require band adjustment.

SPEED SENDER UNIT / SPEEDOMETER GEAR ASSEMBLY
Remove
1. Raise rear of vehicle and place on safety stands. Place drip tray beneath speed sender.
2. Disconnect sender unit electrical connector.
3. Unscrew retaining bolt securing retaining clip and remove retaining clip.
4. Withdraw fitting assembly including driven gear from extension housing.

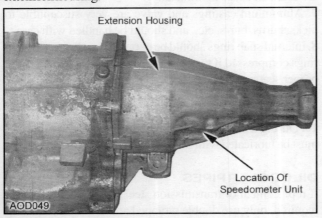

Install
1. Inspect fitting assembly 'O' ring seal and replace it if unsatisfactory.
2. Installation is the reverse of the removal procedure.
3. Tighten retainer bolt.

COOLER REPLACEMENT
The cooler is located inside the radiator, if the cooler is to be replaced the radiator must also be replaced. See cooling system for radiator replacement.
Some vehicles may have an external transmission cooler fitted. This is mounted in front of the radiator.

MAJOR REPAIR

DISMANTLE TRANSMISSION ASSEMBLY
1. From the transmission assembly remove the neutral start switch.

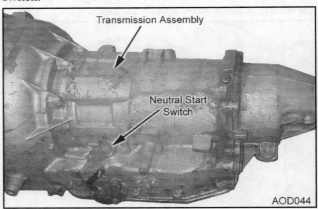

2. Remove the six bolts retaining the extension housing to transmission case and remove the extension housing.

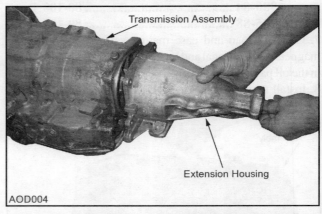

3. Remove the snap ring securing the governor to the output shaft. Slide the governor from the shaft being careful not to lose the governor drive ball.

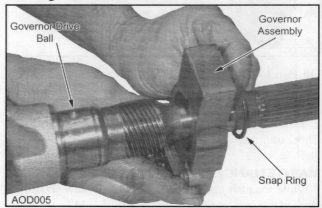

4. Remove the oil pan / sump and gasket.

AOD AUTOMATIC TRANSMISSIONS

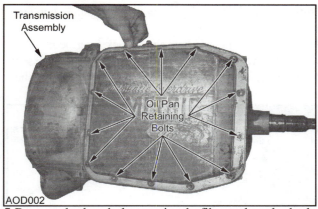

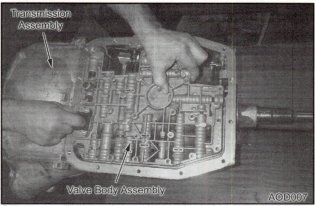

5. Remove the three bolts securing the filter to the valve body and remove filter from assembly.

8. Remove the snap ring retaining the 2-3 accumulator, then remove the accumulator cover, return spring and piston.

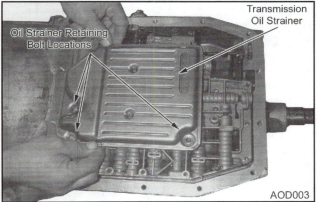

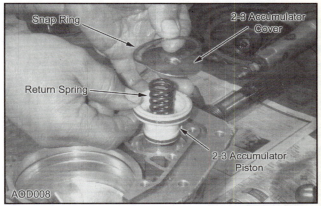

6. Remove all long valve body bolts shown in diagram marked "A", then remove the bolt securing the manual lever detent spring and roller assembly.

9. Remove the snap ring retaining the low-reverse servo, then remove the servo cover, selective piston and return spring from transmission case.

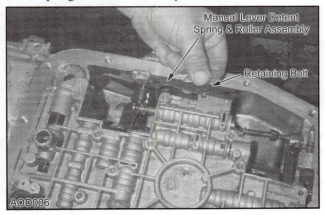

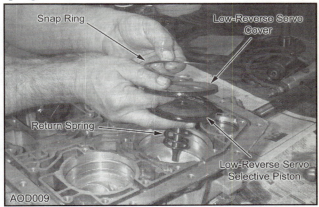

7. Remove the remaining bolts securing the valve body to transmission assembly and then remove valve body from assembly.

10. Remove the snap ring retaining the overdrive servo, then remove the servo cover, piston and the return spring from transmission case.

AOD AUTOMATIC TRANSMISSIONS

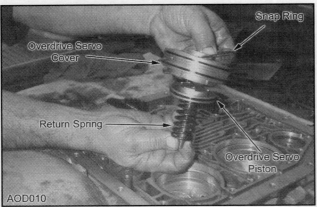

11. Remove the snap ring retaining the 3-4 accumulator, then remove the accumulator cover, return spring and piston from transmission case.

12. From the inner throttle lever remove the throttle tension spring then remove nut retaining the throttle lever to the manual shaft.

13. Remove the retaining pin for the manual shaft by prying it up with a pair of side cutters, then remove manual shaft from transmission case.

14. From the case remove the inner throttle lever and shaft assembly, then remove the inner manual lever and parking pawl actuating rod.

15. From the transmission case remove the parking pawl shaft then remove the parking pawl and spring.

16. From the turbine shaft withdraw the direct driveshaft.

17. Remove the seven bolts retaining the front pump then remove the front pump from the transmission case.

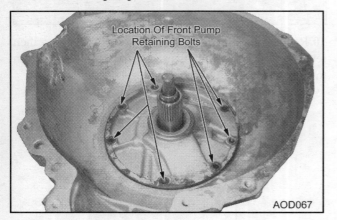

Note: *It may be necessary to use two slide hammers threaded into the pump.*

18. Remove the intermediate clutch pack, intermediate one-way clutch, reverse clutch and forward clutch as an assembly from the transmission case by holding the turbine shaft and withdrawing.

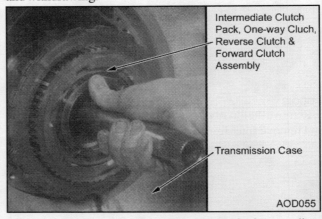

19. From the reverse clutch pack remove the intermediate clutch pack.

20. From the forward clutch and turbine shaft assembly remove the reverse clutch drum and intermediate one-way clutch.

21. From inside the transmission case remove the overdrive band then remove the forward clutch hub and No.3 needle bearing assembly.

22. From inside the transmission case remove the No.4 needle bearing from the top of the reverse sun gear and drive shell assembly, then remove the reverse sun gear and drive shell assembly from transmission case.

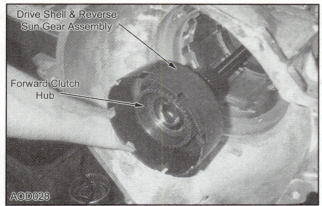

23. Pry the centre support retaining ring from the grove in the transmission case using a large screwdriver, then pry out the anti-clunk spring from between the transmission case and centre support.

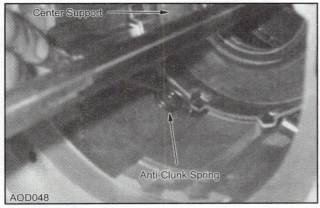

27. From inside the transmission case remove the direct clutch hub then remove the output shaft, ring gear, reverse band and direct clutch as an assembly.

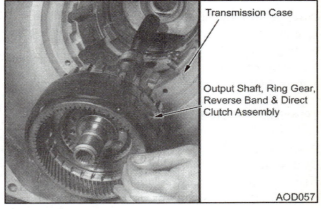

24. From inside the transmission case remove the forward sun gear and No.5 needle bearing assembly.

25. From the transmission case remove the centre support and also remove the planetary carrier assembly.

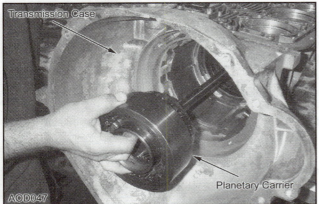

26. Separate the centre support from the planetary carrier then from the planetary carrier assembly remove the planetary one-way clutch, being careful not to lose any springs or rollers.

28. From the ring gear remove the reverse band.

29. From inside the transmission case remove the No.9 needle bearing and where fitted remove the case snap-ring from the case groove.

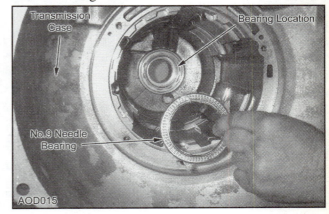

Transmission Case Inspection

1. Inspect the exterior of the transmission case for damage, cracks porosity.

2. Inspect the inside of the transmission casing for damage, nicks and burrs, also inspect case lugs for excessive wear.

3. Inspect for damage to the valve body surface and also check flatness of surface. Check all bores and oil passages for damage, nicks and burrs.

4. Inspect all threaded holes for damage and if required repair

using thread inserts.
5. Inspect the fittings for the oil cooler pipes for damage.
6. Inspect the output shaft bushing, for wear.
7. Inspect the park lock linkage and manual linkage for damage.

Planetary Gear Set Inspection
1. Inspect for worn bushings.
2. Inspect the drive shell, sun gear, planetary carriers and ring gears for damaged or worn teeth and splines.
3. Inspect the thrust bearings for wear or damage.
4. Inspect for wear or damage to the pinion gear bearings.
5. Inspect the one-way clutch rollers and springs for damage, wear or signs of over heating.
6. Inspect for scoring, wear or damage to the race finish.

Output Shaft & Governor Inspection
1. Inspect for damaged or worn splines, scoring or worn bushing races on the output shaft.
2. Inspect governor for stuck valves.
3. Inspect for damage to the governor O-ring grooves.

TRANSMISSION SUB-ASSEMBLIES

Pump Assembly
Dismantle
1. Dislodge the locking tabs on the intermediate clutch spring retainer using a small screwdriver and remove the spring and retainer assembly from the pump assembly.

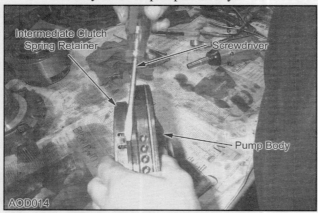

2. From the pump assembly remove the intermediate clutch piston then from the stator support remove the No.1 selective thrust washer.

3. Remove the five bolts securing the stator support then remove the stator support from the pump body.

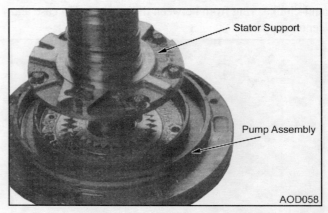

4. From the pump body remove the drive and driven gears.

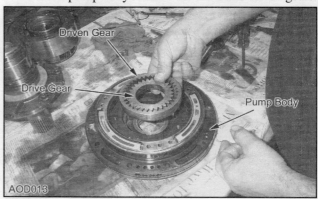

5. Carefully remove the front pump oil seal from pump housing.

Clean & Inspect
1. Using a solvent cleaner, clean the oil pump components then allow to air dry.
2. Inspect the drive and driven gears for damage or scoring.
3. Inspect the pump body and cover for damage such as nicks and burrs.
4. Inspect the sealing ring grooves for damage.
5. Inspect stator shaft bushings for wear and damage.
6. Install the pump body to the cover and inspect for warpage.
7. Ensure oil passages and lubrication holes are clean and not restricted.

AOD AUTOMATIC TRANSMISSIONS

Assembly

1. If front pump body bushing requires replacement, remove bushing from pump body.
2. Fit new bushing with the notch in the pump body bushing aligned with the land in the pump body.
3. Using a bushing installation tool seat the bushing into pump body, then install a new front oil pump seal.
4. If the stator support bushings require replacement, remove bushings from stator support, then install new bushing using a bushing installation tool.
5. Lubricate the pump gears with clean transmission fluid then install the driven gear into pump body ensuring that the reference mark is facing down in the pump body.
6. Install the drive gear to the pump body, ensuring that the flat side of the offset drive tang is facing up.

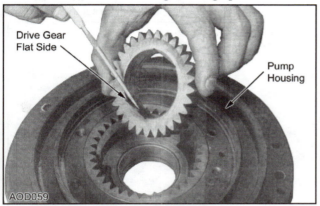

7. To the pump body install the stator support and tighten retaining bolts to specification.

Stator Support Retaining Bolts: **12-16 lb.ft.**

8. To the intermediate clutch piston install the inner and outer seals ensuring the seal lips face into the bore.
9. Lubricate the piston seals and pump body with petroleum jelly then install the piston in the pump body using seal protectors.

10. Ensure piston is seated in the bottom of the bore and that the piston bleed hole is at the top of transmission.
11. To the pump body install the return spring retainer assembly ensuring it snaps into position properly.

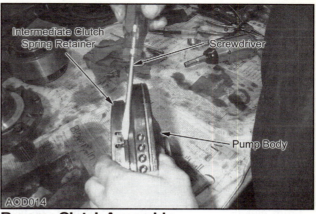

Reverse Clutch Assembly
Dismantle

1. From the reverse clutch drum remove the No.2 thrust washer or needle bearing assembly.
2. From the reverse clutch drum remove the selective snap-ring then remove the pressure plate, friction discs, steel plates and the apply plate from the drum assembly.

3. From the drum assembly remove the reverse clutch wave snap-ring ensuring to keep separate from other snap rings.
4. From the drum assembly remove the reverse clutch piston return spring, thrust spring and the reverse clutch piston.

5. From the reverse clutch piston remove the inner and outer seals.
6. From the clutch drum remove the intermediate one-way clutch retaining snap-ring then remove the intermediate one-way clutch retaining plate.

7. From clutch drum remove the intermediate one-way clutch outer race and the intermediate one-way clutch assembly.

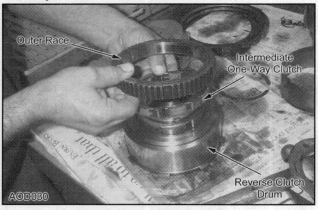

Clean & Inspect

1. Clean components with a suitable cleaning solvent then allow components to air dry.
2. Inspect the bushings and overdrive band for wear and damage.
3. Inspect piston for damage, also inspect piston check ball is clean and moves freely.
4. Inspect clutch plates for overheating and damage.
5. Inspect the friction plates for flaking, cracking, pitting or wear.
6. Inspect the one-way clutch for worn or damaged rollers and also inspect springs for damage or breakage.
7. Inspect for scoring, wear or damage on the race finish.
8. Inspect the input shaft splines for damage.
9. Replace any components in which are damaged or suspect.

Assembly

1. To the reverse clutch piston install the inner square-cut seal, then install the outer square-cut seal and coat seals with petroleum jelly.
Note: *Direction does not matter for square-cut seals.*

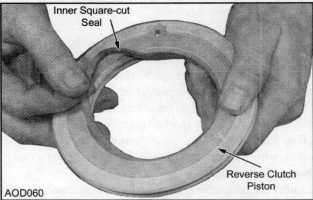

2. To the reverse clutch drum hub install the inner seal protector then install the outer seal protector to the reverse clutch piston.
3. To the reverse clutch drum install the piston pressing down until it is fully seated then remove seal protectors.

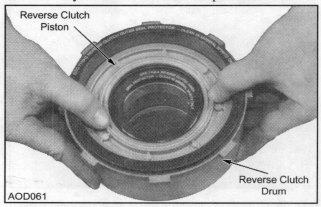

4. To the reverse clutch hub assembly install the thrust spring, then install the Bellville return spring with the tips facing down against the thrust ring.
5. To the reverse clutch drum install the wave snap-ring ensuring the points are down next to the return spring.
6. Using a suitable spring compressor, compress the return spring and seat the wave snap-ring into the groove.

7. To the reverse clutch drum install the reverse clutch apply plate with the flat side facing up, then install a clutch friction plate into drum assembly.
Note: *New friction plates should be soaked in clean*

transmission fluid for 15 minutes prior to installation.
8. Install the remaining steel and friction plates, then install the reverse clutch pressure plate.
9. Install the selective snap-ring ensuring it is seated correctly.

10. To the inner race install the intermediate one-way clutch assembly then to the one-way clutch install the outer race pressing down on race and turning in an anticlockwise direction until fully seated.

11. Lubricate the one-way clutch with clean transmission fluid.
12. To the reverse clutch hub install the retaining plate then install the non-selective snap-ring, ensuring it is fully seated in the groove.

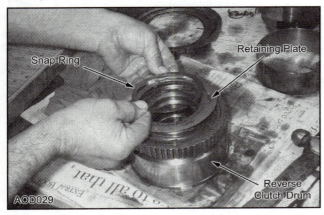

13. Turn the intermediate one-way clutch outer race to ensure it is operating correctly. It should turn in a anticlockwise direction and lock when turned in a clockwise direction.
14. Check operation of the clutch pack using compressed air, the operation should be smooth and there should be no leaks.
15. Check the clearance between the selective snap ring and the pressure plate with a feeler gauge, pressing down lightly on the pressure plate.

Forward Clutch Assembly
Dismantle
1. From the forward clutch housing remove the selective retaining snap-ring, then remove the pressure plate, friction plates, and steel plates from the clutch housing.

2. From the forward clutch housing remove the wave plate, then install a suitable spring compressor and compress the forward clutch return spring.

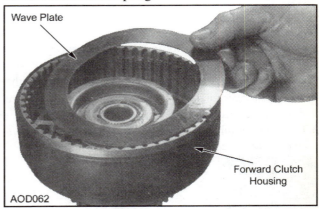

3. Release the snap-ring retaining the return spring then release spring compressor.
4. From the forward clutch housing remove the snap-ring, spring retainer and return spring.

AOD AUTOMATIC TRANSMISSIONS

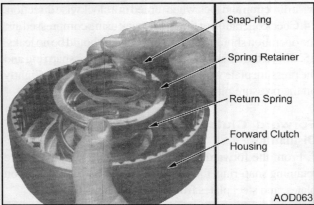

5. From the clutch housing remove the forward clutch piston then remove inner and outer piston seals from the piston.

Clean & Inspect

1. Clean components with a suitable cleaning solvent then allow components to air dry.
2. Inspect the bushing and low-reverse band for wear and damage.
3. Inspect the return springs for overheating or damage.
4. Inspect piston for damage, also inspect housing check balls are clean and moves freely.
5. Inspect clutch plates for overheating and damage.
6. Inspect the friction plates for flaking, cracking, pitting or wear.
7. Replace any components in which are damaged or suspect.

Assembly

1. To the forward clutch piston install the inner and outer seals with the seal lips facing into the bore.
2. To the clutch hub install the inner seal protector then to the forward clutch piston install the outer seal protector. Ensure to lubricate seals and protectors with petroleum jelly.
3. To the forward clutch drum install the piston pressing down until it is fully seated, then remove seal protectors.

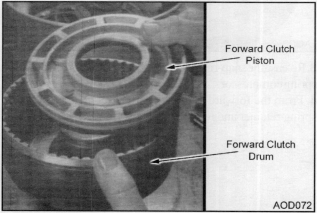

4. To the assembly fit the piston return spring, retainer and snap-ring, then compress the clutch spring with a suitable spring compressor.
5. Fully install the retaining snap-ring ensuring it is fully seated, then remove the spring compressors.
6. To the forward clutch drum install the forward clutch wave plate, then install the steel and friction plates ensuring to start with a steel plate.
Note: *New friction plates should be soaked in clean transmission fluid for 15 minutes prior to installation.*
7. Install the forward clutch pressure plate then install the selective snap-ring ensuring it is seated correctly.

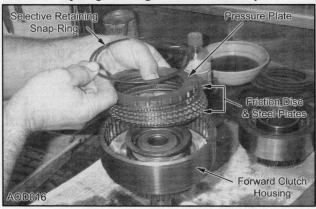

8. Check operation of the clutch pack using compressed air, the operation should be smooth and there should be no leaks.
9. Check the clearance between the selective snap ring and the pressure plate with a feeler gauge, pressing down lightly on the pressure plate.

Direct Clutch Assembly
Dismantle

1. From the direct clutch drum remove the No.7 needle bearing, then from inside the clutch drum remove the thrust spacer or bearing support.

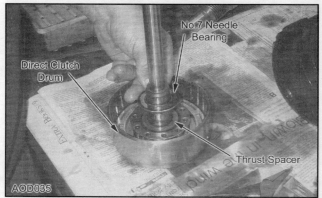

2. Remove the snap ring retaining the output shaft to ring gear, then remove the output shaft from the direct clutch drum and internal ring gear.

130

AOD AUTOMATIC TRANSMISSIONS

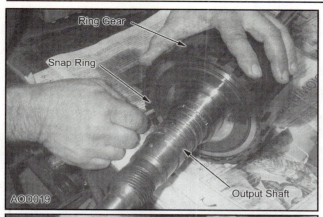

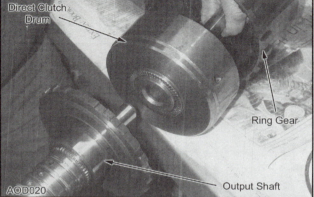

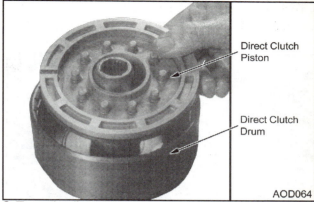

3. From the direct clutch drum remove the No.8 needle bearing, then remove the direct clutch drum from the ring gear.
4. Remove the retaining snap ring from the direct clutch drum then remove the direct clutch pressure plate, friction discs and steel plates.

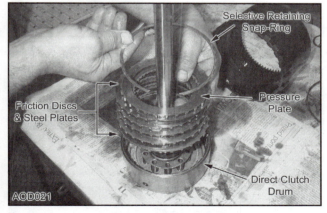

5. Compress the direct clutch return spring with a suitable clutch spring compressor, then remove the retaining snap-ring. Remove spring compressor.
6. From the direct clutch drum remove the direct clutch piston return spring and retainer assembly.
7. From the drum remove the direct clutch piston then remove and discard the piston inner and outer seals.

8. From the direct drum hub remove the inner piston seal, ensure to note the direction of installation.

Clean & Inspect
1. Clean components with a suitable cleaning solvent then allow components to air dry.
2. Inspect the bushing and low-reverse band for wear and damage.
3. Inspect the return springs for overheating or damage.
4. Inspect piston for damage, also inspect piston check ball is clean and moves freely.
5. Inspect clutch plates for overheating and damage.
6. Inspect the friction plates for flaking, cracking, pitting or wear.
7. Replace any components in which are damaged or suspect.

Assembly
1. To the direct clutch drum hub install the inner piston seal by using a seal protector. Ensure to lubricate seal and seal protector before installation, this is to help protect the seal.
2. Ensure the seal is seated correctly with the seal lip facing down.
3. To the direct clutch piston install the outer piston seal with the seal lip facing into drum bore, then lubricate the piston seal and seal protector.
4. Install direct clutch piston into direct clutch drum using the seal protect. Fully seat piston into bore and remove seal protect.

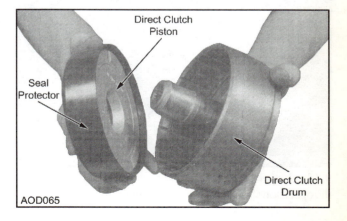

5. To the direct clutch drum install the direct clutch piston return spring and retainer assembly ensuring the springs are over the posts.

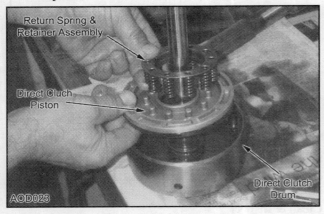

6. Compress the direct clutch return spring with a suitable clutch spring compressor, then install the retaining snap-ring and remove spring compressor.

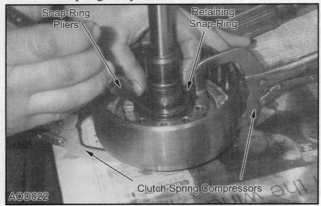

7. To the direct clutch drum install the clutch pack starting with a steel plate and alternating between steel and friction plates.
Note: *New friction plates should be soaked in clean transmission fluid for 15 minutes prior to installation.*
8. Install the direct clutch pressure plate and then install the retaining snap ring ensuring it is seated correctly.

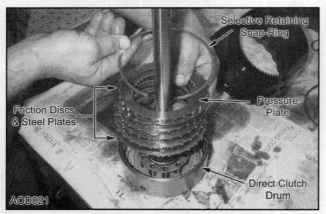

9. Check operation of the clutch pack using compressed air, the operation should be smooth and there should be no leaks.

10. Check the clearance between the selective snap ring and the pressure plate with a feeler gauge, pressing down lightly on the pressure plate.

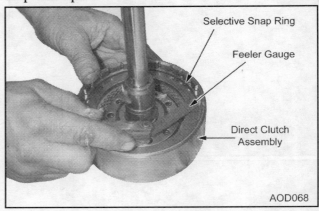

Valve Body Assembly
Dismantle
1. Remove the 11 bolts retaining the reinforcement plates, then from the separator plate remove the detent spring guide bolt.

2. From valve body assembly remove the reinforcement plates, separator plate and gasket.

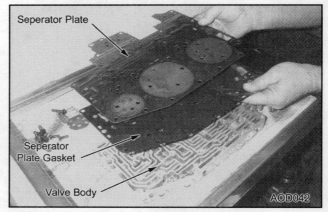

3. From the valve body remove the two relief valves and the 8 (80-81) or 7 (82-88) check balls from valve body.
Note: *Remember location of orange check ball as it is non interchangeable with any others.*

VALVE BODY ASSEMBLY

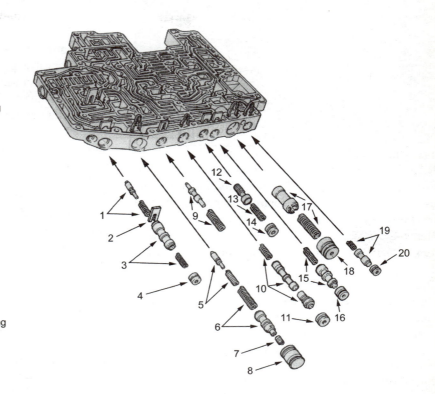

1. 2-3 Capacity Modulator Valve & Spring
2. Spring Retainer Plate
3. Orifice Control Valve & Spring
4. Bore Plug
5. 3-4 TV Modulator Valve & Spring
6. 3-4 Shift Valve & Spring
7. Plug
8. Sleeve
9. TV Limit Valve & Spring
10. 1-2 Shift Valve & Spring
11. Bore Plug
12. Overdrive Servo Regulator Valve
13. Spring
14. Bore Plug
15. 3-4 Shift Valve & Spring
16. Bore Plug
17. 1-2 Accumulator Valve & Spring
18. Bore Plug
19. 1-2 Capacity Modulator Valve & Spring
20. Bore Plug

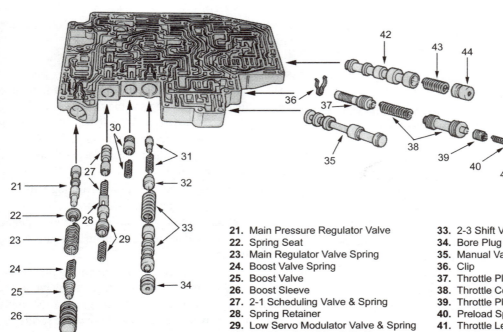

21. Main Pressure Regulator Valve
22. Spring Seat
23. Main Regulator Valve Spring
24. Boost Valve Spring
25. Boost Valve
26. Boost Sleeve
27. 2-1 Scheduling Valve & Spring
28. Spring Retainer
29. Low Servo Modulator Valve & Spring
30. 3-4 Back Out Valve & Spring
31. 2-3 Modulator Valve & Spring
32. 3-2 Control Valve
33. 2-3 Shift Valve & Spring
34. Bore Plug
35. Manual Valve
36. Clip
37. Throttle Plunger
38. Throttle Control Valve & Spring
39. Throttle Plug
40. Preload Spring
41. Throttle Lever
42. 2-3 Back Out Valve
43. Spring
44. Bore Plug

aod071

AOD AUTOMATIC TRANSMISSIONS

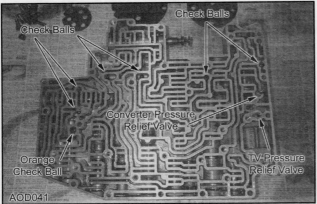

4. From the valve body remove the manual valve.
5. Remove the retaining clip securing the throttle sleeve then remove throttle sleeve, preload spring, throttle plug, throttle pressure control valve, throttle control spring and the throttle plunger from the valve body.
6. Remove the retaining clip securing the bore plug for the 2-3 back out valve, then remove the spring and the 2-3 back out valve.
7. Remove the retaining clip securing the bore plug for the orifice control valve then remove the orifice control valve spring and valve.
8. Remove the retaining plate securing the 2-3 capacity modulator valve spring, then remove spring and 2-3 capacity modulator valve.
9. Remove the retaining clip securing the bore plug for the 3-2 shift valve, then remove the 3-4 shift valve and spring.
10. Remove the 3-4 TV modulator valve spring and valve from the valve body assembly.
11. From the valve body remove the retaining clip securing the throttle plug then remove the sleeve and the throttle plug from the valve body bore.
12. Remove the 3-4 shift valve and spring then remove the 3-4 TV modulator valve spring and valve.
13. Remove the retaining plate securing the TV limit valve and spring then remove spring and valve from valve body assembly.
14. Remove the retaining clip securing the bore plug for the 1-2 shift valve then remove plug, 1-2 shift valve and spring from valve body.
Note: *Some models have a retaining plate, 1-2 shift valve, drive 2 valve and spring.*
15. Remove the retaining plate securing the bore plug for the over drive servo regulator valve, then remove bore plug, spring and the regulator valve.
16. Remove the retaining clip securing the bore plug for the 3-4 shuttle valve, then remove bore plug, 3-4 shuttle valve and spring from valve body.
17. Remove the retaining clip securing the bore plug for the 1-2 accumulator valve then remove the bore plug and O-ring.
18. Remove the 1-2 accumulator valve spring and valve from the valve body.
19. Remove the retaining clip securing the bore plug for the 1-2 capacity modulator valve then remove the modulator valve and spring.
20. Remove the retaining clip securing the boost sleeve then remove the boost sleeve, boost valve, main regulator valve spring, boost valve spring, spring seat and the main pressure regulator valve.
21. Remove the retaining plate securing the low servo modulator valve spring then remove valve spring and the low servo modulator valve.
22. Remove the retaining plate securing the 2-1 scheduling valve spring then remove the 2-1 scheduling valve spring and valve.
23. Remove the retaining plate securing the 3-4 back out valve spring then remove spring and 3-4 back out valve from valve body.
24. Remove the retaining clip securing the bore plug for the 2-3 shift valve then remove bore plug, 2-3 shift valve and where fitted remove the 3-2 control valve.
25. From the valve body assembly remove the shift valve spring, modulator valve spring and the 2-3 TV modulator valve.

Clean & Inspect
1. Ensure all components are carefully laid out in order of removal.
2. Clean all valves, springs and bushings carefully and air dry.
3. Inspect all valves and bushings for scoring, cracks or any other form of damage.
4. Inspect the springs to ensure they are not distorted, broken or any collapsed coils.
5. Carefully inspect the valve body bores for scoring, cracks or any other form of damage.

Assembly
1. To the valve body assembly install the 2-3 TV modulator valve, modulator valve spring and the shift valve spring.
2. To the valve body install the 3-2 control valve, 2-3 shift valve, bore plug and bore plug retaining clip.
3. To the valve body install the 3-4 back out valve, spring and install the spring retaining plate.
4. To the valve body install the 2-1 scheduling valve and spring then install the spring retaining plate.
5. To the valve body assembly install the low servo modulator valve, valve spring and the retaining plate to secure the low servo modulator valve spring.
6. To the valve body install the main pressure regulator valve, spring seat, boost valve spring, main regulator valve spring, boost valve and the retaining clip to secure valve assembly.
7. To the valve body install the modulator valve spring, 1-2 capacity modulator valve and then install the bore plug and retaining clip.
8. To the valve body install the 1-2 accumulator valve and valve spring then install the bore plug and secure with the retaining clip.

AOD AUTOMATIC TRANSMISSIONS

9. To the valve body install the 3-2 shuttle valve spring, shuttle valve and bore plug, then install the retaining clip to secure valve assembly into valve body.
10. To the valve body install the overdrive servo regulator valve, spring and bore plug then secure with retaining plate.
11. To the valve body install the 1-2 shift valve spring, shift valve, bore plug and secure assembly with retaining clip.

Note: *Some models have a retaining plate, 1-2 shift valve, drive 2 valve and spring.*

12. To the valve body assembly install the TV limit valve, valve spring and secure into valve body by installing retaining plate.
13. To the valve body install the 3-4 TV modulator valve and valve spring then install the 3-4 shift valve, sleeve, bore plug and retaining clip.
14. To the valve body install the 3-4 shift valve spring and shift valve then install bore plug and secure with retaining clip.
15. To the valve body install the 2-3 capacity modulator valve, valve spring and secure assembly into valve body with retaining plate.
16. To the valve body install the orifice control valve and valve spring then install bore plug and retaining clip to secure valve assembly.
17. To the valve body install the 2-3 back out valve, valve spring, bore plug and the retaining clip to secure valve assembly.
18. To the valve body install the throttle plunger throttle control spring, throttle pressure control valve, throttle plug, preload spring, throttle sleeve and then secure valve assembly into valve body by installing retaining clip.
19. Install the manual valve into the valve body.
20. To the valve body install the two relief valves and the 8 (80-81) or 7 (82-88) check balls.

Note: *Remember to install orange check ball into correct location as it is non interchangeable with any others.*

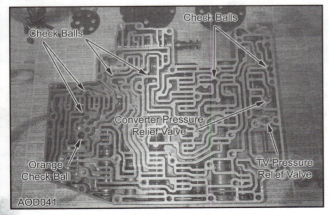

21. To the valve body assembly using a new gasket install the separator plate and the reinforcement plates.

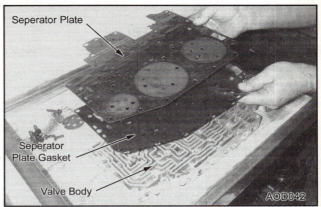

22. To the separator plate install the detent spring guide bolt, then install and tighten the 11 reinforcement plate retaining bolts.

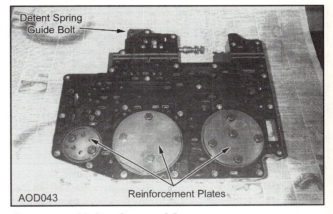

Governor Valve Assembly
Dismantle

1. From the governor body remove cover retaining screws and cover.
2. From the governor assembly remove the screws securing the governor body to the counterweight and separate assembly.
3. From the governor body remove the valve plug and sleeve.
4. Remove the spring retaining clip then remove the spring and governor valve from governor body.
5. From the governor body remove the screen and clean all components in a suitable cleaning solvent and allow to air dry.

Inspect

1. Inspect the governor for stuck valves.
2. Inspect the all components for wear, scoring and damage.
3. Inspect O-ring grooves for damage.

Assembly

1. To the governor body install the screen, then install the governor valve.
2. To the governor body install the valve spring and secure in place with retaining clip.
3. To the governor body install the valve sleeve and plug.
4. To the governor assembly install the counterweight and tighten retaining screws to specification.

AOD AUTOMATIC TRANSMISSIONS

GOVERNOR ASSEMBLY

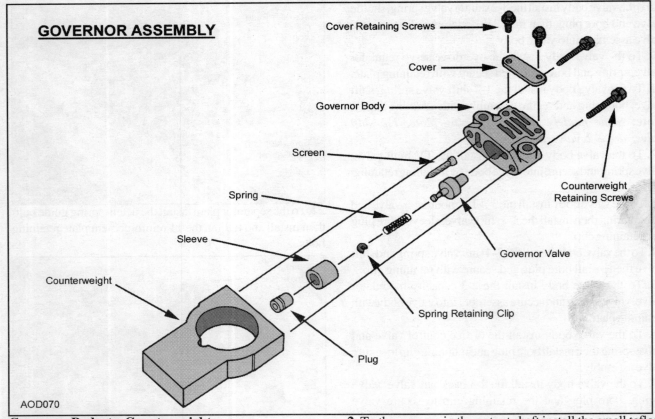

Governor Body to Counterweight:
  1980 .... 80-120 lb.in.
  1981-88 .... 50-60 lb.in.

5. To the governor body install the cover plate and tighten retaining screws to specification.

Governor Body Cover to Governor Body:
  1980 .... 34-50 lb.in.
  1981-88 .... 20-30 lb.in.

TRANSMISSION ASSEMBLY

When assembling transmission lubricate all moving parts with clean transmission fluid or petroleum jelly.
Secure all thrust washers and check balls into position using petroleum jelly.

1. To the grooves in the output shaft install the large output shaft seal rings, ensure all rings are locked together properly.

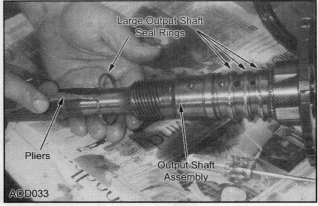

2. To the grooves in the output shaft install the small teflon seal rings.

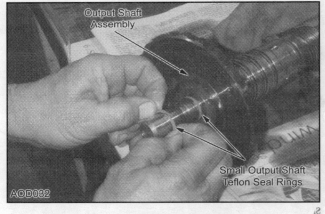

3. Install the thrust spacer over the direct clutch hub ensuring the thrust spacer is lubricated with petroleum jelly.
4. Lubricate the No.7 needle bearing with petroleum jelly then install over direct clutch hub onto the thrust spacer.

AOD AUTOMATIC TRANSMISSIONS

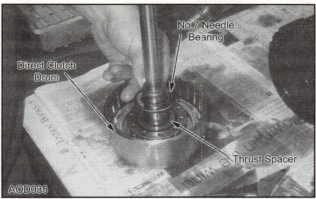

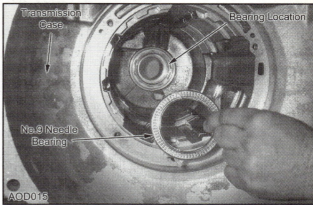

5. Align the friction plates in the direct clutch pack then install the direct clutch hub ensuring it is fully seated.
6. To the direct clutch drum install the No.8 needle bearing and retain with petroleum jelly.

15. To the transmission case install the output shaft assembly ensuring it turns smoothly on the No.9 needle bearing.

7. To the output shaft install the direct clutch, ensuring the drum turns freely.
8. To the direct clutch drum install the ring gear, engaging it into the output shaft hub, then install the hub-to-ring non selective snap ring ensuring it is seated correctly.
9. To the transmission case and parking pawl install the parking pawl shaft, then install the parking pawl return spring.
10. As an assembly install the inner manual lever and parking pawl actuating rod.
11. To transmission case install a new manual lever shaft seal, then with the manual lever attaching nut placed on the shaft of the inner throttle lever install shaft through inner manual lever and shaft seal.
12. Using petroleum jelly lubricate the outer manual lever and shaft assembly then install lever assembly to transmission case.
13. Attach the inner manual lever to the outer manual shaft and tighten lock nut to specification, then install the manual lever retaining pin ensuring not to drive pin in past pan gasket surface.

Manual Lever Lock Nut:
    1980-84 .... 30-40 lb.ft.
    1985-8 .... 19-27 lb.ft.
14. With the No.9 needle bearing lubricated with petroleum jelly install thrust bearing into bottom of transmission case.

16. To transmission case install the non selective snap-ring and ensure it is seated correctly.
Note: *Not all models are fitted with this snap-ring.*
17. To the transmission assembly install the reverse band, ensuring it is seated against the lower band anchor pins.

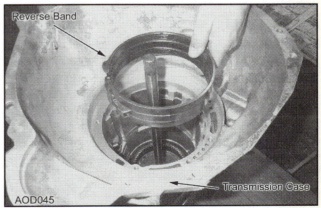

18. Use transmission fluid to lubricate the reverse servo piston seal then install piston and return spring into transmission case.
19. If a new low-reverse servo piston was installed carry out the following procedures to determine the length of the new apply pin.
a) Install the servo piston selection tool and tighten the band apply bolt on the selection tool to 50 lb.in.
b) Fit a dial indicator so the needle is sitting on the flat section

AOD AUTOMATIC TRANSMISSIONS

of the piston and zero dial indicator.

c) Loosen the selector tool bolt until the piston stops against the bottom of the tool and note reading on dial indicator.

d) Check piston travel is within specification, if not replace selective piston.

Piston Travel: 0.112 - 0.237 in.

20. To the reverse servo piston install the reverse servo cover and secure with retaining snap-ring.

21. To the planetary carrier install the one-way clutch, then install the planetary carrier into transmission case ensuring the planetary carrier is fully seated into direct clutch hub.

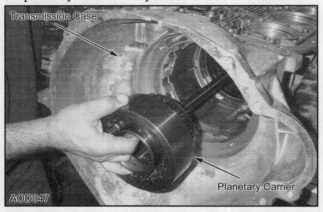

22. Coat No.5 needle bearing with petroleum jelly then install needle bearing to the forward sun gear.

23. To the transmission case install the forward sun gear, ensuring the sun gear is properly meshed with the planetary pinion gears.

24. To the transmission case install the centre support engaging the inner race into the planetary one-way clutch. Ensure to align the notch in the centre support with the overdrive band anchor pin.

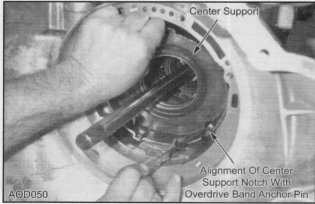

25. To the transmission case install the centre support retaining ring with the ends pointing upwards and ensure the ends are as shown when fully seated.

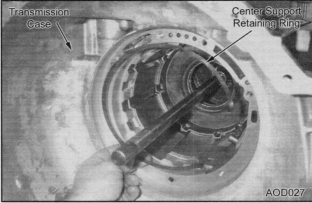

26. To the transmission case between the centre support and case install the anti-clunk spring, ensuring the end of the spring locks into the hole in the case.

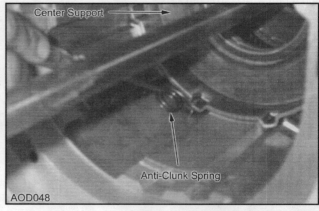

27. To the transmission case install the drive shell and reverse sun gear assembly, ensuring the sun gear is meshed properly and fully seated.

28. To the drive shell install the No.4 needle bearing which has been lubricated with petroleum jelly.

29. To the reverse clutch drum install the No.2 thrust washer which has been lubricated with petroleum jelly.

30. Install the reverse clutch assembly over the turbine shaft and onto the forward clutch, rotating the reverse clutch until all reverse clutch plates seat onto reverse hub.

31. To the forward clutch hub install the No.3 needle bearing which has been lubricated with petroleum jelly, then to the forward clutch drum install the forward hub ensuring it is fully seated.

32. Hold the turbine shaft and to the transmission case install the reverse clutch and forward clutch assembly, rotating assembly locking it into the input shell.

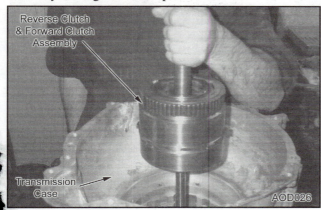

33. To the transmission case install the overdrive band around the reverse clutch drum ensuring it is seated on the anchor pin.
34. To the overdrive servo cover and piston install new seals then lubricate with petroleum jelly.
35. To the overdrive servo piston cover install the piston rotating to prevent damage to seal.
36. To the transmission case install the overdrive servo piston return spring and piston.
37. Ensure the overdrive band is engaged properly with the anchor pin and apply pin then install overdrive servo retaining snap ring.

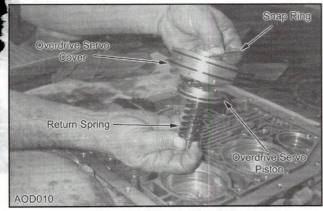

38. To the transmission case install the intermediate clutch pressure plate, then install a clutch friction plate and a steel plate rotating until the same number removed is installed.
Note: *Friction plates should be soaked in transmission fluid for 15 minutes before installation.*

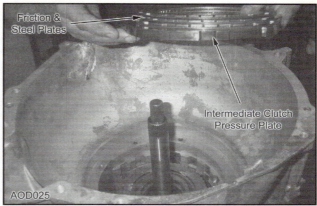

39. To the transmission case install the intermediate clutch selective steel plate.
40. Measure the intermediate clutch clearance.
a) Position a end play gauge bar across pump case mounting surface.
b) Set the depth micrometer/vernier over the intermediate clutch.
c) Read the gauge to determine the depth to the selective plate.
d) If depth is not to specification replace the intermediate clutch selective steel plate.

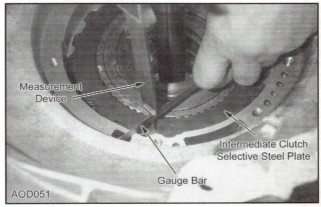

41. Check the transmission endplay.
a) Position a end play gauge bar across pump case mounting surface.
b) Set the depth micrometer/vernier over the clutch drum.
c) Read the gauge to determine the depth to the thrust face.

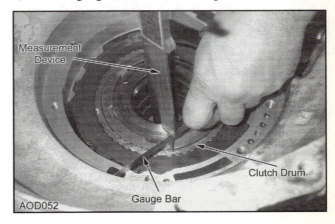

d) Using the depth measured to select the correct No.1 selective thrust washer.

Depth	Washer No.	Washer Size	Washer Colour
1.483-1.500 in.	1	0.050-0.054 in.	Green
1.501-1.517 in.	2	0.068-0.072 in.	Yellow
1.518-1.534 in.	3	0.085-0.089 in.	Natural
1.535-1.551 in.	4	0.102-0.106 in.	Red
1.552-1.568 in.	5	0.119-0.123 in.	Blue

42. To the transmission assembly install the alignments studs to aid in the installation of front pump and gasket.

Note: *Make alignment studs from M8-1.25mm bolts.*

43. To the front pump install the correct No.1 selective thrust washer with petroleum jelly. (correct thrust washer is determined from end play check).

44. To the groove on the front pump body install the square cut front pump O-ring and lubricate with petroleum jelly.

44. To the transmission install a new front pump gasket over guide pins, ensuring it is installed with all holes aligned.

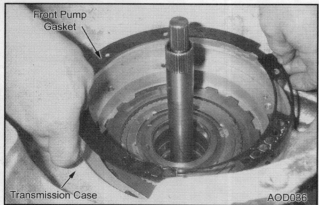

45. To the transmission assembly install the pump and stator support assembly into position and gentle press pump down to seat correctly.

Note: *If guide pins are not available, use a screwdriver to align pump while installing pump assembly.*

46. To the transmission assembly install the seven pump retaining bolts and tighten to specification.

Front Pump Bolts .... 3 - 20 lb.ft

47. Lubricate the 2-3 accumulator piston seals with transmission fluid then install 2-3 accumulator piston into transmission case.

48. To the 2-3 accumulator piston install the accumulator spring, spring cover and secure assembly with retaining snap ring.

49. With new seals on the 3-4 accumulator piston lubricated with transmission fluid install the piston into transmission case.

50. To the 3-4 accumulator piston install the accumulator spring, and the 3-4 accumulator cover which has had the seal lubricated with transmission fluid.

51. Press the 3-4 accumulator cover down into the transmission case and secure with retaining snap ring.

52. Apply air pressure to the indicated apply passages to check the operation of the servos and clutches.

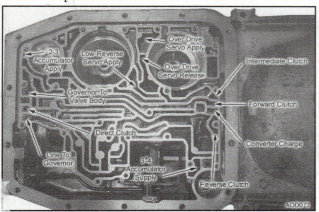

53. To the transmission case install two alignment studs to assist in installation of the valve body and gasket.

54. Install a new valve body gasket to transmission case using alignment studs to position correctly.

55. Install the valve body to transmission case using alignments studs, ensure the TV lever is in contact with the TV valve and the manual lever is fitted between the manual valve lands.

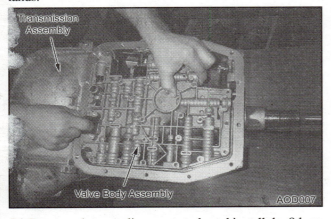

56. Remove the two alignment studs and install the 8 long valve body retaining bolts, tightening by finger only.

57. To the transmission assembly install the detent spring and roller assembly, then install the remaining 15 valve body bolts and finger tighten.

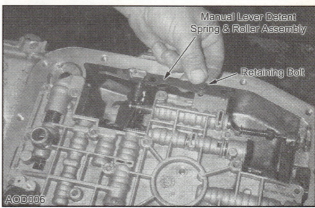

58. Start at the centre of the valve body and tighten retaining bolts to specification working in a spiral pattern outwards.

Valve Body Retaining Bolts: .... 80 - 100 lb.in.

59. Fit the hooked end of the throttle tension spring to the TV lever arm and the straight end against the separator plate in the V notch.

60. To the oil filter install the filter grommet and gasket the using petroleum jelly lubricate the inside of the grommet.

61. To the valve body install the oil filter then tighten retaining bolts to specification.

Oil Filter Retaining Bolts:
    1980-84 .... 80 - 100 lb.in.
    1985-88 .... 80 - 120 lb.in.

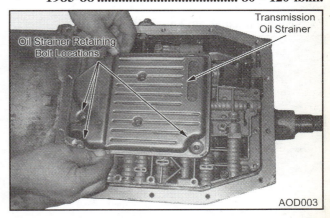

62. To the transmission assembly install a new oil pan gasket then install oil pan (sump) and tighten retaining bolts to specification.

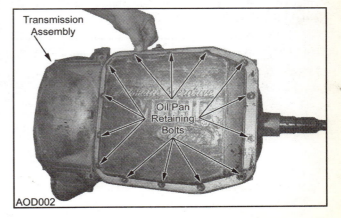

AOD AUTOMATIC TRANSMISSIONS

Oil Pan (sump) Retaining Bolts:
  1980-84 .... 12 - 16 lb.ft.
  1985-88 .... 6 - 10 lb.ft.

63. To the output shaft install the governor with the oil feed holes facing the front of the transmission.

64. To the hole in the output shaft fit the governor drive ball then align the key-way in the governor with the drive ball and slide governor into position.

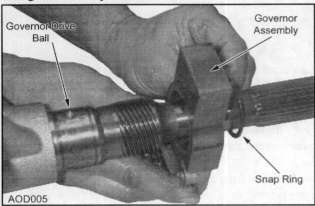

65. Install the retaining snap ring for the governor assembly ensuring it is fully seated into groove.

66. To the transmission case install a new extension housing gasket then install extension housing and tighten retaining bolts to specification.

Extension Housing Bolts: 16 - 20 lb.ft.

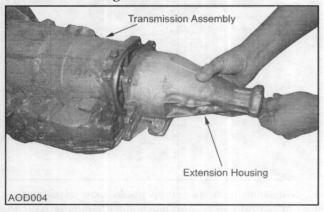

67. To the neutral start switch install a new O-ring then install switch to transmission assembly tightening to specification.

Neutral Start Switch:
  1980-84 .... 8-11 lb.ft.
  1985-88 .... 7-8 lb.ft.

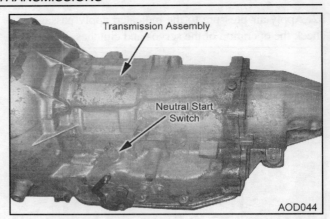

PROBLEM SOLVING & DIAGNOSIS

FLUID CHECK

Transmission fluid changes colour and smell very early in life, these indicators should not necessarily be relied on to diagnose either transmission internal condition nor fluid deterioration.

A dark brown fluid colour, coupled with a delayed shift pattern, may only indicate that the fluid requires replacement and alone, is not a definite indication of a potential transmission failure.

The fluid level should only be checked when the transmission is at normal operating temperature (82-93 degrees Celsius). Transmission fluid colour when new and unused, is red. A red dye is added so that it can be distinguished from other oils and lubricants. The red dye is not an indicator of fluid quality and is not permanent. As the vehicle is driven, the transmission fluid will begin to look darker in colour. The colour will then appear light brown. A DARK brown colour with a distinctively burnt odour MAY indicate fluid deterioration and a need for the fluid to be changed.

Road Test
Drive and Reverse Engagement Shift Check.
1. Start engine.
2. Depress brake pedal.
3. Move gear selector:
    a) 'P' (Park) to 'R' (Reverse)
    b) 'R' (Reverse) to 'N' (Neutral) to 'D' (Drive).
    c) Gear selections should be immediate and not harsh.

AOD AUTOMATIC TRANSMISSIONS

PROBLEM	POSSIBLE CAUSE	CORRECTION
* Slow Initial Engagment	* Improper fluid level * Damaged or improperly adjusted linkage * Contaminated fluid * Faulty clutch and band application, or oil control pressure system.	* Add fluid as required * Repair or adjust linkage * Perform fluid level check * Perform control pressure test
* Rough initial engagement in either forward or reverse	* Improper fluid level * High engine idle * Looseness in driveshaft, U-joints or engine mounts. * Incorrect linkage adjustment * Faulty clutch or band aplication, or oil control pressure system * Sticking or dirty valve body	* Perform fluid level check * Adjust idle to specification * Repair as required * Repair or adjust linkage * Perform control pressure test * Clean, repair or replace valve body
* No drive in any gear	* Improper fluid level * Damaged or improperly adjusted linkage * Faulty clutch or band aplication, or oil control pressure system * Internal linkage * Valve body loose * Faulty clutches * Sticking or dirty valve body	* Perform fluid level check * Repair or adjust linkage * Perform control pressure test * Check and repair as required * Tighten to specification * Perform air pressure test * Clean, repair or replace valve body
* No drive forward - reverse OK	* Improper fluid level * Damaged or improperly adjusted linkage * Faulty clutch or band aplication, or oil control pressure system * Faulty forward clutch or governor * Valve body loose * Sticking or dirty valve body	* Perform fluid level check * Repair or adjust linkage * Perform control pressure test * Perform air pressure test * Tighten to specification * Clean, repair or replace valve body
* No drive, slips or chatters in reverse - forward OK	* Improper fluid level * Damaged or improperly adjusted linkage * Looseness in driveshaft, U-joints or engine mounts. * Bands or clutches out of adjustment * Faulty oil control pressure system * Faulty reverse clutch servo * Valve body loose * Sticking or dirty valve body	* Perform fluid level check * Repair or adjust linkage * Repair as required * Adjust low reverse clutch * Perform control pressure test * Perform air pressure test * Tighten to specification * Clean, repair or replace valve body
* No drive, slips or chatters in first gear in D - all others OK	* Faulty one-way clutch	* Repair or replace one-way clutch
* No drive, slips or chatters in second gear	* Improper fluid level * Damaged or improperly adjusted linkage * Intermediate band out of adjustment * Faulty band or clutch application, or oil pressure control system * Faulty servo and/or internal leaks * Sticking or dirty valve body * Polished, glazed intermediate band or drum	* Perform fluid level check * Repair or adjust linkage * Adjust intermediate band * Perform control pressure test. * Perform air pressure test * Clean, repair or replace valve body * Replace or repair as required
* Starts in high - in D drag or lockup at 1 2 shift pint or in 2 or 1	* Improper fluid level * Damaged or improperly adjusted linkage * Faulty governor * Faulty clutches and/or internal leaks * Valve body loose * Dirty sticking valve body * Poor mating of valve body to case mounting surfaces	* Perform fluid level check * Repair or adjust linkage * Repair or replace governor, clean screen * Perform air pressure test. * Tighten to specification * Clean, repair or replace valve body * Replace valve body or case

AOD AUTOMATIC TRANSMISSIONS

PROBLEM	POSSIBLE CAUSE	CORRECTION
* Starts up in 2nd or 3rd but no lockup at 1-2 shift points	* Improper fluid level * Damaged or improperly adjusted linkage * Improper band and/or clutch application, or oil pressure control system * Faulty governor * Valve body loose * Dirty sticking valve body * Cross leaks between valve body ans case mating surface	* Perform fluid level check * Repair or adjust linkage * Perform control pressure test * Perform governor check. Replace or repair governor, clean screen * Tighten to specification * Clean, repair or replace valve body * Replace valve body and/or case as required
* Shift points incorrect	* Improper fluid level * Improper vacuum hose routing or leaks * Improper operation of EGR system * Linkage out of adjustment * Improper speedometer gear installed * Improper band or clutch application, or oil pressure control system * Faulty governor * Dirty sticking valve body	* Perform fluid level check * Correct hose routing * Repair or replace as required * Repair or adjust linkage * Replace gear * Perform shift test and control pressure test * Repair or replace governor - clean screen * Clean, repair or replace valve body
* No upshift at any speed in D	* Improper fluid level * Vacuum leak to diaphragm unit * Linkage out of adjustment * Improper band or clutch application, or oil pressure control system * Faulty governor * Dirty sticking valve body	* Perform fluid level check * Repair vacuum line or hose * Repair or adjust linkage * Perform control pressure test * Repair or replace governor - clean screen * Clean, repair or replace valve body
* Shifts 1-3 in D	* Improper fluid level * Intermediate band out of adjustment * Faulty front servo and/or internal leaks * Polished, glazed band or drum * Improper band or clutch application, or oil pressure control system * Sticking or dirty valve body	* Perform fluid level check * Adjust band * Perform air pressure test. Repair front servo and/or internal leaks * Repair or replace band or drum * Perform control pressure test * Clean, repair or replace valve body
* Engine over-speeds on 2-3 shift	* Improper fluid level * Linkage out of adjustment * Improper band or clutch application, or oil pressure control system * Faulty high clutch and/or intermediate servo * Sticking or dirty valve body	* Perform fluid level check * Repair or adjust linkage * Perform control pressure test. * Perform air pressure test. Repair as required * Clean, repair or replace valve body
* Mushy 1-2 shift	* Improper fluid level * Incorrect engine idle and/or performance * Improperly adjusted linkage * Intermediate band out of adjustment * Improper band or clutch application, or oil pressure control system * Faulty high clutch and/or intermediate servo release * Polished, glazed band or drum * Dirty sticking valve body	* Perform fluid level check * Tune adjust engine idle as required * Repair or adjust linkage * Adjust intermediate band * Perform control pressure test * Perform air pressure test. Repair as required * Repair or replace as required * Clean, repair or replace valve body
* Rough 1-2 shift	* Improper fluid level * Incorrect engine idle and/or performance * Intermediate band out of adjustment * Improper band or clutch application, or oil pressure control system * Faulty intermediate servo * Dirty sticking valve body	* Perform fluid level check * Tune and adjust engine idle as required * Adjust intermediate band * Perform control pressure test * Air pressure check intermediate servo * Clean, repair or replace valve body

AOD AUTOMATIC TRANSMISSIONS

PROBLEM	POSSIBLE CAUSE	CORRECTION
* Rouh 2-3 shift	* Improper fluid level * Incorrect engine idle and/or performance * Improper band or clutch application, or oil pressure control system * Faulty intermediate servo apply and release and high clutch piston check ball * Dirty sticking valve body	* Perform fluid level check * Tune and adjust engine idle as required * Perform control pressure test * Air pressure test the intermediate servo apply and release and hogh clutch piston check ball. Repair as required * Clean, repair or replace valve body
* Rough 3-1 shift at closed throttle in D	* Improper fluid level * Incorrect engine idle and/or performance * Improperly adjusted linkage * Improper band or clutch application, or oil pressure control system * Faulty governor operation * Dirty sticking valve body	* Perform fluid level check * Tune and adjust engine idle as require * Repair or adjust linkage * Perform control pressure test * Perform governor test. Repair as required * Clean, repair or replace valve body
* No forced downshifts	* Improper fluid level * Improperly adjusted linkage * Improper band or clutch application, or oil pressure control system * Faulty internal kickdown linkage * Dirty sticking valve body	* Perform fluid level check * Repair or adjust linkage * Perform control pressure test * Repaire internal kickdown linkage * Clean, repair or replace valve body
* No 3-1 shift in D	* Improper fluid level * Incorrect engine idle and/or performance * Faulty governor * Dirty sticking valve body	* Perform fluid level check * Tune and adjust engine idle as required * Perform governor test. Repair as required * Clean, repair or replace valve body
* Runaway engine on 3-2 downshift	* Improper fluid level * Improperly adjusted linkage * Improper band or clutch application, or oil pressure control system * Faulty intermediate servo * Faulty intermediat servo * Polished, glazed band or drum * Dirty sticking valve body	* Perform fluid level check * Repair or adjust linkage * Adjust intermediate band * Perform control pressure test * Perform air pressure testcheckthe intermediate servo and/or seals. * Repair or replace as required * Clean, repair or replace valve body
* No engine braking in manual first gear	* Improper fluid level * Improperly adjusted linkage * Band or clutches out of adjustment * Faulty oil pressure control system * Faulty reverse servo * Polished, glazed band or drum	* Perform fluid level check * Repair or adjust linkage * Adjust low-reverse clutch * Perform control pressure test * Perform air pressure test of reverse servo. Repair reverse clutch or rear servo as required * Repair or replace as required

Torque Specifications

Description	lb.ft.
Converter Housing Access Cover	12 - 16
Converter Plug to Converter	8 - 28
Converter to Flywheel	20 - 34
Cooler Line to Case	10 - 14
Extension Housing to Case	3 - 20
Front Pump to Case	3 - 20
Inner Manual Lever to Shaft 1980-84	30 - 40
1985-88	19 - 27
Neutral Start Switch to Case 1980-84	8 - 11
1985-88	7 - 8
Oil Pan to Case 1980-84	12 - 16
1985-88	6 - 10
Outer Throttle Lever to Shaft	12 - 16
Pressure Plug to Case	6 - 12
Stator Support to Pump Body 1980-84	3 - 25
1985-88	12 - 16
Transmission to Engine	40 - 50
Detent Spring Attaching Bolt 1983-84	80 - 100
1985-88	80 - 120
Filter to Valve Body 1980-84	80 - 100
1985-88	80 - 120
Governor Body Cover to Governor Body 1980	34 - 50
1981-88	20 - 30
Governor Body to Counterweight 1980	80 - 120
1981-88	50 - 60
Reinforcing Plate to Valve Body	80 - 100
Separator Plate to Valve Body	80 - 100
Valve Body to Case	80 - 100

BORG-WARNER M51 AUTOMATIC TRANSMISSION

Subject	Page
GENERAL INFORMATION	**147**
Transmission Identification	147
MAINTENANCE AND ADJUSTMENT	**147**
Lubrication	147
Fluid Level	147
Changing Fluid	147
Lubricant	147
Maintain Strainer	147
Maintenance Notes	148
Oil Cooler Pipes	148
Clean and Inspect	148
Console Shift Lever Assembly	149
Removal	149
Installation	149
Accelerator Linkage & Down Shift Cable	149
Check and Adjust	149
Setup For Adjustment Both MPEFI & EFI	149
MPEFI Engines	149
EFI Engines	149
Replace Kickdown Cable	150
Band Adjustment	150
Front Brake Band	150
Rear Brake Band	150
Oil Pan/Sump & Valve Body Assembly	150
Remove	150
Install	151
SERVO VALVES	152
Front & Rear Servos	152
Remove	152
Installation	152
COOLER REPLACEMENT	152
SELECTOR LINKAGE	152
Remove	152
Inspect	152

Subject	Page
Install	152
Adjust	152
Speed Sender Unit and Fitting Assembly	152
Remove	152
Install	152
MAJOR REPAIR	**153**
Dismantle Transmission	**153**
Housing	153
Valve Bodies	155
Pump	157
Front Clutch & Input Shaft Assembly	157
Rear Clutch & Forward Sun Gear Assembly	158
Front Servo	159
Rear Servo	159
Governor	159
Assemble Transmission	**159**
Governor	159
Rear Servo	159
Front Servo	159
Rear Clutch & Forward Sun Gear Assembly	159
Front Clutch & Input Shaft Assembly	160
Pump	161
Valve Bodies	161
Housing	161
PROBLEM SOLVING AND DIAGNOSIS	163
Fluid Checks	163
Oil Pressure Check	164
Road Test	164
Torque Converter Evaluation	164
SPECIFICATIONS	**165**
TORQUE WRENCH SPECIFICATIONS	**165**

GENERAL INFORMATION

Transmission Identification
Transmissions are fitted with and identification plate for easy identification when servicing and repairing.

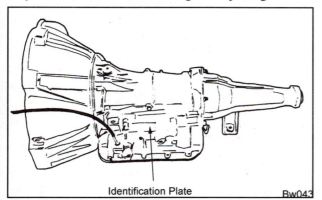

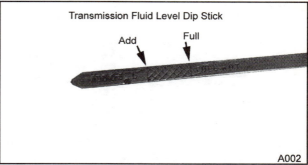

The model code for vehicles equipped with different transmissions are listed in General Information Chapter at the front of this manual.

MAINTENANCE AND ADJUSTMENT

LUBRICATION
If adding or changing the transmission fluid, use only specified Automatic Transmission fluid ESR-M2C163A (Dextron II).

FLUID LEVEL
The dipstick is located at the right rear of the engine near the fire wall. Check fluid level is done in the following procedure:
Parking brake engaged and engine idling with transmission at normal operating temperature, select each gear briefly, and selector the "P" park position.
* The transmission must be at normal operating temperature to obtain an accurate dipstick reading.
* Do not overfill the transmission. Overfilling will cause foaming of the fluid, loss of fluid, shift complaints and possible damage to the transmission.
Remove dipstick and wipe with clean lint free cloth. Turn the engine off, then within 10 sec of turning off replace dipstick into transmission, then remove and check the level. The level must be indicated within the low and full marks on the "hot" range on dipstick, refer below.

NOTE: Ensuring dipstick is properly seated in dipstick tube to prevent fluid contamination. Maintaining transmission fluid at correct level, use recommended fluid in the transmission.

CHANGING FLUID
Overfill the transmission will cause fluid to foaming, loss of fluid, shift complaints and possible damage to the transmission.
1. Raise vehicle and place a large drain tray under transmission oil pan. Clean all dirt from around oil pan and transmission case.
2. Remove all but 2 oil pan retaining bolts, loosen one of the two bolts and tap pan at one corner to break seal loose, allow fluid to drain from the pan.
3. Carefully remove oil pan from the transmission, as pan will still have fluid within it.
4. Clean oil pan and remove gasket, also clean the transmissions pan mounting surface.
5. Install oil pan with a new gasket, tighten bolts to specified torque.
Oil pan bolt torque specification: 15 Nm
6. Pour 3.5L of automatic transmission fluid ESR-M2C163A into the transmission through the dipstick tube.
7. Start engine and allow to idle for at least two minutes. With park brake on, move selector lever momentarily to each position ending in "P" park position.
8. Remove dipstick and wipe with clean lint free cloth. Turn the engine off, then within 10 sec of turning off replace dipstick into transmission, then remove and check the level. The level must be indicated within the low and full marks on the "hot" range on dipstick, refer below.
9. Add more fluid if necessary, until correct level is obtained.

LUBRICANT
8.5 litres including converter ESR-M2C163A (Dextron II)

MAINTAIN STRAINER
Take care when removing sump from transmission as hot oil can cause serious burns. Avoid this by allowing transmission to cool down.
1. Remove the oil pan as described above in the Changing Fluid section, from step 1 to 3.
2. Remove the fluid pipe retainer by removing the two

retaining screws.

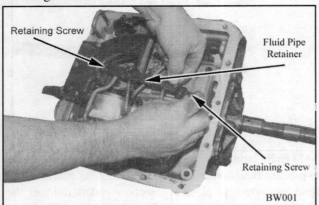

3. Remove the three screws and washers securing the oil filter to the valve body, then remove filter from valve body and gasket.

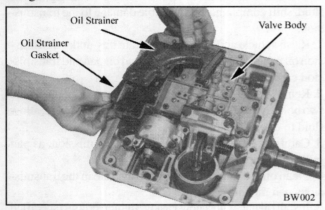

4. Fit the new strainer and gasket into position, and refit the retaining screws, then install the fluid pipe retainer.
5. Replace the oil pan as described above in the Changing Fluid section, from step 4 to 9.

MAINTENANCE NOTES

While maintaining the transmission, all parts should be cleaned and inspected. Individual units should be reassembled before disassembly of other units to avoid confusion and interchanging of parts.
1. Thoroughly clean the exterior before disassembly of the unit.
2. Disassembly and assembly must be made on a clean work bench. Cleanliness is of the utmost importance. The bench tools, and parts must be kept clean at all times.
3. Before installing screws into aluminium parts, dip screws into transmission fluid prevent galling aluminium threads and to prevent screws from seizing.
4. To prevent thread stripping, always use a torque wrench when installing screws.
5. If threads in aluminium parts are stripped or damaged the part can be made serviceable by the use of suitable thread inserts.
6. Protective tools must be used when assembling seals to prevent damage. The slightest flaw in the sealing surface of the seal can cause an oil leak.
7. Aluminium castings and valve are very susceptible to nicks, burns, burrs, etc., and should be handled with care.
8. Internal snap rings should be expanded and external snap rings compressed if they are to be reused. This will ensure proper seating when reinstalled.
9. "O" rings, gaskets and oil seals that are removed should not be reused.
10. Teflon oil seal rings should not be removed unless damaged.
11. During assembly of each unit, all internal moving parts must be lubricated with transmission fluid.

OIL COOLER PIPES

If replacement of transmission steel tubing cooler pipes is required, only use double wrapped and brazed steel tubing meeting transmission manufactures specifications or equivalent. Under no condition use copper or aluminium tubing to replace steel tubing. These materials do not have satisfactory fatigue durability to withstand normal car vibrations. Steel tubing should be flared using the double flare method.

CLEAN AND INSPECT

After complete disassembly of a unit, wash all metal parts in a clean solvent and dry with compressed air. Blow oil passages out and check to make sure they are not obstructed. Small passages should be checked with tag wire. All parts should be inspected to determine which parts are to be replaced.
Pay particular attention to the following:
1. Inspect the magnet in the sump pan for metal filings, to help determine problems with transmission.

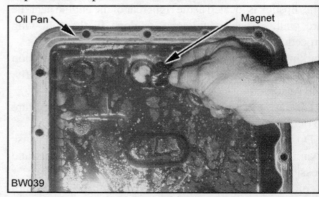

2. Inspect the transmission case for cracking a major problem is cracking in the section shown in below diagram.

BORG-WARNER M51 AUTOMATIC TRANSMISSION

Transmission Housing Cracks

3. Inspect linkage and pivot points for excessive wear.
4. Bearing and thrust surfaces of all parts should be checked for excessive wear and scoring.
5. Check for broken score seal rings, damaged ring lands and damaged threads.
6. Inspect seal and 'O' rings.
7. Mating surfaces of castings should be checked for burrs. Irregularities may be removed by lapping the surface with emery paper. The emery paper is laid on a flat surface, such as a piece of plate glass.
8. Castings should be checked for cracks and sand holes. Do not use solvents on neoprene seals, composition faced clutch plates or thrust washers as damage to parts may occur.

CONSOLE SHIFT LEVER ASSEMBLY
* Column shift autos refer to the Steering Section under Steering Column Removal (Column Shift).
REMOVAL
1. Raise vehicle to enable the shift rod to be disconnected from the shift lever under the vehicle.
2. Loosen the selector lever handle lock nut, then remove the handle, lock control rod, bush and locknut.
3. Centre Console is to be removed as described in Body Chapter under the Floor Pan/Chassis Section, refer to Centre Console Removal.
4. Disconnect the shift indicator light, then unscrew the shift assembly retaining screws and lift the assembly from the floor pan.

INSTALLATION
1. Clean mating surfaces of floor pan and shift lever assembly.
2. Apply a bead of sealer around opening in floor pan between the screw holes.
3. Place the shift lever assemble into the floor pan, then screw the shift assembly retaining screws into position and connect the shift indicator light.
4. Centre Console is to be replaced as described in Body Chapter under the Floor Pan/Chassis Section, refer to Centre Console Installation.
5. Replace the locknut, bush, lock control rod and the handle onto the shift assembly, then tighten the selector lever handle lock nut.
6. Raise vehicle to enable the shift rod to be connected to the shift lever under the vehicle.
7. Adjust linkage as described in this chapter.

ACCELERATOR LINKAGE & DOWN SHIFT CABLE

CHECK & ADJUST
* *Ensure accelerator linkage/cable is correctly adjusted before resetting down shift cable (i.e. Check that wide open throttle can be achieved).*
Set Up For Adjustment Both EFI & MPEFI.
1. Transmission and engine to be at normal operating temperature before ant adjustments are carried out. Engage the hand brake to ensure the vehicle will not move.
2. The pressure outlet at the rear of the transmission will need to have a pressure gauge fitted to it, the gauge will need to read to at least 500 kPa.

MPEFI Engines Adjustment
3. With vehicle running, the idle speed control loom needs to be detached.
4. The engine will now remain at base idle. Then with the transmission in drive alter the adjuster nuts on the cable until the pressure gauge reads a pressure of 450 kPa, then tighten the nuts.
5. Place transmission in the park position, then switch engine off and disconnect the pressure gauge from the transmission.
6. The sleeve will then need to be set with a clearance of 0.25-0.75 mm above the end of the outer casing. Engine must still be at base idle.
7. Attach the idle control valve loom, then road test the vehicle.

EFI Engine Adjustment
8. Vehicles engine not running, fit a 4 mm spacer between the idle speed motor plunger and throttle lever, then start the engine.
9. The idle speed will reset itself in a few minutes, then engine can be turned off and the loom can be disconnected and the
spacer removed.
10. The engine can now be started. Then with the transmission in drive alter the adjuster nuts on the cable until the pressure gauge reads a pressure of 450 kPa, then tighten the nuts.

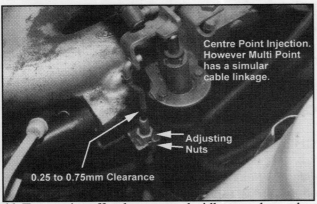

11. Turn engine off and reconnect the idle motor loom, then disconnect the pressure gauge and road test the vehicle.

REPLACE KICKDOWN CABLE:
1. Remove the oil pan as previously described in this chapter.
2. Remove the inner cable from kick down cam located in the transmissions left hand front corner.
3. Unclip the inner cable from throttle lever, then loosen the adjuster screws and disconnect it from its bracket.
4. To remove the assembly from the transmission casing, press the outer cable retaining lugs together from the inside of the transmission and push the assembly out.
5. With new seal fitted to the retainer, push it into the transmission case until the lugs lock into position.
6. Fit the inner cable to the downshift valve cam, then refit the oil pan with a new gasket as described previously in the chapter.
7. Fit the kickdown cable to the adjuster bracket and then to the throttle lever.
8. Ensure cable is placed correctly, then adjust cable as described above.

BAND ADJUSTMENT
Front Brake Band
1. Place vehicle on safety stands.
2. Place an oil collect tray under transmission.
3. Remove oil pan as described above.
4. Loosen adjusting screw locknut, to allow the servo lever to move outwards, then place a 6.35 mm spacer into the gap between the servo piston pin and adjusting screw.

5. The adjusting screw can then be tensioned.
Torque Adjusting screw: 1130 Nm
6. Once screw is tensioned the locknut can then be tightened, then remove the spacer.
7. Refit oil pan as described above.
8. The vehicle can then be taken for a test drive.

Rear Brake Band
1. Place vehicle on safety stands.
2. With adjusting screw locknut loosened, located on the right hand side of the transmission case.
3. Tighten the adjusting screw to a torque of 14 Nm, then slacken adjusting screw 3/4 of a turn.

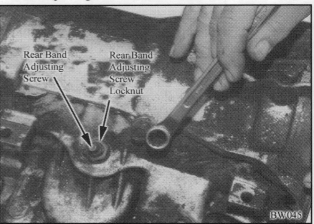

4. Tighten the adjusting screw locknut.
5. Remove vehicle from safety stands and test run.

OIL PAN / SUMP & VALVE BODY ASSEMBLY
Remove
1. Place vehicle on safety stands.
2. Place an oil collection tray underneath the transmission, then lower the oil pan as described above.
3. Disconnect the transfer pipe retainer and transfer pipes, pipes are pushed into the valve body and servo's and many need to be levered from the valve body.
* Do not damage the pipes when levering them from the body.

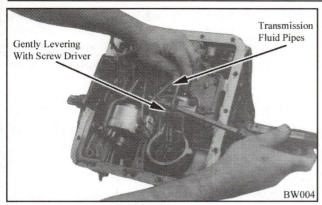

4. Remove the oil strainer as described previously.
5. Unclip the kick down cable from the downshift cam, then the retaining bolts can be removed.

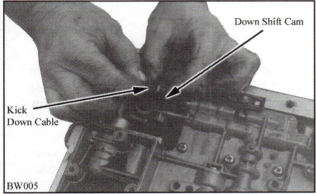

6. There are 3 retaining bolts, 1 was removed when the pipe retaining bracket was removed. The other 2 are at the rear of the valve body and behind the filter they must be withdrawn to allow the valve body to be removed.

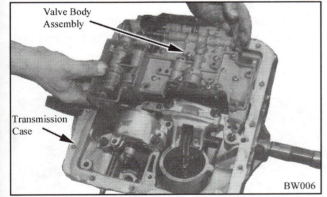

7. The valve body assembly has to be removed evenly to protect the valve body to main casing and pump pipes.

Install

1. Oil pick-up tubes will need to be refitted to the pump if they

have been removed. Ensure "O" ring is fitted to large pipe into pump.
2. The valve body can be lifted into position ensuring that the oil tubes are fitted into the oil tube collector correctly. Ensure the manual control valve has engaged the peg of the operating lever.
3. The valve body retaining bolts can be fitted, the 2 long bolts go to the rear of the valve body and 1 short in the centre of the valve body near the filter, securing the valve body assembly.
4. The kickdown cable is able to be fitted and adjustment checked.

5. Install the fluid pipes to the valve body assembly, then the retaining strap can be fitted into place, 0.4 mm min. clearance must be present between the end of the strap and the filter screen.

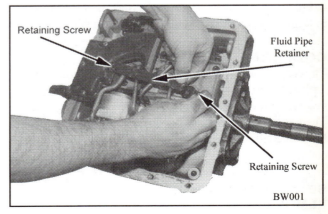

6. Adjust the front band as previously described.
7. Refit oil pan as previously described.
8. Remove from safety stands and road test vehicle.

SERVO VALVES
Front and Rear Servo
Remove
1. Place vehicle on safety stands.
2. Place an oil collection tray underneath the transmission.
3. Detach the oil pan and valve body from the housing.
4. Remove two bolts which attach the particular servo to the transmission case.

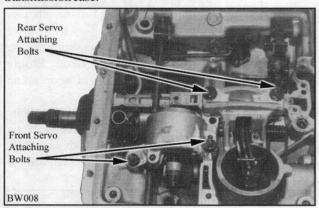

Remove servo take care the operating strut, that transfers the movement from the servos to bands does not fall out and get bent or distorted..

Install
1. Fit operating strut to the servo with petroleum jelly, then manoeuvre into place until strut engages the band.
2. The servo retaining bolts can now be fitted and tensioned. (The front servo bolts are the same) (The rear servo, rear bolt is longer and has a reduced diameter at one end to locate the centre support). Torque bolts to specification.

Front Servo Bolts: 15 Nm
Rear Servo Bolts: 3/8 bolts 30 Nm
5/16 bolts 20 Nm

3. Proceed with band adjustments as previously described.
4. Fit the oil pan as previously described in this chapter.
5. Remove from safety stands and road test vehicle.

COOLER REPLACEMENT
The cooler is located inside the radiator, if the cooler is to be replaced the radiator must also be replaced. See cooling system for radiator replacement.
There is an optional transmission cooler that is mounted in front of the radiator for models that do not have an air-conditioner fitted.

SELECTOR LINKAGE
REMOVE
Set transmission selector to lever to 'PARK' position. Raise front of vehicle. Remove locking bolt, dished washer, flat washer, insulator and sleeve from lower end of selector lever. Slide trunnion from selector rod. Remove retaining nut, rod and lever assembly from the transmission manual shaft.

INSPECT
Check all items for wear and/or damage, replace all worn or damaged items.

INSTALL
Installation is the reverse of the removal procedure. Tighten the nut to the specified torque. Adjust linkage as described below.
Manual shaft nut torque specification: 26-30 Nm

ADJUST
1. Loosen locking bolt at selector lever.
2. Position transmission selector lever in "PARK".
3. Position gear shift lever in 'PARK', then tighten the locking bolt at the selector lever, to the specified torque.
Selector lever locking bolt specification: 18-24 Nm
4. Lower vehicle and test.
5. Ensure that engine can be started only in 'PARK' and 'Neutral'. The Park /Neutral/Backup switch is automatically adjusted when linkage is correctly adjusted.

SPEED SENDER UNIT AND FITTING ASSEMBLY
REMOVE
1. Raise rear of vehicle and place on safety stands. Place drip tray beneath speed sender.
2. Disconnect sender unit electrical connector.
3. Unscrew vehicle speed sender unit retaining bolt and remove.
4. Withdraw fitting assembly including driven gear from case extension.

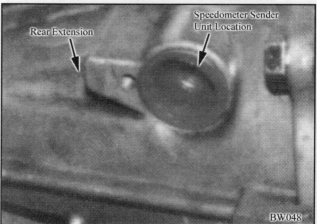

INSTALL
1. Inspect speed sender unit 'O' ring seal and replace it if unsatisfactory.

BORG-WARNER M51 AUTOMATIC TRANSMISSION

2. Installation is the reverse of the removal procedure.
3. Tighten retainer bolt to specified torque.

Retainer bolt torque specification: 8-14 Nm

* The vehicle speed unit is tightened by hand only.

MAJOR REPAIR

Dismantle Transmission Housing

1. Carefully slide the torque converter from the bell housing, placing it on a clean work area, cover pump drive lugs and sleeve to protect from contamination.
2. Loosen the bell housing retaining bolts, place the auto upside down in a transmission cradle with the bell housing over the end of the bench.
3. Undo the speed sensor retaining bolt and slide the unit from the extension housing, then withdraw the bell housing bolts and the bell housing can be levered from the housing if needed.
4. The extension housing bolts can be undone, then slide the extension housing from the transmission case and place to one side.

Press the speedo clip down and withdraw the gear from the output shaft, place gear and clip together on the bench.

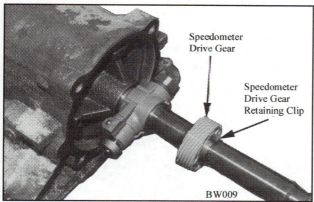

5. The centre support screws can now be removed, which are located 120° from the rear servo on both sides.

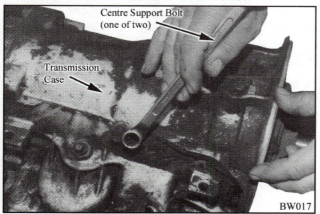

6. Remove oil pan and valve body as previously described in this chapter, also remove the safety 'P'/'N' switch.

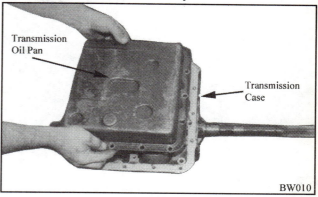

7. Remove the front and rear servo piston assemblies as described previously.

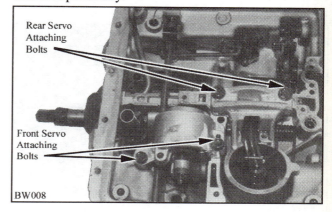

8. Loosen the governor retaining bolt 2.5 turns, then the governor should be able to be slid off the output shaft. Also remove the servos as previously described in this chapter.

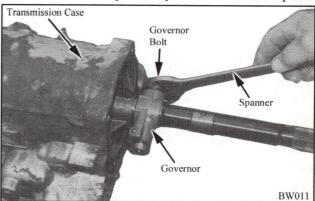

9. The end float of the gear train will need to be checked, this is done by levering the front clutch backwards until there is no movement, then place a dial indicator on the input shaft and release the lever and then levering the assemble towards the dial indicator.

End Float Specifications 0.25-0.74 mm, if not in specs replace shim pack.

10. The transmission fluid pump is retained by 6 bolt, once the bolts have been withdrawn the pump assembly, gasket and

thrust washer can be removed from the housing.

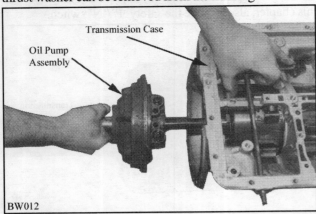

11. Slide the front clutch assembly from the housing, being careful to keep the thrust washers and needle roller bearing in order of where they come from.

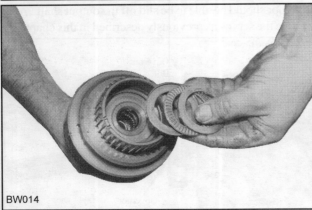

12. Rear clutch and sun gears can now be slid from the casing as an assembly, located behind the assembly is a washer and needle roller thrust bearing which can also be removed and placed in order.

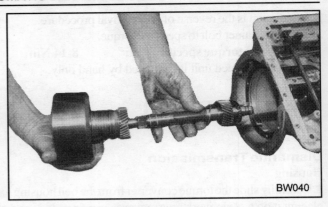

13. Before the centre support can be released the front band will need to be removed by squeezing the top together and sliding out.

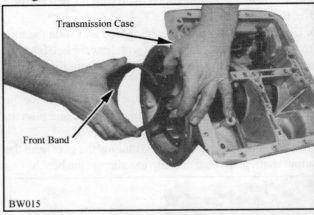

14. Using a rubber mallet lightly hit the output shaft to release the centre support and allow it to be slid from the case.

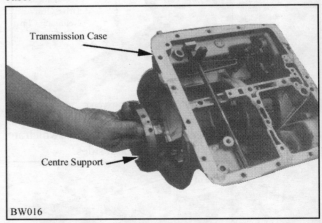

15. Remove the planet gear assembly, needle thrust bearing and steel washer, then the rear band can be removed in a similar way to the front band.

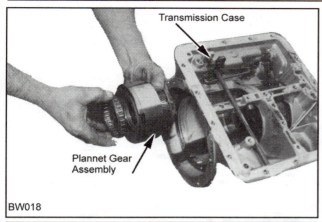

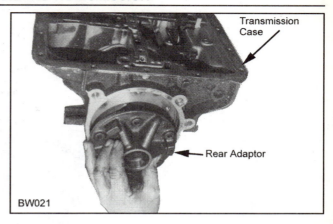

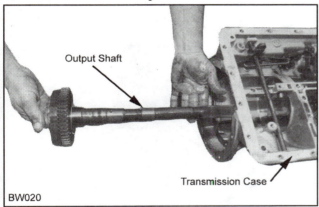

15. Remove the output shaft from the casing, ensuring that the thrust washer is still in place.

16. Loosen and withdraw the rear adaptor retaining bolts and remove the adaptor body and plate from the rear of the transmission case, there will be three rings visible made of cast iron that can not be damaged under any circumstances.

17. To remove the cross shaft, withdraw the spring clip from the end furthest from the shaft to the manual valve lever, then compress the cross shaft spring with the valve lever until the drive pin is released and withdraw the pin from the shaft.

18. Slide the cross shaft from the casing, the manual valve lever spring and detent ball are spring loaded, so do not loose. Withdraw the manual valve lever and parking pawl link after detaching it from the parking pawl operating mechanism.

19. Release the spring clip from the parking pawl operating mechanism, take note of the fitment of the spring before it is released, then withdraw the assembly from the casing.

20. The band adjusters can be removed from the casing, if necessary the parking pawl pivot pin can be removed by pushing the tension pin from the parking pawl pivot pin, then push the parking pawl pivot pin from the casing, and the 2nd pivot pin can be removed by tilting the case and taping in lightly.

Valve Bodies

The valve body parts must be laid out in order when being dismantled to ensure the correct installation on reassembling. The best place to lay them out is on clean paper.

1. If not previously removed withdraw the filter element retaining screws, then detach the filter element from the valve body and place to one side. Slide the reverse pressure boost cam and manual control valve (if fitted).

2. Release down shift cam assembly and bracket from the valve body, placing to one side, then slide the throttle and down shift valves with springs from the valve body.

3. Withdraw the 6 lower valve body screws and 2 upper valve body screws to divide that valve body into two pieces.

4. With the valve body split unscrew the 6 screws from the retaining plates on the upper body, then withdraw the 1-2 shift valve, 2-3 shift valve, 2-3 plunger & spring from one side and the 1-2 plunger & spring from the other side.

5. With the lower valve body facing up on a bench, withdraw the retaining screws for the oil tube collector and the retaining screws for the governor line plate, then lift them away including the separator plate.

6. With the separator plate lifted the 2-3 dump valve (spring

BORG-WARNER M51 AUTOMATIC TRANSMISSION

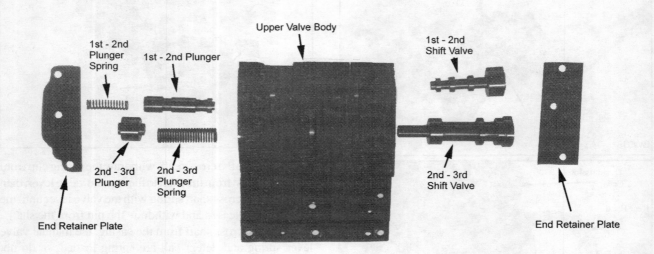

Lower Valve Body Assembly

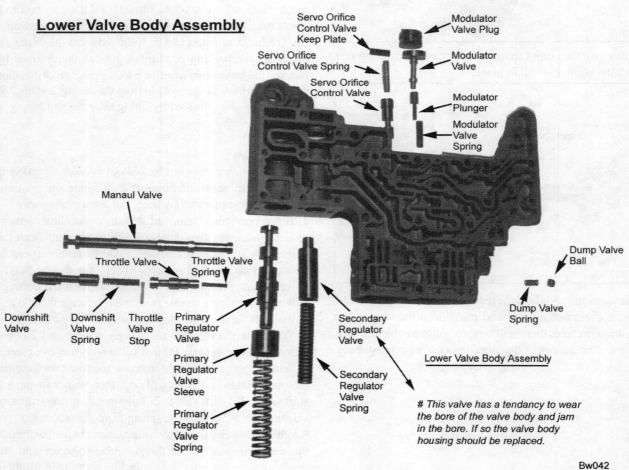

This valve has a tendency to wear the bore of the valve body and jam in the bore. If so the valve body housing should be replaced.

BORG-WARNER M51 AUTOMATIC TRANSMISSION

& ball), throttle valve keep plate and throttle valve stop rollercam be withdrawn and placed to one side.

7. From the lower valve body detach the regulator valve retainer plate, then withdraw the primary regulator valve spring, sleeve and valve, then the secondary regulator spring and valve.

8. Withdraw the orifice control valve keep plate from the lower body, with keep plate withdrawn the orifice control valve and spring can be slid from the lower valve body.

9. Modulator valve dowel pin is to be withdrawn from the valve body to allow the modulator valve plug, plunger, spring and valve to be slid from the lower valve body.

Pump

To divide the pump assembly there is 1 screw and 5 bolts that need to be unscrewed, this will allow the body to be removed from the adaptor.

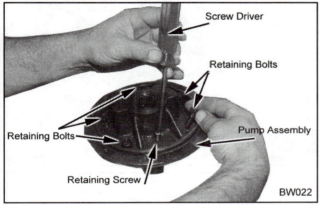

Pump gears will need marking to ensure they are installed correctly, inspect all components and seals for damage, if any need replacing do so prior to assembly.

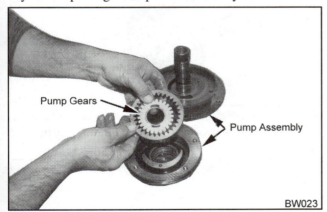

Front Clutch & Input Shaft Assembly

When dismantling this assembly ensure that all components are laid out in order as they are removed from the assembly, this will help with correct installation when assembling.

1. Pry input shaft retaining circlip from the clutch cylinder and remove the input shaft assembly.

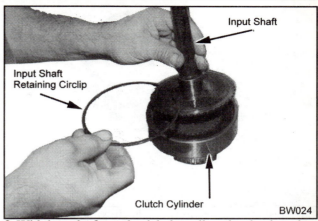

2. Withdraw the front clutch hub to allow the clutch pack to be withdrawn easier, taking note of the order that the steel and composition plates are being removed.

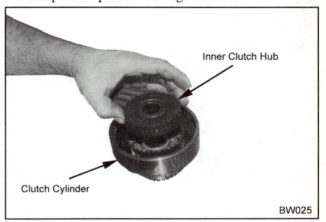

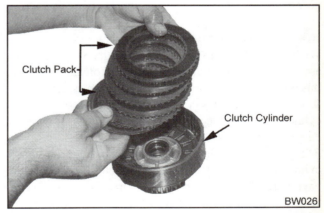

3. The last plate that is removed is a pressure plate which has a wave through it, this can be determined by placing it on a flat surface. Then the lower circlip will need prying from the clutch cylinder to enable the diaphragm spring and piston to be removed.

157

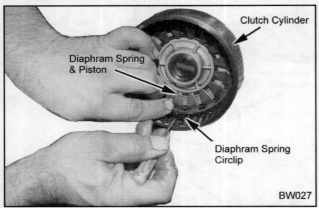

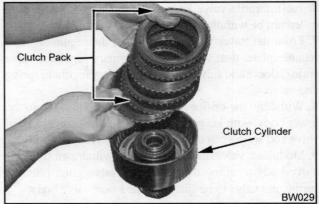

4. The piston is released from the clutch cylinder by applying compressed air to the clutch cylinder piston guide, this will push the piston off its seat and enable it to be removed.

4. Apply the clutch spring compressor to the clutch spring, compressing the spring to enable the circlip to be release. Then remove the circlip, compressor, retainer, and spring.

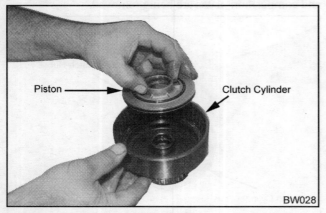

5. All components will need inspection and be replaced if necessary.

Rear Clutch & Forward Sun Gear assembly
When dismantling this assembly ensure that all components are laid out in order as they are removed from the assembly, this will help with correct installation when assembling.

2. Pull the forward sun gear shaft from the rear clutch cylinder, then pry the sealing rings from the shaft with out damaging the shaft.

3. Pry the clutch plate retaining circlip from the clutch cylinder, then withdraw the pressure plate. The clutch pack have three different plate designs and must be replaced in the same order as they are removed, they use a fibre plate, flat steel plate and a dished steel plate.

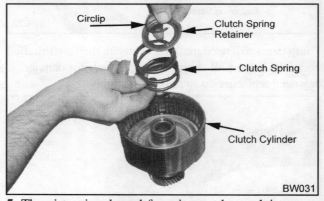

5. The piston is released from its seat by applying compressed air to the port located beside the sealing ring near the front drum.

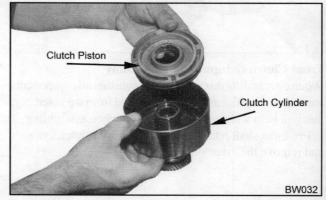

Front Servo

Press the piston guide down the servo housing bore until the circlip is clear of the guide and is able to be released from the housing.

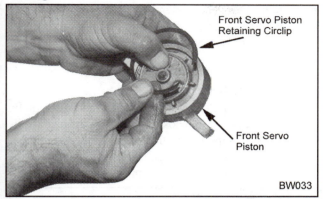

Once the circlip has been removed from the housing release the piston guide and allow the spring to push the piston and guide from the housing, then withdraw the piston from the guide.

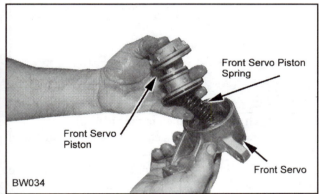

All seals are to be replaced with new seals before assembly.

Rear Servo

To withdraw the piston from the assembly depress the straight arm of the spring, then disconnect it from the lug cast in the servo body. Spring can then be withdrawn as well as the piston.

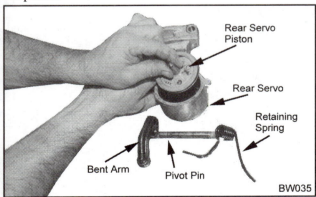

If the lever is to be disconnected, push the retaining pin from the housing using a 3 mm drift.

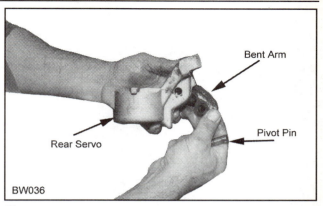

Governor

The governor is dismantled by disconnecting the circlip from the weight stem and sliding the weight from the stem, then the stem, valve and spring are all withdrawn through the main shaft bore of the governor.

Assemble Transmission
Governor

Place the weight stem, spring and valve into position through the governor main bore, then slide weight into place and fit the circlip.

Rear Servo

Replace the seals, install the piston spigot to the seat of the operating lever, then move the piston into the bore, then apply spring to pivot pin and engage the bent arm to the servo lever, press the straight spring arm to connect the servo body lug.

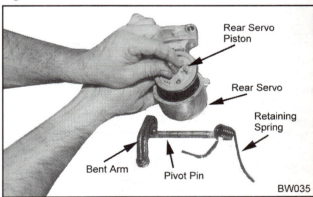

Front Servo

All seals are to be replaced with new seals before assembly, if lever has be disconnected, fit into place and push the retaining pin into the housing using a 3 mm drift.

Install the piston into the guide, then place the spring, piston and guide into the housing, then press the piston guide down the servo housing bore compressing the spring until the circlip grove is clear of the guide and the circlip is able to be installed into the housing.

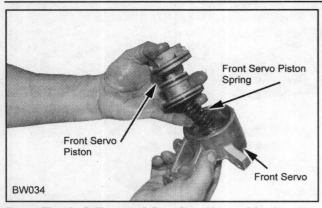

Rear Clutch & Forward Sun Gear Assembly

All seals are to be replaced with new seals before assembly, also inspect the needle roller bearings that support the forward sun gear shaft.

1. Place the piston into position in the rear clutch cylinder, pressing it into place by hand, then fit the spring, retainer and compressor into place and compress the spring until circlip groove is visible, then install circlip and remove the compressor.

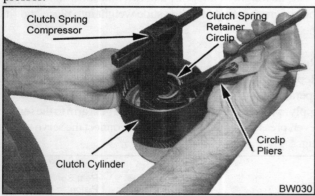

2. Install the clutch plates into the rear clutch cylinder in the reverse order as they were removed, starting with a outer spline, then inner spline, as follows below:

   * dished - fibre - flat - fibre - dished - fibre - flat - fibre - dished - fibre *

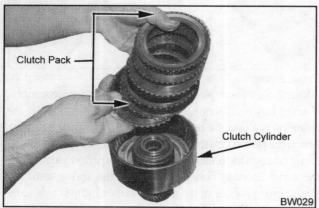

The dish drops in towards the piston when assembling the plates.

3. Once the clutch plates are fitted into place the pressure plate and circlip are able to be fitted into position and secure the clutch pack into the housing.

4. Replace the seal on the forward sun gear shaft, then fit the forward needle thrust race, placing the forward sun gear shaft into the rear clutch assembly.

5. Install the seals to the forward sun gear shaft and then fit the needle thrust race and steel washer onto the rear of the forward sun gear shaft.

Front Clutch & Input Shaft Assembly

All seals are to be replaced with new seals before assembly.

1. (a) Place the piston into position and push down until it is fully seated, then install the diaphragm spring, retaining it with the circlip. Once the circlip has been installed the pressure plate and clutch plates can be fitted.

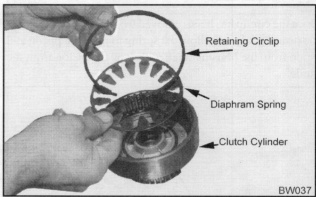

(b) The clutch plates are fitted in the order of:

   * steel - fibre - steel - fibre - steel - fibre - steel - fibre - steel - fibre *

The steel plates have an outer spline and the fibre plates have an inner spline.

2. The clutch clearances need to be checked after installation, this is done by applying a 3.0 kg load to the clutch pack, then measuring the distance from the input shaft seat to the top of the clutch pack, using vernia callipers is the easiest way of measuring this distance.

   * Clearance should be 0.38 mm maximum

If out of specs use external tooth plates to bring within specifications.

3. Install the inner front clutch hub aligning the inner toothed plates, until the hub has bottomed out in the front clutch cylinder, then fit input shaft into position and install the circlip, ensuring that it is locked in its groove properly.

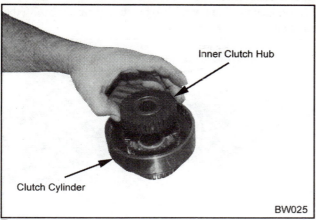

Pump
Replace all seals and components that are damaged in any way before assembling the pump body to the adaptor. Fit the pump gears into the pump body, then aligning up the holes in the pump adaptor with the pump body segment.

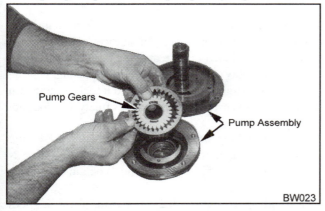

When pump body and adaptor are aligned with each other install the retainer bolts and screw, tightening to the correct tension.

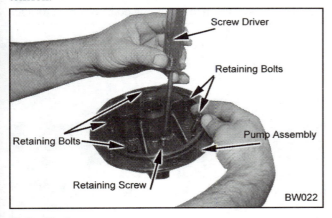

Valve Body
Valve body parts were laid out in order when dismantled to provide easier installation on reassembling.

1. In the lower valve body install the modulator valve spring, plunger, valve, plug and then plug dowel to secure components into place.

2. The servo orifice valve and spring can be fitted into the housing and secured using the valve keep plate

3. Install the secondary regulator valve and spring, then the primary regulator valve, sleeve and spring. Once they are fitted the regulator valve retainer plate can be installed, the springs will need to be compressed to install the retaining screws.

4. The 2-3 dump valve (spring & ball), throttle valve keep plate and throttle valve stop roller will need installing before the separator plate can be fitted.

5. With the lower valve body facing up on a bench place the separator plate, governor line plate and oil tube collector into place, then install the retaining screws for the governor line plate and oil tube collector tensioning them to correct tension.

6. The upper valve body can have the 2-3 plunger, spring, 2-3 shift valve and the 1-2 shift valve fitted into one side, the 1-2 plunger and spring fitted into the other side. The retainer plates can then be installed and screws tensioned.

7. Place the upper valve body onto the lower valve body securing them together with 6 lower valve body screws and 2 upper valve body screws.

8. Slide the throttle valve spring and valve, then the down shift valve spring and valve, then the manual valve into the valve body before securing the down shift cam assembly and bracket on the valve body.

9. Install the filter element and filter element retaining screws, then the reverse pressure boost cam and manual control valve can be reinstalled (if originally fitted).

Housing
1. Replace the band adjuster into the case and if the parking pawl pivot pin needs to be refitted to the casing repeat the remove process in reverse.

2. Place the park pawl operating mechanism into position in the case, the spring is to be fitted the same way as it was removed, and the spring clip to be installed.

3. Connect the park pawl linkage to the operating mechanism, then lower the manual valve lever into place with detent ball & spring fitted and slide the cross shaft through the lever.

4. Install the spring clip in place, then the cross shaft spring can be compressed with the manual valve lever, until the drive pin is able to be inserted into the shaft. Once the drive pin is in place the manual valve lever can be released into position.

5. Replace the adaptor body and plate into place over the output shaft, once the adaptor body and plate are aligned, insert the retaining bolts tensioning them to the correct torque.

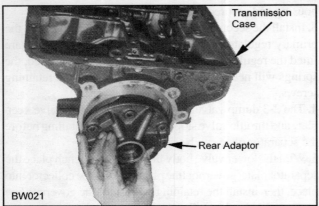

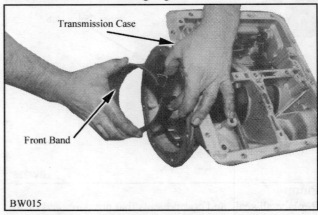

6. The thrust washer is to be installed to the transmission casing, where it aligns with lugs in the casing to stop thrust washer turning. Fit the output shaft assembly in the casing.

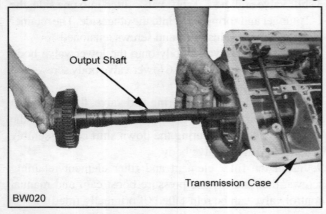

7. The one way clutch outer race can be fitted into the planet gear carrier making sure the lugs are engaged. Install the retaining circlip and then the one way clutch.

8. The centre support is to be fitted to the planetary gear assembly with the centre boss inside the one way clutch. On the rear of the planet gear assemble fit the steel washer, lip facing out, and then the needle thrust race.

9. Install the rear band into the casing, placed on the adjuster.

10. Carefully manoeuvre the planet gear assembly and centre support as one into the casing slotting correctly into place with the ring gear and aligning centre support with the pre-dismantle markings. Fit the retaining bolts in through the casing to the centre support.

11. Replace the front band into position the casing with the band attached to the casing lug.

12. The next process is to fit the front clutch to the rear clutch, fit the steel thrust washer then the needle roller bearing to the front of the rear clutch. Carefully slide the two clutch packs together.

13. (a) Before installing the clutch assemblies into the casing, ensure that the needle thrust race and steel thrust washer are positioned at the rear of the front sun gear shaft, then the assembly can be installed into the casing.

(b) Once the assembly is fully installed into the casing turn the assembly to ensure that it all moves freely and does not bind up.

14. When installing the pump the preload will need setting, if the reading obtained on the dismantling procedure is incorrect the shims will need altering to obtain the correct reading before the pump is fitted.

End Float Specifications 0.25-0.74 mm, if not in specs replace shim pack.

15. Once the correct shim thickness is obtained, fit the shims to the face of the pump, then install the pump into the casing, then install and tension the retaining bolts to correct torque.

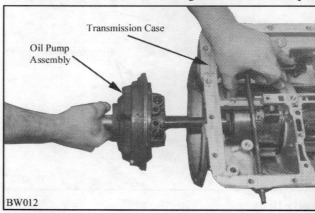

16. Position the governor drive hole up, then install the governor into place over the output shaft, the cast projection towards the rear of the assembly. The locking screw can then be tensioned to the correct torque.

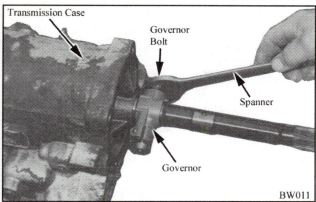

17. Refit the servos and valve body as previously described in this chapter, then adjust the bands as previously described in this chapter.

18. Replace oil pan as previously described in this chapter, also fit the safety 'P'/'N' switch into place.

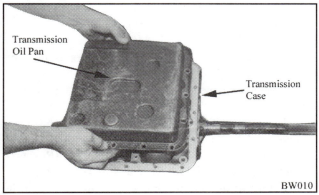

19. With the speedo clip positioned on the output shaft, slide the gear over the output shaft and the clip until gear locks into the clip.

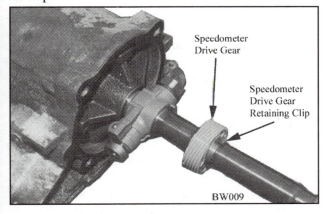

20. Slide the extension housing into place on the transmission case, then the extension housing bolts can be fitted and tensioned.

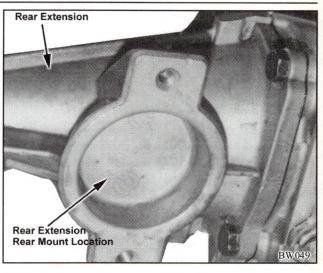

21. Slide the speed sensor unit into the extension housing, then install and tension the speed sensor retaining bolt.

22. Fit the bell housing into place tipping lightly with a soft face hammer if needed, insert and tension the bell housing retaining bolts. Remove the transmission from the cradle and place with the bell housing over the end of the bench.

23. Carefully slide the torque converter over the input shaft, taking care not to damage the front pump seal. Transmission can then be installed into the vehicle.

PROBLEM SOLVING & DIAGNOSIS

FLUID CHECK

Transmission fluid changes colour and smell very early in life, these indicators should not necessarily be relied on to diagnose either transmission internal condition nor fluid deterioration. The chart on the next page shows that a dark brown fluid colour, coupled with a delayed shift pattern, may only indicate that the fluid requires replacement and alone, is not a definite indication of a potential transmission failure.

The fluid level should only be checked when the transmission reaches normal operating temperature (82-93 degrees Celsius).

Transmission fluid colour when new and unused, is red. A red dye is added so that it can be distinguished from other oils and lubricants. The red dye is not an indicator of fluid quality and is not permanent. As the vehicle is driven, the transmission fluid will begin to look darker in colour. The colour will then appear light brown. A DARK brown colour with a distinctively burnt odour MAY indicate fluid deterioration and a need for the fluid to be changed.

Details of transmission oil pressure check procedures refer to 'Oil pressure check information' chart at the start of this chapter.

BORG-WARNER M51 AUTOMATIC TRANSMISSION

OIL PRESSURE CHECK
Preliminary Check Procedure
Check transmission oil level and condition
Check and adjust Kickdown Cable
Check outside manual linkage and correct
Check engine tune

Engine Idle Test
With pressure gauge fitted to the transmission, hand brake applied and service brake applied, start the vehicle and check the fluid pressures in all gears.

The pressure should be within the specs indicated on the Pressure Table under the specifications section of this chapter.

Stall Test
With pressure gauge fitted to the transmission, hand brake applied and service brake applied, start the vehicle and check the fluid pressures in all gears at full throttle.

The pressures and speeds should be within the specs indicated on the Pressure Table under the specifications section of this chapter.

Engine not to be held at full throttle for any longer than 5 sec, then select 'N' and run at about 1200 rpm to cool torque converter before continuing.

After Cut Back
With pressure gauge fitted to the transmission, this test is conducted on the road. Accelerating at full throttle and the pressure should drop at modulator operation.

The pressure should be within the specs indicated on the Pressure Table under the specifications section of this chapter.

ROAD TEST
Drive and Reverse Engagement Shift Check.
1. Start engine.
2. Depress brake pedal.
3. Move gear selector:
   a) 'P' (Park) to 'R' (Reverse)
   b) 'R' (Reverse) to 'N' (Neutral) to 'D' (Drive).
   c) Gear selections should be immediate and not harsh.

Transmission Upshifts
With gear selector in 'D' :-
1. Accelerate using a steady increasing throttle application.
2. Note the shift speed point gear engagements for:
   a) 2nd gear
   b) 3rd gear

Throttle Downshift
At a speed of 70-90 km/h, quickly depress the accelerator to half open position and observe:
   Transmission downshift to 2nd gear immediately.

Full Throttle (Detent) Downshift
Operate the vehicle at 30 km/h in 'D', then quickly depress to wide open throttle position and observe:
   Transmission downshifts to 1st gear immediately.

Manual Downshift
1. Operate the vehicle at 65 km/h in 'D', then release the accelerator pedal (closed throttle position) and simultaneously move the gear selector to 1st gear, and observe:
   a) Transmission downshifts 3rd to 2nd gear immediately.
   b) Vehicle should slow under engine braking.
   c) Should downshift 2nd to 1st gear under 30 km/h..
2. Operate the vehicle at 30 km/h in 1st.
   Check the transmission for no up shifts, slippage and squawking.

Manual Gear Range Selection.
Manual Third "D".
1. With vehicle stopped, place gear selector in 'D' (Drive) and accelerate to observe:
   a) The first to second gear shift point.
   b) The second to third gear shift point.

Manual Second (2).
1. With vehicle stopped, place gear selector in '2' (second) and accelerate to observe:
   a) The first to second gear shift point.
2. Accelerate to 60 km/h and observe:
   a) That a second to third gear shift does not occur.

Manual First (1)
1. With vehicle stopped, place gear selector in '1' (first) and accelerate to 40 km/h and observe:
   a) That no upshift occurs.

Reverse.
1. With vehicle stopped. Place gear selector in 'R' (Reverse) and slowly accelerate to observe reverse gear operation.

* This publication does not include all possible throttle positions and the corresponding shift point information. Actual shift points will vary in accordance with transmission build variation.

Kickdown Cable
Kickdown adjustments are important for Borg Warner automatic transmissions as this also controls the transmission pressure. Kickdown slipping will occur if the kickdown cable is not hooked up at all.

TORQUE CONVERTER EVALUATION
Torque Converter Stator
The torque converter stator roller clutch can have one of two different type malfunctions:
a) Stator assembly freewheels in both directions.
b) Stator assembly remains locked up at all times.

Condition A:- Poor Acceleration, Low Speed
The vehicle tends to have poor acceleration from a standstill. The engine tune is correct and the transmission is in first (1st) gear when starting out.

Checking for poor performance in 'D' (Drive) and 'R' (Reverse) will help determine if the stator is free wheeling at all times.

Condition B:- Poor Acceleration, High Speed
Engine rpm and car speed limited or restricted at high speeds.

BORG-WARNER M51 AUTOMATIC TRANSMISSION

Performance when accelerating from a standstill is normal. Engine may overheat. Visual examination of the converter may reveal a blue colour from over heating.

If converter has been removed, the stator roller clutch can be checked by inserting a finger into the splined inner race of the roller clutch and trying to turn the race in both directions. The inner race should turn freely clockwise, but not turn or be very difficult to turn counter-clockwise.

The Converter Should be Replaced if:-
Leaks externally, such as the hub weld area.
Converter has an imbalance which can not be corrected.
Converter is contaminated with engine coolant containing anti freeze.

The Converter Should Not be Replaced if:-
The oil has an odour, is discoloured, and there is no evidence of metal or clutch facing particles.
The threads in one or more of the converter bolt holes are damaged. Correct with thread insert.

SPECIFICATIONS

Trans Models

Application	Ford No.	Borg Warner No.
EFI Engines :		
3.9L	87DA-7000-BE	BW0551-000002
3.2L	87DA-7000-CE	BW0551-000003
MPEFI Engines :		
3.9L	87DA-7000-AE	BW0551-000001

Lubricant
8.5 litres including converter ESR-M2C163A
(Dextron II)

Gear Ratios:
Reverse (R) 2.09:1
Drive (D) 1.00:1
Second (2) 1.45:1
First (1) 2.39:1

Shift Points
Diff Ratio 2.77:1 3.9L MPEFI

Manual	Shift	Throttle	Km/h
D	1-2	KD	74-83
D	2-3	KD	125-133
D	3-2	KD	109-117
D	3-1	KD	50-60
Manual	Shift	Throttle	Km/h
D	1-2	Zero	17-21
D	2-3	Zero	19-24
D	3-2	Zero	11-15
1	3-1	Zero	40-50

Diff Ratio 2.77:1 3.9L EFI

Manual	Shift	Throttle	Km/h
D	1-2	KD	72-82
D	2-3	KD	120-130
D	3-2	KD	105-115
D	3-1	KD	48-58
Manual	Shift	Throttle	Km/h
D	1-2	Zero	16-21
D	2-3	Zero	18-23
D	3-2	Zero	10-15
1	3-1	Zero	38-48

Diff Ratio 2.77:1 3.2L EFI

Manual	Shift	Throttle	Km/h
D	1-2	KD	67-77
D	2-3	KD	115-124
D	3-2	KD	99-109
D	3-1	KD	44-54
Manual	Shift	Throttle	Km/h
D	1-2	Zero	16-21
D	2-3	Zero	18-23
D	3-2	Zero	10-15
1	3-1	Zero	38-48

Control Pressure (kPa)

Trans Model	Idle	Stall	Rev Idle
87DA-7000-BE	420-500	1420-1820	420-500
87DA-7000-CE	420-500	1750-2200	1100-1380
87DA-7000-AE	420-500	1700-2100	1100-1380

Torque Converter:

Stall Speed	R.P.M.
3.2L EFI	1750-1850
3.9L EFI	1970-2070
3.9L MPEFI	2000-2100

Torque Wrench Spec. Nm

Converter Housing to Engine 40
Transmission Case to Converter Housing 20
Extension Housing to Transmission 55
Converter to Flywheel/Drive plate 35
Converter Housing Lower Cover to Housing 15
Transmission Oil Pan (Sump) 15
Front Servo to Transmission Case 3.2L EFI 15
Rear Servo to Transmission Case
        except 3.9L (2x3/8 bolts) 30
        3.9L (1x5/16 bolt) 20
Downshift Valve Cam Bracket to Valve Body 10
Fluid Cooler Line to Case 20
Front Pump to Case 20
Governor body to Shaft 40

BTR 85/91/93/95/97 LE AUTOMATIC TRANSMISSIONS

Subject	Page
MAINTENANCE AND ADJUSTMENT	**167**
Lubrication	167
Fluid Level	167
Changing Fluid	167
Lubricant	167
Maintain Strainer	167
Maintenance Notes	168
Oil Cooler Pipes	168
Clean and Inspect	169
Console Shift Lever Assembly	**169**
Removal	169
Installation	169
Band Adjustment	**169**
Front Band	169
Rear Band	169
Oil Pan/Sump & Valve Body Assembly	**169**
Removal	169
Valve Body Dismantle	169
Valve Body Assembly	170
Install	170
SERVO VALVES	**171**
Front Servo Remove	171
Front Servo Installation	171
Rear Servo Remove	171
Rear Servo Installation	171
COOLER Replacement	**172**
SELECTOR LINKAGE Adjustment	**172**
Speed Sender Unit and Fitting Assembly	**172**
Remove	172
Install	172
MAJOR REPAIR	**172**
Transmission Assembly	172
Dismantle	172
Transmission Case	173
Forward Clutch Cylinder	174
C3 Clutch Cylinder	175
Planet Carrier & Centre Support	176
Pump	176
Assemble	176
Rear Band Assembly	177
Output Shaft and Ring Gear Assembly	177
Rear Servo Assembly	178
Planet Gear Carrier & Centre Support	178
Extension Housing	179
Front Servo Assembly	179
Front Band Assembly	179
C2/C4 Clutch Assembly	180
C3 Clutch, Reverse & Forward Sun Gear	181
Forward Sun Gear & C3 Clutch Pack	182
C1 Clutch Overdrive & Input Shaft	182
Pump Cover & Converter Support	183
Valve Body, Oil Filter & Pan	185
PROBLEM SOLVING AND DIAGNOSIS	**186**
Oil Pressure Check	186
Hydraulic Diagnosis	186
Road Test	186
Torque Convertor Clutch Diagnosis	187
Torque Converter Evaluation	187
EA/ED SPECIFICATIONS	**189**
EA/ED TORQUE WRENCH SPECIFICATIONS	**190**
EF/EL & AU SPECIFICATIONS	**191**
EF/EL & AU TORQUE WRENCH SPECIFICATIONS	**192**

BTR 85/91/93/95/97 LE AUTOMATIC TRANSMISSIONS

GENERAL INFORMATION

The illustration on this page shows the Falcon 85/91/93/95/97LE automatic transmissions.

A metal identification plate is attached to the transmission. The model code for vehicles equipped with different transmissions are listed in General Information Chapter at the front of this manual.

MAINTENANCE AND ADJUSTMENT

LUBRICATION
If adding or changing the transmission fluid, use only specified Automatic Transmission fluid TQ95 (Castrol).

FLUID LEVEL
The dipstick is located in the right section of engine compartment. To check level, follow this procedure:
Apply parking brake and with engine idling and transmission at normal operating temperature, engage each gear briefly, ending with selector in "N" neutral.
* The transmission must be at normal operating temperature to obtain an accurate dipstick reading.
* The transmission should not be overfilled, otherwise the transmission fluid will cause undue transmission-fluid high pressure, this could result in fluid leakages, foaming and difficulty in gear changes.
Withdraw dipstick and wipe clean with a lint free cloth. Install dipstick into transmission, withdraw and check level. The level must be within "hot" range on dipstick, refer below.

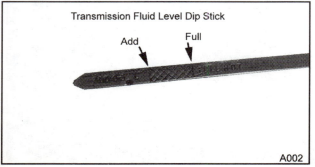

NOTE: * Avoid entry of dirt into transmission by ensuring that dipstick is properly seated. Maintaining transmission to correct level with recommended fluid is essential for correct operation of unit.
** A fluid flow test should be conducted. If less than 4 litres /minute flow it will indicate a problem, possibly with radiator and transmission will overheat, causing internal damage.

CHANGING FLUID
* The transmission should not be overfilled, otherwise the transmission fluid will cause undue transmission-fluid high pressure, this could result in fluid leakages, foaming and difficulty in gear changes.
1. Raise vehicle and place a large drain tray under transmission oil pan.
2. Remove transmissions drain plug and allow fluid to drain, refer below.
3. Remove oil pan retaining bolts and tap pan at one corner to break it loose, allow fluid to drain and then remove pan.

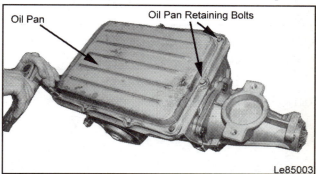

4. Clean transmission case gasket surface and oil pan.
5. Install oil pan with a new gasket, tighten bolts to specified torque.
Oil pan bolt torque specification: 4.5 Nm
6. Firstly pour sufficient automatic transmission fluid TQ95 to bring fluid level to lower mark on dipstick. Add automatic transmission fluid into transmission through dipstick hole.
7. Start engine and allow to idle for at least two minutes. With park brake on, move selector lever momentarily to each position ending in "N" neutral position.
8. Add sufficient automatic transmission fluid to bring fluid level to lower mark on dipstick. Re-check fluid level after transmission has reached operating temperature. The fluid level should be between upper and lower marks of "HOT" range on dipstick. Insert the dipstick fully to prevent dirt entry into transmission.

LUBRICANT
10.0 litres including converter   TQ95 (Castrol).

MAINTAIN STRAINER
* Take care when removing sump from transmission as hot oil can cause serious burns. Avoid this by allowing transmission to cool down.

1. Raise vehicle and support on safety stands.
2. Clean all dirt from around oil pan and transmission case, place drain tray under transmission.
3. Hold oil pan in place, leaving one bolt loose at the front of the oil pan, remove the remaining bolts. Allow the rear of the oil pan to drop, emptying oil into drain tray.
4. Remove remaining bolt and oil pan and empty fluid from pan.

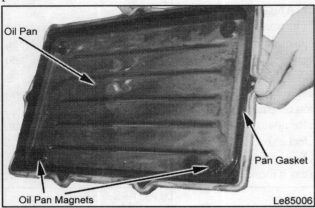

5. If necessary, remove strainer, by releasing retaining clip, also remove 'O'-ring and discard.

6. If necessary install new strainer and 'O' ring.
7. Clean oil pan and case mating surfaces. Check that magnets are functional and located in the designated position in the oil pan.
8. Install new seal and reinstall oil pan. Tighten bolts to specified torque.

Oil pan bolt torque specification: **4.5 Nm**

9. Lower vehicle and add automatic transmission fluid. Check transmission fluid level.

MAINTENANCE NOTES

* While maintaining the transmission, all parts should be cleaned and inspected. Individual units should be reassembled before disassembly of other units to avoid confusion and interchanging of parts.

1. Thoroughly clean the exterior before disassembly of the unit.
2. Disassembly and assembly must be made on a clean work bench. Cleanliness is of the utmost importance. The bench, tools, and parts must be kept clean at all times.

3. Before installing screws into aluminium parts, dip screws into transmission fluid prevent galling aluminium threads and to prevent screws from seizing.
4. To prevent thread stripping, always use a torque wrench when installing screws.
5. If threads in aluminium parts are stripped or damaged the part can be made serviceable by the use of suitable thread inserts.
6. Protective tools must be used when assembling seals to prevent damage. The slightest flaw in the sealing surface of the seal can cause an oil leak.
7. Aluminium castings and valve are very susceptible to nicks, burns, burrs, etc., and should be handled with care.
8. Internal snap rings should be expanded and external snap rings compressed if they are to be reused. This will ensure proper seating when reinstalled.
9. "O" rings, gaskets and oil seals that are removed should not be reused.
10. During assembly of each unit, all internal moving parts must be lubricated with transmission fluid.

OIL COOLER PIPES

If replacement of transmission steel tubing cooler pipes is required, only use double wrapped and brazed steel tubing meeting transmission manufactures specifications or equivalent. Under no condition use copper or aluminium tubing to replace steel tubing. These materials do not have satisfactory fatigue durability to withstand normal car vibrations.
Steel tubing should be flared using the double flare method.

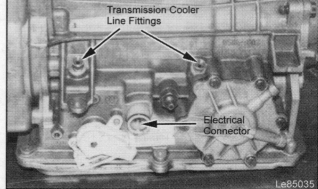

CLEAN AND INSPECT

After complete disassembly of a unit, wash all metal parts in a clean solvent and dry with compressed air. Blow oil passages out and check to make sure they are not obstructed. Small passages should be checked with tag wire. All parts should be inspected to determine which parts are to be replaced.

Pay particular attention to the following:
1. Inspect linkage and pivot points for excessive wear.
2. Bearing and thrust surfaces of all parts should be checked for excessive wear and scoring.
3. Check for broken score seal rings, damaged ring lands and damaged threads.
4. Inspect seal and 'O' rings.
5. Mating surfaces of castings should be checked for burrs. Irregularities may be removed by lapping the surface with emery paper. The emery paper is laid on a flat surface, such as a piece of plate glass.
6. Castings should be checked for cracks and sand holes.
* Do not use solvents on neoprene seals, composition faced clutch plates or thrust washers as damage to parts may occur.

CONSOLE SHIFT LEVER ASSEMBLY
Removal
1. Remove centre console from vehicle as described in body chapter.
2. Raise vehicle. From beneath vehicle, disconnect rod from shift lever by removing nut securing trunnion to lever.
3. Disconnect park/neutral/reverse switch electrical connector.
4. Lower vehicle, then remove screws securing selector shift lever assembly to floor pan and remove assembly.

Installation
1. Clean mating surfaces of floor pan and shift lever assembly.
2. Apply a bead of sealer around opening in floor pan between screw holes.
3. Install selector lever assembly using retaining screws.
4. The remainder of the installation is the reverse of the removal procedure.
5. Adjust linkage

BAND ADJUSTMENT
Front Band
1. Loosen the lock nut on the band adjusting bolt.
2. Tighten band adjusting bolt to initial specification.
Front Band Adjusting Screw: 10 Nm
3. Unscrew the band adjusting bolt exactly three (3) turns.
4. Use a spanner to grip adjusting bolt in place and tighten lock nut to specification.
Front Band Adjusting Screw Lock Nut: 40 Nm

Rear Band
1. Loosen the lock nut on the band adjusting bolt.
2. Tighten band adjusting bolt to initial specification.

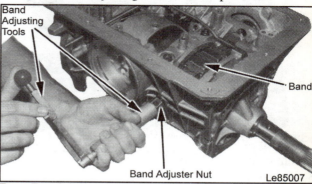

Rear Band Adjusting Screw: 15 Nm
3. Unscrew the band adjusting bolt exactly one (1) turn.
4. Use a spanner to grip adjusting bolt in place and tighten lock nut to specification.
Front Band Adjusting Screw Lock Nut: 40 Nm

OIL PAN / SUMP & VALVE BODY ASSEMBLY
Remove
1. Place vehicle on safety stands.
2. Place an oil collection tray underneath the transmission.
3. Remove the oil pan / sump and seal.
4. Remove the filter, then disconnect the solenoid wires from each solenoid.

5. The manual valve link lever must be removed from the manual valve link.
6. Remove the valve body assembly by pulling down evenly.

Valve Body Dismantle
* **Valve body problems are usually caused by the electrical solenoids more than the valves them selves.**
1. Remove the retainer plate for the detent spring and also remove the spring, then pull out the manual valve.
2. Make note of the angle the solenoid terminals make with the valve body for assembly.

BTR 85/91/93/95/97 LE AUTOMATIC TRANSMISSIONS

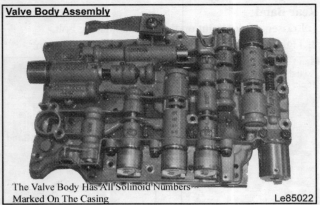

Valve Body Assembly

The Valve Body Has All Solinoid Numbers Marked On The Casing. Le85022

3. Remove the S1, S2 and S3 solenoids also remove the No. 3 solenoid sleeve.
4. Remove the CAR valve but do not remove the sleeve.
5. Remove the S4 solenoid, sleeve and BAR valve, but do not remove the BAR valve sleeve.
6. Remove the S5 solenoid, S6 solenoid and assembly, (damper valve, supply valve and the spring).
7. Remove the 25 retaining screws, then lift the upper valve body and separator plate from the lower valve body as an assembly.
8. Lay the upper valve body on the bench then remove the separator plate and gaskets.
9. Five nylon check balls will be exposed, remove these from the upper valve body, then remove the two filters from the lower valve body. Plus a large nylon check ball.
10. Turn the valve body over so the keeper plates securing the 1-2, 2-3 and 3-4 shift valves fall out, then remove shift valves.
11. Remove the 4-3 sequence valve keeper by depressing the 4-3 sequence valve, then remove the valve plug, valve and spring.
12. Remove the keeper pin for the damper valve, then remove the valve, and spring.
13. Remove the keeper pin for the line pressure release valve, then remove a disc if one is fitted plus, spring and valve.
14. Adjacent to the BAR valve drive out the roll pin, then remove spring plus ball check valve.
15. Adjacent to the 3-4 shift valve drive out the roll pin, then remove the spring and ball check valve.

Valve Body Assembly

1. Clean the upper and lower valve bodies and all components then dry with compressed air.
2. Inspect valve body ports, holes and cavities for imperfections and wear.
3. Install the locating pin for the detent lever.
4. To the valve body install the S5 damper spring, piston and the retaining pin, then install the 1-2 shift valve, plug and the retaining plate.
5. To the valve body install the 3-4 shift valve and secure with retaining plate, then install the 2-3 shift valve and retaining plate.
6. To the valve body install the 4-3 sequence valve, spring, plug and secure with retaining plate.
7. To the valve body install the nylon ball, then install the two filters for S5 and S6 solenoids.
8. To the lower valve body install the lower valve body gasket, then install the five nylon check balls in the upper valve body in same locations as removed.
9. To the upper valve body install the gasket and the separator plate.
10. Carefully install the upper valve body assembly to the lower valve body assembly, install retaining screws and tighten to specification in order shown.

Valve body upper to lower retaining screws: 15 Nm

11. To valve body assembly install the band apply regulator valve, inner spring, valve, outer spring, plunger and the solenoid sleeves, then install the S4 solenoid and tighten retainer screw to specification.

S4 solenoid retainer screw: 15 Nm

12. To valve body assembly install the clutch apply regulator valve and associated components, (inner spring, valve, outer spring, plunger and the solenoid sleeve) then install the S3 solenoid and tighten retainer screw to specification.

S 3 solenoid retainer screw: 15 Nm

13. To valve body install the solenoid supply valve and spring, then install the No. 6 damper sleeve and components, (spring, plunger, retaining pin and the locating pin) then install the S 6 solenoid.
14. To the valve body install the S2 solenoid (2-3 shift valve solenoid), then install the S1 solenoid (3-4 shift valve solenoid).
15. Install the S5 solenoid and earth wire into position and secure with retaining screw, tighten to specification.

S5 solenoid retainer screw: 15 Nm

16. On the side of the valve body adjacent to the 3-4 shift valve, install the line 70 ball and spring, plus retaining pin.
17. Next to the BAR valve, install the manual feed ball and spring assembly plus retaining pin.
18. The line pressure valve, spring, disc and retaining pin is to be installed next.
19. Install the manual shift valve, then install the detent spring, support plate and screw, tighten to specification.

Detent spring assembly retaining screw: 20 Nm

Install

1. Lift valve body into position, install retaining screws and tighten in order as shown on previous page to specification.

Valve body retaining screws: 15 Nm

2. Connect the manual valve lever link to the manual valve, then check the detent roller is aligned.

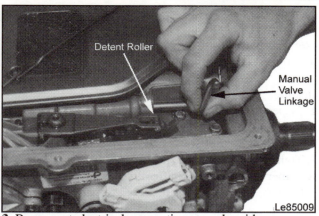

3. Reconnect electrical connections to solenoids.
4. Install the filter into position ensuring to firstly lubricate the 'O' ring, then install the retaining clip.
5. Refit oil pan / sump and a new gasket.
6. Tighten the sump bolts to specification.

Torque Transmission Oil Sump   4.5 Nm

7. Fill transmission with fluid.
8. Remove from safety stands and road test vehicle.

SERVO VALVES
Front Servo
 Remove
1. Remove the circlip retaining servo cover.

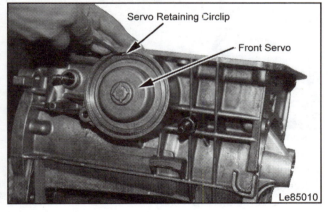

2. Force out the servo piston by screwing in the band adjuster.
3. Remove servo piston and do not slacken off band adjuster until servo piston is back in transmission during installation.

Install
1. Before installation inspect piston and 'O' rings, if damaged or warn replace.
2. Install the servo piston ensuring to lubricate the 'O' rings with transmission fluid. Ensure the strut is engages with piston rod.
3. Apply pressure to piston while loosening band adjuster, then install cover and retaining circlip.
4. Adjust the bands as previously described.
5. Fill transmission with fluid.

Rear Servo
 Remove
1. Place vehicle on safety stands.
2. Place an oil collection tray underneath the transmission.
3. Remove the oil pan / sump, seal and filter.
4. Remove the bolts securing the servo cover to the transmission, then remove the servo assembly.

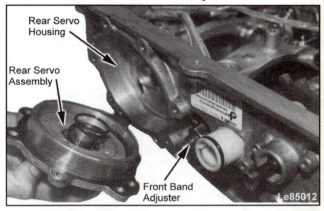

5. Separate the piston from the housing. Remove the gasket and 'O' rings, replace with new ones on assembly.

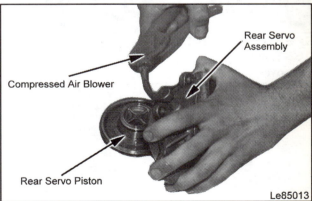

Install
1. Lubricate all 'O' rings, then install assembly into transmission case.
2. Install and tighten cover retaining bolts to specification.

Servo Cover retaining bolts: 20 Nm.

3. The band struts must be positioned.
4. Install filter, sump gasket and sump, then check the band adjustment.

5. Refill with transmission fluid and inspect fluid levels.

COOLER REPLACEMENT

The cooler is located inside the radiator, if the cooler is to be replaced the radiator must also be replaced. See cooling system for radiator replacement.

There is an optional transmission cooler that is mounted in front of the radiator for models that do not have an air-conditioner fitted.

SELECTOR LINKAGE ADJUSTMENT

1. Loosen clamp nut at the slotted rod.
2. Position transmission selector lever in 'D'.
3. Position gear shift lever in 'D', then install the 6mm setting in into the boss on the case passing through the hole in the lever.
4. Hold the selector against its stop in 'D', then tighten clamp nut.
5. Lower vehicle and test.
6. Ensure that engine can be started only in 'PARK' and 'Neutral'. The Park /Neutral/Backup switch is automatically adjusted when linkage is correctly adjusted. It can also be tested for correct operation using a ohm meter.

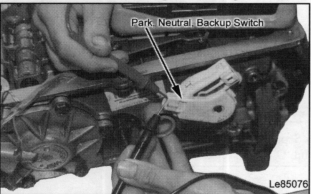

SPEED SENDER UNIT AND FITTING ASSEMBLY

Remove

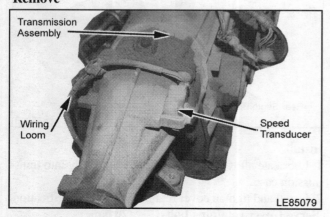

1. Raise rear of vehicle and place on safety stands. Place drip tray beneath speed sender.
2. Disconnect sender unit electrical connector.
3. Remove vehicle speed sender unit by unscrewing.
4. Unscrew bolt securing fitting assembly retainer to extension and remove retainer. Withdraw fitting assembly including driven gear from case extension.

Install

1. Inspect fitting assembly 'O' ring seal and replace it if unsatisfactory.
2. Installation is the reverse of the removal procedure.
3. Tighten retainer bolt to specified torque.

Retainer bolt torque specification: 8 Nm

* The vehicle speed unit is tightened by hand only.

MAJOR REPAIR

TRANSMISSION ASSEMBLY.

Dismantle

1. Remove the converter housing from transmission then install transmission in a transmission cradle on a clean work bench.

2. Remove the oil pan / sump and gasket.
3. Remove the filter retainer and filter, then disconnect the solenoid wires from each solenoid.
4. Remove the manual valve lever to link, then remove the screws securing the valve body.
5. Remove the valve body assembly by pulling down evenly.
6. Remove the circlip, retaining servo cover.
7. Remove servo piston by forcing out by screwing in the band adjuster, then remove servo piston.
8. Remove the bolts securing the rear extension and remove rear extension.

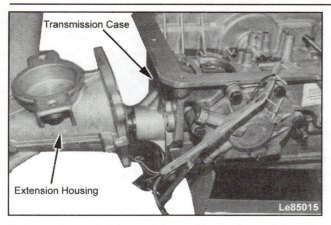

9. Remove speedo drive gear by pushing in the retaining clip and sliding speedo drive gear from shaft.
10. Remove the 'O' ring from the input shaft and remove the oil pump retaining bolts.
11. Using a puller and adaptors remove the pump from the transmission case.

14. Remove the two bolts securing the centre support assembly then remove the circlip for the centre support.
15. From the transmission case remove as an assembly the centre support, 1-2 one way clutch, planetary gears including the output shaft.

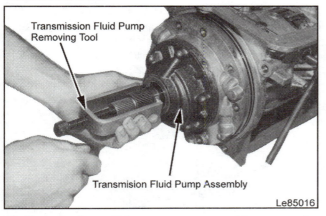
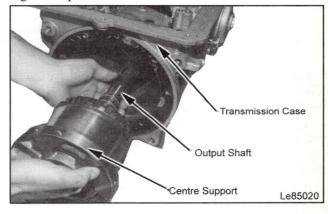

12. From the front of the case, as an assembly remove the input shaft, forward clutch cylinder and overdrive shaft.

16. Remove the bolt securing the parking rod cam plate, then remove the cam plate.
17. From the transmission case remove the rear band struts and rear band.

Transmission Case

1. From the transmission case remove the inhabiter switch, and using the tool E1540 remove the cross shaft seals.

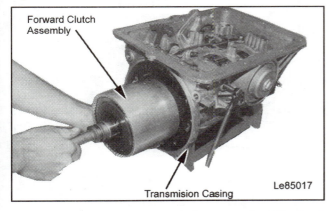
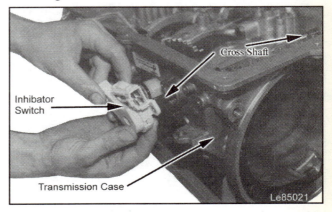

13. Remove from the transmission case the C3 clutch cylinder, sun gears, front band struts and the front band.

2. From the cross shaft remove the cir-clips, release the drive pin from selector quadrant by pulling the shaft.

3. Press the pin from the cross-shaft using special tool E1539, then slide the cross shaft from the transmission case.
4. Remove the park rod and manual valve lever, then disconnect (press in side lugs) the wiring loom plug from the case.
5. From the front of the transmission case disconnect the No. 7 solenoid wire, then retainer for the wiring connector, connector and loom.

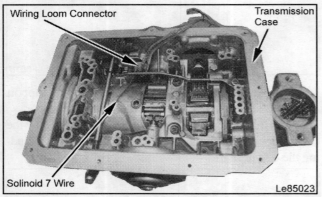

6. From the case remove the parking pawl pivot, pawl and spring.
7. From the case remove the rear servo lever and shaft, then remove the rear servo cover and piston assembly.
8. Remove the release exhaust valve for the front servo, then remove both band adjusters.
9. It is not necessary to remove the park rod lever from the transmission case unless it is being replaced.
Removal of park rod lever.
a) Remove the circlip from the inner most end of the shaft then gently at the outer end of the shaft tap to release from case.
b) Gently punch the pin from the inside of the case, then remove the lever and spring from transmission case.
10. Inspect the output shaft bushing in case, the cooler line fittings and the case for water and damage. Any component damage replace before assembly.

Forward Clutch Cylinder

1. From the input shaft remove the thrust bearing and adjustment shims, then at the front of the clutch cylinder remove the circlip and remove the input shaft.

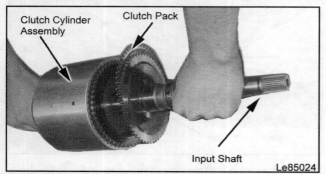

2. Remove the overdrive shaft and the C1 clutch hub assembly, as shown.

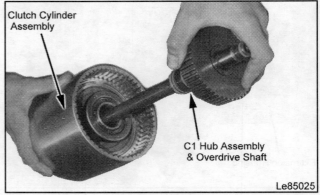

3. From the clutch cylinder remove the C1 clutch plates, then remove the C3 clutch hub circlip and remove clutch hub.
4. From clutch cylinder remove the C2/C4 clutch hub components, then from the C4 hub remove the thrust bearing.
5. Remove the clutch plates for the C2 clutch.
6. From the opposite end of the clutch cylinder remove the C4 clutch sleeve, clutch plates and the two wave washers.

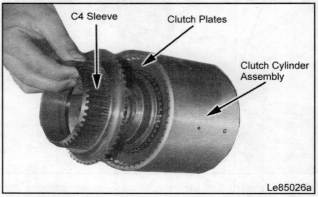

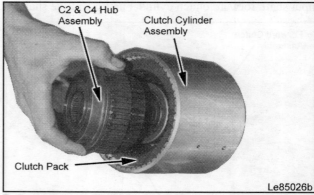

7. Separate the C2 & C4 clutch hubs by rotating one hub clockwise and withdrawing, then remove the 3-4 one way clutch.

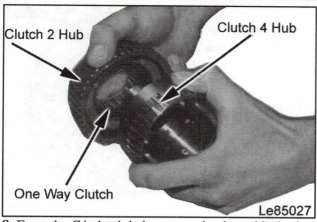

8. From the C4 clutch hub remove the thrust block, then install the clutch cylinder on the special tool E1543 ensuring the C2/C4 end facing up.

9. Compress the piston return spring, then remove the retaining circlip and remove the circlip, keeper and the spring.

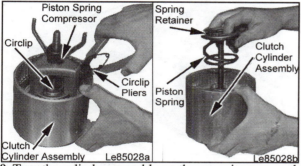

10. Turn the cylinder assembly up the opposite way on the special tool, and remove the C1 clutch piston return spring by compressing the C1 piston return spring, then remove the retaining circlip and remove the circlip, keeper and the spring.

11. Apply compressed air to the apply ports of the cylinder and remove the pistons.

C3 Clutch Cylinder

1. Slide the forward sun gear and thrust bearing away from the assembly.

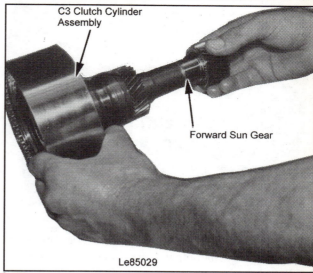

2. Then remove the thrust bearing assemblies, nylon thrust bearing and support, needle thrust bearing and block.

3. Install the clutch cylinder to the tool E1543, then compress the piston return spring and remove the circlip, keeper and spring.

4. Remove the 'O' ring for the reverse sun gear, then remove the cir-clip securing the clutch plates and remove clutch plates.

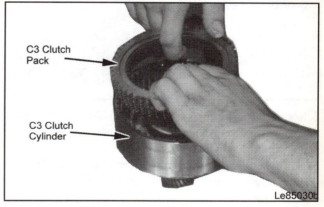

5. Apply compressed air to the apply port on the bearing journals between the iron sealing rings of the cylinder and remove the pistons.

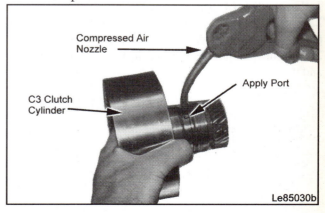

6. Remove the rear (reverse) sun gear.

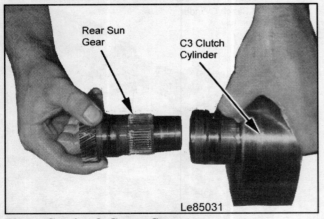

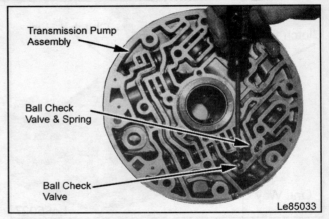

Planet Carrier & Centre Support

1. From the output shaft slide the planet carrier and centre support, then from the output shaft and planet carrier remove the thrust bearings.

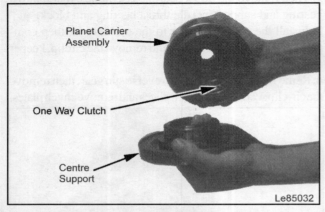

2. Rotate the centre support anticlockwise to release it from the planet carrier, then remove the one way clutch from the planet carrier.
3. From the planet carrier remove the circlip retaining the one way clutch outer race and remove the race.
4 From the planet carrier remove the one way clutch retainer.

Pump

1. Remove the wiring loom, and the No. 7 solenoid.
2. From the cover plate remove the 5 bolts and 5 screws and remove the cover plate.
3. From the pump cover remove the two ball check valves and the spring.

4. From the cover remove the retaining pins securing the 4 valves, then remove the 4 sealing plugs and valves.
5. From the outer edge of the pump cover remove the 'O' ring seal, then remove the inner and outer gears from the pump body.

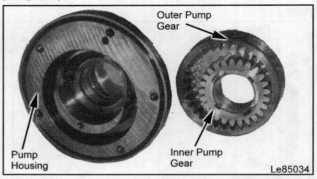

6. From the pump body remove the 'O' ring seal, and the lip seal from the front of the body.

Assemble

1. To the transmission case install all the plugs, fittings and breather, then in any sections requiring sealant apply, sealant. Inspect that any orifices including breather and lube fitting in rear of case are clean and not blocked.
2. Install the BIR valve and spring to the transmission case, then secure in position with circlip.
3. To the transmission case install the rear servo lever and pivot pin.
4. Install the park rod lever, spring and pivot pin into the transmission case, ensuring the lever pivots freely and the spring fully returns the lever.
5. To the transmission case install the parking pawl, spring and pivot pin.
6. To the park lever install the park rod and ensure that the cam collar moves on the rod without catching.
7. From the linkage side of the case start to install the cross shaft, installing the inhibitor switch end first, then install the anti rattle spring to the shaft.
8. Install the manual valve detent lever, ensuring it aligns with the cross shaft bore in the case, then push the shaft through the detent lever until it starts in the opposite side of

the case.

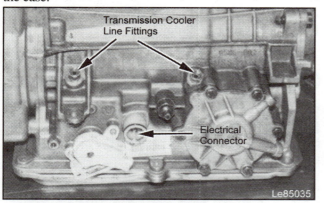

9. Using the special tool E1539 install the detent lever drive pin in the shaft, until the tool bottoms.
10. Install the spring retaining circlip and the end float circlip to the shaft, then using tool E1541 install the cross shaft seals.

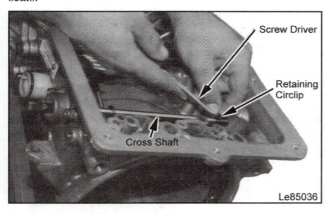

11. Install the inhibitor switch, then inspect the wiring loom for damage then install into case, the S7 solenoid wire is installed behind the park rod and cross shaft, then the S7 solenoid terminal is located in the pump mounting flange at the front.

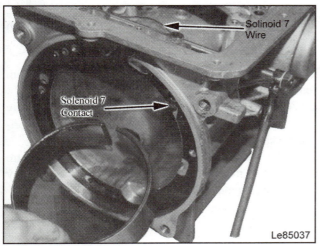

12. Install to the case the ten pin connector, then install the spring retainer, then connect the internal loom to the connector.

Rear Band Assembly

1. Inspect the band for any cracks or deterioration and if damaged replace band, if using a new band insure to soak in transmission fluid for six minutes before assembly.
2. To the transmission case install the rear band, then install the apply strut to the rear band and servo lever.

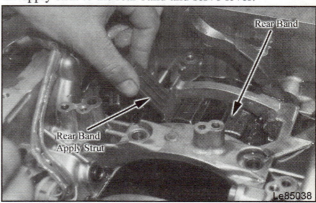

3. To the band install the reaction strut, them install the adjuster screw engaging the strut and on the end of the adjuster install the "C" clip.

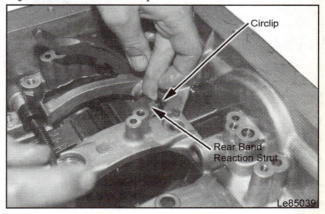

4. Slacken off the band adjustment then install the cam plate and tighten screws to specification.

Cam Plate Retaining Screws: 20 Nm

Output Shaft and Ring Gear Assembly

1. If the output shaft bush is damaged replace the bush, also inspect the ring gear, if damaged replace the ring gear.
2. Inspect the sealing ring grooves for damage, if so, use a small file to remove any burrs. Apply transmission fluid to the sealing ring.
3. Install sealing ring (have the diagonal cut at the top, this will help keep the seal in position) to the output shaft, then install the ring gear to the output shaft and secure with circlip.

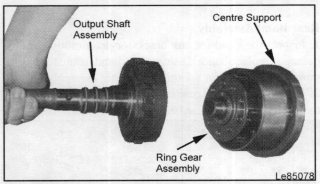

4. To the output shaft install the No. 10 thrust bearing assembly.

5. Carefully install the output shaft assembly into the transmission case, then lubricate the bush and install the speedo drive gear.

Rear Servo Assembly
Inspect the piston 'O' rings and gasket for damage, it is good policy to use new "O" rings and gasket.

1. Fit the three 'O' rings and gasket to cover.
2. Apply transmission fluid to lubricate the servo piston 'O' rings, then install the 'O' rings to the piston and install the piston to the cover, ensuring the 'O' ring is not damaged during compression.
3. To the piston spigot fit and align the spring, then install the servo rod in the spigot and install assembly to transmission case.

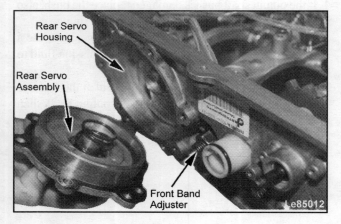

4. Install and tighten retaining bolts to specification. (use loctite 567 or equivalent on bolts)

Rear Servo Cover retaining bolts: **20 Nm**

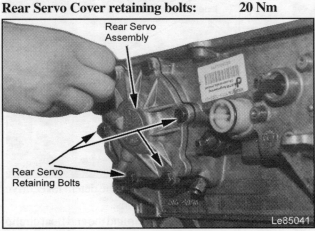

5. Install the wiring loom upwards and retain with clip.

Planet Gear Assembly Carrier and Centre Support
1. Inspect the carrier and planet gear assembly for damage, replace or repair if necessary, also check pinions turn with ease and that the free play is to specification 0.1 - 0.5 mm.

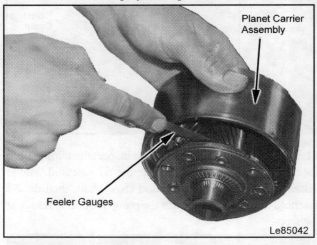

2. With the inner edge facing down install the one way clutch retainer to the carrier, the one way clutch race and sprag assembly must be in excellent condition.

3. Inside the drum install the outer race, then secure with retaining circlip.

4. With the lip edge facing upwards install the one way clutch into the outer race, apply transmission fluid to lubricate the sprags.

5. Ensure the plugs are properly installed to the centre support, then install the centre support into the one way clutch, rotation must be anticlockwise only.

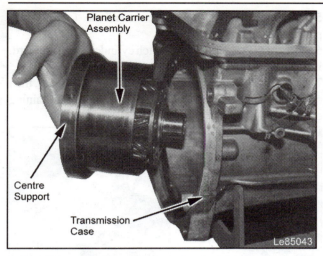

6. Install into the rear of the carrier the No. 9 needle thrust bearing, use petroleum jelly to position and lubricate.
7. To the transmission case install the planet carrier and centre support assembly aligning the bolt holes for the centre support, then loosely install the centre support retaining bolts.
8. Install the retaining circlip, then remove retaining bolts, coat with loctite 222 and reinstall to centre support. Tighten to specification.

Centre Support Retaining Bolts: **25 Nm**

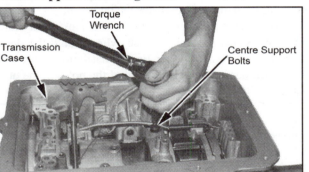

9. Adjust the rear band to specification as described in appropriate section of chapter.

Extension Housing Assembly
1. Inspect the housing rear bushing and replace if required, replace the rear oil seal is also a good policy.
2. Install a new gasket to the extension housing, then install the rear extension and tighten retaining bolts to specification.

Rear Extension Retaining Bolts: **60 Nm**

Front Servo Assembly
1. Apply transmission fluid to the cover 'O' ring and piston 'O' rings, then install the 'O' rings.
2. (85 LE) Apply transmission fluid to sealing rings and install to push rod.
3. To the front servo cover install the piston push rod assembly, do not damage 'O' ring.
4. To the transmission case install the front servo assembly, take care not to damage the 'O' ring.

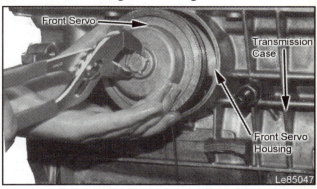

5. Compress the servo cover and install the retaining circlip.

Front Band Assembly
1. Inspect the band for deterioration or damage, if installing a new band it needs to be soaked for 5-6 minutes in transmission fluid.
2. Install the front band adjuster screw to the transmission case, then position the strut retainer on the band.
3. To the transmission case install the front band assembly it must be seated correctly and not caught on the case side.

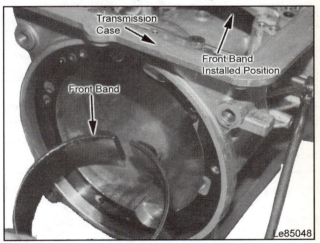

4. Install the reaction strut to its retaining clip, then install the it to the band and adjuster screw.

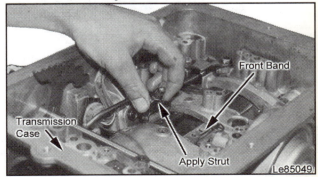

5. Install the apply strut in the retaining clip, and fit the clip

with the front band and servo piston rod as shown.
6. Loosen off the band adjustment to enable the clutch cylinder to be fitted.

C2/C4 Clutch Assembly

\# All cylinder bore feed ducts and piston bleed ducts must be clear and clean.

\# Apply transmission fluid to all 'O' rings and to both pistons, then install the 'O' rings to the inner grooves and the larger 'O' rings to the outer grooves.

\# C2 clutch piston is prone to cracking around centre bore, this will cause pressure to be applied to C4 clutch at the same time and burn out clutches.

1. To the C2 piston fit the C4 piston, ensuring the bleed orifices are aligned and that the C4 piston outer 'O' ring is not damaged.

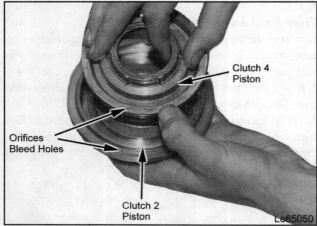

2. With the C2/C4 opening of the clutch cylinder facing upward, then install into the cylinder the C2/C4 piston assembly until the C2 piston enters the inner diameter of the cylinder, ensuring the bleed ducts are aligned with the holes in the outside of the cylinder.

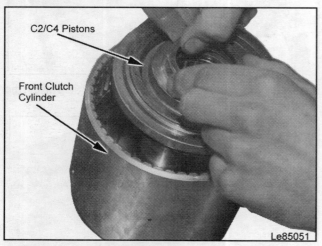

3. To the piston fit the piston return spring and spring retainer, then compress the spring using tool E1543 and install the retaining circlip.

4. Check the C1 piston check valves are operating OK.

5. Lubricate all C1 'O' rings, then install the 'O' rings into position.

6. With the C1 opening of the clutch cylinder facing upward, install into the cylinder the C1 piston assembly.

7. To the piston fit the piston spring and spring retainer, then compress the spring using tool E1543 and install the retaining circlip.

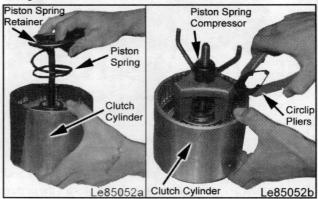

8. To the cylinder install the C2 wave washer with the top of the washer covering one of the C2 piston bleed ducts.

9. Measure the thickness of the flange of the C2 piston, write this down for later use.

10. Into the C2 actuating sleeve install the C4 clutch plates and wave washer starting with a steel plate, ensuring the rounder edge of the steel plates facing down.

11. Position the cylinder horizontally then install the clutch plate and sleeve assembly to the cylinder until the sleeve contacts the C2 wave washer. Ensure that the top of one wave of the washer is aligned with one of the holes in the outer surface of the cylinder.

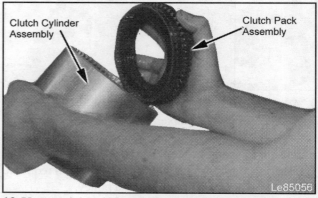

12. Use special tool No. 1545 and vernier callipers to check the C4 clutch pack clearance, pressure plate thickness plus a clearance of 1.4-1.8mm, if not as specified, correct with selective plates.

C4 Clutch Pack Clearance: 6.4 - 6.65mm

BTR 85/91/93/95/97 LE AUTOMATIC TRANSMISSIONS

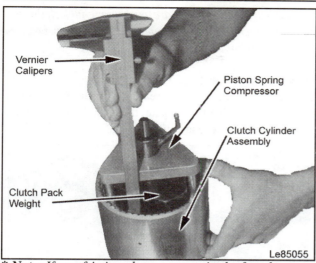

Note: If new friction plates are required, after clearance is checked remove friction plates and soak in transmission fluid for six minutes. Reassemble.

13. Over the inner hub install the thrust plate, then install the C2 clutch plates into the cylinder starting with a friction disc.

14. Using only the weight from special tool No. 1545 check the C2 clutch pack clearance from the friction plate surface to the C3 hub locating step.

C2 Clutch Pack Clearance: 0.8 0 1.05 mm

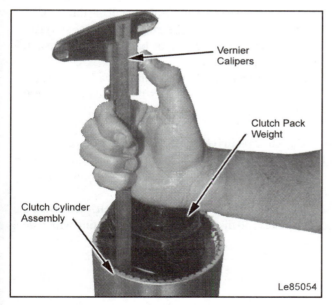

Note: If new friction plates are required, after clearance is checked remove friction plates and soak in transmission fluid for six minutes. Reassemble.

15. Lubricate the 3-4 OWC and the C2 OWC, install the 3-4 OWC then, install the C2 OWC and end caps to the C2 hub.

16. To the C4 hub install the nylon thrust washer aligning the tangs, as shown.

17. Assemble the C4 hub and the C2 clutch and OWC assembly, then check that while looking at the C2 section of the C4/C2 hub assembly the C2 will turn anticlockwise only.

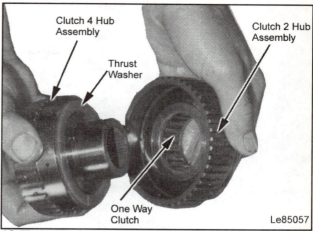

18. Fit the No.5 thrust bearing to the C4 hub, then remove all the C2 clutch plates.

19. Assembly and locate the C2/C4 hub assembly in the C4 clutch plates, then reinstall the C2 clutch plates and C3 hub. Lock these in position with circlip.

C3 Clutch, Reverse Sun Gear & Forward Sun Gear Assemblies

1. Inspect the cylinder ducts are clean, then measure the C3 cylinder bush O.D. and the I.D. of centre support, if not compatible, replace damaged part.

2. Apply transmission fluid to the sealing ring and install into the sealing ring grooves of the C3 cylinder.

3. Check the all surfaces and thrust face of the reverse sun gear, then using new clean transmission fluid lubricate the 'O'ring and install it the reverse sun gear seal groove.

4. To the C3 cylinder install the reverse sun gear, make sure that the 'O' ring is not damaged.

5. Apply new clean transmission fluid to the 'O' rings for the C3 piston, then install the small 'O' ring to the inner groove and larger 'O' ring to the outer groove of the C3 piston.

6. Align and install the C3 piston to the cylinder until the piston fits into the inner diameter of the cylinder.

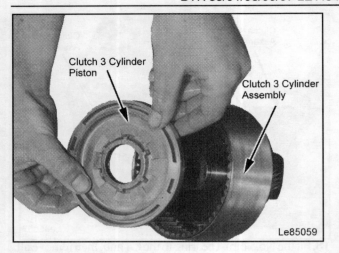

7. To the piston install the spring and spring retainer, then compress the spring using tool E1543 and install the retaining circlip.
8. To the C3 piston face install the C3 wave plate ensuring one top of the wave plate covers one of the piston ducts, then install the clutch plates and discs starting with a steel plate.
9. Fit the pressure plate ensuring it is aligned and the counterbore surface is not against the clutch plates, then install the retaining circlip.
10. Using only the weight from special tool No. 1545 check the clutch clearance as follows:
a) Install the weight to the pressure plate and measure the distance from top of the pressure plate to the end of the cylinder. Record reading.
b) Lift pressure plate up against the circlip, then measure the distance from the top of the pressure plate to the end of the cylinder. Record reading.

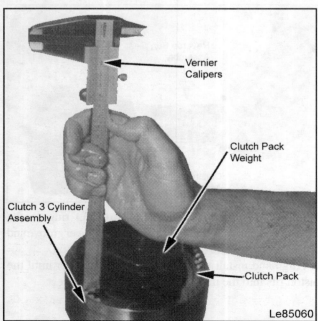

c) Subtract the second reading from the first reading, this new reading is the clutch pack clearance.

Note: If new friction plates are used, after clutch clearance is measured remove friction plates and soak in transmission fluid for six minutes. Reassemble.

Forward Sun Gear & C3 Clutch Pack
1. Install No. 7 needle thrust bearing over the forward sun gear with the washer face to gear, then install the C3 clutch assembly over the forward sun gear shaft.

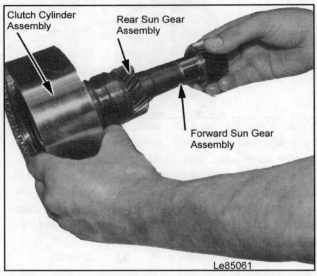

2. Over the reverse sun gear firmly install the thrust plate.
3. Install No. 6 needle thrust bearing over reverse sun gear to the thrust plate, ensuring that the bearing lugs locate in the thrust plate counterbore.
4. To the thrust plate fit the plastic thrust washer, then install the assembly against the No.6 thrust bearing over the forward sun gear.

C1 Clutch Overdrive Shaft & Input Shaft
1. Inspect the surfaces of the overdrive shaft, if faulty repair or replace, also inspect the input shaft, then coat the sealing rings with petroleum jelly.
2. Fit the sealing rings to the overdrive shaft, then install the clutch plates and discs into the cylinder starting with a steel plate.

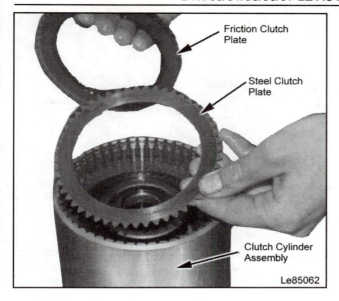

3. Using special tool E1545 check the clutch pack clearance while supporting 2 kg weight, measure the clearance between the friction disc and input shaft locating step. If not correct clearance is not obtained correct using selective plates.

C1 Clutch Pack Clearance: 0.70 - 0.90 mm

Note: If new friction plates are used, after clutch clearance is measured remove friction plates and soak in transmission fluid for six minutes. Reassemble.

4. If the C1 clutch hub fits loosely on the overdrive shaft, the shaft and hub are not repairable and must be replaced.
5. To the cylinder hub install the small nylon thrust spacer coated in petroleum jelly, then carefully without damaging the sealing rings install the overdrive shaft into the C1 cylinder.

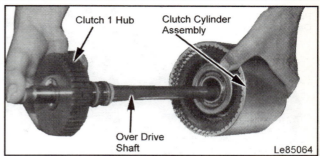

6. Install the bronze C1 hub thrust washer into position, then install the input shaft into the cylinder and retain using the circlips.
7. Apply petroleum jelly to both front and rear sealing rings and then outer 'O' ring, then install to input shaft.
8. To the overdrive shaft install the No. 8 thrust bearing and the spigot fits into the forward sun gear.
9. To the C3 clutch and sungear assembly install the C1/C2/C4 clutch assembly, then install this complete unit into transmission case.

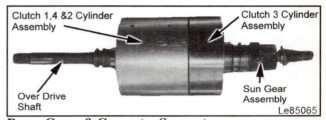

Pump Cover & Converter Support

1. Inspect the pump body for foreign matter or damage, also inspect the bush to ensure it is firmly fixed in the drive gear, then to the pump body install a new seal so it is flush with the front face.
2. Using new clean transmission fluid lubricate the bush, drive and driven gears, then install the driven and drive gears, ensuring the side marked top is facing upward.

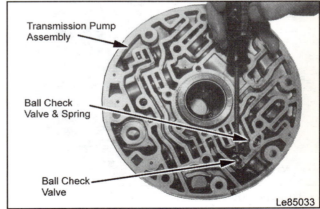

3. Using a straight edge and feeler gauge check the pump end clearance, to adjust clearance if not to specification replacement of gears is required.

Pump End Clearance Specification: 0.04 - 0.018 mm

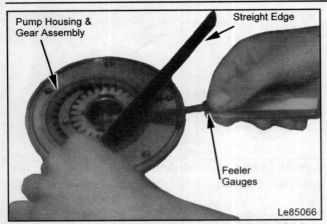

4. Using transmission fluid lubricate the pump body 'O' ring, then install 'O' ring to pump body.

5. Inspect the pump cover for damage and that no foreign matter is in the cover, lubricate all components before installation.

6. To the pump cover install the primary regulator valve, ensuring that the 'O' ring compression is not excessive then secure with retaining pin.

7. To the pump cover install the converter clutch regulator valve and plug, check that the 'O' ring is not being damaged then secure with retaining pin.

8. To the pump cover install the converter clutch control valve, spring and plug, check that the 'O' ring is not being damaged, then secure with retaining pin.

9. To the pump cover install the C1 bias valve spring, valve and plate, check that the 'O' ring is not being damaged, then secure with retaining pin.

10. Install the two steel balls and spring, then install the gasket to the pump cover, apply petroleum jelly to hold the gasket in position.

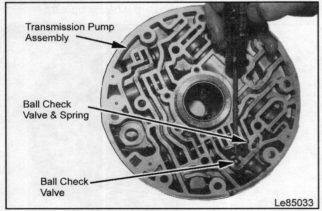

11. To the pump cover install the cover plate and the solenoid wiring retainer, then tighten retaining screws to specification.

Pump Cover Plate Retaining Screws: 18 Nm

12. Install the No. 7 solenoid, wiring must not be able to contact the input shaft or C1/C2 clutch cylinder.

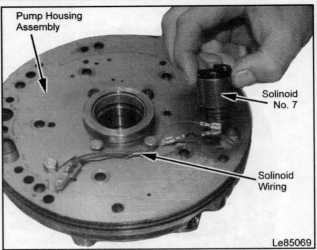

13. Using the alignment tool E1536 install the pump cover, then tighten the retaining bolts and crescent screw to initial specification, make sure the pump cover is aligned. Tighten retaining bolts and crescent screw to final specifications.

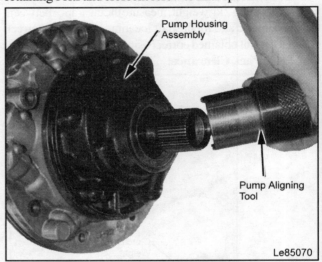

Pump Bolts & Crescent Screw Initial: 14 Nm
Pump to Pump Cover Bolts Final: 27 Nm
Crescent Screw Final: 19 Nm

14. Install pump gasket and pump to the transmission case, take care not to damage the sealing rings. Tighten the retaining bolts to specification.

Pump Assembly to Transmission Case Bolts: 30 Nm

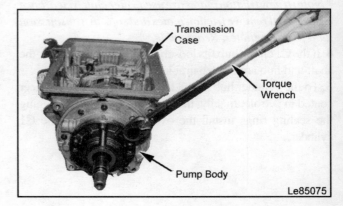

15. Check the transmission end float by:

a) Install a dial indicator to the transmission case with the needle resting on the input shaft.

b) Push down with a weight to the input shaft of approx. 25 kg, then zero the dial indicator.

c) Lever the forward clutch cylinder forward using a screw driver, and record reading.

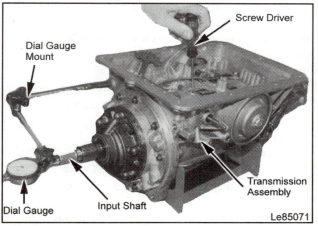

Transmission End Float 85LE: 0.4 - 0.55 mm
Transmission End Float 95LE: 0.5 - 0.65 mm

d) If the end float is greater than specification and is unshimmed, add shims between the No.4 bearing and input shaft bearing to adjust end float.

e) If there are no shims and the end float is under 0.4 mm (85LE) 0.5 mm (95LE) or over 1.65 mm the transmission needs attention by pulling down for inspection. Because components are either installed incorrectly or not within specification.

16. Adjust the front band as described in appropriate section of this chapter.

Valve Body Oil Filter & Pan Assembly

1. Lift the valve body into position, install retaining screws and tighten to specification.

Valve body retaining screws: 15 Nm

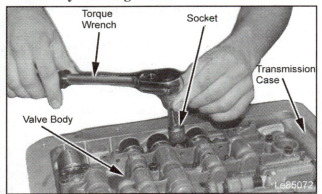

2. Install manual valve lever to manual valve link, then check the alignment of the detent roller.

3. Reconnect electrical connections to solenoids.

4. Using automatic transmission fluid lubricate the 'O' ring for the filter, then install 'O' ring to filter.

5. Install the filter to the valve body assembly, then secure filter with retainer.

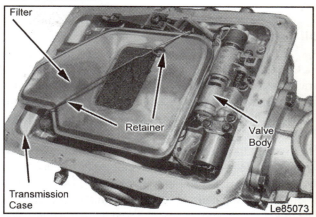

6. Inspect the oil pan and ensure the four magnets are in each of the corners, then install to oil pan gasket to the pan.

7. Install the oil pan to the transmission case and tighten retaining bolts to specification in correct order.

Oil Pan Retaining bolts: 4.5 Nm

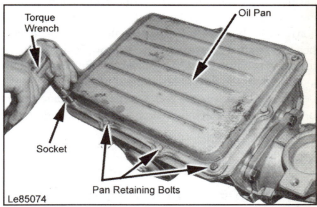

8. Install the torque converter housing to the transmission case, install and tighten the retaining bolts.

Torque Converter Housing Bolts: 60 Nm

PROBLEM SOLVING & DIAGNOSIS

Oil Pressure Check

FLUID CHECK
Transmission fluid changes colour and smell very early in life, these indicators should not necessarily be relied on to diagnose either transmission internal condition nor fluid deterioration.

The chart on the next page shows that a dark brown fluid colour, coupled with a delayed shift pattern, may only indicate that the fluid requires replacement and alone, is not a definite indication of a potential transmission failure.

The fluid level should only be checked when the transmission reaches normal operating temperature (82-93 degrees Celsius).

Transmission fluid colour when new and unused, is red. A red dye is added so that it can be distinguished from other oils and lubricants. The red dye is not an indicator of fluid quality and is not permanent. As the vehicle is driven, the transmission fluid will begin to look darker in colour. The colour will then appear light brown. A DARK brown colour with a distinctively burnt odour MAY indicate fluid deterioration and a need for the fluid to be changed.

Details of transmission oil pressure check procedures refer to 'Oil pressure check information' chart at the start of this chapter.

HYDRAULIC DIAGNOSIS

OIL PRESSURE CHECK INFORMATION
Preliminary Check Procedure
* Check transmission oil level and condition
* Check outside manual linkage and correct
* Check engine tune
* Install oil pressure gauge
* Connect tachometer to engine
* Check oil pressure as follows:

Minimum Kickdown Line Pressure Check
Set the Kickdown cable to specification; and with the brakes applied, take the line pressure readings in the ranges and at the engine r.p.m.'s indicated in the chart below.
Full Kickdown Line Pressure Check
Full Kickdown line pressure readings are obtained by tying or holding the Kickdown cable to the full extent of it's travel; and with the brakes applied, take the line pressure readings in the ranges and at the engine r.p.m.'s indicated in the chart shown later.
NOTICE - Total running time for this combination not to exceed 2 mins.
CAUTION - Brakes must be applied at all times.

Road Test
Drive and Reverse Engagement Shift Check.
1. Start engine.
2. Depress brake pedal.
3. Move gear selector:
   a) 'P' (Park) to 'R' (Reverse)
   b) 'R' (Reverse) to 'N' (Neutral) to 'D' (Drive).
   c) Gear selections should be immediate and not harsh.

Upshifts and Torque Converter Clutch (TCC) Application
With gear selector in 'D' :-
1. Accelerate using a steady increasing throttle application.
2. Note the shift speed point gear engagements for:
   a) 2nd gear
   b) 3rd gear
   c) Overdrive
3. Note the speed shift point for the Torque Converter Clutch (TCC) application. This should occur while in 3rd gear.
IMPORTANT
The TCC will not engage if engine coolant temperature is below 45 degrees Celsius or road speed is to low.

Part Throttle Downshift
At a speed of 70-90 km/h, quickly depress the accelerator to half open position and observe:
   a) TCC releases.
   b) Transmission downshift to 2nd gear immediately.

Full Throttle (Detent) Downshift
Operate the vehicle at 70-90 km/h in 'D', then quickly depress to wide open throttle position and observe:
   a) TCC releases.
   b) Transmission downshift to 2nd gear immediately.

Manual Downshift
1. Operate the vehicle at 70-90 km/h in 'D', then release the accelerator pedal (closed throttle position) and simultaneously move the gear selector to 'D' (Drive), and observe:
   a) TCC release occurs at zero throttle.
   b) Transmission downshift to 2nd gear immediately.
   c) Engine should slow vehicle.
2. Operate the vehicle at 70-80 km/h in 'D'.
Release the accelerator pedal and simultaneously move the gear selector '2' (second) gear position, and observe:
   a) TCC release occurs at zero throttle.
   b) Transmission downshift to 2nd gear immediately.
   c) Engine should slow vehicle.
3. Move gear selector to 'D' and accelerate to 40 km/h Release the accelerator pedal (closed throttle position) and simultaneously move the gear selector to '1' (first) gear and observe:
   a) Transmission downshift to 1st gear immediately.
   b) Engine should slow vehicle.

Coastdown Downshift

1. With the gear selector in 'D', accelerate to engage 4th gear with TCC applied (approx. 75km/h).
2. Release the accelerator pedal (closed throttle position) and lightly apply the brakes to observe:
   a) TCC release occurs at zero throttle.
   b) The point at which downshift occurs.

Manual Gear Range Selection.

Manual Third "D".
1. With vehicle stopped, place gear selector in 'D' (Drive) and accelerate to observe:
   a) The first to second gear shift point.
   b) The second to third gear shift point.

Manual Second (2).
1. With vehicle stopped, place gear selector in '2' (second) and accelerate to observe:
   a) The first to second gear shift point.
2. Accelerate to 60 km/h and observe:
   a) That a second to third gear shift does not occur.
   b) That TCC does not engage.

Manual First (1)
1. With vehicle stopped, place gear selector in '1' (first) and accelerate to 40 km/h and observe:
   a) That no upshift occurs.
   b) That TCC does not engage.

Reverse.
1. With vehicle stopped. Place gear selector in 'R' (Reverse) and slowly accelerate to observe reverse gear operation.

* This publication does not include all possible throttle positions and the corresponding shift point information. Actual shift points will vary in accordance with transmission build variation.

Torque Converter Clutch Diagnosis

Functional Check Procedure
1. Install a tachometer.
2. Operate the vehicle until operating temperature is reached.
3. Drive vehicle at 80-88 km/h with light throttle (road load)
4. Release the throttle to allow the TCC to disengage, then reapply throttle slowly and notice if engine speed drops.

Torque Converter Evaluation

Torque Converter Stator
The torque converter stator roller clutch can have one of two different type malfunctions:
a) Stator assembly freewheels in both directions.
b) Stator assembly remains locked up at all times.

Condition A:- Poor Acceleration, Low Speed
The vehicle tends to have poor acceleration from a standstill. The engine tune is correct and the transmission is in first (1st) gear when starting out.
Checking for poor performance in 'D' (Drive) and 'R' (Reverse) will help determine if the stator is free wheeling at all times.

Condition B:- Poor Acceleration, High Speed
Engine rpm and car speed limited or restricted at high speeds. Performance when accelerating from a standstill is normal.
Engine may overheat. Visual examination of the converter may reveal a blue colour from over heating.
If converter has been removed, the stator roller clutch can be checked by inserting a finger into the splined inner race of the roller clutch and trying to turn the race in both directions. The inner race should turn freely clockwise, but not turn or be very difficult to turn counter-clockwise.

The Converter Should be Replaced if:-
Leaks externally, such as the hub weld area.
Converter has an imbalance which can not be corrected.
Converter is contaminated with engine coolant containing anti freeze.

The Converter Should Not be Replaced if:-
The oil has an odour, is discoloured, and there is no evidence of metal or clutch facing particles.
The threads in one or more of the converter bolt holes are damaged. Correct with thread insert.

Harsh Gear Change

No S5 solenoid controls shift pressures between gears and may cause harsh shifting if not operating correctly. Replacement of solenoid is only option as cleaning is not possible with solenoid.

Tightening Sequence For Valve Body To Case Bolts LE85000

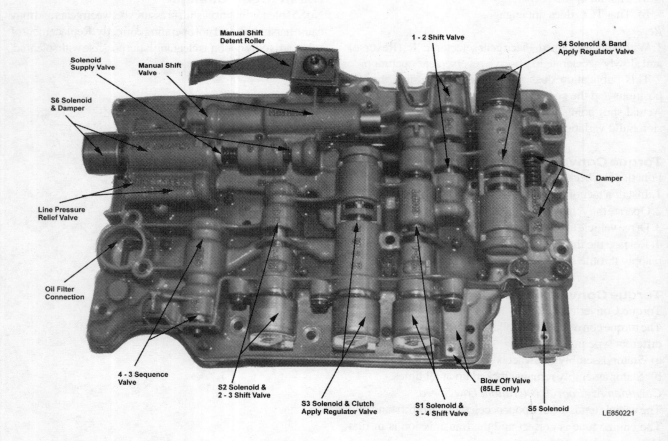

EA/ED SPECIFICATIONS

TRANSMISSION
Application & Code:
85LE	6 Cylinder	90 DA 7000 AA
91LE	6 Cylinder (XR6)	91 DA 7000 AA/BA
95LE	8 Cylinder	91 DA 7000 CA

Lubricant: 10.0 litres TQ95 (castrol)
(including converter)

Gear Ratios:
Reverse	2.09:1
Fourth	0.68:1
Third	1.00:1
Second	1.45:1
First	2.39:1

CONVERTER:
Stall Speed:
85LE	1750 - 1950 rpm.
91LE	2000 - 2200 rpm.
95LE	2000 - 2400 rpm.

Mean Diameter of Fluid Circuit: 279.4
Torque Multiplication: 2.1 (max)

GEAR TRAIN END FLOAT
85 LE	0.40 - 0.55 mm
91/95 LE	0.50 - 0.65 mm

GEAR SET PINION END FLOAT
All Transmissions 0.10 - 0.50 mm

CLUTCH PLATES
	Steel		Composition
C1	5	*2	5
C2	4	*2	5
C3	4	*2	4
C4	4	*1	3

* Number of selective thickness steel plates to achieve specified clutch pack clearance.

LINE PRESSURE (HOT)
	85LE	91/95LE
Idle - Drive	500 - 700	450 - 750
Stall - Drive	1425 - 1750	1400 - 1800
Idle - Reverse	620 - 1050	700 - 1200
Stall - Reverse	1850 - 2100	1970 - 2220

SHIFT SPEEDS

Economy Mode 3.9 Litre MPEFI 3.23:1 Diff Ratio
Shift	0% throttle	40% throttle	100% throttle
1-2	13	25	65
2-3	23	51	109
3-4	38	81	160
L-U	69	109	163

Performance Mode 3.9 Litre MPEFI 3.23:1 Diff Ratio
Shift	0% throttle	40% throttle	100% throttle
1-2	13	44	69
2-3	27	76	114
3-4	39	106	161
L-U	75	126	163

Economy Mode 3.9 Litre EFI 3.08:1 Diff Ratio
Shift	0% throttle	40% throttle	100% throttle
1-2	14	21	65
2-3	22	43	110
3-4	38	70	166
L-U	57	98	169

Performance Mode 3.9 Litre EFI 3.08:1 Diff Ratio
Shift	0% throttle	40% throttle	100% throttle
1-2	14	38	69
2-3	24	68	114
3-4	41	105	166
L-U	72	127	171

Economy Mode 4.0 Litre MPEFI 3.27:1 Diff Ratio (XR6 3.45:1 Diff Ratio)
Shift	0% throttle	40% throttle	100% throttle
1-2	13(13)	28(28)	65(63)
2-3	23(22)	58(58)	109(107)
3-4	35(35)	85(85)	160(149)
L-U	82(80)	109(109)	163(151)

Performance Mode 4.0 Litre MPEFI 3.27:1 Diff Ratio (XR6 3.45:1 Diff Ratio)
Shift	0% throttle	40% throttle	100% throttle
1-2	15(15)	48(48)	69(65)
2-3	29(29)	84(83)	114(109)
3-4	44(44)	115(115)	162(153)
L-U	84(82)	162(153)	163(163)

Economy Mode 5.0 Litre MPEFI 3.27:1 Diff Ratio
Shift	0% throttle	40% throttle	100% throttle
1-2	14	30	66
2-3	24	57	111
3-4	39	83	160
L-U	68	107	168

Performance Mode 5.0 Litre MPEFI 3.27:1 Diff Ratio
Shift	0% throttle	40% throttle	100% throttle
1-2	14	45	68
2-3	28	78	117
3-4	41	109	162
L-U	77	129	175

KICKDOWN MAXIMUM SPEEDS (km/h)

85 LE	Shift	Economy Mode	Performance Mode
	4-3	152	156
	4-2	99	102
	4-1	53	55
	3-2	99	102
	3-1	53	55
	2-1	53	55

95 LE	Shift	Economy Mode	Performance Mode
	4-3	149	151
	4-2	102	108
	4-1	50	50
	3-2	102	108
	3-1	50	50
	2-1	50	50

91 LE (XR6)	Shift	Economy Mode	Performance Mode
	4-3	144 (140)	151 (150)
	4-2	102 (100)	102 (102)
	4-1	55 (55)	55 (55)
	3-2	102 (100)	103 (102)
	3-1	55 (55)	55 (55)
	2-1	55 (55)	55 (55)

MANUAL DOWNSHIFT MAXIMUM SPEEDS

85LE (downshifts are inhibited above these speeds. km/h)
- Manual 2-1   60
- Manual 3-2   115
- Manual 4-3   145 (MPEFI)   120 (EFI)

95LE (downshifts are inhibited above these speeds. km/h)
- Manual 2-1   60
- Manual 3-2   115
- Manual 4-3   165
- Manual 4-2   87 (direct 4-2)
- 87 & 115 (4-3-2 sequence)

91LE (downshifts are inhibited above these speeds. km/h)
- Manual 2-1   59
- Manual 3-2   116
- Manual 4-3   160
- Manual 4-2   87 (direct 4-2)
- 87 & 115 (4-3-2 sequence)

91/95LE	Gear	Idle	Stall
	Drive	450-750	1400-1800
	Reverse	700-1200	1970-2220

TORQUE CONVERTER:

Stall Speed	R.P.M.
85LE	1750-1950
91LE	2000-2200
95LE	2000-2400

Torque Specifications

DESCRIPTION	Nm
Converter Housing to Engine	60
Transmission Case to Converter Housing	60
Extension Housing to Transmission	60
Converter to Flywheel/Drive plate	60
Converter Housing Lower Cover to Housing	15
Converter housing to Engine Brace	40
Engine Brace to Cylinder Block	40
Transmission Oil Pan (Sump)	4.5
Valve Body to Transmission Case	15
Upper Valve Body to Lower Valve Body	15
On/Off Solenoids Valve Body	15
Detent Spring	20
Rear Servo Cover	20
Band Adjusting Screw Locknut to Case	40
Fluid Cooler Line to Case	16
Fluid Cooler Line to Radiator	20
Fluid Cooler Line Tube Nuts	20
Front Pump to Case	30
Pump to pump cover	25
Cover Plate to Pump Cover	18
Cover Plate to Crescent	18
Centre Support to Case	25
Parking Prawl	20
Speedo Transducer	8
Line Pressure Take Off Plug	5

EF / EL & AU / AUII SPECIFICATIONS

TRANSMISSION
Application:	93LE	6 Cylinder
	97LE	8 Cylinder
Lubricant:	10.0 litres	TQ95 (castrol)
(including converter)		
Gear Ratios:	Reverse	2.09:1
	Fourth	0.68:1
	Third	1.00:1
	Second	1.45:1
	First	2.39:1

CONVERTER
Stall Speed:	93LE	2000 - 2200 rpm.
	97LE	2000 - 2400 rpm.
Mean Diameter of Fluid Circuit:		279.4
Torque Multiplication:		2.1 (max)

GEAR TRAIN END FLOAT
91/95 LE   0.50 - 0.65 mm

GEAR SET PINION END FLOAT
All Transmissions   0.10 - 0.50 mm

CLUTCH PLATES
	Steel		Composition
C1	5	*2	5
C2	4	*2	5
C3	4	*2	4
C4	4	*1	3

* Number of selective thickness steel plates to achieve specified clutch pack clearance.

LINE PRESSURE (HOT)   93/97LE
Idle- Drive	450 - 750
Stall- Drive	1400 - 1800
Idle- Reverse	700 - 1200
Stall- Reverse	1970 - 2220

SHIFT SPEEDS

Economy Mode (km/h)   4.0 Litre MPEFI
(except column shift wagon, Fairlane and LTD)

Shift	0% throttle	40% throttle	100% throttle
1-2	15	26	73
2-3	22	54	123
3-4	70	101	175
M3L-U	42	64	123
3L-U	42	64	123

Normal Mode (km/h)   4.0 Litre MPEFI
(except column shift wagon, Fairlane and LTD)

Shift	0% throttle	40% throttle	100% throttle
1-2	15	50	71
2-3	27	85	129
3-4	60	117	179
M3L-U	54	92	129
4L-U	88	120	179

Economy Mode (km/h)   4.0 Litre MPEFI
(column shift wagon, Fairlane and LTD)

Shift	0% throttle	40% throttle	100% throttle
1-2	15	26	73
2-3	22	57	123
3L-U	37	90	175
M3L-U	42	64	123
4L-U	85	105	175

Normal Mode (km/h)   4.0 Litre MPEFI
(except column shift wagon, Fairlane and LTD)

Shift	0% throttle	40% throttle	100% throttle
1-2	15	50	71
2-3	27	85	129
3-4	60	117	179
M3L-U	54	92	129
4L-U	88	120	179

Economy Mode (km/h)   5.0 Litre SEFI

Shift	0% throttle	40% throttle	100% throttle
1-2	14	29	65
2-3	23	56	108
3-4	38	81	156
4L-U	61	104	163

Normal Mode (km/h)   5.0 Litre SEFI

Shift	0% throttle	40% throttle	100% throttle
1-2	14	44	66
2-3	27	76	114
3-4	39	106	158
4L-U	72	111	170

Economy Mode (km/h)   I6HO (EF / EL)

Shift	0% throttle	40% throttle	100% throttle
1-2	15	31	64
2-3	23	58	107
M3L-U	60	60	107
3-4	36	86	152
4L-U	77	96	152

BTR 85/91/93/95/97 LE AUTOMATIC TRANSMISSIONS

Normal Mode (km/h) I6HO (EF / EL)

Shift	0% throttle	40% throttle	100% throttle
1-2	15	47	67
2-3	31	82	114
M3L-U	60	82	114
3-4	45	118	163
4L-U	84	126	175

Economy Mode (km/h) XR6 & XR8 (AU / AUII)

Shift	0% throttle	40% throttle	100% throttle
1-2	13	28	59
2-3	23	54	104
3-4	37	78	102
L-U	63	102	160

Normal Mode (km/h) XR6 & XR8 (AU / AUII)

Shift	0% throttle	40% throttle	100% throttle
1-2	13	42	67
2-3	27	74	108
3-4	39	104	122
L-U	73	122	180

KICKDOWN MAXIMUM SPEEDS (km/h)

93 LE	Shift	Economy Mode	Normal Mode
	4-3	147	154
	4-2	106	112
	4-1	55	55
	3-2	106	112
	3-1	55	55
	2-1	55	55

97 LE	Shift	Economy Mode	Normal Mode
	4-3	149	151
	4-2	102	108
	4-1	57	57
	3-2	102	108
	3-1	57	57
	2-1	57	57

93 LE (I6HO)	Shift	Economy Mode	Normal Mode
	4-3	149	159
	4-2	104	108
	4-1	58	58
	3-2	104	108
	3-1	58	58
	2-1	58	58

MANUAL DOWNSHIFT MAXIMUM SPEEDS

93LE (downshifts are inhibited above these speeds. km/h)

Manual 2-1	75
Manual 3-2	116
Manual 4-3	160
Manual 4-2	87 (direct 4-2)
	115 (4-3-2 sequence)

97LE (downshifts are inhibited above these speeds. km/h)

Manual 2-1	75
Manual 3-2	115
Manual 4-3	165
Manual 4-2	87 (direct 4-2)
	115 (4-3-2 sequence)

TORQUE CONVERTER:

Stall Speed	R.P.M.
93LE	2000-2200
97LE	2000-2400

Torque Specifications

DESCRIPTION	Nm
Converter Housing to Engine	60
Transmission Case to Converter Housing	54-68
Extension Housing to Transmission	54-68
Converter to Flywheel/Drive plate	60
Converter Housing Lower Cover to Housing	24-34
Converter housing to Engine Brace	40
Engine Brace to Cylinder Block	40
Transmission Oil Pan (Sump)	4-6
Valve Body to Transmission Case	8-13
Upper Valve Body to Lower Valve Body	11-16
On/Off Solenoids Valve Body	8-12
Detent Spring	20-22
Rear Servo Cover	20
Band Adjusting Screw Locknut to Case	40
Fluid Cooler Line to Case	16
Fluid Cooler Line to Radiator	20
Fluid Cooler Line Tube Nuts	20
Front Pump to Case	30
Pump to pump cover	24-27
Cover Plate to Pump Cover	18
Cover Plate to Crescent	16-19
Centre Support to Case	20-27
Parking Prawl	16-22
Speedo Transducer	8
Line Pressure Take Off Plug	6-9

3 spd. PARTIAL SYNCHRONIZED MANUAL TRANSMISSION

Subject	Page
GENERAL INFORMATION	**193**
Service Information	193
Recommended Lubricant	193
Checking Transmission Lubricant Level	193
Draining & Refilling Transmission	194
MAINTENANCE	**194**
Transmission Extension Seal	**194**
Removal	194
Installation	194
MAJOR SERVICE REPAIRS	**194**
Dismantle	194
Clean and Inspect Transmission	196
Synchronizers	**196**
Dismantle	196
Assemble	197
Cluster Gear & Countershaft	197
Assemble	197
Assemble Transmission	197
PROBLEM DIAGNOSIS	**200**
SPECIFICATIONS	**200**
TORQUE WRENCH SPECIFICATIONS	**200**

GENERAL INFORMATION

Ford used a Borg Warner 3 spd. Partial Synchronized manual transmission on their XK (1960) to XA (1973) series vehicles.

The three speed manual transmission is a Borg Warner model 0501 series, this was the standard manual transmission for many of the six cylinder vehicles, also in particular commercials such as utilities and vans and was only available as column shift.

SERVICE INFORMATION
Attached to the left-hand side of the transmission extension, is a tag which provides the transmission serial No. and assembly part No. These numbers provide coded information which is relevant to transmission application and replacement part interpretation, and should be referred to when ordering replacement parts.

Recommended Lubricant

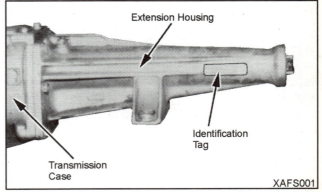

For Borg Warner 3 spd. partial synchronized manual transmission is ESW-M2C37 SAE 30.
The transmission lubricant capacity is: 1.9 Litres

Checking Transmission Lubricant Level.
To check level, remove filler plug on the side of transmission case. The level is correct when lubricant is at bottom of plug hole.

3 spd. PARTIAL SYNCHRONIZED MANUAL TRANSMISSION

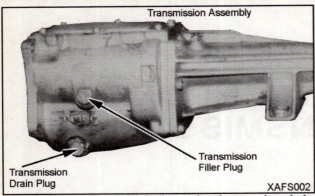

* Ensure that the vehicle is on level ground and the transmission is cold.

Draining and Refilling Transmission
Periodic lubricant changes are not necessary. The lubricant must be replaced when overhauling the transmission or when operating the vehicle under severe driving conditions

MAINTENANCE

TRANSMISSION EXTENSION SEAL
Removal
1. Disconnect battery earth lead and raise vehicle (front and rear) and support on safety stands.
2.(a) Remove propeller shaft.
(b) Place a drain tray beneath transmission extension.
3. Remove seal using seal remover.

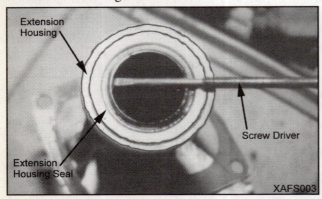

4.(a) Inspect seal lip surface on slip yoke of propeller shaft for damage.
(b) Clean (or replace) as necessary.

Installation
Installation of the seal is the reverse of REMOVAL procedures, noting the following points:
1.(a) Apply a little transmission lubricant to seal lip.
(b) Install seal into the extension with a seal insertion tool.
(c) Torque all bolts to specification.
2. Check transmission lubricant level as previously described in this Chapter.

MAJOR SERVICE REPAIRS

TRANSMISSION ASSEMBLY
DISMANTLE
1. Thoroughly clean exterior of transmission assembly.
2.(a) Remove transmission drain plug with a socket.
(b) Allow transmission lubricant to drain into a container. The drain plug is located on the lower left-hand side of the transmission case.
3. Withdraw speedo driven gear assembly from the transmission extension.
4. Withdraw the clutch folk and throw out bearing, then the bell housing from the transmission casing.

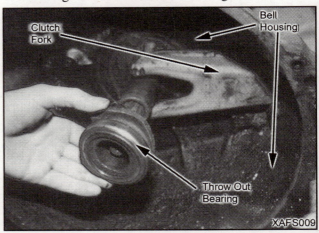

5. Release the extension housing retaining bolts then withdraw the extension housing.

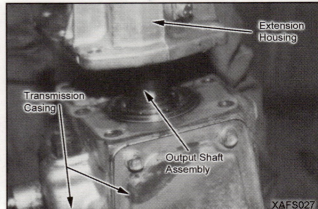

6. Release speedo drive gear clip. (Depress speedometer drive gear clip to remove.)

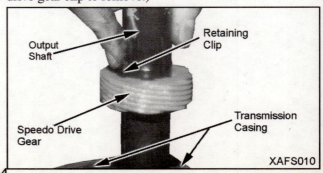

3 spd. PARTIAL SYNCHRONIZED MANUAL TRANSMISSION

7. Release the top inspection cover plate and withdraw.
8.(a) Withdraw front maindrive gear bearing retainer (3 attaching cap screws) to transmission case.

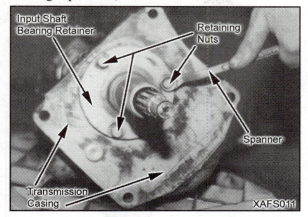

(b) Carefully lever bearing retainer from transmission case with a screwdriver, to break retainer to case seal.
9.(a) Use a soft drift to knock the countershaft through from the front to allow the lock plate to be removed.
(b) Slide the lock plate from the counter shaft and reverse idler gear shaft.
(c) Push countershaft out through rear of case with dummy countershaft tool.

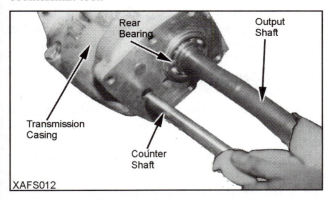

(d) Lower the countershaft and dummy shaft to the case bottom.
10.(a) Pull out input shaft from front of case.
(b) Withdraw third gear synchronizer ring.
11. Release the rear (output shaft) bearing outer circlip.
12. Move second and third speed gearshift cam into third gear position.
13.(a) Knock out taper pins from each gearshift camshaft (underneath transmission).

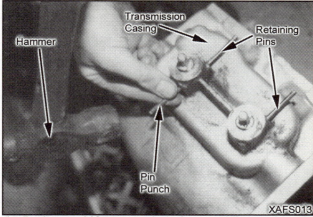

(b) Push gearshift cam and shaft assemblies against the inside of the case.
14.(a) Push the output shaft assembly forward so that the output shaft bearing moves through into the gear case.
(b) Move the mainshaft assembly away from the gearshift forks.
15.(a) Move the first and reverse sleeve and gear forward (do not move first and reverse gearshift fork) into first speed position.
(b) Withdraw first and reverse gearshift fork.
(c) Withdraw second and third gearshift fork.
16. Move the second and third speed synchro outer sleeve rearwards into second gear position.
17.(a) Withdraw output shaft assembly through top of gear case.
(b) Align input shaft end of out put shaft with the cut out section in the casing.

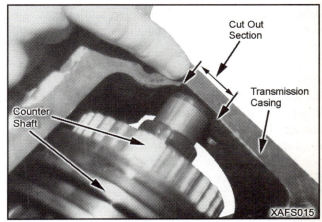

19.(a) Knock out reverse idler gear and cluster gear assembly.
(b) Lift the counter shaft assembly from the transmission casing.

3 spd. PARTIAL SYNCHRONIZED MANUAL TRANSMISSION

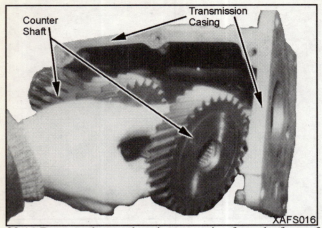

20.(a) Remove the synchronizer snap ring from the front of the output shaft and slide off the second and third speed synchronizer assembly and the second gear with its blocker ring.
(b) Take note of the synchronizer assembly hub end positions to help assembly.
21.(a) Withdraw the output shaft bearing snap ring and spacer from the output shaft
(b) Slide the bearing from the output shaft.
22. Withdraw first and reverse slide gear from output shaft.
23. Clean and inspect all components, replace damaged components.

Clean and Inspect Transmission
Thoroughly wash all components in a suitable cleaning solvent. Dry components with clean, dry compressed air.
1. Inspect the following components for any cracks or defects that may cause lubricant leakage: transmission case, rear extension, case cover and maindrive gear bearing retainer.
2. Check all machined faces for burrs, and (if possible), dress them off with a fine mill file.
3. Clean magnet located in the bottom of transmission case.
4.(a) Inspect all roller and needle bearing assemblies closely, and replace if there is any sign of wear.
(b) Inspect mainshaft and internal surfaces of gears where needle bearings come in contact.
5. Inspect all gears for excessive wear, chips or cracks.

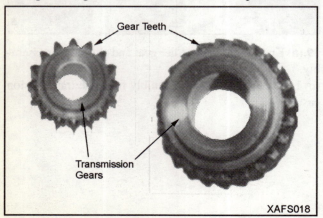

Replace any that are worn or damaged.
6. Check synchronizer teeth on blocking rings and gears. Replace any components that is worn or damaged.
7.(a) Inspect synchronizer hubs, sleeves, inserts and springs for damage or war.
(b) Check that the synchronizer sleeves slide freely on their hubs.
(c) Replace any worn component.
8. Inspect reverse idler gear shaft and replace if worn.

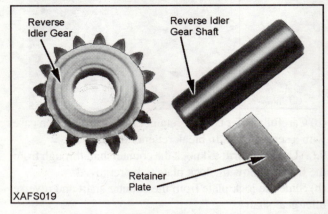

9. Check all thrust washers and replace any that are worn.
10. Inspect all shift control component contact and sliding surfaces for wear, scratches, projections of other damage.
11. Inspect breather (located in transmission extension) to make sure it is not blocked.

SYNCHRONIZERS
Dismantle
* Before dismantling any synchronizers, paint or etch an alignment mark on each of the synchronizer sleeves and hubs.
* Do not mix parts from one synchronizer assembly to another.

2nd & 3rd Speed Synchronizer Assembly
1. Remove both synchronizer springs with a screwdriver.
2. Separate sleeve from hub and remove the 3 synchronizer inserts.

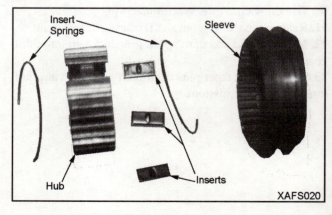

196

3 spd. PARTIAL SYNCHRONIZED MANUAL TRANSMISSION

Assemble
2nd & 3rd Speed Synchronizer Assembly
1. Fit lubricated synchronizer sleeve to inner hub with sleeve selector groove and hub inner spline protrusion at opposite ends.
2. Slide sleeve across hub until three second and third speed shift plates can be fitted into the slots in the inner hub.
3. Fit two second and third speed syncro springs under the shift plates behind the pads.

*Note: The spring tangs should be located in the same shift plate. The springs should be installed with the free ends opposite.

CLUSTER GEAR & COUNTERSHAFT
Assemble

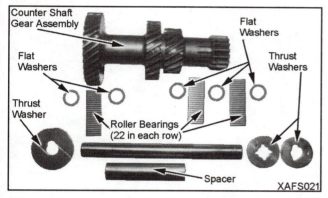

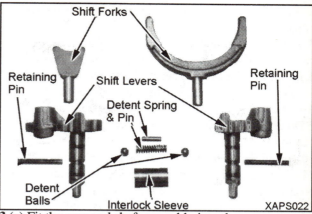

1. Insert dummy countershaft and spacer into cluster gear.
2.(a) Fit a set of 22 lubricated needle rollers at the front (largest gear end) of the cluster.
(b) Fit two sets of 22 lubricated needle rollers at either end of the cluster.
(c) Separate the rollers with cluster gear needle roller retainer washer.
3. Fit cluster gear needle roller retainer washers at each end of the dummy countershaft, together with two thrust washers at the rear (small steel washer to cluster, engage tangs with slots in gears) (small bimetal to case, engage tangs with slot in case) of the cluster gear, and one thrust washer (large bimetal engage tang with slot in case) at the front end of the gear.
* These may be retained with grease.

ASSEMBLE TRANSMISSION.
* On assembly, coat all bearing surfaces, shafts, gears, blocking rings, cones and oil seals with transmission lubricant.

1.(a) Hold 1 ball in rear of interlock sleeve with the use of grease.
(b) Fit sleeve into case.
2.(a) Fit cam and shaft assembly to case in neutral position.
(b) Ensure that the interlock sleeve ball is in extended detent notch of the cam.

3.(a) Fit the cam and shaft assembly into the case.
(b) Push the cam against the side of the case so that the interlock sleeve hole is not blocked.
4.(a) Fit interlock pin, spring and second ball.
(b) Move the cam and shaft assembly into third gear position, so that extended detent notch of the cam retains the ball and spring.
5.(a) Install lubricated reverse idler gear and bush assembly and shaft with bevelled ends of the gear teeth forward.
(b) Shaft must be inserted so that the locking groove is flush with the outside face of the gear case, and face towards the cluster gear shaft hole.

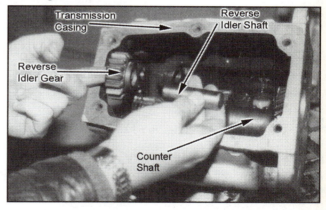

6.(a) Assemble cluster gear, dummy countershaft and bearings as previously outlined
(b) Place the cluster assembly in the bottom of the gear case.

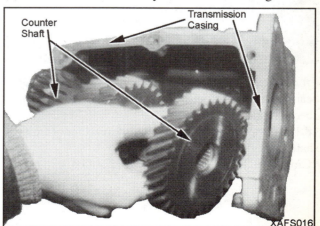

(c) Ensuring that the tabs of the thrust washers fit the grooves of the case.

7. Assemble second and third speed synchro assembly as previously described.

8. Fit 1st and reverse slide gear to the output shaft assembly.

9.(a) Install output shaft bearing, spacer and snap ring.

(b) Fit appropiate snap ring to achieve specifications

* Do not fit snap ring to outside diameter of output shaft bearing.

10. Install 2nd speed gear block ring.

11.(a) Install the output shaft with the inner hub inner spline protrusion facing the front of the transmission case.

(b) Install snap ring and check end float specification then remove snap ring.

12. Shift 2nd & 3rd synchro sleeve to engage 2nd drive gear.

14.(a) Position the gearshift camshafts to the side of the case, so that 3rd and neutral are still held by the cams.

(b) Tilt the mainshaft away from the camshafts.

15.(a) Move the gear shift forks into position in the camshaft assembly.

(b) Move the output shaft assembly so the 2nd and 3rd speed fork line up with the second and third speed synchro sleeve, moving it along until the groove in the 1st reverse fork lines up with the slide gear.

(c) Lift the output shaft assembly to engage the forks, in the synchro sleeve and sliding gear.

16. Move the camshafts into position and fit the tapered retaining pins into the case.

17.(a) Slide the output shaft backwards into the rear bearing until the bearing outer snap ring can be fitted.

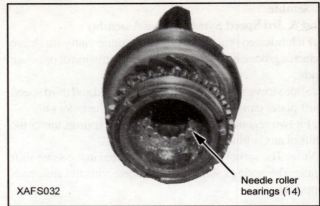

19. Install the input shaft assembly to the case checking the output shaft spigot is correctly positioned.

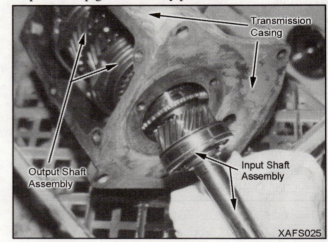

(b) Install the bearing retainer, 3 bolts and lock washers, tighten to specification.

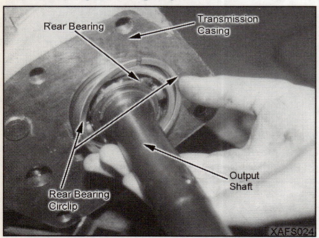

(b) Fit the oil slinger between the gear teeth, input shaft bearing with outside snap ring fitted, spacer and snap ring, check end float specification.

18. Install the needle rollers (14) into the rear bore of the input shaft bearing.

*Grease will help retain the rollers in position.

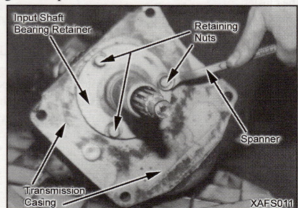

20. Turn the transmission upside down carefully and mesh the cluster gear.

21. From the rear of the transmission install the countershaft (plain end first) pushing out the dummy shaft. Push the shaft until the locking plate slot is flush with outside rear of the case.

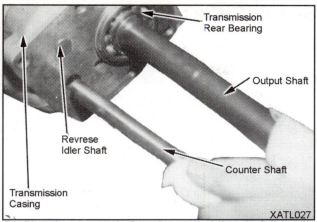

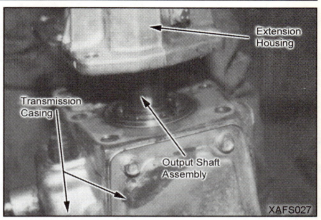

(b) Slots in countershaft and reverse idler shaft must be adjacent & parallel.

(c) Install and tap (shafts) home, the locking plate into the slots of both shafts.

24. Install gear shift control levers and tighten nuts to specification.

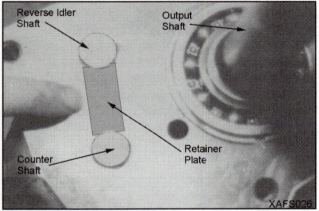

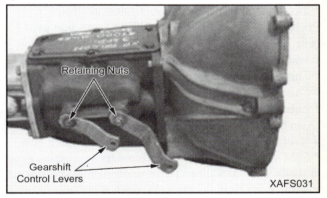

22. Install the speedo drive clip first and gear onto the main shaft (clip flanged end towards the case).

25. Install drain plug to specification.

26. Install top cover with new gasket and tighten 6 bolts to specification.

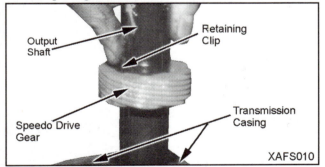

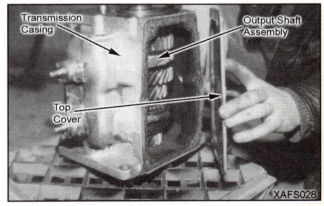

23.(a) Fit extension housing with new gasket to rear of transmission and torque to specification.
(b) Check rear bushing inside diameter before installation.
(c) Install new breather to extension housing if removed.

27.(a) Fit transmission to vehicle as previously described.
(b) Fill transmission with specified fluid as previously described.
(c) Test transmission in all gears.

PROBLEM DIAGNOSIS

Problem: Transmission shift hard/heavy!
Possible Causes and Remedies:
* Clutch adjustment incorrect. Remedy - Adjust clutch.
* Clutch pedal high effort. Remedy - Lubricate or replace as required.
* Shifter shaft binding. Remedy - Check for misspositioned selector arm roll pin, loose cover bolts, worn shifter shaft or shaft bores, distorted oil seal or transmission extension not aligned with case.
* Internal bind in transmission caused by shift forks, selector plates of synchronizer assemblies. Remedies - Remove, dismantle and inspect transmission. Replace worn or damaged components as necessary.
* Incorrect lubricant. Remedy - Drain and refill.

Problem: Gear clash when shifting from one gear to gear.
Possible Causes and Remedies:
* Clutch adjustment incorrect. Remedy - Adjust clutch.
* Clutch cable binding. Remedy - Lubricate or replace.
* Lubricant level low or incorrect lubricant. Remedies - Drain and refill transmission and check for lubricant leaks if level was low. Repair as necessary.
* Gear shift components or synchronizer assemblies worn or damaged. Remedies - Remove, dismantle and inspect transmission. Replace worn or damaged parts.

Problem: Transmission noisy!
Possible Causes and Remedies:
* Lubricant incorrect or level low. Remedies - Refill transmission. Check for leaks and repair as necessary.
* Clutch housing-to-engine, or transmission-to-clutch housing bolts loose. Remedy - Re-torque bolts.
* Gearshift mechanism, transmission gears or bearing components worn or damaged. Remedies - Replace worn or damaged components as necessary.

Problem: Jumps out of gear!
Possible Causes and Remedies:
* Offset lever damper sleeve worn or lever loose. Remedies - Remove gearshift lever and check for loose offset lever or damper sleeve.
* Gearshift mechanism, shift forks, selector plates, interlock plate, selector arm or shift cover worn or damaged. Remedies: Remove, dismantle and inspect transmission cover assembly. Replace worn or damaged components. * Gear teeth worn or tapered, synchronizer assemblies worn or damaged, excessive end play caused by worn thrust washers or mainshaft gears. Remedies - Remove, dismantle and inspect transmission. Replace worn or damaged components.

SPECIFICATIONS

Type: .... Borg Warner Partial Synchronized 3 speed
Lubrication: ESW-M2C37 SAE30
Capacity: .... 1.9 litre

End Float Clearances (mm):
1st & 2nd Gear 0.15-0.48
Input Shaft Bearing (max) 0.10
Output Shaft Bearing (max) 0.10

Gear Ratio:		
	1st Gear	2.95:1
	2nd Gear	1.69:1
	3rd Gear	1.00:1
	Reverse	3.80:1

Torque Specifications

Description	Nm
Clutch Bell Housing to Engine	47 - 60
Transmission to Clutch Bell Housing	50 - 57
Rear Extension to Transmission	57 - 68
Transmission Cover	19 - 26
Input Bearing Retainer Bolts	26 - 34
Operating Lever Retainer Nuts	24 - 31
Drain Plug	14 - 27
Filler Plug	14 - 27
Reverse Light Switch	20 - 27
Speedometer Sender Unit Retainer Bolt	10 - 15

3 spd. FULLY SYNCHRONIZED MANUAL TRANSMISSION

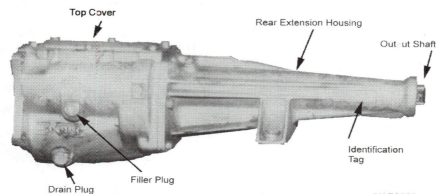

Borg Warner 3 Speed Fully Synchronized Transmission

Subject	Page
GENERAL INFORMATION	202
Service Information	202
Recommended Lubricant	202
Checking Transmission Lubricant Level	202
Draining & Refilling Transmission	202
MAINTENANCE	202
Transmission Extension Seal	202
Removal	202
Installation	202
Back-Up Lamp Switch	202
Test	202
Removal	203
Installation	203

Subject	Page
Major Repairs & Rebuild	203
Transmission Dismantle	203
Clean and Inspect Transmission	205
Synchronizers	206
Dismantle	206
Assemble	206
Cluster Gear & Counter Shaft	207
Assemble	207
Assemble Transmission	207
PROBLEM DIAGNOSIS	211
SPECIFICATIONS	211
TORQUE WRENCH SPECIFICATIONS	211

3 spd. FULLY SYNCHRONIZED MANUAL TRANSMISSION

GENERAL INFORMATION

Ford used a Borg Warner series 0501 fully synchronized manual transmission as optional equipment from XR to XA models, then as standard equipment for XB to XF six cylinder base models and commercial vehicles such as utilities and vans.

The transmission was only released as column shift option.

SERVICE INFORMATION

Attached to the left-hand side of the transmission extension, is a tag which provides the transmission serial No. and assembly part No. These numbers provide coded information which is relevant to transmission application and replacement part interpretation, and should be referred to when ordering replacement parts.

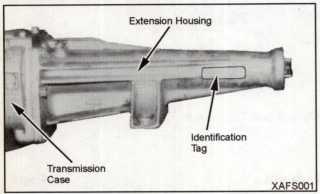

Recommended Lubricant

For Borg Warner 3 spd. Fully Synchronized manual transmission is ESW-M2C37 SAE 30. The transmission lubricant capacity is: 1.9 Litres

Checking Transmission Lubricant Level.

To check level, remove filler plug on the side of transmission case. The level is correct when lubricant is at bottom of plug hole.

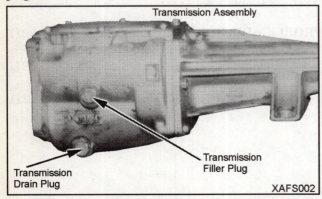

Ensure that the vehicle is on level ground and the transmission is cold.

Draining and Refilling Transmission

Periodic lubricant changes are not necessary. The lubricant must be replaced when overhauling the transmission or when operating the vehicle under severe driving conditions

MAINTENANCE

TRANSMISSION EXTENSION SEAL
Removal
1. Disconnect battery earth lead and raise vehicle (front and rear) and support on safety stands.
2. (a) Remove propeller shaft (refer to **PROPELLER SHAFT & UNIVERSAL JOINTS** Chapter in this Manual).
(b) Place a drain tray beneath transmission extension.

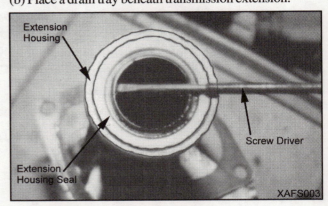

3. Remove seal using seal remover.
4. (a) Inspect seal lip surface on slip yoke of propeller shaft for damage.
(b) Clean (or replace) as necessary.

Installation
Installation of the seal is the reverse of REMOVAL procedures, noting the following points:
1. (a) Apply a little transmission lubricant to seal lip.
(b) Install seal into the extension with a seal insertion tool.
(c) Torque all bolts (see TORQUE SPECIFICATIONS Section of this Chapter).
2. Check transmission lubricant level as previously described in this Chapter.

BACKUP LAMP SWITCH
Test
1. Jack up vehicle (front and rear) and support on safety stands as previously described.
2. Disconnect wiring harness connector from back-up lamp switch.
 The switch is located on the right-hand side of the transmission case At the back of the shift levers.
3. Connect an ohmmeter across the switch terminals.
4. (a) With transmission control lever in any position other than reverse, the ohmmeter should shown open circuit (infinity ohms).
(b) With the control lever in the reverse position the ohmme-

ter should register a resistance.
(c) If ohmmeter readings indicate that switch is faulty, remove switch as per following instructions.

Removal
1. Jack up vehicle (front and rear) and support on safety stands as previously described.
2.(a) Disconnect wiring harness connector from switch.
(b) Loosen and remove switch from transmission case.

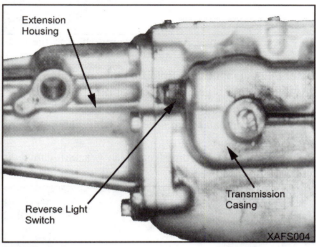

Installation
1. Make sure all threads of switch are clean.
2. Apply sealant or use thread sealing tape, to switch threads if applicable.
3. Fit and tension switch to specifications..
Make sure sealant (or thread sealing tape) does not extend beyond switch thread end.
4.(a) Refit wiring harness connector to switch
(b) Remove safety stands and lower vehicle to ground.
(c) Check back-up lamp operation.

MAJOR REPAIR & REBUILD

TRANSMISSION DISMANTLE
1. Thoroughly clean exterior of transmission assembly.
2.(a) Remove transmission drain plug with a socket.
(b) Allow transmission lubricant to drain into a container.
* The drain plug is located on the lower left-hand side of the transmission case.
3. Release the speedo driven gear assembly from the transmission extension housing.
4. Withdraw the clutch folk and throw out bearing, then the bell housing from the transmission casing.

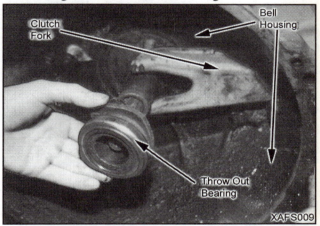

5. Release the extension housing retaining bolts then withdraw the extension housing.

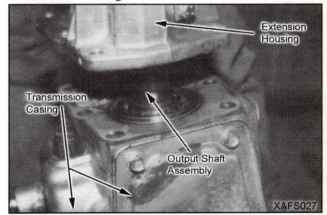

6. Release speedo drive gear clip. (Depress speedometer drive gear clip to remove.)

3 spd. Fully SYNCHRONIZED MANUAL TRANSMISSION

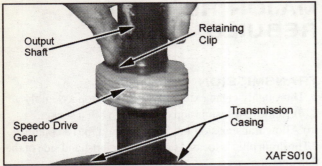

7.(a) Remove back-up lamp switch from transmission case.
(b) Release the top inspection cover plate and withdraw.

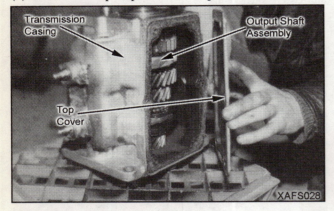

8.(a) Withdraw front maindrive gear bearing retainer (3 attaching cap screws) to transmission case.

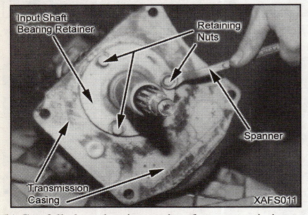

(b) Carefully lever bearing retainer from transmission case with a screwdriver, to break retainer to case seal.
9.(a) Use a soft drift to knock the countershaft through from the front to allow the lock plate to be removed.
(b) Slide the lock plate from the counter shaft and reverse idler gear shaft.
(c) Push countershaft out through rear of case with dummy countershaft tool.

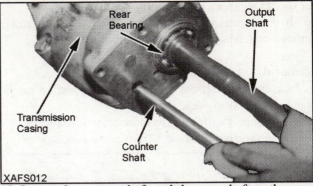

(d) Lower the countershaft and dummy shaft to the case bottom.
10.(a) Pull out input shaft from front of case.
(b) Withdraw third gear synchronizer ring.
11. Release the rear (output shaft) bearing outer circlip.
12. Move second and third speed gearshift cam into third gear position.
13.(a) Knock out taper pins from each gearshift camshaft (underneath transmission).

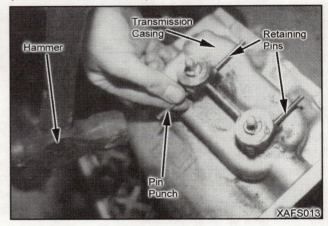

(b) Push gearshift cam and shaft assemblies against the inside of the case.
14.(a) Push the output shaft assembly forward so that the output shaft bearing moves through into the gear case.
(b) Move the main shaft assembly away from the gearshift forks.
15.(a) Move the first and reverse sleeve and gear forward (do not move first and reverse gearshift fork) into first speed position.
(b) Withdraw first and reverse gearshift fork.
(c) Withdraw second and third gearshift fork.

3 spd. Fully Synchronized Manual Transmission

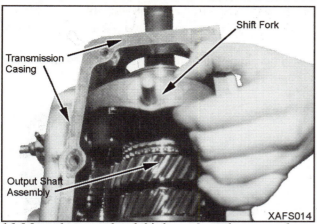

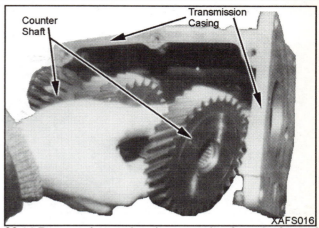

16. Move the second and third speed synchro outer sleeve rearwards into second gear position.

17.(a) Withdraw output shaft assembly through top of gear case.

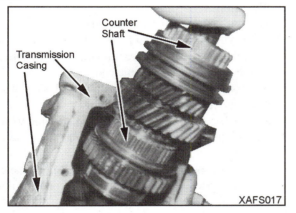

(b) Align input shaft end of out put shaft with the cut out section in the casing.

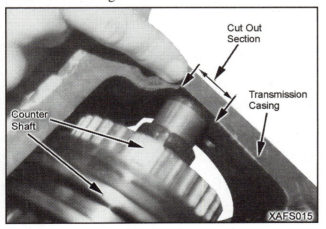

19.(a) Knock out reverse idler gear and cluster gear assembly.
(b) Lift the counter shaft assembly from the transmission casing.

20.(a) Remove the synchronizer snap ring from the front of the output shaft and slide off the second and third speed synchronizer assembly and the second gear with its blocker ring.
(b) Take note of the synchronizer assembly hub end positions to help assembly.

21.(a) Withdraw the output shaft bearing snap ring and spacer from the output shaft
(b) Slide the bearing from the output shaft.

22.(a) Release the first speed synchronizer and reverse gear assembly snap ring from the output shaft.
(b) Withdraw the synchronizer and gear assembly from the output shaft.

23. Clean and inspect all components, replace damaged components.

Clean and Inspect Transmission

Thoroughly wash all components in a suitable cleaning solvent. Dry all components with clean and dry compressed air.

1. Inspect the following components for any cracks or defects that may cause lubricant leakage: transmission case, rear extension, case cover and maindrive gear bearing retainer.

2. Check all machined faces for burrs, and (if possible), dress them off with a fine mill file.

3. Clean magnet located in the bottom of transmission case.

4.(a) Inspect all roller and needle bearing assemblies closely, and replace if there is any sign of wear.
(b) Inspect mainshaft and internal surfaces of gears where needle bearings come in contact.

5. Inspect all gears for excessive wear, chips or cracks. Replace any that are worn or damaged.

3 spd. FULLY SYNCHRONIZED MANUAL TRANSMISSION

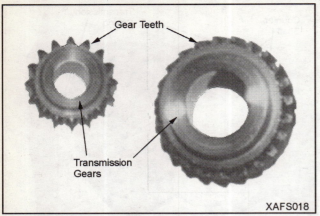

6. Check synchronizer teeth on blocking rings and gears. Replace any components that is worn or damaged.
7.(a) Inspect synchronizer hubs, sleeves, inserts and springs for damage or war.
(b) Check that the synchronizer sleeves slide freely on their hubs.
(c) Replace any worn component.
8. Inspect reverse idler gear shaft and replace if worn.

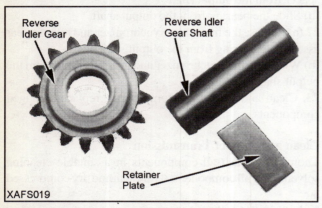

9. Check all thrust washers and replace any that are worn.
10. Inspect all shift control component contact and sliding surfaces for wear, scratches, projections of other damage.
11. Inspect breather (located in transmission extension) to make sure it is not blocked.

SYNCHRONIZERS
Dismantle
* Before dismantling any of the synchronizers, paint or etch an alignment mark on each of the synchronizer sleeves and hubs.
* Do not mix parts from one synchronizer assembly to another.

1st & Reverse Synchronizer Assemblies
1. Withdraw 1st gear synchronizer ring, then the two synchronizer springs with a screwdriver.
2. Separate sleeve from hub and remove the 3 synchronizer inserts.

2nd & 3rd Speed Synchronizer Assembly
1. Remove both synchronizer rings, then the two springs with a screwdriver.
2. Separate sleeve from hub and remove the 3 synchronizer inserts.

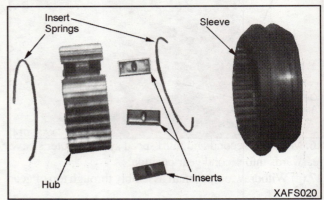

Assemble
1st & Reverse Synchronizer Assembly
1. Lubricate synchro sleeve and reverse gear and fit to the inner hub with the teeth of the gear and the synchro spring groove of the inner hub at the same ends.
2. Fit three first speed shifting plates into the hub slots, with plate pads in the recessed end of the hub.
3. Fit two synchro springs under the shift plates, the white painted spring in the spring groove of the hub, the other in the hub end recess.
* **Note:** The springs are not identical. The spring tangs should locate on opposite sides of the same shift plate, so that the spring openings do not line up.

2nd & 3rd Speed Synchronizer Assembly
1. Fit lubricated synchronizer sleeve to inner hub with sleeve selector groove and hub inner spline protrusion at opposite ends.
2. Slide sleeve across hub until three second and third speed shift plates can be fitted into the slots in the inner hub.
3. Fit two second and third speed syncro springs under the shift plates behind the pads.
* **Note:** The spring tangs should be located in the same shift plate. The springs should be installed with the free ends opposite.

CLUSTER GEAR & COUNTERSHAFT

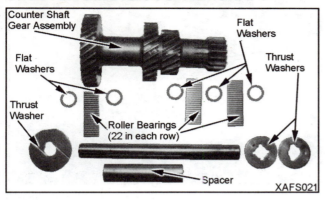

XAFS021

Assemble

1. Insert dummy countershaft and spacer into cluster gear.
2. (a) Fit a set of 22 lubricated needle rollers at the front (largest gear end) of the cluster.
(b) Fit two sets of 22 lubricated needle rollers at either end of the cluster.
(c) Separate the rollers with cluster gear needle roller retainer washer.
3. Fit cluster gear needle roller retainer washers at each end of the dummy countershaft, together with two thrust washers at the rear (small steel washer to cluster, engage tangs with slots in gears) (small bimetal to case, engage tangs with slot in case) of the cluster gear, and one thrust washer (large bimetal engage tang with slot in case) at the front end of the gear.
* These may be retained with grease.

TRANSMISSION ASSEMBLY

* *On assembly, coat all bearing surfaces, shafts, gears, blocking rings, cones and oil seals with transmission lubricant.*

1. (a) Hold 1 ball in rear of interlock sleeve with the use of grease.
(b) Fit sleeve into case.
2. (a) Fit cam and shaft assembly to case in neutral position.
(b) Ensure that the interlock sleeve ball is in extended detent notch of the cam.

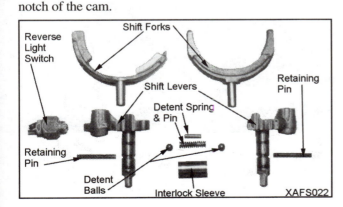

XAFS022

3. (a) Fit the cam and shaft assembly into the case.
(b) Push the cam against the side of the case so that the interlock sleeve hole is not blocked.
4. (a) Fit interlock pin, spring and second ball.
(b) Move the cam and shaft assembly into third gear position, so that extended detent notch of the cam retains the ball and spring.
* Interlock sleeves are selectively fitted for axial movement of 0.05-0.254 mm in all gear selection positions.
5. (a) Install lubricated reverse idler gear and bush assembly and shaft with bevelled ends of the gear teeth forward.
(b) Shaft must be inserted so that the locking groove is flush with the outside face of the gear case, and face towards the cluster gear shaft hole.

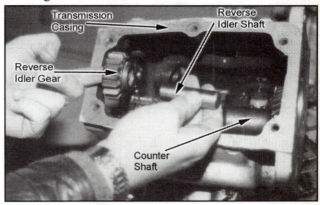

6. (a) Assemble cluster gear, dummy countershaft and bearings as previously outlined
(b) Place the cluster assembly in the bottom of the gear case.

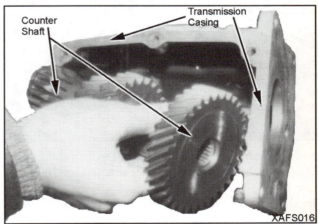

XAFS016

(c) Ensuring that the tabs of the thrust washers fit the grooves of the case.
7. (a) Assemble first and reverse speed synchro assembly as previously described.
(b) Assemble second and third speed synchro assembly as previously described.
8. (a) Fit 1st speed block ring to 1st speed gear.
(b) Fit 1st speed synchro and reverse gear sleeve assembly.
9. (a) Fit snap ring to output shaft, make sure reverse gear sleeve teeth face towards the rear of the case.

3 spd. FULLY SYNCHRONIZED MANUAL TRANSMISSION

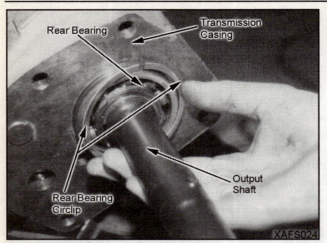

(b) Check end float and fit appropriate snap ring to achieve specifications
10.(a) Install output shaft bearing, spacer and snap ring.
(b) Fit appropriate snap ring to achieve specifications
* Do not fit snap ring to outside diameter of output shaft bearing.
11. Install 2nd speed gear block ring.
12.(a) Install the output shaft with the inner hub inner spline protrusion facing the front of the transmission case.

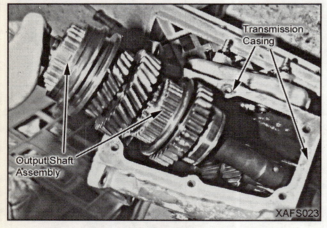

(b) Install snap ring and check end float specification.
13.(a) Shift 2nd & 3rd synchro sleeve to engage 2nd drive gear.
(b) Shift 1st & reverse synchro sleeve to engage 1st drive gear.
14. Through the top of the case fit the output shaft assembly.
15.(a) Position the gearshift camshafts to the side of the case, so that 3rd and neutral are still held by the cams.
(b) Tilt the mainshaft away from the camshafts.
16.(a) Move the gear shift forks into position in the camshaft assembly.
(b) Move the output shaft assembly so the 2nd and 3rd speed fork line up with the second and third speed synchro sleeve, moving it along until the groove in the 1st reverse fork lines up with the sleeve.
(c) Lift the output shaft assembly to engage the forks, in the synchro sleeve and reverse sliding gear and sleeve.

17. Move the camshafts into position and fit the tapered retaining pins into the case.

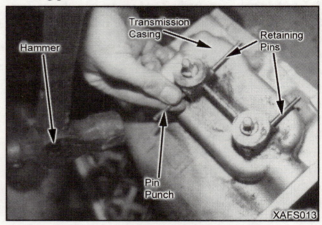

18.(a) Slide the output shaft backwards into the rear bearing until the bearing outer snap ring can be fitted.
(b) Fit the oil slinger between the gear teeth, input shaft bearing with outside snap ring fitted, spacer and snap ring, check end float specification.

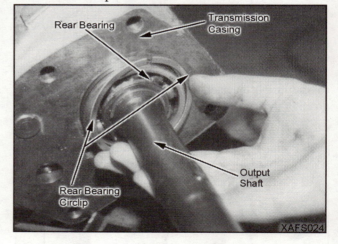

19. Install the needle rollers (14 - 6 cylinder, 15 - 8 cylinder) into the rear bore of the input shaft bore.
* Grease will help retain the rollers in position.

3 spd. FULLY SYNCHRONIZED MANUAL TRANSMISSION

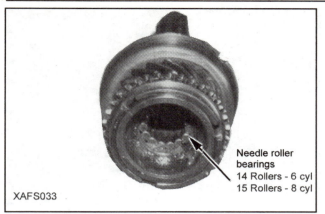

20.(a) Install the input shaft assembly to the case checking the output shaft spigot is correctly positioned.

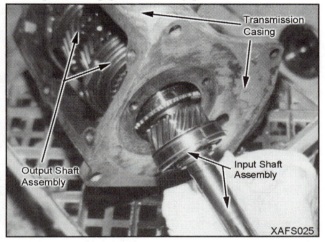

(b) Install the bearing retainer, 3 bolts and lock washers, tighten to specification.

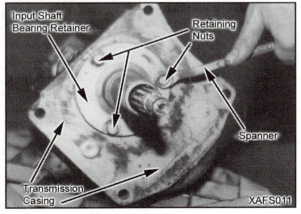

21. Turn the transmission upside down carefully and mesh the cluster gear.

22.(a) From the rear of the transmission install the countershaft (plain end first) pushing out the dummy shaft. Push the shaft until the locking plate slot is flush with the outside rear of the case.

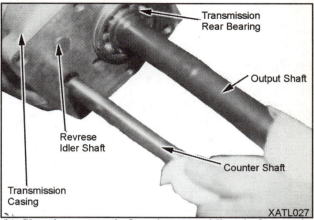

(b) Slots in countershaft and reverse idler shaft must be adjacent & parallel.
(c) Install and tap (shafts) home, the locking plate into the slots of both shafts.

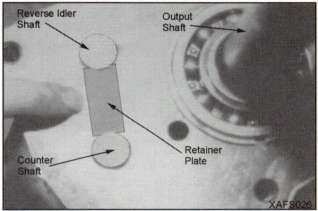

23. Install the speedo drive clip first and gear onto the main shaft (clip flanged end towards the case).

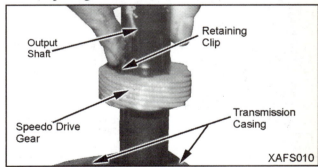

24.(a) Fit extension housing with new gasket to rear of transmission and torque to specification.
(b) Check rear bushing inside diameter before installation.
(c) Install new breather to extension housing if removed.

209

3 spd. FULLY SYNCHRONIZED MANUAL TRANSMISSION

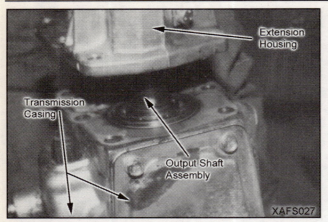

25. Install gear shift control levers and tighten nuts to specification.

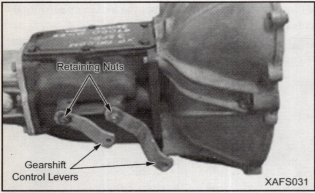

26.(a) Install new welsh plug if removed.
(b) Install filler plug to specification.
(c) Install drain plug to specification.

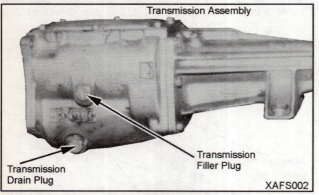

27. Install top cover with new gasket and tighten 6 bolts to specification.

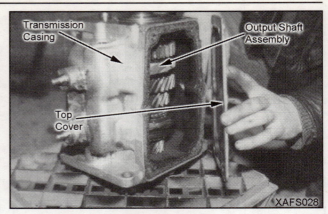

28.(a) Fit transmission to vehicle.
(b) Fill transmission with specified fluid as previously described.
(c) Test transmission in all gears.

3 spd. FULLY SYNCHRONIZED MANUAL TRANSMISSION

PROBLEM DIAGNOSIS

Problem: Transmission shift hard/heavy!
Possible Causes and Remedies:
* Clutch adjustment incorrect. Remedy - Adjust clutch.
* Clutch pedal high effort. Remedy - Lubricate or replace as required.
* Shifter shaft binding. Remedy - Check for mispositioned selector arm roll pin, loose cover bolts, worn shifter shaft or shaft bores, distorted oil seal or transmission extension not aligned with case.
* Internal bind in transmission caused by shift forks, selector plates of synchronizer assemblies. Remedies - Remove, dismantle and inspect transmission. Replace worn or damaged components as necessary.
* Incorrect lubricant. Remedy - Drain and refill.

Problem: Gear Clash when shifting from one gear to another!
Possible Causes and Remedies:
* Clutch adjustment incorrect. Remedy - Adjust clutch.
* Clutch cable binding. Remedy - Lubricate or replace.
* Lubricant level low or incorrect lubricant. Remedies - Drain and refill transmission and check for lubricant leaks if level was low. Repair as necessary.
* Gear shift components or synchronizer assemblies worn or damaged. Remedies - Remove, dismantle and inspect transmission. Replace worn or damaged parts.

Problem: Transmission noisy!
Possible Causes and Remedies:
* Lubricant incorrect or level low. Remedies - Refill transmission. Check for leaks and repair as necessary.
* Clutch housing-to-engine, or transmission-to-clutch housing bolts loose. Remedy - Re-torque bolts.
* Gearshift mechanism, transmission gears or bearing components worn or damaged. Remedies - Replace worn or damaged components as necessary.

Problem: Jumps out of gear!
Possible Causes and Remedies:
* Offset lever damper sleeve worn or lever loose.
Remedies - Remove gearshift lever and check for loose offset lever or damper sleeve.
* Gearshift mechanism, shift forks, selector plates, interlock plate, selector arm or shift cover worn or damaged.
Remedies - Remove, dismantle and inspect transmission cover assembly. Replace worn or damaged components.
* Gear teeth worn or tapered, synchronizer assemblies worn or damaged, excessive end play caused by worn thrust washers or mainshaft gears.
Remedies - Remove, dismantle and inspect transmission. Replace worn or damaged components as necessary.

SPECIFICATIONS

Fully Synchronized 3 speed
Lubrication
Capacity .... 1.9 litre
Type .... ESW-M2C37 SAE 30
End Float Clearances (mm)
1st & 2nd Gear 0.15-0.48
Input Shaft Bearing (max) 0.10
Output Shaft Bearing (max) 0.10

Gear Ratio	6cyl.	8cyl.
1st Gear	2.95:1	2.71:1
2nd Gear	1.69:1	1.69:1
3rd Gear	1.00:1	1.00:1
Reverse	3.67:1	3.367:1

Torque Specifications

Description	Nm
Transmission to Clutch Bell Housing	40 - 55
Rear Extension to Transmission	60 - 75
Transmission Cover	11 - 16
Input Bearing Retainer Bolts	27 - 34
Operating Lever Retainer Nuts	27 - 34
Drain Plug	27 - 34
Filler Plug	27 - 34
Reverse Light Switch	20 - 27
Speedometer Gear/Cable Retainer Bolt	10 - 15

4 spd. MANUAL TRANSMISSIONS (Top Loader)

Subject	Page
GENERAL INFORMATION	213
Service Information	213
Recommended Lubricant	213
Checking Transmission Lubricant Level	213
Draining & Refilling Transmission	213
MAINTENANCE	214
Transmission Extension Seal	214
Removal	214
Installation	214
Back-Up Lamp Switch	214
Test	214
Removal	214
Installation	214

Subject	Page
Major Service Repairs	214
Transmission Rebuild	214
Transmission Dismantle	214
Clean and Inspect Transmission	215
Synchronizers	216
Dismantle	216
Assemble	216
Main Shaft	216
Input Shaft	217
Shift Arm Assembly	217
Counter Shaft	217
Reverse Idler Gear	217
Assemble Transmission	217
PROBLEM DIAGNOSIS	220
SPECIFICATIONS	220
TORQUE WRENCH SPECIFICATIONS	220

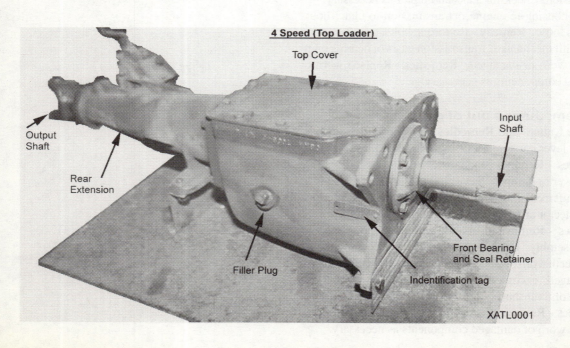

4 Speed (Top Loader)

XATL0001

4 spd. MANUAL TRANSMISSIONS - (Top Loader)

GENERAL INFORMATION

The top loader transmission was initially available for XR and XT GT Falcons, then became an option with most Falcon from XW to XB series vehicles and co-manufactured Fairlane and LTD vehicles.

The floor mounted control lever operates a linkage mechanism which extends from the transmission extension to the transmission case shift levers. The 1st/2nd, 3rd/4th and reverse shift forks are mounted in the side of the transmission.

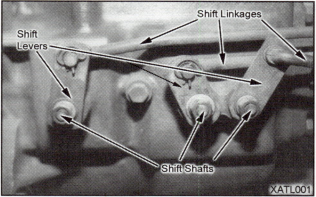

Power Flow of the transmission is the maindrive gear (3rd, 2nd and 1st speed gears) are in constant mesh with the cluster gear; therefore with the engine running and the clutch engaged, torque is imparted to the maindrive gear and through the cluster gear to the 3rd, 2nd and 1st speed gears at all times.

SERVICE INFORMATION

Attached to the right-hand side of the transmission case, is a tag which provides the transmission serial No. and assembly part No.

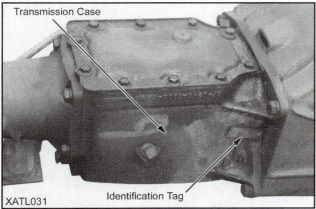

These numbers provide coded information which is relevant to transmission application and replacement part interpretation, and should be referred to when ordering replacement parts.

Recommended Lubricant ESP-M2C-33F Grade 80W
The transmission lubricant capacity is: 2.2 Litres

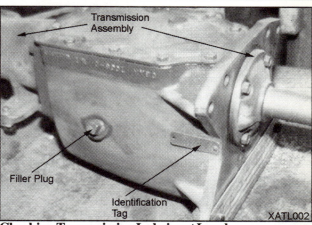

Checking Transmission Lubricant Level.
To check level, remove filler plug on the side of transmission case. The level is correct when lubricant is at bottom of plug hole.

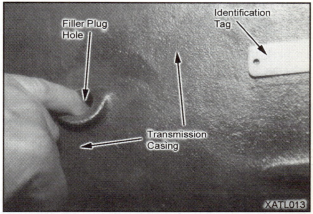

* Ensure that the vehicle is on level ground and the transmission is cold.

Draining and Refilling Transmission
Periodic lubricant changes are not necessary. The lubricant must be replaced when overhauling the transmission or when operating the vehicle under severe driving conditions

MAINTENANCE

Transmission Extension Seal
Removal
1. Disconnect battery earth lead and raise vehicle (front and rear) and support on safety stands.
2.(a) Remove tail shaft.
(b) Place a drain tray beneath transmission extension.
3. Remove seal using seal remover.
4.(a) Inspect seal lip surface on slip yoke of propeller shaft for damage.
(b) Clean (or replace) as necessary.

Installation
Installation of the seal is the reverse of REMOVAL procedures, noting the following points:
1.(a) Apply a little transmission lubricant to seal lip.
(b) Install seal into the extension with a seal insertion tool.
(c) Torque all bolts (see TORQUE SPECIFICATIONS Section of this Chapter).
2. Check transmission lubricant level as previously described in this Chapter.

BACKUP LAMP SWITCH
Test
The switch is located on the left-hand side of the extension housing incorporated in the shift assembly.

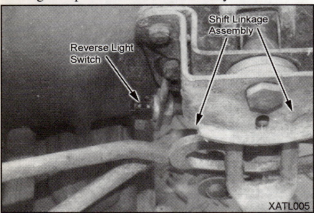

1. Jack up vehicle (front and rear) and support on safety stands as previously described.
2. Disconnect wiring harness connector from back-up lamp switch.
3. Connect an ohmmeter across the switch terminals.
4.(a) With transmission control lever in any position other than reverse, the ohmmeter should shown open circuit (infinity ohms).
(b) With the control lever in the reverse position the ohmmeter should show continuity.
(c) If ohmmeter readings indicate that switch is faulty, remove switch as per following instructions.

Removal
1. Jack up vehicle (front and rear) and support on safety stands as previously described.
2.(a) Disconnect wiring harness connector from switch.
(b) Loosen and remove switch from transmission case.

Installation
1. Make sure all threads of switch are clean.
2. Apply sealant P/N3835214 or equivalent, or use thread sealing tape, to switch threads if applicable.
3. Install and torque switch.
* Make sure sealant (or thread sealing tape) does not extend beyond switch thread end.
Torque: 20 - 27 Nm.
4.(a) Refit wiring harness connector to switch
(b) Remove safety stands and lower vehicle to ground.
(c) Check back-up lamp operation.

MAJOR SERVICE REPAIRS

TRANSMISSION REBUILD
Dismantle Transmission
1. **Thoroughly** clean exterior of transmission assembly.
2.(a) Remove transmission drain plug with a socket and ratchet (if fitted).
(b) Allow transmission lubricant to drain into a container.
3. Withdraw speedometer drive assembly from the transmission extension.
4. Release the inspection cover retaining bolts, then withdraw the cover.

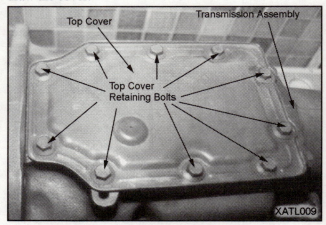

5. Withdraw the input shaft retainer bolts, then slide the input shaft retainer from the transmission assembly.
6. Loosen extension housing bolts, then withdraw the bolts and extension housing from the assembly.
7. Drive the counter shaft from the transmission case using a dummy shaft, then allow the counter shaft to drop to the bottom of the case.
8. Position the 3rd/4th shift lever in the 3rd gear position,

4 spd. MANUAL TRANSMISSIONS - (Top Loader)

then the 1st/2nd shift lever and reverse shift lever in the neutral position.

9. Release the 3rd/4th shift rail detent bolt, spring and detent (located outside case), then withdraw the set screw, detent spring and plug.

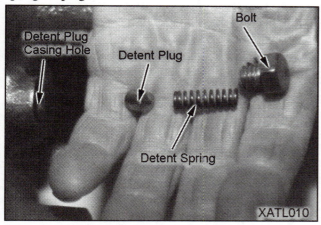

Note: Keep detent plugs and springs identified, to help assembly into original positions, otherwise gear selection could be difficult.

10. Withdraw shift fork attaching screw, tap 3rd/4th rail out to remove expansion plug, then slide shaft from the casing.
11. Withdraw shift fork attaching screw, slide 1st/2nd rail out from the casing, then withdraw the detent plug and interlock pin.
12. Withdraw from the output shaft the speedo gear and retaining clips, then the rear bearing retaining circlip, and bearing.
13. Pull input shaft and synchronizer ring from the transmission casing.

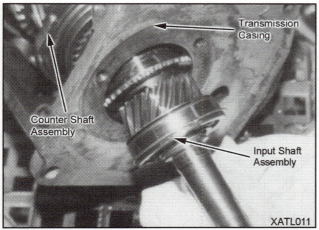

14. With output shaft to the opposite side of the case to the shift forks, withdraw the shift forks, then lift the output shaft from the casing.
15. Release the reverse shift fork screw, turn shift rail and withdraw from the rear of the case, then the fork, detent plug and spring can be withdrawn.
16. Slide reverse idler shaft from the case, then withdraw reverse idler gear and counter shaft from casing.

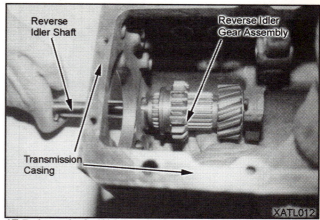

17. Release the 3rd/4th synchronizer snap ring, then withdraw the synchronizer and third gear from the output shaft.
18. Release the second gear snap ring, then pull the thrust washer, second gear and synchronizer ring from the output shaft.
19. Release the 1st/2nd synchronizer snap ring, then withdraw the synchronizer, synchronizer ring and first gear from the output shaft.

Clean And Inspect Transmission

Thoroughly wash all components in a suitable cleaning solvent. Dry all components with clean and dry compressed air.

1. Inspect the following components for any cracks or defects that may cause lubricant leakage: transmission case, rear extension, case cover and maindrive gear bearing retainer.
2. Check all machined faces for burrs, and (if possible), dress them off with a fine mill file.
3. Clean magnet located in the bottom of transmission case.
4.(a) Inspect all roller and needle bearing assemblies closely, and replace if there is any sign of wear.
(b) Inspect mainshaft and internal surfaces of gears where needle bearings come in contact.
5. Inspect all gears for excessive wear, chips or cracks. Replace any that are worn or damaged.

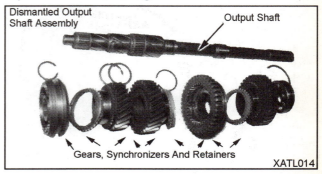

6. Check synchronizer teeth on blocking rings and gears. Replace any components that are worn or damaged.
7.(a) Inspect synchronizer hubs, sleeves, inserts and springs for damage or war.

4 spd. MANUAL TRANSMISSIONS - (Top Loader)

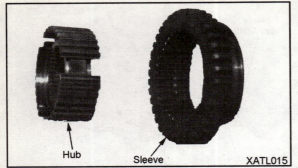

(b) Check that the synchronizer sleeves slide freely on their hubs.
(c) Replace any worn component.
8. Inspect reverse idler gear shaft and replace if worn.
9. Check all thrust washers and replace any that are worn.
10. Inspect all shift control component contact and sliding surfaces for wear, scratches, projections of other damage.
11. Inspect breather (located in transmission extension) to make sure it is not blocked.

Synchronizers
Dismantle
* Before dismantling any of the synchronizers, paint or etch an alignment mark on each synchronizer sleeve and hub.
* Do not mix parts from one synchronizer assembly to another.

1st & 2nd Synchronizer Assemblies
1. Remove both synchronizer springs with a screwdriver.
2. Separate sleeve from hub and remove the 3 synchronizer inserts.

3rd & 4th Speed Synchronizer Assembly
1. Remove both synchronizer springs with a screwdriver.
2. Separate sleeve from hub and remove the 3 synchronizer inserts.

Assemble
1st & 2nd Synchronizer Assembly

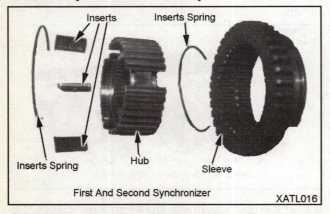

1. Fit lubricated synchronizer sleeve to inner hub with sleeve selector groove and hub inner spline protrusion at opposite ends.
2. Slide sleeve across hub until three shift plates can be fitted into the slots in the inner hub.
3. Install two synchronizer springs under the shift plates behind the pads with the long lug of each spring in the same shift plate.
* The spring tangs should locate on opposite sides of the same shift plate so that the spring openings do not line up.

3rd & 4th Speed Synchronizer Assembly

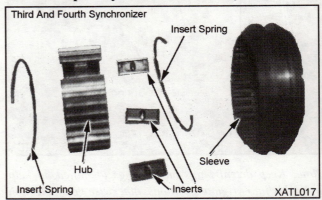

1. Fit lubricated synchronizer sleeve to inner hub with sleeve selector groove and hub inner spline protrusion at opposite ends.
2. Slide sleeve across hub until three shift plates can be fitted into the slots in the inner hub.
3. Install two synchronizer springs under the shift plates behind the pads with the long lug of each spring in the same shift plate.
* The spring tangs should locate on opposite sides of the same shift plate so that the spring openings do not line up.

Mainshaft Assemble
1. Lubricate the first gear bore and fit synchronizer ring.
2. Place the first gear assembly and 1st/2nd synchronizer to the output shaft, then retain using snap ring.

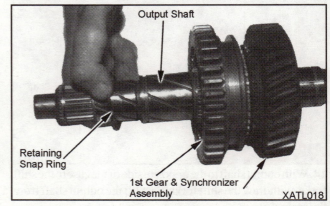

3.(a) Fit the synchronizer ring to the 2nd gear, then the second gear assembly can be slide into place on the output shaft, engaging the 1st/2nd synchronizer.
(b) Fit the thrust washer to the back of the 2nd gear, then retain components using the snap ring.

4 spd. MANUAL TRANSMISSIONS - (Top Loader)

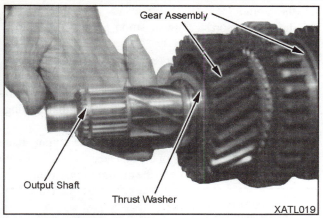

4.(a) Fit the synchronizer ring to the 3rd gear, then slide the gear into place on the output shaft.
(b) Place the 3rd/4th synchronizer into place on the output shaft until it engages with the 3rd gear, then retain using snap ring.

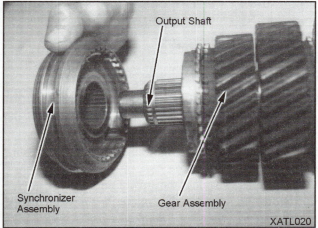

* The mainshaft is now completely assembled ready for assembly into the case.

Input Shaft
1. Release the bearing retaining snap ring, then using suitable adaptor press bearing from thew shaft.
2. Fit new bearing by pressing it onto the input shaft, then retain using snap ring.

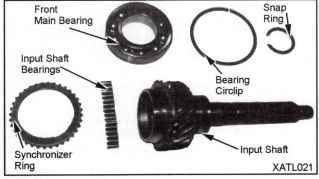

Shift Arm Assemblies
1. Withdraw the shift arms, then pry seals from the arms.
2. Fit new seals to the arms, then slide the arms into the casing.

Counter Shaft
1. Slide dummy shaft out of the counter shaft gear assembly allowing the roller bearing to fall out of either end.
* 22 roller bearings at each end.

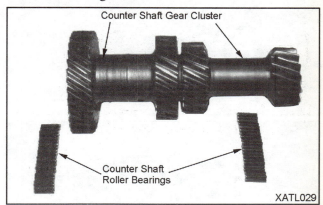

2. Inspect roller bearings, replace if damaged.
3. Fit dummy shaft, then position the roller bearing, ensuring there are 22 in either end.

Reverse Idler Gear
1. Withdraw the slide gear from the idler gear, then withdraw the dummy shaft from the idler gear.
2. Withdraw the retaining washers from either end of the gear and allow the roller bearing to fall out.
* 22 roller bearing at either end of the idler gear, total of 44.
3. Apply grease to the idler gear bore, then fit the dummy shaft into position.
4.(a) Fit the 22 roller bearings (new or old) to one end of the idler gear, then fit the retaining washer.
(b) Fit the remaining 22 roller bearings to the other end of the idler gear, then fit the second retaining washer.
5. Refit the sliding gear to the reverse idler gear.

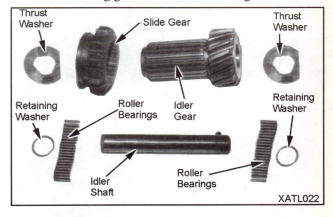

Assemble Transmission
1.(a) With counter shaft gear assembled and lubricated, position the thrust washer in the case.
(b) lower the counter shaft into position, aligning the bores and fitting the counter shaft.
(c) Using feeler gauges, check that the gear end play is correct before proceeding.

4 spd. MANUAL TRANSMISSIONS - (Top Loader)

Gear shift cams install from inside case to outside as shown xatl034

(d) Refit the dummy shaft and lower the counter gear assembly to the bottom of the casing.

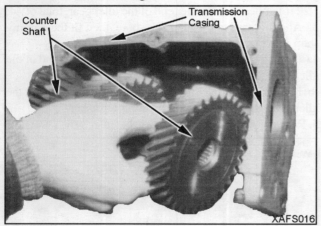

2.(a) With reverse idler gear and thrust washers lubricated, fit

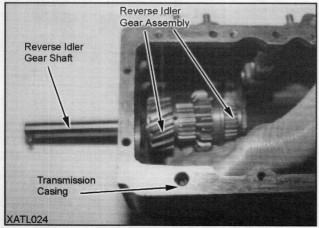

into the casing.
(b) Slide the support shaft into position, pushing the dummy shaft out.
(c) Check the bearing end play using feeler gauges, if correct leave installed in position.
3. With the reverse gear shift rail detent spring, plug and shift fork held in place, fit the rail then secure fork with the retaining screw.
4.(a) Fit the thrust washer in position on the output shaft holding it hard against back of the first gear.
(b) Lower the output shaft into the transmission casing.

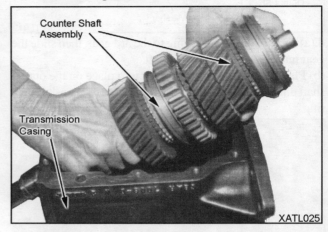

(c) Fit the shift forks onto the gear synchronizers, then position them correctly in the casing.
5.(a) Fit detent plug to detent bore, then position reverse shift rail in neutral.
(b) Fit the inter lock pin in the 3rd/4th shift rail.
(c) Slide the 3rd/4th shift rail into place aligning the shift fork.

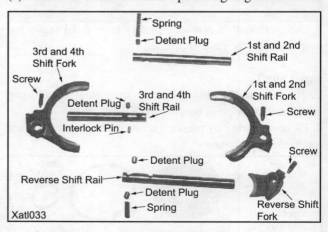

(d) Secure the fork with the retaining screw, then fit the detent plug, spring and retaining bolt.
6.(a) Fit the detent plug in the bore, then slide the 1st/2nd shift rail into position aligning the shift fork.
(b) Fit the detent plug and spring, then secure using the set screw.
7.(a) Fit the bearings (15) in the back of the input shaft, then place the synchronizer ring on the first gear.

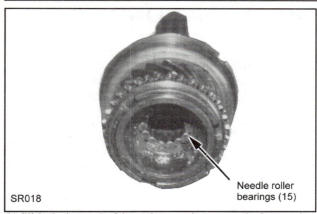

(b) Slide the input shaft into place on the output shaft, ensuring that the synchronizer ring aligns with the synchronizer hub.

8. With new seal fitted to the input shaft bearing retainer, position it in place, then retain with bolts, tension to correct specification.

9. Fit the output shaft bearing, pressing it into place, then retain

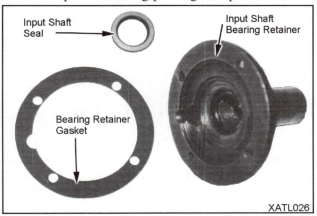

using the snap ring.

* Ensure the thrust washer is still in place.

10.(a) Fit the speedo drive gear to the output shaft using clips

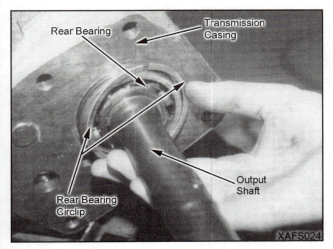

to retain correctly.

(b) Stand case assembly with input shaft down, then align counter shaft gear assembly with case bores.

(c) Fit the counter shaft from the back, withdrawing the dummy shaft at the same time.

11.(a) Position a new extension housing gasket on the casing,

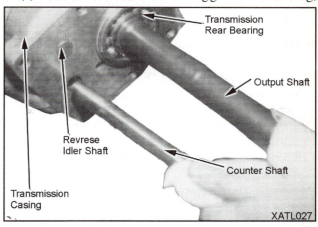

then lower the extension housing onto the casing.

(b) Fit retaining bolts tensioning to specification.

12.(a) Fit the filler plug, then pour specified fluid over the gears while turning the shaft.

(b) Ensure that all shift levers work in every gear position.

13.(a) With sealer applied to expansion plug, fit the plug in the 3rd/4th shift rail bore.

(b) Position new cover gasket to the case, then fit the cover and cover bolts tensioning to specifications.

14. Fit the transmission in the vehicle, then fill with fluid to the

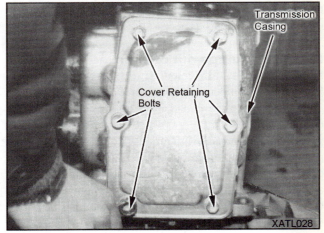

correct level.

PROBLEM DIAGNOSIS

Problem: Transmission shift hard/heavy!
Possible Causes and Remedies:
* Clutch adjustment incorrect. Remedy - Adjust clutch.
* Clutch pedal high effort. Remedy - Lubricate or replace as required.
* Shifter shaft binding. Remedy - Check for mispositioned selector arm roll pin, loose cover bolts, worn shifter shaft or shaft bores, distorted oil seal or transmission extension not aligned with case.
* Internal bind in transmission caused by shift forks, selector plates of synchronizer assemblies. Remedies - Remove, dismantle and inspect transmission. Replace worn or damaged components as necessary.
* Incorrect lubricant. Remedy - Drain and refill.

Problem: Gear Clash when shifting from one gear to another!
Possible Causes and Remedies:
* Clutch adjustment incorrect. Remedy - Adjust clutch.
* Clutch cable binding. Remedy - Lubricate or replace.
* Lubricant level low or incorrect lubricant. Remedies - Drain and refill transmission and check for lubricant leaks if level was low. Repair as necessary.
* Gear shift components or synchronizer assemblies worn or damaged. Remedies - Remove, dismantle and inspect transmission. Replace worn or damaged parts.

Problem: Transmission noisy!
Possible Causes and Remedies:
* Lubricant incorrect or level low. Remedies - Refill transmission. Check for leaks and repair as necessary.
* Clutch housing-to-engine, or transmission-to-clutch housing bolts loose. Remedy - Re-torque bolts.
* Gearshift mechanism, transmission gears or bearing components worn or damaged. Remedies - Replace worn or damaged components as necessary.

Problem: Jumps out of gear!
Possible Causes and Remedies:
* Offset lever damper sleeve worn or lever loose. Remedies - Remove gearshift lever and check for loose offset lever or damper sleeve.
* Gearshift mechanism, shift forks, selector plates, interlock plate, selector arm or shift cover worn or damaged. Remedies: Remove, dismantle and inspect transmission cover assembly. Replace worn or damaged components. * Gear teeth worn or tapered, synchronizer assemblies worn or damaged, excessive end play caused by worn thrust washers or mainshaft gears. Remedies - Remove, dismantle and inspect transmission. Replace worn or damaged components as necessary.

SPECIFICATIONS

Lubrication
Capacity .... 2.2 litre
Type ESP-M2C-83C   80W

End Float Clearances (mm)
1st Speed Gear .... 0.05 - 0.69
2nd Speed Gear .... 0.15 - 0.43
3rd Speed Gear .... 0.13 - 0.51
Countershaft Gear .... 0.102 - 0.459
Reverse Idler Gear .... 0.102 - 0.459
Input Shaft Bearing (max) 0.10
Output Shaft Bearing (max) 0.10

Gear Ratio
1st Gear	2.78:1
2nd Gear	1.93:1
3rd Gear	1.36:1
4th Gear	1.00:1
Reverse	2.78:1

Torque Specifications

Description	Nm
Transmission to Clutch Bell Housing	50 - 57
Extension Housing to Transmission	57 - 68
Transmission Cover	19 - 26
Operating Lever Retainer Nuts	24 - 31
Filler Plug	14 - 27
Shift Fork to Shift Rail	14 - 27
Input Shaft Bearing Retainer Bolts	26 - 34

BORG WARNER 4spd (0503 series) SINGLE RAIL MANUAL TRANSMISSION

Subject	Page
GENERAL INFORMATION	222
Service Information	222
Recommended Lubricant	222
Checking Transmission Lubricant Level	222
Draining & Refilling Transmission	222
MAINTENANCE	222
Transmission Extension Seal	222
Removal	222
Installation	222
Back-Up Lamp Switch	223
Test	223
Removal	223
Installation	223
Gear Shift Lever	223
Removal	223
Installation	223
Major Service Repairs	223
Transmission Dismantle	223
Clean and Inspect Transmission	225
Mainshaft Assembly Inspection	227
Main Shaft	227
Dismantle	227
Assemble	228
Synchronizers	228
Dismantle	228
Assemble	228
Counter Shaft	228
Dismantle	228
Assemble	228
Maindrive Gear	229
Dismantle	229
Assemble	229
Assemble Transmission	229
PROBLEM DIAGNOSIS	232
SPECIFICATIONS	232
TORQUE WRENCH SPECIFICATIONS	232

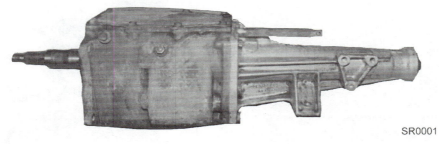

Borg Warner Single Rail 4 Speed

SR0001

GENERAL INFORMATION

The 4 speed Borg Warner 0503 single rail transmission was available on XB, XC, XD, XE & XF series Falcon vehicles and co-manufactured Fairlane and LTD vehicles. Also TC to TF series Cortina vehicles.

The floor mounted control lever operates a shift rail which extends from the transmission extension through into the transmission case directly into the shift forks.

SERVICE INFORMATION

Attached to the side of the transmission case, is a tag which provides the transmission serial No. & assembly part No.

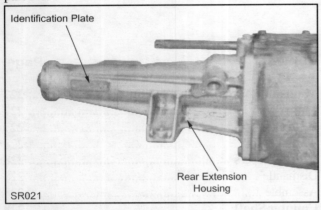

The model code for vehicles equipped with different transmissions are listed in General Information Chapter at the front of this manual.

Recommended Lubricant

For Borg Warner manual transmissions is ESP-M2C-33F Grade 80W
The transmission lubricant capacity is: 2.8 Litres

Checking Transmission Lubricant Level.

To check level, remove filler plug on the side of transmission case. The level is correct when lubricant is at bottom of plug hole.

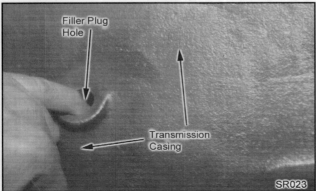

* Ensure that the vehicle is on level ground and the transmission is cold.

Draining and Refilling Transmission

Periodic lubricant changes are not necessary. The lubricant must be replaced when overhauling the transmission or when operating the vehicle under severe driving conditions

MAINTENANCE

Transmission Extension Seal
Removal
1. Disconnect battery earth lead and raise vehicle (front and rear) and support on safety stands.
2. (a) Remove propeller shaft.
(b) Place a drain tray beneath transmission extension.
3. Remove seal using seal remover.
4. (a) Inspect seal lip surface on slip yoke of propeller shaft

for damage.
(b) Clean (or replace) as necessary.

Installation

Installation of the seal is the reverse of REMOVAL procedures, noting the following points:
1. (a) Apply a little transmission lubricant to seal lip.
(b) Install seal into the extension with a seal insertion tool.
(c) Torque all bolts (see TORQUE SPECIFICATIONS

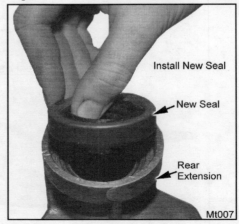

Section of this Chapter).
2. Check transmission lubricant level as previously de-

scribed in this Chapter.

BACKUP LAMP SWITCH
Test
The switch is located on the right-hand side of the gear shift assembly.

1. Jack up vehicle (front and rear) and support on safety

stands as previously described.
2. Disconnect wiring harness connector from back-up lamp switch.
3. Connect an ohmmeter across the switch terminals.
4. (a) With transmission control lever in any position other than reverse, the ohmmeter should shown open circuit (infinity ohms).
(b) With the control lever in the reverse position the ohmmeter should show continuity.
(c) If ohmmeter readings indicate that switch is faulty, remove switch as per following instructions.

Removal
1. Jack up vehicle and support on safety stands.
2. (a) Disconnect wiring harness connector from switch.
(b) Loosen and remove switch from transmission case.

Installation
1. Make sure all threads of switch are clean.
2. Apply sealant P/N3835214 or equivalent, or use thread sealing tape, to switch threads if applicable.
3. Install and torque switch.
* Ensure sealant does not extend beyond switch thread end.

Backup lamp switch: **150 lb. in.**

4. (a) Refit wiring harness connector to switch
(b) Remove safety stands and lower vehicle to ground.
(c) Check back-up lamp operation.

GEAR SHIFT LEVER
Removal
1. Remove centre console cover.
2. Remove screw securing the control lever to lever of control housing and bend back retaining tags then unscrew gear shift lever.

Installation
1. (a) Clean threads of lever to lever securing screw of control housing.
(b) Apply Loctite 620 (or equivalent) to screw threads.
2. Place control lever on side of control housing lever and install, then tighten retaining screw and bend over tabs.
3. (a) Install seal to seal retainer of control lever.
(b) Install cover cap of centre console.

MAJOR SERVICE & REPAIRS

TRANSMISSION ASSEMBLY

Dismantle Transmission
1. Thoroughly clean exterior of transmission assembly.
2. (a) Remove transmission drain plug, then allow transmission lubricant to drain into a container.
3. Remove speedometer cable and driven gear assembly of speedometer from the top of transmission extension.
4. Remove the pin retaining the gear shift connecting rod and gearshift rail, then remove the three screws retaining gearshift assembly to extension housing.

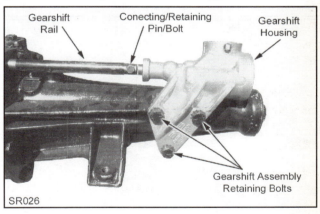

5. Remove the rear extension retaining bolts and remove extension housing, then depress speedometer drive gear retaining lug down and slide gear from output shaft.

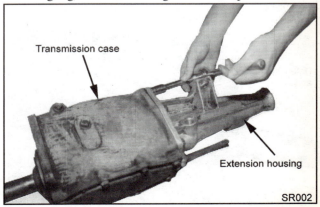

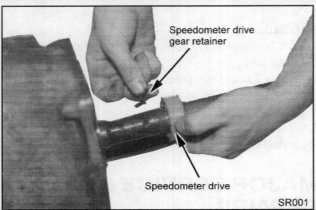

6. From the front of the transmission remove the front bearing retainer, then remove top cover.

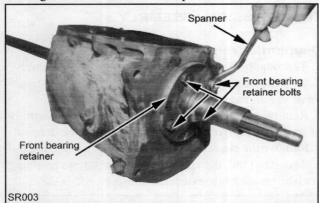

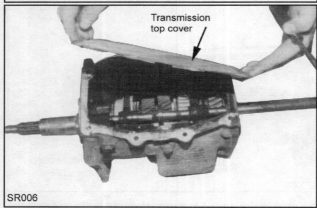

7. Remove the detent screw from the transmission then remove the spring and detent pin from screw location.

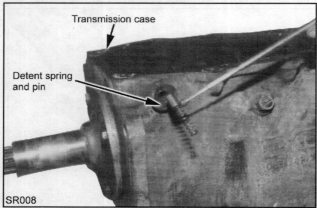

8. Turn the gearshift rail and partially pull outward to free operating pin then press operating pin from shaft.

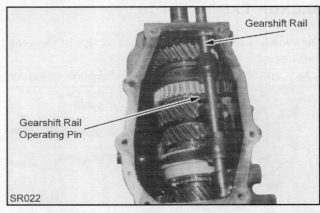

9. Fully remove gearshift rail from transmission by sliding outward toward rear of transmission then remove the shift forks and interlock.

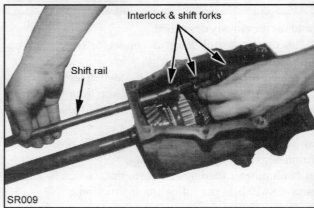

10. Using a dummy shaft drive the counter gear shaft out of the transmission from the rear of the case.

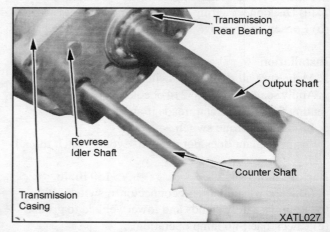

11. From the front of the transmission case pull the input shaft and gear assembly out.

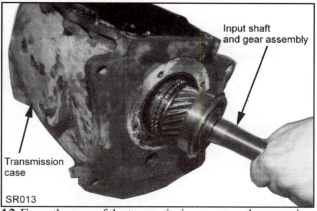

12. From the rear of the transmission remove the snap ring securing the mainshaft bearing, then push mainshaft so the mainshaft bearing pushes through into the transmission casing.

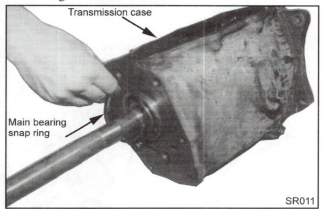

13. Remove the mainshaft and gear assembly from the transmission, then lift the counter gear assembly from the transmission case.

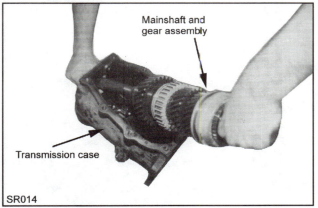

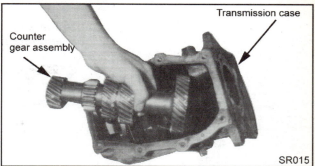

14. Push the reverse idler gear shaft out of the transmission then remove the reverse idler gear.

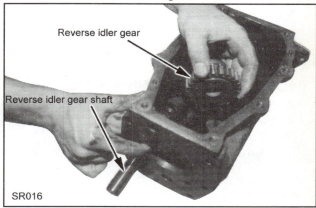

15. Remove the nut and retaining pin for the reverse lever then remove lever from transmission case.

CLEAN AND INSPECT TRANSMISSION

Thoroughly wash all components in a suitable cleaning solvent. Dry all components with clean and dry compressed air.

1. Inspect the following components for any cracks or defects that may cause lubricant leakage: transmission case, rear extension, case cover and maindrive gear bearing retainer.

2. Check all machined faces for burrs, and (if possible), dress them off with a fine mill file.

3. (a) Inspect all roller and needle bearing assemblies closely, and replace if there is any sign of wear.

(b) Inspect mainshaft and internal surfaces of gears where needle bearings come in contact.

5. Inspect all gears for excessive wear, chips or cracks.

BORG WARNER 4spd SINGLE RAIL MANUAL TRANSMISSION (0503)

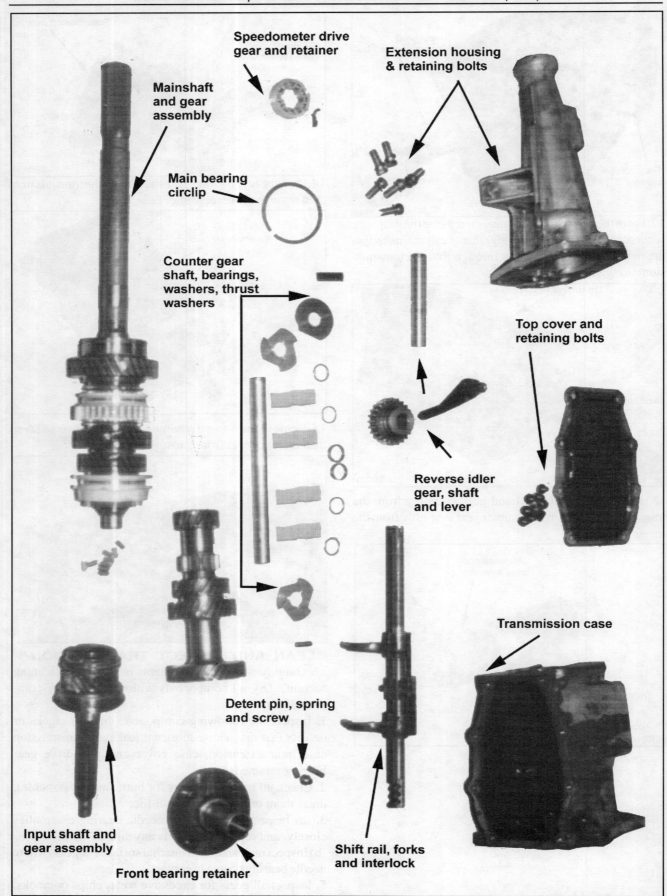

BORG WARNER 4spd SINGLE RAIL MANUAL TRANSMISSION (0503)

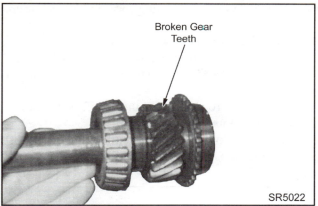

Replace any that are worn or damaged.

6. Check synchronizer teeth on blocking rings and gears. Replace any components that are worn or damaged.

7. (a) Inspect synchronizer hubs, sleeves, inserts and springs for damage or war.
(b) Check that the synchronizer sleeves slide freely on their hubs.
(c) Replace any worn component.

8. Inspect reverse idler gear shaft and replace if worn.

9. Check all thrust washers and replace any that are worn.

10. Inspect all shift control component contact and sliding surfaces for wear, scratches, projections of other damage.

11. Inspect breather (located in transmission extension) to make sure it is not blocked.

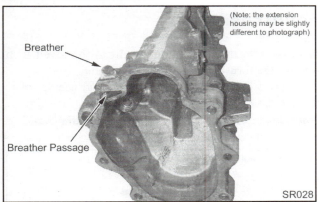

MAINSHAFT ASSEMBLY INSPECTION

Before dismantling the mainshaft assembly, the first speed, second speed and third speed gear end floats should be checked for end float.

End Float specification:
- Third Speed Gear: 0.127 to 0.508 mm
- Second Speed Gear: 0.15 to 0.43 mm
- First Speed Gear: 0.05 to 0.69 mm

If the end float of any gear is not with in specification the following dimensions must be checked after dismantle to determine which component must be replaced to bring the end float within specifications.

1st Speed Gear Width: 53.47-53.54 mm

1st and 2nd Synchro Hub-width to 1st speed thrust face 15.32 - 15.42 mm
1st and 2nd Synchro Hub- width from 2nd gear thrust face to snap ring thrust face: 22.48 - 22.58 mm
2nd Speed Gear width: 46.63-46.71 mm
3rd Speed Gear width: 46.36-46.43 mm
3rd and 4th Synchro Hub width: 22.48-22.58 mm

MAINSHAFT

Dismantle

1. From the front of the mainshaft remove the snap ring, then remove the 3rd and 4th synchronizer assembly.

2. From the main shaft remove the 3rd speed blocker ring and 3rd speed gear.

3. Rear Bearing
(a) Remove the snap ring.
(b) With a universal type puller
(c) Press on the rear end of the mainshaft to remove the rear bearing and first speed gear.

If you press on the front face of the second speed gear you will damage the mainshaft. A snap ring that is hidden, holds the second speed gear and the first and second gear synchronizer in place.

4. From the main shaft remove the snap ring for the 1st & 2nd synchronizer inner hub, hub and reverse sliding gear.

5. Remove the second speed gear and blocker ring by supporting the front face of the second speed gear and pressing on the rear end of the mainshaft.

When pressing on the front face of the second speed gear always ensure that the faces of the second speed gear, the end of the mainshaft and the blocks mounted on the press are square to each other.

Do not press on the thrust face flange of the mainshaft.

6. 3rd and 4th synchronizer.
(a) From the synchro hub slide off the synchronizer sleeve.
(b) Remove the springs and shift plates.

8. 1st and 2nd speed synchronize
(a) From the synchro hub slide off the synchronizer sleeve.
(b) Remove the springs and shift plates.

Assembly
1. Assemble the synchronizer assemblies as described under synchronizer assemblies.
2. Lubricate the bore of the second speed gear and to mainshaft with the blocker ring.

Slots in blocker rings: 8.76 - 9.14 mm wide.

3. With the reverse gear sleeve gear teeth towards the front install the 1st & 2nd speed synchronizer assembly, then install snap ring with thickness to keep end float within specification.

Hub end float specification: 0.0-0.1 mm

2. Lubricate the bore of the first speed gear and install to mainshaft with the blocker ring, then install the mainshaft bearing and retaining snap ring
3. Lubricate the bore of the third speed gear and to the mainshaft install gear with blocker ring.
4. Lubricate the third & fourth speed synchronizer assembly, with the inner hub spline to the front install to mainshaft and snap ring.
5. Check the end float of all gears to ensure they are within specification.
6. Engage third gear with the third and fourth synchronizer sleeve and engage second gear with the first and second synchronizer sleeve.

SYNCHRONIZERS
Dismantle
* Before dismantling any of the synchronizers, paint or etch an alignment mark on each of the synchronizer sleeves and hubs.
* Do not mix parts from one synchronizer assembly to another.

1st & 2nd Synchronizer Assemblies
1. Remove both synchronizer springs with a screwdriver.
2. Separate sleeve from hub and remove the 3 synchronizer inserts.

3rd & 4th Speed Synchronizer Assembly
1. Remove both synchronizer springs with a screwdriver.
2. Separate sleeve from hub and remove the 3 synchronizer inserts.

Assemble
1st & 2nd Synchronizer Assembly
1. Fit lubricated synchronizer sleeve to inner hub with sleeve selector groove and hub inner spline protrusion at opposite ends.
2. Slide sleeve across hub until three shift plates can be fitted into the slots in the inner hub.
3. Install two red synchronizer springs under the shift plates behind the pads with the long lug of each spring in the same shift plate.
* The spring tangs should locate on opposite sides of the same shift plate so that the spring openings do not line up.

3rd & 4th Speed Synchronizer Assembly
1. Fit lubricated synchronizer sleeve to inner hub with sleeve selector groove and hub inner spline protrusion at opposite ends.
2. Slide sleeve across hub until three shift plates can be fitted into the slots in the inner hub.
3. Install two yellow synchronizer springs under the shift plates behind the pads with the long lug of each spring in the same shift plate.

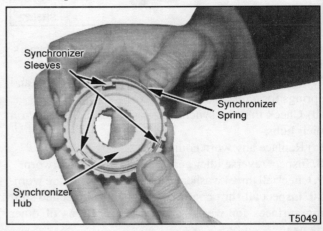

* The spring tangs should locate on opposite sides of the same shift plate so that the spring openings do not line up.

COUNTERSHAFT
Dismantle
1. Remove the dummy shaft if not already removed, then remove the thrust washers from either end.
2. Remove the needle roller bearings and needle roller thrust washers from either end.

Note: *In each end there are three thrust washers and 48 needle roller bearings.*

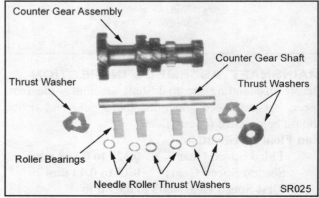

Assemble
1. To the gear assembly install the dummy countershaft.
2. To each end of the gear install a roller thrust washer, set on 24 roller bearings, a second roller thrust washer and 24 bearings then a third thrust washer.
3. To the Rear of the gear assembly (small end) install the

bronze thrust washer and then the steel thrust washer, the bronze washer has 2 tags to lock into shaft and the tag on the steel washer faces outward.

4. To the opposite end install the bronze thrust washer with the singe tag which faces outward.

Note: *Grease can be used to hold thrust washers to end of shaft.*

MAINDRIVE GEAR
Dismantle
1. From the gear bore remove the needle roller bearings, there should be 15 bearings.
2. Remove the snap ring securing maindrive bearing to the shaft then remove maindrive bearing and oil slinger.

Assemble
1. Install the oil slinger and bearing, then install the main bearing retaining snap ring.
Note: *Use snap ring size which will maintain minimum endfloat specification.*
Main bearing endfloat specification: 0.0 - 0.1 mm
2. To the main drive gear fit the fourth speed synchronizer blocker ring, then install the 15 needle roller bearings retaining with grease.

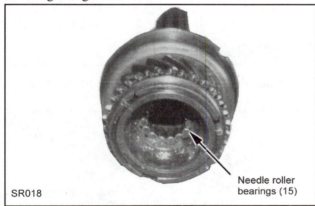

ASSEMBLE TRANSMISSION
1. Install reverse idler gear and bush assembly to the reverse idler shaft, faces back of transmission case.
2. Install the reverse gear lever to transmission case and install retaining pivot pin.

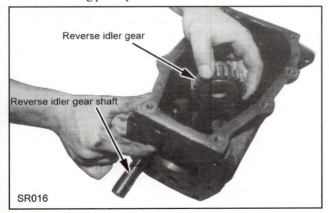

3. Install the cluster gear assembly to the bottom of the transmission case ensuring tangs on thrust washers sit into the case grooves.

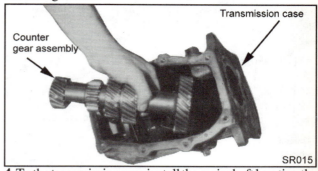

4. To the transmission case install the mainshaft locating the bearing in the case then gently tap the mainshaft assembly with a soft hammer to fully install bearing and install snap ring.

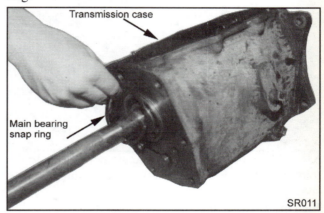

5. Install the input shaft to transmission, gently tap with soft hammer to fully install then install snap ring.

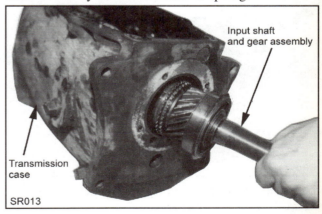

6. Turn the transmission case to allow the counter gear assembly to drop into position, ensure the assembly has meshed correctly with main gear assembly by rotating main shaft.
7. Drive in the counter gear shaft knocking out the dummy shaft at the same time, then to the end install the locking plate between the counter gear shaft and reverse idler shaft.

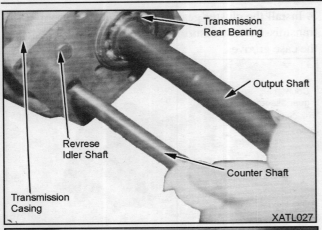

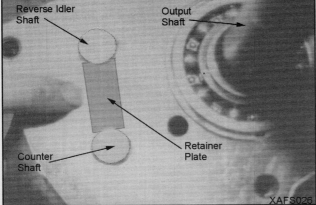

8. Install the bearing retainer using a new gasket to the transmission case and tighten the four retaining bolts to specification.

Bearing retainer bolts: **20-25 lb.ft.**

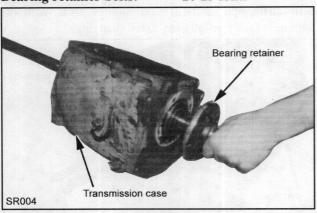

9. To the mainshaft install the speedometer drive gear securing in place with gear clip.

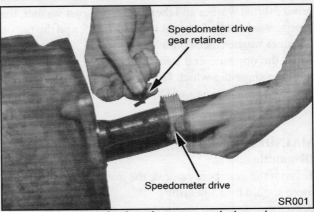

10. Install the extension housing to transmission using a new gasket, then tighten bolts to specification.

Extension housing bolts: **61-75 Nm**

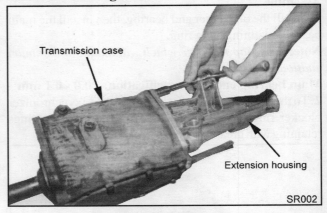

11. Position the synchronizer sleeves in neutral position then install the shift forks into position.

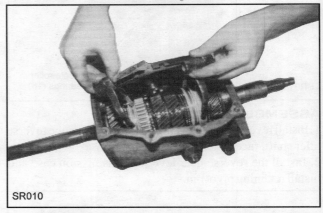

12. Between the two forks install the interlock spool, then install the detent shaft through the rear extension and case.

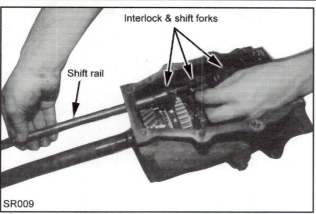
SR009

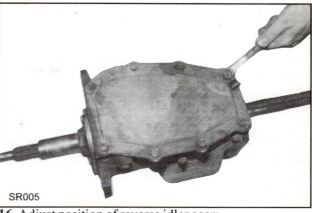
SR005

13. Press the shift pin into shaft then slide shaft forward to sit pin in the interlock spool slot.

14. Install the detent pin, spring and screw, tighten screw to specification.

Detent screw torque specification: 34-41 Nm

16. Adjust position of reverse idler gear:
(a) Ensure gear shift rail is in neutral, then turn pin until it becomes tight.
(b) Back of pin slightly then tighten lock nut to specification.

Ecentric pin torque specification: 27-34 Nm

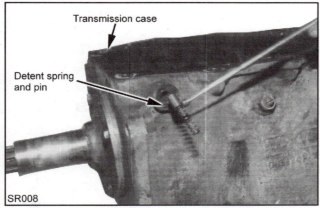
SR008

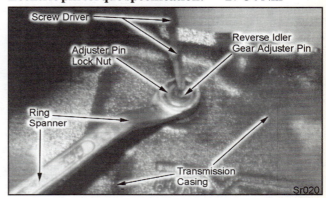
Sr020

17. To the extension housing install the gearshift housing assembly and tighten bolts to specification.

Gearshift housing assembly: 51-75 Nm

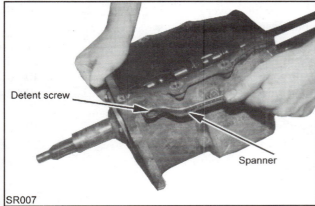
SR007

15. Install the top cover to case using a new gasket and tighten bolts to specification.

Top cover to case bolts: 11-16 Nm

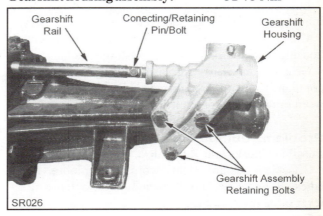
SR026

18. Install the roll pin into the gearshift rail and gearshift rod by pressing in.

PROBLEM DIAGNOSIS

Problem: Transmission shift hard/heavy!
Possible Causes and Remedies:
* Clutch adjustment incorrect. Remedy - Adjust clutch.
* Clutch pedal high effort. Remedy - Lubricate or replace as required.
* Shifter shaft binding. Remedy - Check for mispositioned selector arm roll pin, loose cover bolts, worn shifter shaft or shaft bores, distorted oil seal or transmission extension not aligned with case.
* Internal bind in transmission caused by shift forks, selector plates of synchronizer assemblies. Remedies - Remove, dismantle and inspect transmission. Replace worn or damaged components as necessary.
* Incorrect lubricant. Remedy - Drain and refill.

Problem: Gear Clash when shifting from one gear to another!
Possible Causes and Remedies:
* Clutch adjustment incorrect. Remedy - Adjust clutch.
* Clutch cable binding. Remedy - Lubricate or replace.
* Lubricant level low or incorrect lubricant. Remedies - Drain and refill transmission and check for lubricant leaks if level was low. Repair as necessary.
* Gear shift components or synchronizer assemblies worn or damaged. Remedies - Remove, dismantle and inspect transmission. Replace worn or damaged parts.

Problem: Transmission noisy!
Possible Causes and Remedies:
* Lubricant incorrect or level low. Remedies - Refill transmission. Check for leaks and repair as necessary.
* Clutch housing-to-engine, or transmission-to-clutch housing bolts loose. Remedy - Re-torque bolts.
* Gearshift mechanism, transmission gears or bearing components worn or damaged. Remedies - Replace worn or damaged components as necessary.

Problem: Jumps out of gear!
Possible Causes and Remedies:
* Offset lever damper sleeve worn or lever loose. Remedies - Remove gearshift lever and check for loose offset lever or damper sleeve.
* Gearshift mechanism, shift forks, selector plates, interlock plate, selector arm or shift cover worn or damaged. Remedies: Remove, dismantle and inspect transmission cover assembly. Replace worn or damaged components.
* Gear teeth worn or tapered, synchronizer assemblies worn or damaged, excessive end play caused by worn thrust washers or mainshaft gears. Remedies - Remove, dismantle and inspect transmission. Replace worn or damaged components as necessary.

SPECIFICATIONS

Borg Warner 4 speed 0503
Lubrication

Capacity	2.2 litre
Type	ESP-M2C-83C 80W

End Float Clearances (mm)

1st Speed Gear	0.05-0.69
2nd Speed Gear	0.15-0.43
3rd Speed Gear	0.13-0.51
Input Shaft Bearing (max)	0.10
Output Shaft Bearing (max)	0.10

Gear Ratio	Carburettor	E.F.I.
1st Gear	3.43:1	3.50:1
2nd Gear	1.99:1	1.99:1
3rd Gear	1.43:1	1.32:1
4th Gear	1.00:1	1.00:1
Reverse	3.29:1	3.47:1

Torque Specifications

Description	Nm
Clutch Bell Housing to Engine	47-60
Transmission to Clutch Bell Housing	60-75
Extension Housing to Transmission	60-75
Transmission Cover	10-15
Input Bearing Retainer Bolts	27-35
Operating Lever Retainer Nuts	27-35
Detent Pin Screw	35-40
Drain Plug	40-50
Filler Plug	40-50
Reverse Light Switch	20-27
Speedometer Sender Unit Retainer Bolt	10-15

BORG WARNER 4spd (0506 series) & 5spd (0507 series) SINGLE RAIL MANUAL TRANSMISSION's

Subject	Page
GENERAL INFORMATION	234
Recommended Lubricant	234
Checking Transmission Lubricant Level	234
Draining & Refilling Transmission	234
MAINTENANCE	234
Transmission Extension Seal	234
Removal	234
Installation	234
Back-Up Lamp Switch	234
Test	234
Removal	235
Installation	235
Gear Shift Lever	235
Removal	235
Installation	235
MAJOR SERVICE REPAIRS	235
Transmission Assembly	235
Transmission Dismantle	234
Clean and Inspect Transmission	238
Mainshaft Assembly Inspection	239

Subject	Page
Sub Assemblies	239
Main Shaft	239
Dismantle	239
Assemble	239
Synchronizers	240
Dismantle	240
Assemble	240
Cluster Gear & Main Drive Gear Bearing	240
Replacement	240
Top Cover Assembly	240
Dismantle	240
Assemble	241
Assemble Transmission	242
PROBLEM DIAGNOSIS	247
SPECIFICATIONS	247
TORQUE WRENCH SPECIFICATIONS	247

GENERAL INFORMATION

The 4 speed (0506) and the 5 speed (0507) single rail transmissions became available on XE and XF Falcon series vehicles and co-manufactured Fairlane and LTD vehicles.

The 4 and 5 speed transmissions exactly the same except the 5 speed has the addition of a 5th gear assembly included outside the transmission case in the extension housing.

The floor mounted control lever operates a shift rail which extends from the transmission extension through into the transmission case directly into the shift forks.

Attached to the side of the transmission case, is a tag which provides the transmission serial No. & assembly part No.

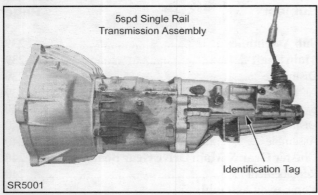

The model code for vehicles equipped with different transmissions are listed in General Information Chapter at the front of this manual.

Recommended Lubricant
For Borg Warner manual transmissions is ESP-M2C-33F Grade 80W.
The transmission lubricant capacity is: 2.8 Litres.

Checking Transmission Lubricant Level.
To check level, remove filler plug on the side of transmission case. The level is correct when lubricant is at bottom of plug hole.

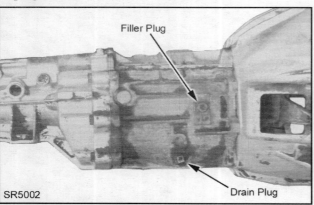

* Ensure that the vehicle is on level ground and the transmission is cold.

Draining and Refilling Transmission
Periodic lubricant changes are not necessary. The lubricant must be replaced when overhauling the transmission or when operating the vehicle under severe driving conditions

MAINTENANCE

Transmission Extension Seal
Removal
1. Disconnect battery earth lead and raise vehicle (front and rear) and support on safety stands.
2. (a) Remove propeller shaft.
(b) Place a drain tray beneath transmission extension.
3. Remove seal using seal remover.
4. (a) Inspect seal lip surface on slip yoke of propeller shaft for damage.
(b) Clean (or replace) as necessary.

Installation
Installation of the seal is the reverse of removal procedures, noting the following points:
1. (a) Apply a little transmission lubricant to seal lip.
(b) Install seal into the extension with a seal insertion tool.
(c) Torque all bolts to specification.
2. Check transmission lubricant level as previously described in this Chapter.

BACKUP LAMP SWITCH
Test
1. Jack up vehicle (front and rear) and support on safety stands as previously described.
2. Disconnect wiring harness connector from back-up lamp switch.
The switch is located on the right-hand side of the gear shift assembly.

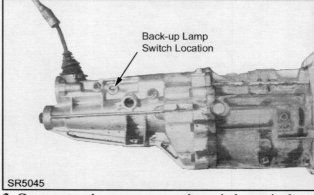

3. Connect an ohmmeter across the switch terminals.
4. (a) With transmission control lever in any position

other than reverse, the ohmmeter should shown open circuit (infinity ohms).
(b) With the control lever in the reverse position the ohmmeter should show continuity.
(c) If ohmmeter readings indicate that switch is faulty, remove switch as per following instructions.

Removal
1. Jack up vehicle (front and rear) and support on safety stands as previously described.
2. (a) Disconnect wiring harness connector from switch.
(b) Loosen and remove switch from transmission case.

Installation
1. Make sure all threads of switch are clean.
2. Apply sealant P/N3835214 or equivalent, or use thread sealing tape, to switch threads if applicable.
3. Install and torque switch.
* Make sure sealant (or thread sealing tape) does not extend beyond switch thread end.

Backup lamp switch: **150 lb. in.**

4. (a) Refit wiring harness connector to switch
(b) Remove safety stands and lower vehicle to ground.
(c) Check back-up lamp operation.

GEAR SHIFT LEVER
Removal
1. Remove centre console cover.
2. Remove screw securing the control lever to lever of control housing and bend back retaining tags then unscrew gear shift lever.

Installation
1. (a) Clean threads of lever to lever securing screw of control housing.
(b) Apply Loctite 620 (or equivalent) to screw threads.
2. Place control lever on side of control housing lever and install, then tighten retaining screw and bend over tabs.
3. (a) Install seal to seal retainer of control lever.
(b) Install cover cap of centre console.

MAJOR SERVICE & REPAIRS

TRANSMISSION ASSEMBLY

Dismantle Transmission
1. Thoroughly clean exterior of transmission assembly.
2. (a) Remove transmission drain plug with a socket and ratchet, then allow transmission lubricant to drain into a container, then remove reverse lamp switch.
3. Remove the pin retaining the gear shift connecting rod and gearshift rail, then remove the gearshift link and damper block from extension housing.

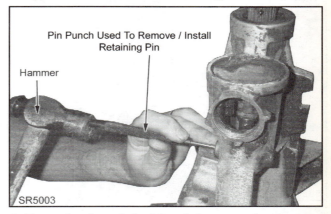

4. From the front left side of the extension housing remove the 5th gear interlock sleeve adaptor and mounting bolt.

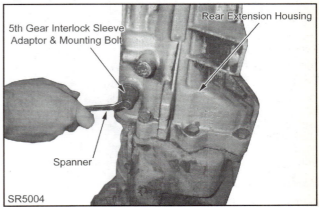

5. Remove the rear extension housing retaining bolts and remove extension housing.

BORG WARNER 4spd SINGLE RAIL (0506) & 5spd SINGLE RAIL (0507) MANUAL TRANSMISSION's

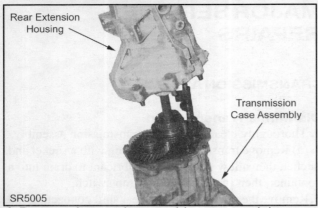

6. Remove the speedometer drive gear retaining snap rings and slide drive gear from mainshaft.

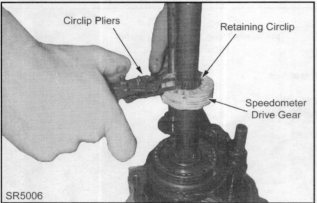

7. From the front of the transmission remove the clutch housing assembly and bearing adjustment shims.

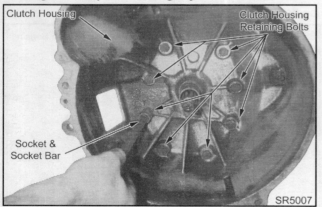

8. From transmission assembly remove top cover retaining bolts and remove top cover from transmission assembly.

9. From the reverse lever shaft remove the inner snap ring then push reverse lever shaft through case and remove the reverse lever, reverse gear fork and torsion spring.

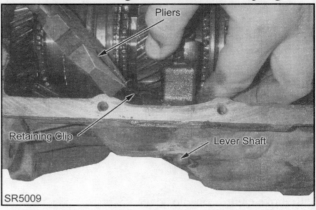

10. From the 5th gear selector lever pin remove the inner snap ring then remove selector lever pin and 5th gear selector lever.

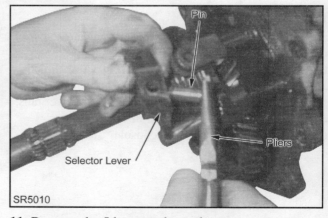

11. Remove the 5th gear selector lever mount.

236

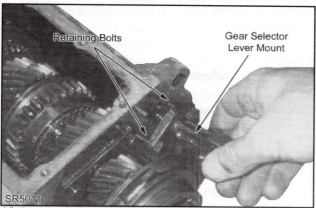

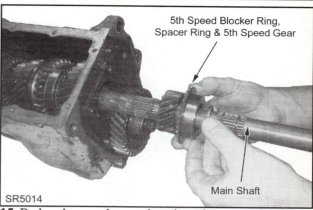

12. Insert a feeler gauge between the 5th fear synchro hub and snap ring, measuring end float to ensure it is within specification.

5th Gear End Float: 0.12 - 0.50 mm

15. By hand move the synchronizer sleeves to simultaneously engage both 4th and 2nd gears.
16. From 5th driving gear remove bolt and lock washer, then remove the 5th speed driving gear.

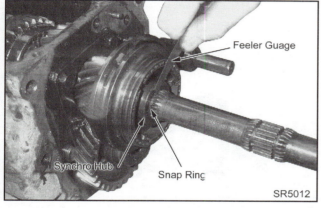

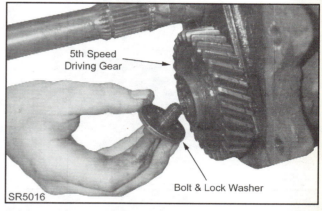

If not to specification check the 5th speed gear width and the 5th gear synchro hub width from fifth gear thrust face to snap ring thrust face to determine which components need replacing.

5th Speed Gear Width: 44.56 - 44.46 mm
Gear Synchro Hub Width: 24.08 - 23.98 mm

13. Remove the snap ring retaining the 5th gear synchro hub then remove synchro assembly and selector fork.

17. Remove the thrust plate for the rear bearings then remove both rear bearing cups and also remove the 2 front bearing cups.

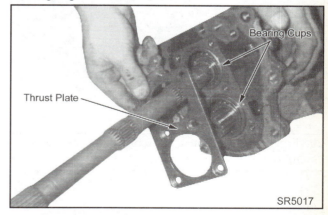

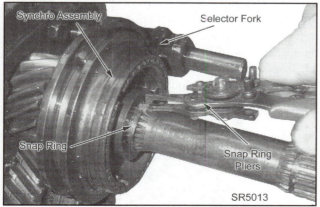

18. From the front of the transmission case pull the input shaft and gear assembly out, then ensure the 3-4 synchronizer hub is in neutral position and remove the 4th speed blocker ring.

14. From the main shaft remove the 5th speed blocker ring, spacer ring and 5th speed gear.

BORG WARNER 4spd SINGLE RAIL (0506) & 5spd SINGLE RAIL (0507) MANUAL TRANSMISSION's

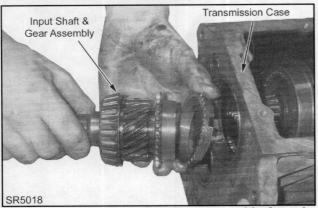

19. Remove the mainshaft and gear assembly from the transmission, then remove the reverse idler shaft and gear.

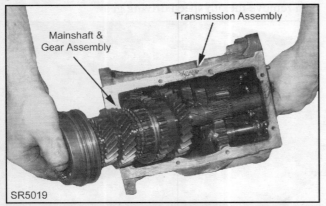

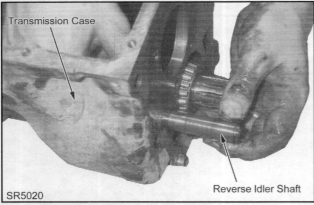

20. From transmission case remove the cluster gear assembly.

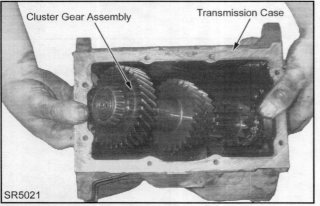

CLEAN AND INSPECT TRANSMISSION

Thoroughly wash all components in a suitable cleaning solvent. Dry all components with clean and dry compressed air.

1. Inspect the following components for any cracks or defects that may cause lubricant leakage: transmission case, rear extension, case cover and main drive gear bearing retainer.

2. Check all machined faces for burrs, and (if possible), dress them off with a fine mill file.

3. (a) Inspect all roller and needle bearing assemblies closely, and replace if there is any sign of wear.

(b) Inspect mainshaft and internal surfaces of gears where needle bearings come in contact.

5. Inspect all gears for excessive wear, chips or cracks. Replace any that are worn or damaged.

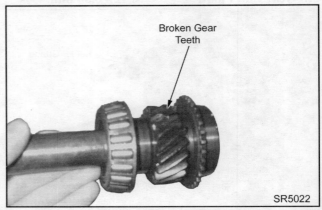

6. Check synchronizer teeth on blocking rings and gears. Replace any components that are worn or damaged.

7. (a) Inspect synchronizer hubs, sleeves, inserts and springs for damage or wear.

(b) Check that the synchronizer sleeves slide freely on their hubs.

(c) Replace any worn component.

8. Inspect reverse idler gear shaft and replace if worn.

9. Check all thrust washers and replace any that are worn.

10. Inspect all shift control component contact and sliding surfaces for wear, scratches, projections of other damage.

11. Inspect breather (located in transmission extension) to make sure it is not blocked.

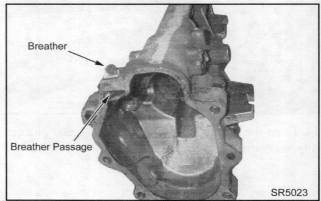

BORG WARNER 4spd SINGLE RAIL (0506) & 5spd SINGLE RAIL (0507) MANUAL TRANSMISSION's

MAINSHAFT ASSEMBLY INSPECTION
Before dismantling the mainshaft assembly, the first speed, second speed and third speed gear end floats should be checked for end float.

Third Speed Gear End Float: 0.12 - 0.50 mm

Second Speed Gear End Float: 0.16 - 0.40 mm

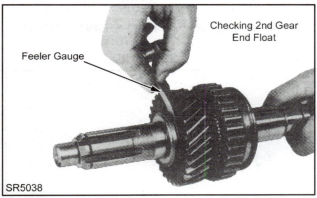

First Speed Gear End Float: 0.15 - 0.74 mm

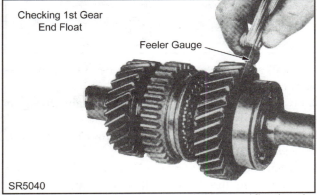

If the end float of any gear is not with in specification the following dimensions must be checked after dismantle to determine which component must be replaced to bring the end float within specifications.
1st Speed Gear Width: 40.32 - 40.38 mm
1st and 2nd Synchro Hub-width to 1st speed thrust face   15.34 - 15.39 mm
1st and 2nd Synchro Hub- width from 2nd gear thrust face to snap ring thrust face: 22.48 - 22.58 mm
2nd Speed Gear width: 38.18 - 38.26 mm
3rd Speed Gear width: 39.42 - 39.50 mm

3rd and 4th Synchro Hub width: 22.48-22.58 mm

MAINSHAFT
Dismantle
1. From the front of the mainshaft remove the snap ring, then remove the 3rd and 4th synchronizer assembly.
2. From the main shaft remove the 3rd speed blocker ring and 3rd speed gear.
3. Rear Bearing
(a) Remove the snap ring.
(b) With a universal type puller
(c) Press on the rear end of the mainshaft to remove the rear bearing and first speed gear.
* *If you press on the front face of the second speed gear you will damage the mainshaft. A snap ring that is hidden, holds the second speed gear and the first and second gear synchronizer in place.*
4. From the main shaft remove the snap ring for the 1st & 2nd synchronizer inner hub, hub and reverse sliding gear.
5. Remove the second speed gear and blocker ring by supporting the front face of the second speed gear and pressing on the rear end of the mainshaft.
* *When pressing on the front face of the second speed gear always ensure that the faces of the second speed gear, the end of the mainshaft and the blocks mounted on the press are square to each other.*
* *Do not press on the thrust face flange of the mainshaft.*
6. 3rd and 4th synchronizer.
(a) From the synchro hub slide off the synchronizer sleeve.
(b) Remove the springs and shift plates.
8. 1st and 2nd speed synchronize
(a) From the synchro hub slide off the synchronizer sleeve.
(b) Remove the springs and shift plates.

Assembly
1. Assemble the synchronizer assemblies as described under synchronizer assemblies.
2. Lubricate the bore of the second speed gear and to mainshaft with the blocker ring.
Slots in blocker rings: 8.76 - 9.14 mm wide.
3. With the reverse gear sleeve gear teeth towards the front install the 1st & 2nd speed synchronizer assembly, then install snap ring with thickness to keep end float within specification.
Hub end float specification: 0.0-0.1 mm
2. Lubricate the bore of the first speed gear and install to mainshaft with the blocker ring, then install the mainshaft bearing and retaining snap ring
3. Lubricate the bore of the third speed gear and to the mainshaft install gear with blocker ring.
4. Lubricate the third & fourth speed synchronizer assembly, with the inner hub spline to the front install to

mainshaft and snap ring.
5. Check the end float of all gears to ensure they are within specification.
6. Engage third gear with the third and fourth synchronizer sleeve and engage second gear with the first and second synchronizer sleeve.

SYNCHRONIZERS
Dismantle
* Before dismantling any of the synchronizers, paint or etch an alignment mark on each of the synchronizer sleeves and hubs.
* Do not mix parts from one synchronizer assembly to another.

1st & 2nd Synchronizer Assemblies
1. Remove both synchronizer springs with a screwdriver.
2. Separate sleeve from hub and remove the 3 synchronizer inserts.

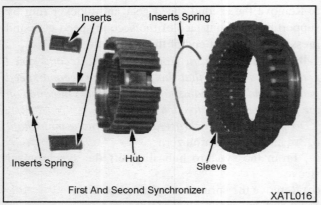
First And Second Synchronizer   XATL016

3rd & 4th Speed Synchronizer Assembly
1. Remove both synchronizer springs with a screwdriver.
2. Separate sleeve from hub and remove the 3 synchronizer inserts.

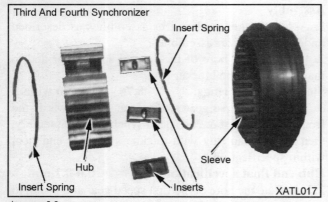
Third And Fourth Synchronizer   XATL017

Assemble
1st & 2nd Synchronizer Assembly
1. Fit lubricated synchronizer sleeve to inner hub with sleeve selector groove and hub inner spline protrusion at opposite ends.
2. Slide sleeve across hub until three shift plates can be fitted into the slots in the inner hub.
3. Install two red synchronizer springs under the shift plates behind the pads with the long lug of each spring in the same shift plate.
* The spring tangs should locate on opposite sides of the same shift plate so that the spring openings do not line up.

3rd & 4th Speed Synchronizer Assembly
1. Fit lubricated synchronizer sleeve to inner hub with sleeve selector groove and hub inner spline protrusion at opposite ends.
2. Slide sleeve across hub until three shift plates can be fitted into the slots in the inner hub.
3. Install two yellow synchronizer springs under the shift plates behind the pads with the long lug of each spring in the same shift plate.
* The spring tangs should locate on opposite sides of the same shift plate so that the spring openings do not line up.

CLUSTER GEAR or MAIN DRIVE GEAR BEARING
Replacement

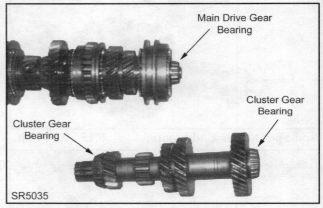
SR5035

1. Install a bearing separator to the bearing behind the bearing rollers.
2. Press on the end of the cluster gear or main drive gear shaft to remove bearing.
Note: *Ensure the bearing separator jaws do not press on the gear teeth.*
3. Fit new bearing to assembly and install into position using a bearing installation tool or steel tube.

TOP COVER ASSEMBLY
Dismantle
1. From the top cover remove the detent screw, detent spring and detent pin.

BORG WARNER 4spd SINGLE RAIL (0506) & 5spd SINGLE RAIL (0507) MANUAL TRANSMISSION's

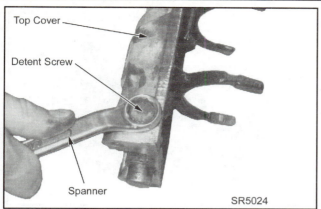

2. From the gear shift rail hole in the front face of the transmission cover remove the metal cup plug.

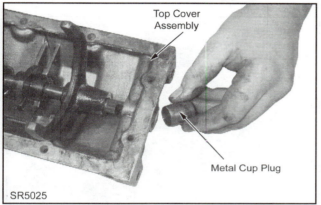

3. Rotate and move forward the gearshift rail so the operating pin is free from the interlock spool, then remove operating pin.

4. Completely remove the gearshift rail and remove the gearshift forks and interlock spool.
5. Remove the 5th gear operating pin.

Assemble

1. To the shift rail install the biasing cam then install the 5th gear operating pin.

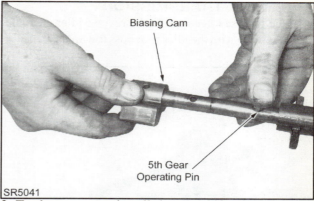

2. To the top cover install the gearshift rail and fit the gearshift forks and interlock spool while installing shift rail.
3. Rotate and move forward the gearshift rail so the hole for the operating pin is free from the interlock spool and with the detent flats facing upwards install the operating pin.

4. Slide gearshift rail back so that the gearshift operating pin is in line with the flange of the interlock spool then rotate shift rail so the shift rail detents are in-line with the detent hole.
5. To the top cover install the detent pin, detent spring and detent screw.

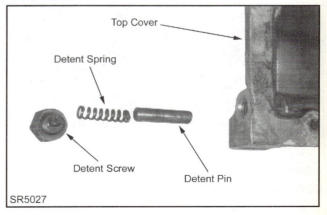

6. Do not install the cap plug at this stage.

ASSEMBLE TRANSMISSION

1. To the reverse idler shaft fit the reverse idler gear and bush assembly with the idler gear boss towards the rear of the case.

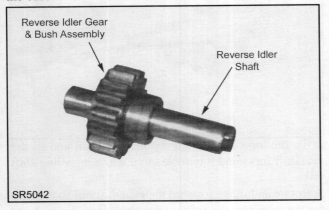

2. Install the reverse idler shaft assembly to the transmission case with the snap ring groove at the rear of the case then secure with snap ring.

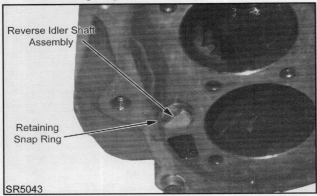

3. To the bottom of the transmission case install the cluster gear assembly so the bearing cones sit rearward of the bearing bores.

4. To the transmission case install the mainshaft assembly locating the bearing into the case bore.

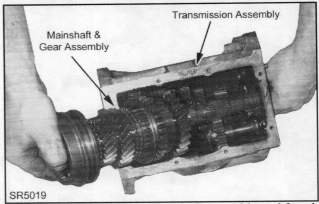

5. To the case install the input shaft assembly and fourth speed blocker ring, then position the cluster gear into position.

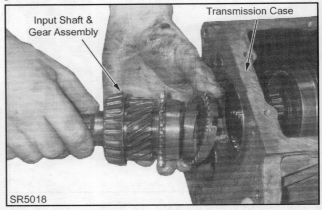

6. Install the bearing cups for the mainshaft and rear cluster gear, then install the rear bearing retainer and tighten retaining screws and bolts to specification.

Rear Bearing Retainer Screws: 20 - 25 Nm
Rear Bearing Retainer Hex Bolts: 24 - 27 Nm

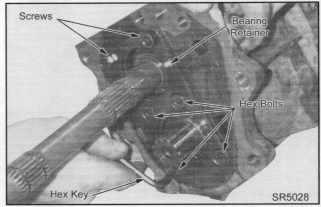

7. To the transmission case assembly install the clutch housing and two bearing shims, then tighten clutch housing bolts to specification.

Clutch Housing Bolts: 47 - 60 Nm

BORG WARNER 4spd SINGLE RAIL (0506) & 5spd SINGLE RAIL (0507) MANUAL TRANSMISSION's

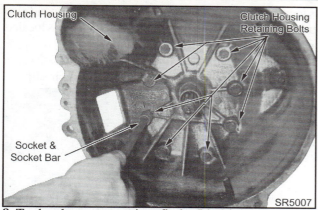

8. To the cluster gear spigot fit the 5th driving gear, then to the bolt apply Loctite 601 and fit bolt and washer, do not tighten.

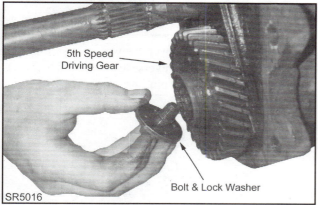

9. Fit the 5th speed gear, then with the outside diameter chamfer facing shaft abutment shoulder, assemble spacer ring.

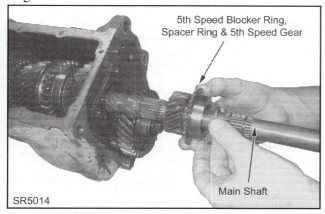

10. Align splines in synchro hub with splines on main shaft and ensure slots in 5th gear blocking ring slots align with shift plates, then slide synchro assembly with selector fork on to main shaft.

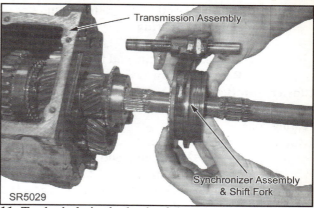

11. To the hole in the back of the gear case slide in the selector fork and fit synchro assembly snap ring. Snap ring should give a maximum axial end float of 0.17mm.

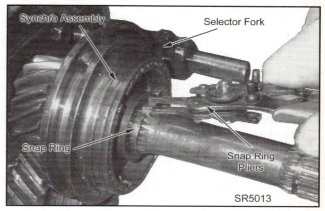

12. By hand simultaneously select reverse and fourth gears, then tighten the 5th driving gear locking bolt to specification.
5th Driving Gear Lock Bolt: 70 - 80 Nm

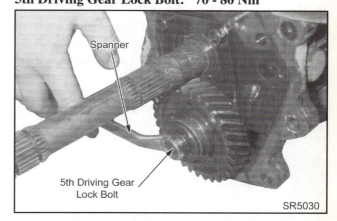

13. Position the transmission back into neutral then position gear assembly into second gear.
14. Determine correct shim size for tapered roller bearings.
Main drive Gear Bearing
a) Gauge the depth of the bearing bore in the clutch housing.
b) Gauge the stand-out height of the bearing cup from the front face of the transmission.

Example:	Housing Depth	6.20 mm
	Height of Bearing	3.38 mm
	=	2.82 mm
	Less 0.25mm min. end float	
	Required Shim =	2.795 mm

Cluster Gear Bearing
c) Gauge depth from front face of transmission case to bearing cone.

Example:	Depth of Cone:	2.24 mm
	Less 0.025mm min. end float	
	Required Shim =	2.215 mm

15. Check the bearing end float of the main drive gear and cluster gear.

a) Install the shims calculated in the above procedure, then position transmission assembly in the vertical position sitting on the clutch housing.

b) To the back face of the case mount a magnetic dial indicator and magnetic clutch stand.

c) To the output shaft apply an axial force of 5 - 7kg, while at the same time turning the output shaft to ensure bearings are properly seated.

Note: *Turn output shaft at least 12 times.*

d) Position the dial indicator needle on top of the output shaft and zero dial indicator.

e) Pry the 5th gear upward and note the reading on the dial indicator (end float).

f) Follow the same procedure to check the cluster gear bearing end float.

End Float Specification:
    Main shaft: 0.025 - 0.127 mm
    Cluster Gear: 0.025 - 0.127 mm

16. If end float of either shaft is not within specification remove clutch housing and install correct size shims to bring end float within specification.

17. To the back face of the transmission case install the 5th gear selector lever mount and tighten the two bolts to specification.

5th Gear Selector Lever Mount Bolts: 70 - 80 Nm

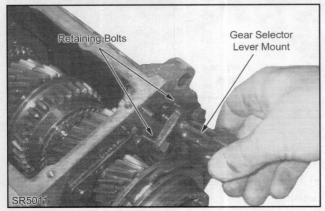

18. To the 5th gear selector lever mount fit the 5th gear selector lever.

19. Ensuring that the flange of the 5th gear interlock spool is located in the slot in the 5th gear selector lever and also ensure the tongue on the end of the selector lever is located in the slot in the 5th gear selector fork.

20. To the hole in the selector lever and mount slide in the 5th gear selector lever pin and install retaining cir-clip.

21. Fit into position the reverse lever, reverse fork and torsion spring, then to the reverse lever shaft fit a new O-ring and outer snap ring or pin.

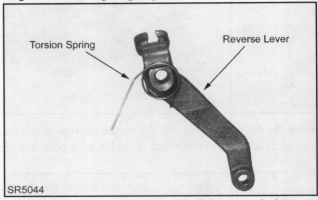

22. Install shaft assembly through hole in transmission case then fit inner snap ring or pin.

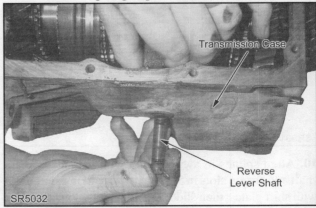

Note: *Correct installation of pin is required, refer to diagram.*

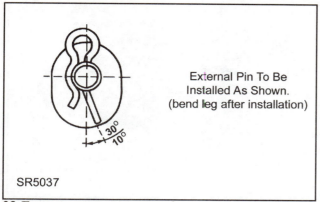

23. Ensure correct movement of reverse idler gear by hand, then ensure that the 1st and 2nd synchro sleeve is in the 1st gear position.
24. To the top cover install a bead of gasket silastic then with top cover in first gear position install top cover and finger tighten retaining bolts.

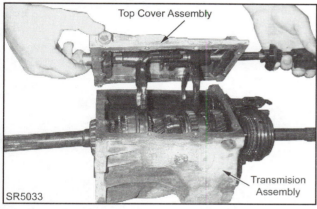

25. Install the two upper clutch housing bolts then tighten the eight top cover bolts to specification.
Upper Clutch Housing Bolts: 40 - 55 Nm
Top Cover Bolts: 10 - 12 Nm

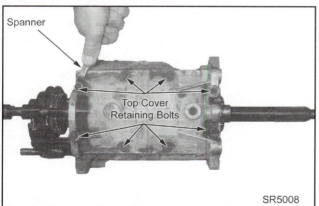

26. Through the access hole in the clutch housing install the metal cup plug to the shift rail hole in the top cover, using jointing compound to seal.
27. To the mainshaft install the speedometer drive gear and secure in position with the two retaining snap rings.

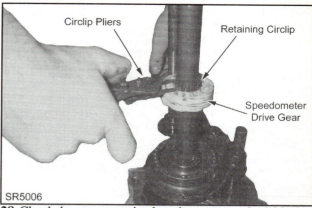

28. Check the rear extension housing to ensure both biasing mechanism plunger screws are backed out as far as possible and the plungers are pressed back into housing.

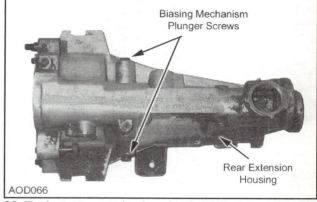

29. To the rear extension housing install a 1.5mm bead of gasket silastic and fill the bottom of the reverse lamp pocket with MIC75B grease.
30. Install extension housing being careful not to damage oil seal and bushing, then install the six retaining bolts with lock washers and tighten to specification.
Extension Housing Bolts: 40 - 55 Nm

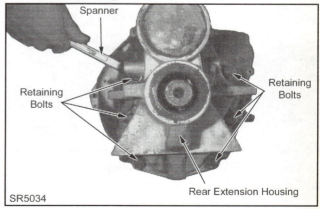

31. To rear extension housing install the reverse lamp switch.

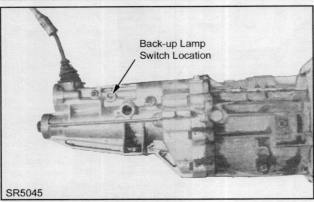

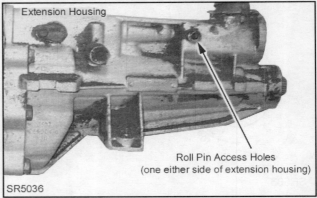

32. To the rear extension housing install the 5th interlock spool adaptor and bolt and tighten bolt to specification.
5th interlock bolt: 24 - 27 Nm

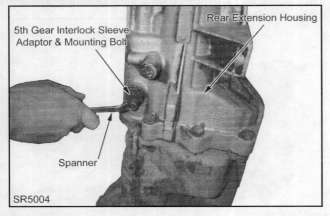

36. To the housing install a new metal plug ensuring that the bottom of the plug is abutting the machined shoulder of housing.

37. Coat threads of biasing mechanism screws with Loctite 222 and tighten screws.

33. Lubricate the gear lever plastic damper block then install damper block into extension housing over the end of the shift rail.

34. Press roll pin into gearshift link and rail.

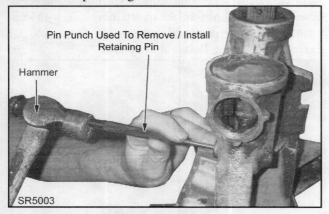

35. To the roll pin access holes in the gearshift housing install the 2 plastic cup plugs.

BORG WARNER 4spd SINGLE RAIL (0506) & 5spd SINGLE RAIL (0507) MANUAL TRANSMISSION's

PROBLEM DIAGNOSIS

Problem: Transmission shift hard/heavy!
Possible Causes and Remedies:
* Clutch adjustment incorrect. Remedy - Adjust clutch.
* Clutch pedal high effort. Remedy - Lubricate or replace as required.
* Shifter shaft binding. Remedy - Check for miss-positioned selector arm roll pin, loose cover bolts, worn shifter shaft or shaft bores, distorted oil seal or transmission extension not aligned with case.
* Internal bind in transmission caused by shift forks, selector plates of synchronizer assemblies. Remedies - Remove, dismantle and inspect transmission. Replace worn or damaged components as necessary.
* Incorrect lubricant. Remedy - Drain and refill.

Problem: Gear Clash when shifting from one gear to another!
Possible Causes and Remedies:
* Clutch adjustment incorrect. Remedy - Adjust clutch.
* Clutch cable binding. Remedy - Lubricate or replace.
* Lubricant level low or incorrect lubricant. Remedies - Drain and refill transmission and check for lubricant leaks if level was low. Repair as necessary.
* Gear shift components or synchronizer assemblies worn or damaged. Remedies - Remove, dismantle and inspect transmission. Replace worn or damaged parts.

Problem: Transmission noisy!
Possible Causes and Remedies:
* Lubricant incorrect or level low. Remedies - Refill transmission. Check for leaks and repair as necessary.
* Clutch housing-to-engine, or transmission-to-clutch housing bolts loose. Remedy - Re-torque bolts.
* Gearshift mechanism, transmission gears or bearing components worn or damaged. Remedies - Replace worn or damaged components as necessary.

Problem: Jumps out of gear!
Possible Causes and Remedies:
* Offset lever damper sleeve worn or lever loose. Remedies - Remove gearshift lever and check for loose offset lever or damper sleeve.
* Gearshift mechanism, shift forks, selector plates, interlock plate, selector arm or shift cover worn or damaged. Remedies: Remove, dismantle and inspect transmission cover assembly. Replace worn or damaged components.
* Gear teeth worn or tapered, synchronizer assemblies worn or damaged, excessive end play caused by worn thrust washers or mainshaft gears. Remedies - Remove, dismantle and inspect transmission. Replace worn or damaged components as necessary.

SPECIFICATIONS

Borg Warner 4 speed (0506 series) & 5 speed (0507 series)

Lubrication
Capacity	2.8 litre
Type	ESP-M2C-83C 80W

End Float Clearances (mm)
1st Speed Gear	0.15 - 0.74
2nd Speed Gear	0.16 - 0.40
3rd Speed Gear	0.12 - 0.50
5th Speed Gear	0.12 - 0.50
Input Shaft Bearing (max)	0.025 - 0.127
Output Shaft Bearing (max)	0.025 - 0.127

Gear Ratio	4spd.	5spd.
1st Gear	3.47:1	3.47:1
2nd Gear	1.96:1	1.96:1
3rd Gear	1.26:1	1.26:1
4th Gear	1.00:1	1.00:1
5th Gear	——	0.79:1
Reverse	3.37:1	3.37:1

Torque Specification Nm

Clutch Bell Housing to Engine	47 - 60
Transmission to Clutch Bell Housing	40 - 55
Extension Housing to Transmission	40 - 55
Transmission Cover	10 - 12
Input Bearing Retainer Bolts	27 - 35
Lower Transmission Cover	12 - 18
Input Bearing Retainer	27 - 35
Operating Lever Retainer Nuts	27 - 35
Rear Bearing Retainer Bolts	24 - 27
Rear Bearing Countersunk Screws	20 - 25
5th Driving Gear Bolt	70 - 80
Detent Bolt Top Cover	14 - 20
Drain Plug	40 - 50
Filler Plug	40 - 50
Reverse Light Switch	20 - 27
Speedometer Sender Unit Retainer Bolt	10 - 15

T5 & M57 - 5 SPEED MANUAL TRANSMISSION

Subject	Page
GENERAL INFORMATION	249
MAINTENANCE	249
Checking and Replacing Transmission Oil	249
Speedo Sender	249
Remove	249
Install	249
Reversing Light Switch	249
Remove	249
Install	249
Extension Housing Rear Seal	250
Remove	250
Install	250
Shift Lever and Boot Assembly	250
Remove	250
Install	250
MAJOR REPAIR & REBUILD	250
Dismantle	250
Assembly	252
GEAR & SHAFT ASSEMBLIES	254
Output Shaft and Gear Assemblies	254
Dismantle	254
Clean	255
Inspect	255
Transmission Case Inspection	256
Assembly	256
Synchronizes	257
Dismantle	257
Assembly	258
Shift Cover	258
Dismantle	258
Assembly	258
Input Shaft Bearing	259
Remove	259
Install	259
Input Shaft to Output Shaft Bearing Cup	260
Remove	260
Install	260
Bearing Retainer Seal - Front	260
Remove	260
Install	260
Counter Shaft Bearing - Front	260
Remove	260
Install	260
Bearing Inspection	260
Bearing Raceways	260
Inspect	260
Bearing External Surfaces	260
PROBLEM SOLVING & DIAGNOSIS	261
EA-ED SPECIFICATIONS	261
EF/EL SPECIFICATIONS	262
AU/AU11 SPECIFICATIONS	262
TORQUE WRENCH SPECIFICATIONS	262

GENERAL INFORMATION

This transmission is fully synchronised with the 1st, 2nd, 3rd and 4th gears located in the transmission case. Fifth gear is an overdrive gear, and situated in the rear extension
This transmission is used extensively with Ford vehicles.

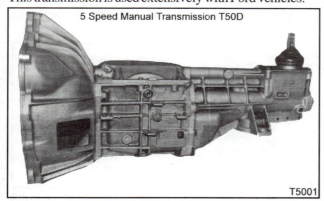
5 Speed Manual Transmission T50D
T5001

Gears are shifted via a single shifting lever mounted in a shift box (turret) at the top and rear of the rear extension. There are two shift forks 1st/2nd and 3rd/4th located in the transmission case top cover with 5th and reverse shifting mechanism at the rear of the case in the rear extension.

Maintenance

Checking and Replacing Transmission Oil

Position an oil catching tray under the transmission, make sure it has the capacity to hold the oil from the transmission (if oil level is at the full level the transmission will hold 2.05 litres).
Remove the drain plug from the lower right side of the transmission, if the vehicle has been recently driven take care as the oil could be hot enough to burn skin on contact.
Replace the drain plug and tighten to specification.

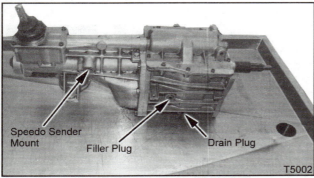
Speedo Sender Mount — Filler Plug — Drain Plug
T5002

Drain Plug torque specification: 35 Nm

Remove the filler plug approximately half way up the right side of the transmission, fill the transmission with the correct amount of specified oil.
Oil Capacity of Transmission: 1.9 litres
See Specifications For Type Of Transmission Oil

Check oil level by inserting your finger into the oil filler hole to check on oil level. The oil level should be at the same level as the filler plug, but so high that oil will run out when the plug is removed.
Replace oil filler plug and tighten plug to specification.
Filler Plug specified torque: 35 Nm

Speedo Sender
Remove
1. Disconnect the wiring connection.
2. Remove the clamp securing the unit to the transmission.
3. Remove sender unit from transmission.

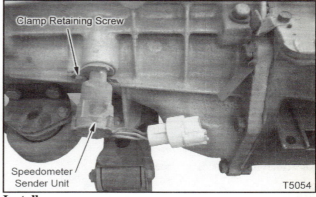
Clamp Retaining Screw — Speedometer Sender Unit
T5054

Install
1. Install a new 'O' ring to sender unit.
2. Install sender unit into transmission, install clamp and tighten securing bolt.
3. Reconnect wiring loom connector.

Reversing Light & Neutral Drive Switch
Remove
Detach wiring connectors, then with a 22mm socket unscrew the switch from the left side of the transmission case, neutral/drive switch is located on the top front of the box. Ensure to remove neutral/drive switch pin from casing as well.

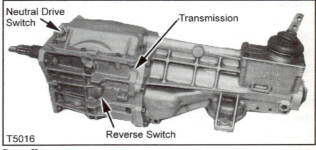
Neutral Drive Switch — Transmission — Reverse Switch
T5016

Install
Check threads of switches, apply Teflon tape to switch, install switches and tighten to specification, remember to replace neutral/drive switch pin.
Reverse Light Switch specified torque: 25Nm

Extension Housing Rear Seal
Remove
1. Jack vehicle up and safely support vehicle to allow access to the transmission and drive / tail shaft..
2. (a) Place a drain tray beneath transmission extension.
(b) Remove drive / tail shaft as described in Tail / Drive Shaft and Universal Joints chapter in this manual.
3. Remove seal using seal remover and discard seal.

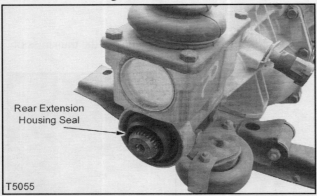

4. (a) Inspect seal lip surface on slip yoke of propeller shaft for damage.
(b) Clean (or replace) as necessary.

Install
1. (a) Apply a little transmission lubricant to seal lip.
(b) Install seal into the extension with a seal insertion tool.
2. Replace tail / drive shaft as described in Tail / Drive Shaft and Universal Joints chapter in this manual.
3. Check transmission lubricant level as previously described in this Chapter.

Shift Lever and Boot Assembly
Remove
1. Remove the gearshift knob (unscrew) from the gear shift lever, take care and ease the boot from the console and raise the boot over and off the gear lever, then repeat procedure for floor boot.
2. Remove centre console if required or from the top of the console opening remove the two bolts securing the shift lever to the transmission and remove the lever.

Install
1. Install the gear shift lever to the transmission lever, tighten the bolts. Install the boot and retainer over the gear shift lever secure it to floor and repeat procedure for console boot pressing the retainer lugs into the console.
2. Install the knob onto the shift lever tighten, so that the gear position markings on the knob are correct.

Major Repairs and Rebuild
Dismantle
1. Drain transmission fluid before placing transmission on a clean bench to enable a complete pull down and rebuild. Drain plug on R/H side of casing.
2. Remove the backup lamp and neutral/drive switches, as well as neutral/drive switch pin.

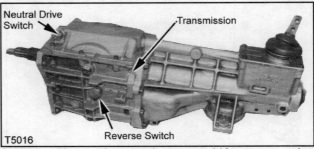

3. With shift lever in neutral, remove shift cover securing bolts, & pry shift cover from shift pot.

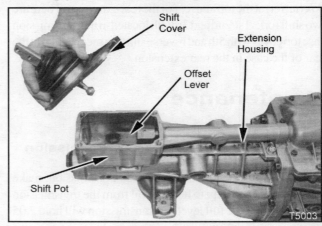

4. With pin punch and hammer, move offset lever roll pin through shifter shaft.
5. Loosen and remove extension housing bolts, pry the extension housing from the case, carefully breaking the seal.
6. Extension housing and offset lever can then be slid backwards from the case.

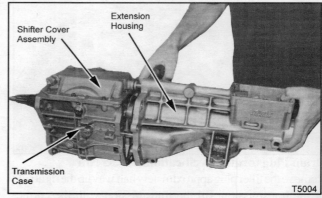

7. Lift the offset lever from the shifter pot and remove the roll pin, detent spring and detent ball from the detent plate.

T5 & M57 - 5 SPEED MANUAL TRANSMISSION

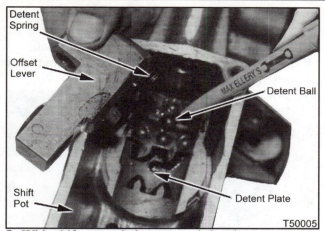

T50005

8. With shift cover bolts removed, break case-to-cover bond.

9. Lift shift cover, tilting it towards the right side of casing, fifth/reverse shift lever will need to be disengaged from shift cover before removal.

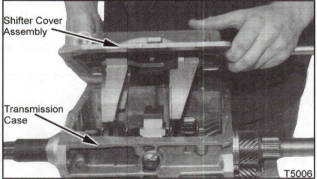

T5006

10. Fifth/reverse shift lever pivot pin removal, release C-clip using pliers, then loosen pivot pin with Torque bit driver, and remove.

11. The fifth gear synchronizer snap ring, retainer, reverse cone and synchronizer blocking ring can be withdrawn from the countershaft by releasing snap ring with circlip pliers.

12.(a) Now fifth gear, shift fork, shift rail and synchronizer can be removed as a complete assembly.

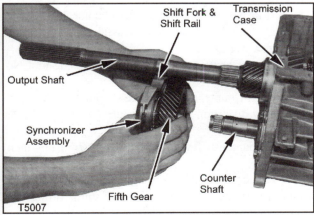

T5007

(b) When the assembly has passed over the end of the countershaft it will have to be twisted to release the ball stud from the fifth/reverse shift lever.

13. Remove input shaft bearing retainer plate bolts and retainer plate, marking top of retainer to help with assembly.

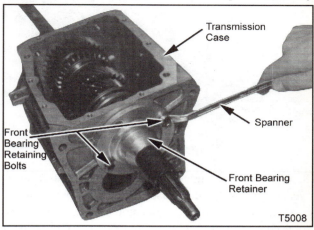

T5008

14. Input shaft has a cut out section on the 4th gear clutching teeth which will need aligning with countershaft to enable the removal of the input shaft from the case.

***Take care not to drop or loose the 15 bearings of the back of the input shaft when removing it from the case.**

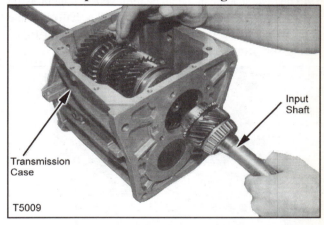

T5009

15. Remove speedo drive gear from output shaft.

16. Move output shaft backwards to release bearing race from its bond to the case. Remove bearing race rearward off output shaft.

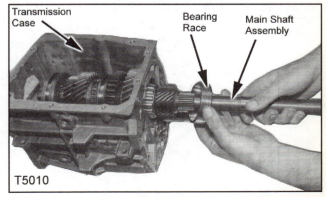

T5010

17. Tip front of output shaft upward then lift, this will help you to remove the output shaft assembly from the case.

T5 & M57 - 5 SPEED MANUAL TRANSMISSION

18. Withdraw from the case the fifth/reverse shift lever, reverse shift fork and reverse positioning spring. When replacing the case the reverse positioning spring anchor pin will need to be removed by withdrawing the Tizz bushing from the anchor bolt and then the anchor bolt itself.

* Take note of shift lever, shift fork and inhibitor spring positions prior to removal, and the rotation of the reverse positioning spring, for assembly purposes.

19. The reverse idler shaft can be removed by punching the roll pin from the shaft, then slide reverse idler shaft out of the case, withdrawing the reverse idler gear and over-travel rubber stop from casing at the same time.

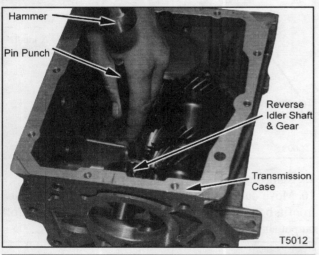

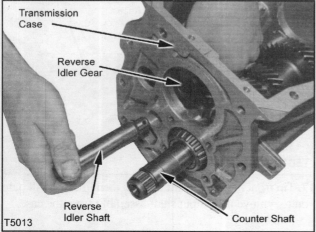

20. Flatten countershaft retainer tabs and remove retainer bolts. Then countershaft retainer and shim/s and rear counter shaft bearing race can be removed from counter shaft.

* If race is locked in casing work the shaft back and forth to released its bond from the case.

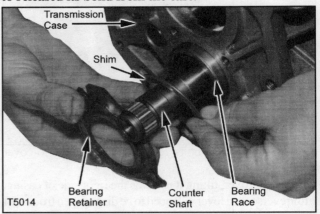

21. Using tools No. E1673 & E1673U15A remove bearing from counter shaft being careful not to damage shaft or bearing.

22. Remove counter shaft in same manner as output shaft was removed.

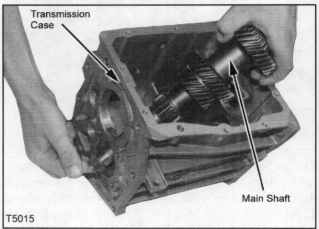

Assembly

1. Using tool No. E7518B install front counter shaft bearing onto shaft, then install counter shaft into case in reverse procedure as removal.

2. Fit counter shaft rear bearing to shaft using tool No. E7518B.

CAUTION: Counter shaft must be supported correctly to prevent any distortion of the case during bearing installation.

* Support counter shaft with steel bar that is 7mm (1/4 inch) thick.

3. Fit rear counter shaft bearing race into position and replace counter shaft bearing retainer and shims, fitting bolts and tighten to specification

Rear Counter Gear Shaft Bearing Housing: 20Nm.

* This should be done initially without any shims installed.

T5 & M57 - 5 SPEED MANUAL TRANSMISSION

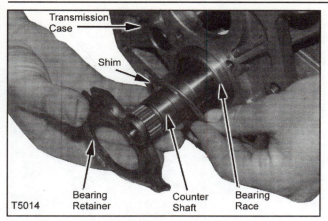

4. End play to be measured using dial indicator, if measurements not within specs install or remove shims as necessary, from between counter shaft bearing race and retainer.

Counter Shaft End Play:

EA/EB:	0.08 - 0.10 mm
EF/EL:	0.013 - 0.102 mm
AU/AUII:	0.013 - 0.102 mm

When counter shaft end play is correct bend retainer tabs over ensuring retaining bolts are secured.

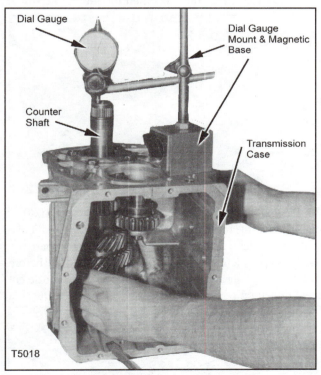

5. Fit reverse idler gear, reverse idler shaft, rubber overtravel stop and shaft into case, with shift lever groove towards rear of casing, .
6. With pin punch, install roll pin into idler shaft.
7. Pipe Sealant with Teflon is to be applied to the reverse positioning spring anchor pin threads upon installation, then tighten to specifications.

Reverse Idler anchor Pin: 8-15Nm

Install Tizz bushing over anchor pin head by softly tapping into place with hammer.

8. Fit fifth/reverse shift lever, reverse shift fork and reverse positioning spring in shift lever.
9. With reverse idler gear in neutral position, align reverse shift fork on reverse idler gear and push down until engaged correctly into reverse idler gear.

* The reverse positioning spring rotation should be counter clockwise into its correct installed place.

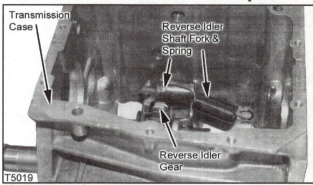

10. Output shaft assembly can now be fitted into the casing.

* Apply multi-purpose grease to the thrust bearing and race. Install the 15 roller bearings into input shaft.

11. The input shaft can be fitted into the casing, with the synchronizer teeth flat aligned with counter shaft.

* Make sure 3-4 synchronizer blocking ring is correctly located.

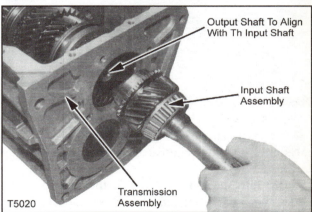

12. Fit bearing cap into bearing retainer, without shims at this point.

Fit with narrow or smaller notch upward, do not apply sealant until later. Tighten retaining bolts to specification.

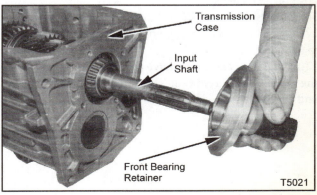

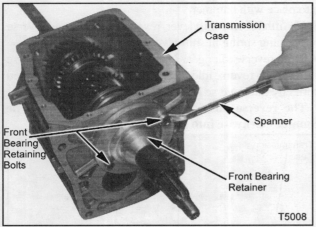

Input Shaft Bearing retaining bolts: 15-27 Nm

13. Output shaft rear bearing race can be fitted using soft face hammer if necessary to tap into place.

14. (a) Now fifth gear, shift fork, shift rail and synchronizer can be fitted into the casing as an assembly.
(b) When the assembly is being fitted it will have to be twisted to engage the ball stud to the fifth/reverse shift lever.
* Shift rail must slide through return spring.

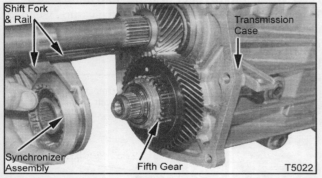

15. The fifth gear synchronizer snap ring, retainer, reverse cone and synchronizer blocking ring can be replaced onto the countershaft, and ensure that the snap ring is correctly in place.
* **Spacer tabs must be locked into the counter shaft splines, the reverse cone tab should be vertical for the rear extension installation.**
* **do not install the pivot pin until the ball stud for the shift lever and shift ball is fully engaged.**

16. With teflon applied to pivot pin threads, install it into position and tension.

5th Gear Shift Lever Pivot Pin: 34 - 47 Nm

17. Fit C-Clip on shift lever pivot pin, and speedometer gear to output shaft.
* **Install the speedometer drive gear and retaining clip to the output shaft, retaining clip must lock into the gear and the shaft.**

18. Apply small amount of silicone Sealer RTV Silastic 1080 or equivalent to the shift cover assembly, align shift cover tilting it slightly to the right side of the transmission and place down into position.
* **All synchronizes must be in the neutral position to allow the shift forks in the cover which must also be in neutral position to function properly.**

19. Fit shift cover securing bolts, tightening to specified torque.

Transmission Cover bolt specified torque: 12Nm

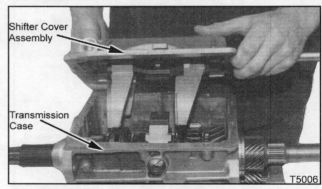

20. Place a bead of Silicone Sealer RTV Silastic 1080 or equivalent to the rear extension, before fitting apply silicone sealer to the lubrication funnel and fit to counter shaft.

21. Apply petroleum jelly to the detent spring and ball before installation, fit spring to offset lever, and detent ball to detent plate in neutral position, placing offset lever in shifter pot

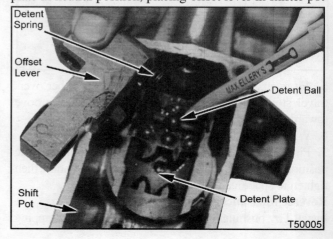

with spring over detent ball.

22. Fit extension housing into position, with offset lever press down and aligned on the detent spring and ball, then slide lever and housing into place. Ensuring reverse cone tag engages the recess in the housing.

23. (a) Fit and tension extension housing retaining bolts.

Extension Housing bolts specified torque: 50-60Nm

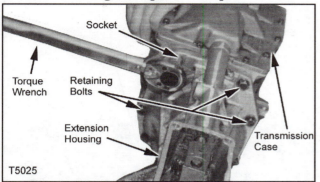

(b) Align the hole in the shifter shaft and offset lever, then fit roll pin, use pin punch and hammer.

* **Check output shaft end play now.**

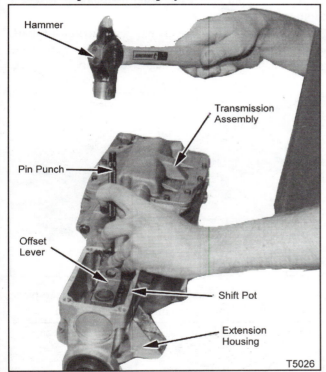

24. Output shaft gear train end play will need to be measured as follows:

* Turn transmission so it is vertical with output shaft pointing up with the dial indicator mounted on extension housing.
* Turn both input and output shafts to allow them to settle, then zero the dial indicator.
* Using a wood block, lift the input shaft up and record the dial indicator reading.

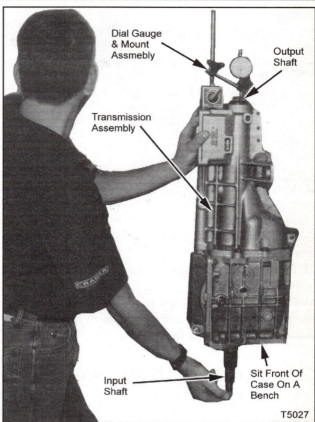

* **Install a shim that is the same thickness of the dial indicator recording which will give zero end play.**

Note: With zero end play at specification, it is acceptable to have a plus or minus .050mm (0.002 inch) tolerance. If the shim is too thick it will overload the bearing.

The thickest shim is to be installed against the front bearing cup.

25. Turn over transmission to excess front bearing retainer and remove, when the required shims are in place and bearing race is installed, applying sealant to the bearing retainer before installation..

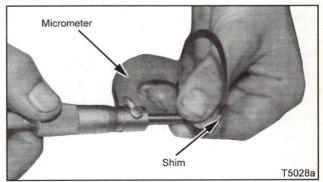

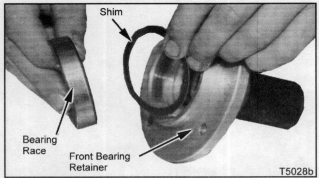

26. Install bearing retainer as described previously, tighten retaining bolts to specified torque.

Main Drive Bearing Retainer: 15-25Nm

CAUTION: Take care not to allow sealer to enter the bearing retainer notch.

27. Fit shifter cover to shifter pot and tighten the retaining bolts to specification.

Shift Cover to Shift Pot Bolts: 8-15Nm

28. Fit and tension drain and filler plugs to specification.

Drain Plug specified torque: 35 Nm.

Gear and Shaft Assemblies

Output Shaft and Gear Assemblies
* Gear and shaft assemblies may not require to be dismantled. Inspect all gears, synchronizes, bearings and shaft surfaces

Dismantle

Section A & B for Sprint & GT only:

(a) Press the bearing from the output shaft using bearing puller and press.

(b) Remove snap ring from the shaft.

1. Remove 3rd gear, 3rd/4th synchronizer and blocking ring as an assembly by pressing them from the output shaft.

2. (a) Slide needle bearing from output shaft, then spacer.

(b) Fifth gear snap ring can then by removed using circlip pliers.

(c) Press fifth gear from the output shaft.

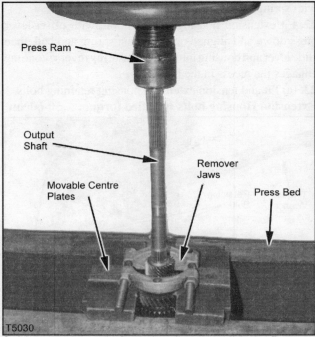

3. (a) Press output shaft rear bearing, then slide the first gear from the shaft.

* There is a snug fit between the sleeve and output shaft.

(b) Slide needle bearing and sleeve as an assembly from the output shaft, then using a magnet or pointy nose pliers withdraw roll pin from the shaft.

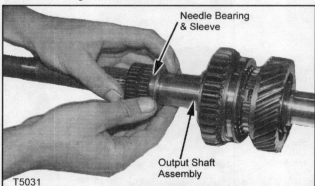

4. From the output shafts longer end slide the three-piece first gear synchronizer blocking ring assembly off.

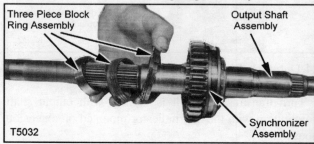

5. Second gear snap ring and thrust washer can be removed from the shaft, then the second gear and the 2nd gear needle bearing and spacer.

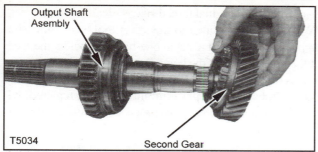

6. (a) Disconnect spiral snap ring from its retaining groove and slide from shaft, then remove thrust washer from shaft as well.
(b) Press the 2nd gear synchronizer blocking ring assembly, and 1st/2nd synchronizer from output shaft.

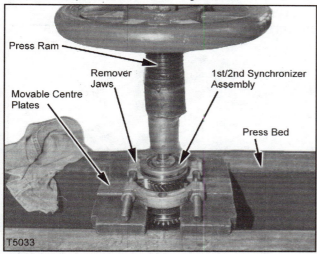

7. Detent ball and spring can be removed from the output shaft synchro hub.
* The 1st/2nd speed synchronizer, hub and output shaft are serviced as a complete assembly. No attempt should be made to separate the hub from the shaft.
8. The sleeve, springs and inserts can be removed from hub after putting alignment marks on hub and sleeve. The springs, inserts and detent ball and spring are not serviceable. If hub or sleeve is worn or damaged, output shaft and synchronizer are to be replaced as an assembly.

Cleaning
Using cleaning solvent to clean all the components of the gearbox except for the seals and 'O' rings. Remove all debris from transmission components using a brush, screw driver or scraper, do not damage any of the components.

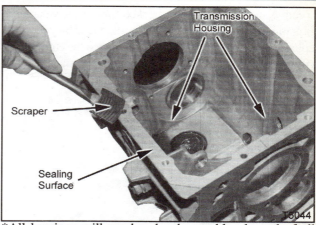

*All bearings will need to be thoroughly cleaned of all lubricants, by rotating the bearings in cleaning fluid and using a brush on them to dislodge any grime.
*Once all components have been cleaned, dry them off with compressed air, do not allow the bearing to spin when doing this, as damage may occur.
*Bearing will need inspecting and if they are found to be serviceable they can then be packed with a multipurpose grease and placed where they will stay clean and free of foreign matter. Refer to 'Bearing Inspection'.
*The casing bottom magnet will need to be cleaned with kerosene or mineral spirits to remove all traces of metal particles, then dry with compressed air.

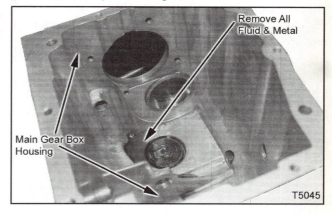

Inspect
*The transmission component housing will need to be inspected very carefully for cracks, fractures, broken or worn component mounts and damaged threads, also any other damage that could cause transmission misalignment and failure.
* Any damage to flat mounting surfaces that need to mount flush and seal will need to be cleaned to obtain the sealing surface that is required. Any that are bent or distorted will need to be replaced.
*Ensure the transmission vent hole is not blocked. The shift lever and cover assembly will need to be checked for wear, damage and distortion on all parts, if excessive wear found to be in the assembly the damaged components will need replacing.

*Teeth on all gears must be checked for brakes, wear, and chipping. If any gears are found to be damaged they must be replaced. If counter shaft gears are damaged the entire shaft will nee replacing as the gears are part of the shaft.

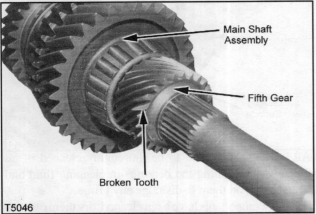

*Any shafts that have been bent or distorted, or have damage to the splines and bearing surfaces will need to be replaced. Check the speedometer drive gear to ensure that the teeth have not been stripped or damaged, if it needs replacing the correct size gear must be fitted.

*All bushes and seal in the transmission should be replaced on a rebuild, otherwise they should be thoroughly inspected for wear or damage and replaced if any is found.

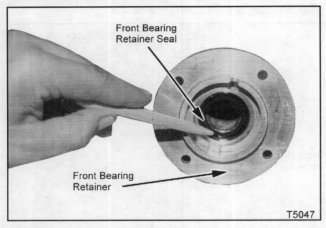

*The synchronizer sleeves must be free moving on their hubs and aligned correctly. The synchronizer blocking rings must be checked for widened index slots, rounded clutch teeth, and smooth internal surfaces (must have machined grooves), and should have a distance of not be less than 0.5mm (0.020 inch) from the synchronizer blocking ring face to the clutch teeth on the gear.

Transmission Case Inspection

*For damaged threads in aluminium transmission case, the most effective form of repair is using a helicoil kit that may be purchased from local automotive part suppliers.

*To repair damaged thread, drill it out, using the drill size described in the helicoil kit. Use the tap size described to cut a new thread large enough to take the helicoil, which after it is installed, the original thread size is obtained again..

*With the helicoil fitted to the insert tool, screw into the tapped hole and until it sits in one-half turn below the face of the housing. Bend the helicoil tang up and down until it breaks off at the notch.

*Once the helicoil is in place, the thread is fully repaired and serviceable again. Repeat this procedure to all threads that need repairing.

Assembly

1. 1st/2nd synchronizer hub detent ball and spring can be fitted.

2. (a) Fit 1st/2nd synchronizer assembly onto the output shaft, then the three-piece 1st gear synchronizer blocking ring to the output shaft, slide on as an assembly.

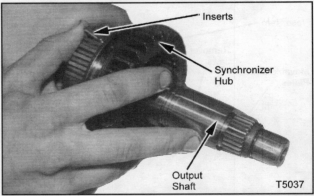

(b) Fit the three-piece 2nd gear synchronizer blocking ring to the output shaft, fit as an assembly.

* Note: The synchronizer blocking ring slots must be aligned with 1st/2nd synchronizer tabs.

Synchronizer assemblies are described under 'Synchronizer Dismantle and Assembly'.

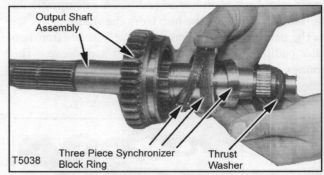

3. (a) Fit thrust washer and then spiral snap ring, use Spiral Snap Ring Replacer.

(b) Replace 2nd gear needle bearing and spacer to output shaft, then fit second gear over the output shaft and seat it on the needle roller.

* The 2nd gear slots must be aligned with tabs on synchronizer blocking ring assembly.

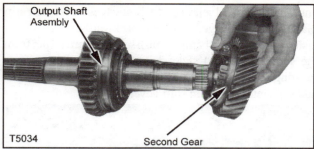

4. Fit 2nd gear thrust washer by sliding it over the shaft and then using snap ring pliers fit the snap ring into place.
5. Roll pin will need to be fitted into the output shaft, then slide the 1st gear sleeve with needle roller bearing fitted over the output shaft and into place ensuring to align the notch with the roll pin.
* **Use pencil magnet if required for the roll pin.**
6. (a) Fit first gear over the needle roller and into place on the output shaft.
* **The first gear slots must be aligned with tabs on first gear synchronizer blocking ring assembly.**

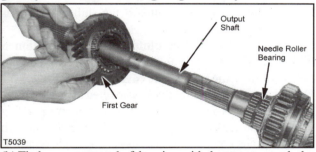

(b) Fit the rear output shaft bearing with the taper towards the rear of the shaft, ensure that it is seated properly.
7. (a) Apply a small amount of petroleum jelly to the fifth gear splines before installation, then place gear into position on the output shaft.
(b) Press the gear carefully onto the output shaft with a capped length of pipe, 31.75mm ID x 356mm (1-1/4 inch ID x 14 inch).
\# **Note: The output shaft and gear splines should be aligned with care. If the splines are not aligned in the correct manner, the gear will damage the splines as it is pressed onto the output shaft.**
8. Fit fifth gear snap ring into its retaining groove on the output shaft using circlip pliers, then fit the spacer and needle bearing into place on the output shaft.

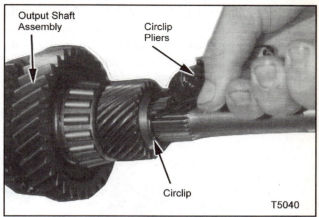

9. Press the 3rd/4th synchronizer blocking ring and third gear onto the output shaft carefully aligning it with the splines..
* **Check that the synchronizer hub faces the shortest end of output shaft before pressing the various parts onto the shaft. The synchronizer and third gear will need to kept as a unit so the synchronizer blocking ring is still aligned.**
Section A & B for Sprint and GT only
(a) Replace snap ring from the shaft.
(b) Press bearing onto output shaft.

Synchronizes
Dismantle
* **These operations apply to all synchronizer assemblies, gear synchronizes which are different in design, procedures are noted.**
1. Alignment marks need to be applied to the synchronizer sleeves and hubs to ensure that they are reassembled correctly.
2. (a) The insert retainer which is fitted to the 5th gear synchronizer will need to be removed, this is the only synchronizer with it fitted.
(b) Lever the two synchronizer retaining springs from the hub using a screw driver, then withdraw the inserts.
* **1st/2nd gear synchronizer hub is only serviceable as an assembly incorporating the output shaft, as the synchronizer hub is pressed with an interference fit onto the output shaft and no attempt to separate the hub and shaft should be made.**

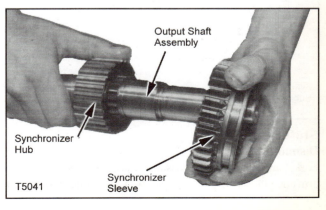

3. (a) The 1st/2nd will need to be slowly and carefully slid off the hub to prevent losing the detent ball and spring.
(b) The other gear synchronizer sleeve can be slid off without worrying about detent balls and springs going missing.
*Ensure that the sleeves and hubs are marked

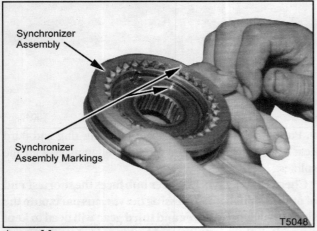

Assembly
* The synchronizer sleeve and hub alignment marks must be aligned for assembly. The sleeve and hub must be held square during assembly to prevent jamming. The sleeve must not be forced onto the hub.
1. Slide the sleeve onto the hub and then install the inserts into the sleeve and hub, once in position the retaining springs can be fitted to the inside of the hub to hold the inserts in place.
2. The 5th gear synchronizer assembly will need the Reverse Blocking Ring fitted to the synchronizer.
3. The detent ball and spring will need to be fitted into the hub of the 1st/2nd gear synchronizer before the sleeve, inserts and retaining springs are fitted.
Assemble retaining springs, inserts and sleeve onto hub. Refer to diagram for placing of the retaining springs and inserts.

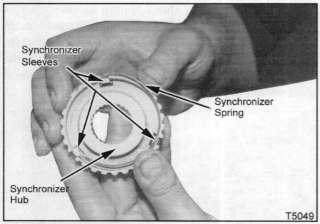

Shift Cover
Dismantle
Forks must be marked for assembly purposes. With selector arm and plates in the Neutral position and rotate shifter shaft anti clockwise until selector arm disengages the selector arm plate, once disengaged pull shaft backwards.
Using pin punch and hammer push selector arm roll pin from the shifter shaft and slide shaft from the cover using a twisting motion to withdraw. Remove shift forks, roll pin and shift interlock from shift cover.

Assembly
New O-ring seal must be fitted if the shifter cover was dismantled.
* **The narrow side of selector interlock plate is positioned in the shift cover slot. The control selector arm roll pin hole is toward the rear of the cover.**
*With control selector interlock plate fitted as an assembly, place shift forks in the cover with there corresponding identification marks. With shift shaft lubricated slide through shift cover and components until its hard through the cover.
***1-2 shift fork is the larger fork of the two, and the offset faces the rear of the cover. The 3-4 gear shift selector arm plate, the smaller plate is fitted under the 1-2 gearshift selector arm plate.**
CAUTION: The roll pin is installed just below the selector arm surface. If the roll pin is not countersunk the result may be interference between the pin and interlock plate during shifts.

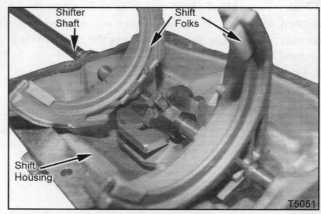

*Ensure flat on shifter shaft is facing upward and install the control selector arm roll pin using a pin punch.

T5 & M57 - 5 SPEED MANUAL TRANSMISSION

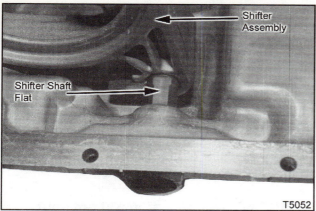

Input Shaft Bearing
Remove
*Input shaft bearing will need to be carefully pressed form the shaft.

Install
*The bearing will need to be pressed back onto the input shaft.

Input Shaft to Output Shaft Bearing Cup
For the Sprint & GT only.
Remove
Remove bearing cup from the end of the input shaft using a bearing cup puller and slide hammer.

Install
Bearing cup will need to be pressed into the input shaft pocket with a bearing cone replacement tool.
CAUTION: Ensure bearing cup is fully seated.

Bearing Retainer Seal, Front
Remove
Bearing race and shim need removing, then pry seal from the bearing retainer using a screw driver, careful not to damage the bearing retainer.

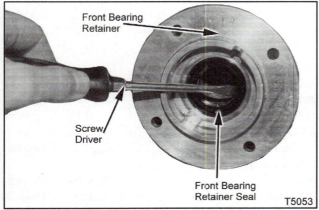

Install
Fit new seal using the appropriate seal installer, then replace the shims and bearing race into the bearing retainer.

* If the transmission is being overhauled with a new seal, the end play shim is not installed.

Front Counter Shaft Bearing Race
* Remove the front counter shaft bearing race if it is showing evidence of wear or damage. Loctite and sealer will need to be applied if a bearing is to be installed.
* Replace the "O" ring with a new "O" ring if replacing the front bearing.

Remove
1. Mount the case in a press and press the old bearing out, however support the press properly other wise the transmission case could distort.

Install
1. O-ring fitted to bearing race.
2. Loctite and sealer will need to be applied to the outer surface of the bearing.
3. Position the bearing race at the case, press the bearing cone into place.

Bearing Inspection
Bearing Raceways
Inspect
Inner Raceway: While holding outer ring stationary, rotate inner ring at least three revolutions. Inspect the raceway of the inner ring from both sides for pits or spalling. A bearing assembly should be replaced when damaged. Light particle indentation is allowable.
Outer Ring Raceway: While holding inner ring stationary, rotate outer ring at least three revolutions. Inspect the raceway of the outer ring from both as with the raceway of the inner ring. If the raceway is spalled or pitted, replace the bearing assembly. Light particle indentation is allowable.
Bearing External Surfaces
The bearing must be replaced if damage is found in any of the following areas:
Radial cracks on front and rear faces of outer or inner rings. Cracks on outside diameter of outer ring (particularly around snap ring groove). Deformation or cracks in ball cage (particularly around rivets).

Spin Test
Lubricate bearing raceways with a slight amount of clean automatic transmission fluid turn the bearing back and forth slowly until the raceways and balls are coated.
With bearing in vertical position. Vertical movement between inner and outer rings is allowable. Spin outer ring several times by hand. If there is roughness or vibration, the bearing should be cleaned again and re-lubricated. Roughness could be foreign particles in the bearing. If bearing is still rough after cleaning and relubricating several times, it must be replaced.
Repeat the above with the bearing in the horizontal position.

PROBLEM SOLVING & DIAGNOSIS

PROBLEM - Transmission noisy in gear.
Cause: Lubricate level low or wrong type.
Action: Fill to bottom of filler plug hole with lubricant.
Cause: Transmission to flywheel housing and flywheel housing to engine block bolts loose.
Action: Tighten bolts to specification.
Cause: Pilot bushing worn or damaged.
Action: Remove transmission.
If noise is howling during start-up, check pilot bushing. Check for loose flywheel and housing alignment.
Cause: Improper transmission pilot engagement into flywheel housing.
Action: Replace housing or input shaft bearing retainer as required.
Cause: Worn or damaged internal components.
Action: Disassemble transmission. Inspect input, output and counter shaft bearings, gear and gear teeth for wear and damage.

PROBLEM - Transmission shifts hard.
Cause: Improper clutch release.
Action: Inspect & adjust or replace clutch.
Cause: Internal shift mechanism binding.
Action: Remove transmission and free up shift mechanism.
Cause: Synchronizer sleeve to hub fit.
Action: Remove and check for burrs or fit.
Cause: Binding condition between input shaft and crank shaft pilot bearing.
Action: Check alignment and service as required.
Cause: Improper Fluid.
Action: Drain and refill with specified fluid or equivalent to bottom of filler plug hole.

PROBLEM - Transmission will not shift into one gear - All other gears OK.
Cause: Floor shift, interference between shift handle and console or floor cut out.
Action: Adjust console or cut out floorpan to eliminate interference.
Cause: Restricted travel of internal shifter components.
Action: Remove transmission.
Inspect shift rail and fork system, synchronizer system and gear clutch teeth for restricted travel.

PROBLEM - Transmission is locked in one gear. It cannot be shifted out of that gear.
Cause: Internal Shifter components worn or damaged.
Action: Remove transmission.
Inspect the problem gear or gearshift rails, fork and synchronizer for wear or damage.
Cause: Selector arm finger broken.
Action: Remove transmission.
Replace selector arm assembly.
Cause: Bent shifter forks at pads and selector slot.
Action: Service or replace as required.

PROBLEM - Transmission will not shift into reverse (all others shifts OK).
Cause: Worn or damaged internal components.
Action: Remove transmission.
Check for damaged reverse geartrain, misaligned reverse relay lever, shift rail and fork system.

EA/EB SPECIFICATIONS

TRANSMISSION
Type .... 5-Speed Manual
Model T50D
Lubricant:
-6 cyl .... ESR-M2C-163A (DEXTRON II)
-V8 .... Shell XGO 75/90 Gear Oil
-Sprint .... ESR-M2C-163A (DEXTRON II)
Dry Capacity .... 1.9 litres

GEAR RATIOS

	5.0L Sprint	5.0L V8	4.0L I6	3.2 & 3.9L I6
1st	3.35:1	2.95:1	3.25:1	3.50:1
2nd	1.99:1	1.94:1	1.99:1	2.14:1
3rd	1.33:1	1.34:1	1.29:1	1.39:1
4th	1.00:1	1.00:1	1.00:1	1.00:1
5th	0.73:1	0.73:1	0.72:1	0.78:1
Reverse	2.76:1	2.76:1	3.15:1	3.39:1

GEAR END FLOAT & CLEARANCES
Output Shaft
1st Gear .... 0.18 - 0.33 mm
2nd Gear .... 0.18 - 0.76 mm
3rd Gear .... 0.18 - 0.69 mm
Countershaft
5th Gear .... 0.04 - 0.98 mm
Countershaft End Float .... 0.08 - 0.10 mm
Output Shaft Bearing Adjustment .... 0.05 mm preload
.... to 0.05 end float

T5 & M57 - 5 SPEED MANUAL TRANSMISSION

EF/EL SPECIFICATIONS

TRANSMISSION
Type .... 5-Speed Manual
Model T50D
Lubricant .... ESR-M2C-163A (DEXTRON II)
Oil Additive .... Lubrizol 7906
Dry Capacity .... 1.9 litres

GEAR RATIOS:

	5.0L (V8)	4.0L (I6)
1st	2.95:1	3.25:1
2nd	1.94:1	1.99:1
3rd	1.34:1	1.29:1
4th	1.00:1	1.00:1
5th	0.73:1	0.72:1
Reverse	2.76:1	3.15:1

GEAR END FLOAT & CLEARANCES
Output Shaft
1st Gear .... 0.18 - 0.33 mm
2nd Gear .... 0.23 - 0.66 mm
3rd Gear .... 0.23 - 0.58 mm
Countershaft
5th Gear .... 0.13 - 0.86 mm
Countershaft End Float .... 0.013 - 0.102 mm
Output Shaft Bearing Adjustment . 0.01-0.10 mm preload

AU/AUII SPECIFICATIONS

TRANSMISSION
Type .... 5-Speed Manual
Model M57
Lubricant .... ESR-M2C-163A (DEXTRON II)
Oil Aditive .... Lubrizol 7906
Dry Capacity .... 1.9 litres

GEAR RATIO:

	5.0L V8	4.0L VCT XR6	4.0L 16&HP XR6
1st	2.95:1	3.05:1	3.35:1
2nd	1.94:1	1.99:1	1.93:1
3rd	1.34:1	1.29:1	1.29:1
4th	1.00:1	1.00:1	1.00:1
5th	0.73:1	0.72:1	0.73:1
Reverse	2.76:1	3.15:1	3.15:1

GEAR END FLOAT & CLEARANCES
Output Shaft
1st Gear .... 0.18 - 0.33 mm
2nd Gear .... 0.23 - 0.66 mm
3rd Gear .... 0.23 - 0.58 mm
Countershaft
5th Gear .... 0.13 - 0.86 mm
Countershaft End Float .... 0.013 - 0.102 mm
Output Shaft Bearing Adjustment . 0.01-0.10 mm preload

Torque Specifications Nm

Drain Plug 35
Filler Plug 35
5th/Reverse Shift Lever Pivot Pin 60
Back Up Lamp Switch 25
Case Cover to Transmission Case Attaching Bolt 12
Extension to Transmission Case Attaching Bolt 50
Transmission Case to Clutch Housing Bolt 65
Propeller Shaft Rear Universal Joint 12
Rear Counter Gear Shaft Bearing Housing 20
Reverse Idler anchor Pin: 8-15
Input Shaft Bearing retaining bolts: 15-27
5th Gear Shift Lever Pivot Pin: .... 34 - 47
Main Drive Bearing Retainer: 15-25
Shift Cover to Shift Pot Bolts: 8-15

Memo